The Progressive Tradition
Eighty Years of *The Political Quarterly*

WILEY-BLACKWELL

The Progressive Tradition

Eighty years of
The Political Quarterly

Edited by
Andrew Gamble
Tony Wright

Wiley-Blackwell
In association with *The Political Quarterly*

Bernard Crick, 1929–2008

Contents

CONTENTS

Notes on Contributors

Ron Amann (1943–) was Professor of Comparative Politics (formerly of Soviet Politics), University of Birmingham, 1986–2003, now Emeritus.

Samuel Beer (1911–2009) was a Harvard political scientist who was a close observer of British government and politics, on which he published a number of notable books.

Gordon Brown (1951–) was elected as a Labour MP in 1983, became Chancellor of the Exchequer 1997–2007, and party leader and Prime Minister 2007–2010.

George Douglas Howard Cole (1889–1959) was a social thinker, economist and historian, and a prolific author; he was the leading theorist of guild socialism in the early part of the twentieth century.

Margaret Cole (1893–1980) was a writer, activist, educationalist and historian who edited the diaries of Beatrice Webb.

Bernard Crick (1929–2008) was Professor of Politics at Birkbeck College, a political reformer and public intellectual, author of *In Defence of Politics* (1962) and *George Orwell: A Life* (1980). He was an influential co-editor of *The Political Quarterly* from 1966 to 1980 and subsequently chair of the journal board.

Colin Crouch (1944–) is Professor of Governance and Public Management at the Business School of Warwick University and External Scientific Member of the Max-Planck-Institute for the Study of Societies at Cologne. He a former editor and chair of *The Political Quarterly*.

Hugh Gaitskell (1906–1963) was leader of the Labour party (1955–1963), but died before he could contest the 1964 general election. He was succeeded by Harold Wilson.

Paul Hirst (1947–2003) was Professor of Social Theory at Birkbeck College, who made important contributions to pluralist political theory and to the analysis of globalisation.

John Maynard Keynes (1883–1946) was the most influential economist of the twentieth century; his *General Theory of Employment, Interest and Money* (1936) equipped governments—which he advised—with 'Keynesianism' as the approach to economic management.

John Mackintosh (1929–1978) was an academic and Labour politician who was a co-editor of *The Political Quarterly* with Bernard Crick from 1975 to 1978.

Robert Trelford McKenzie (1917–1981) was a Canadian who taught political science at the LSE, author of *British Political Parties* (1963) and a pioneer of election broadcasting.

David Marquand (1934–) is a former Labour MP, historian and political writer who was Principal of Mansfield College, Oxford, and is a former editor of *The Political Quarterly*.

© 2010 The Author. The Political Quarterly © 2011 The Political Quarterly Publishing Co. Ltd
Published by Blackwell Publishing Ltd, 9600 Garsington Road, Oxford OX4 2DQ, UK and 350 Main Street, Malden, MA 02148, USA

Kingsley Martin (1897–1969) was an academic, journalist and campaigner, who edited the *New Statesman*; he was a co-founder of *The Political Quarterly* and briefly, an editor of the journal in its first year.

Bhikhu Parekh (1935–) is Emeritus Professor of Political Philosophy at the Universities of Westminster and Hull. He is a Labour peer and has published extensively in the field of political philosophy.

Ben Pimlott (1945–2004) was an outstanding and prolific historian, biographer and public intellectual, author of major studies of Hugh Dalton and Harold Wilson, commentator in the press, editor, campaigner and Fabian. He was Warden of Goldsmith College at the time of his death.

William Alexander Robson (1895–1980) was a founder and co-editor of *The Political Quarterly*, serving for almost 45 years as editor, and for many years held the Chair in Public Administration at the LSE.

Richard Henry Tawney (1880–1962) was a social philosopher, moralist and economic historian, whose work provided a powerful indictment of the moral and practical inadequacy of a society based only upon possessive individualism.

Anthony Wedgwood Benn (1925–) is a former cabinet minister and one of the longest-serving Labour MPs who in later years often opposed the leadership of his party.

David Willetts (1956–) is Conservative MP for Havant and Minister of State (Minister for Universities and Science), Department for Business, Innovation and Skills.

Bernard Williams (1929–2003) was the outstanding moral philosopher of his age who made important contributions to public debate on ethical issues.

Shirley Williams (1930–) is a former Labour MP and minister, who co-founded the Social Democratic Party and has served as Leader of the Liberal Democrats in the House of Lords.

Leonard Woolf (1880–1969) was co-editor of *The Political Quarterly* from 1932 to 1958 and subsequently its first literary editor; he wrote widely on international issues.

Barbara Wootton (1897–1988) was a pioneer social scientist who developed evidence-based public policy, served on a wide range of public bodies, and was one of the first life peers.

Preface

PERHAPS the most remarkable attribute of a quarterly political journal launched eighty years ago, in 1930, is that it has survived. Yet it has not only survived, but prospered; and over these past eighty years it has published some of the best political writing, by the best public intellectuals of their day. A sample only of this rich inheritance is represented here, in this eightieth anniversary volume.

The origins of *The Political Quarterly* are vividly described in the article by William Robson, its founding spirit and first editor, who persuaded Bernard Shaw to stump up some serious money to get it going. Watching the slaughter of the First World War as a young airman, Robson 'determined to devote my working life if I survived to studying the forces which influence the lives of men and women in society, and doing what I could towards improving their condition and clearing up the hideous mess I saw around me'.

With others of like mind, such as Kingsley Martin and Leonard Woolf, this ambition found its practical expression in the project for 'a serious political review in which progressive ideas could be discussed at adequate length'. Progressive ideas were those which sought to make Britain and the world a better place, wherever those ideas came from. The purpose was practical, not theoretical. The task was to 'provide a bridge between the world of thought and the world of action'. This became the mission statement of the journal, which it has endeavoured to sustain over the years.

In recent times this ambition has become even more urgent, as academic social science has seemed to remove itself from the world and to speak only to itself in an esoteric language unintelligible to citizens at large. The reward system of the academy has also not encouraged the role of public intellectual. *The Political Quarterly* has always stood out against these malign tendencies. The need for a coherent and practical progressivism that links thought and action, and expresses itself in a way that engages its audience, is today more necessary than ever.

On the inside cover of every copy of the journal is the declaration, penned by Bernard Crick (former editor and longtime presiding spirit) that 'the tradition of the journal has always been to accept articles written in plain English, without jargon, that deal with issues of political importance or provide background material or basic speculation directly related to those issues'. As current editors, that is the tradition which we endeavour to continue. It is also the tradition that is exemplified by the articles collected here.

The book is dedicated to the memory of Bernard Crick; and we are very grateful to Emma Anderson for her invaluable assistance in bringing it together for publication.

Tony Wright
Andrew Gamble

© 2011 The Author. The Political Quarterly © 2011 The Political Quarterly Publishing Co. Ltd
Published by Blackwell Publishing Ltd, 9600 Garsington Road, Oxford OX4 2DQ, UK and 350 Main Street, Malden, MA 02148, USA

The Founding of *The Political Quarterly*

WILLIAM ROBSON

Vol. 41, no. 1, January–March 1970

I CONCEIVED the idea in 1927 of a serious political review in which progressive ideas could be discussed at adequate length, and shortly afterwards I found that Kingsley Martin had arrived at a similar idea. We felt the need for a forum where a philosophy, a policy and a programme could be hammered out for the socialist movement, which was growing in strength but was lacking a coherent body of ideas. The existing quarterly and monthly reviews were either quite general in their interests, or conservative or right wing liberal in outlook, or moribund. Some of our elders and betters whose support we sought were of the opinion that the day of the quarterly had passed. This view seemed to be confirmed by the demise of the *Edinburgh Review*, once the most famous and politically influential of periodicals, in 1929, a few months before *The Political Quarterly* began publication. *The Westminster Review* had come to an end in 1914.

Kingsley Martin and I took the lead in bringing the idea to fruition. We were then junior members of the teaching staff of the London School of Economics and Political Science. We were both convinced of the need for a political review and were prepared to devote a great deal of time and energy to getting it established. We worked closely together despite the fact that in the autumn of 1927 Martin went north to join the *Manchester Guardian* as a leader writer.

No one would embark on the arduous and time-consuming enterprise of launching a new review unless he were impelled by very strong motives, especially if it meant starting from scratch without money, publishing facilities, or even an established reputation. My own motives were of two kinds: emotional and intellectual.

My emotional drive originated in the First World War, in which I had served in the Royal Flying Corps and later in the Royal Air Force. One great difference between the First and Second World Wars was that the great mass of even educated people were taken completely by surprise when the guns started firing in August 1914, whereas before 1939 the attention of the whole world had been rivetted for years on the menacing acts and attitudes of Nazi Germany, Fascist Italy and Imperial Japan. In the newspapers and on the radio the ravings of Hitler and Mussolini, the warnings of Churchill and the call to resistance of Roosevelt made the expectation of war so widespread and the suspense so great that it was almost a relief when it actually started. Moreover, everyone knew what the Second World War was about, whereas in common with millions of other young men I had volunteered for service on patriotic grounds knowing absolutely nothing about the real causes of the war, or its aims, or of international relations.

The First World War was so traumatic an experience that to this day I cannot bear to read novels or to see plays or films which remind me of the fearful slaughter, the massacre of the cream of the youth, the incompetence and callousness of the high command, the shameless profiteering at home, the mud and hopelessness of the war of attrition. Almost all the friends and acquaintances with whom I had grown up were killed—I still feel acutely that I am one of the few who survived that lost generation.

The morale of the British forces reached its lowest point in 1917. The scale of the slaughter, the absence of any peace aims other than the slogan that we were fighting 'to make the world safe for democracy', and the feeling that a war of attrition might last indefinitely, had very serious effects on the soldiers both of Britain and France.

With many others I went through a mood of deep depression in that crucial year of the war. But strangely enough a little later I underwent an experience which was the secular equivalent of a religious conversion. I determined to devote my working life if I survived to studying the forces which influence the lives of men and women in society, and doing what I could towards improving their condition and clearing up the hideous mess I saw around me.

At the time I was completely ignorant of economics, politics, sociology, social psychology, law and the other relevant subjects. I recall that in the autumn of 1917 I began to read on a remote airfield *The Wealth of Nations*, partly because it was the only book I had heard of which sounded as though it might be of some help in my self-appointed future task and partly because the title offered a promise of something opposed to the death of nations then in process.

After the war I went tentatively to the London School of Economics—it was my first experience of a university—to see if I could get the knowledge and insight I wanted. I came into contact with some remarkable thinkers both there and outside, and in due course I gained a sufficient number of degrees to qualify as a social scientist. But the more I came to know about the social sciences the wider the gulf seemed to be between relevant knowledge and action which might be of help to humanity. So when in due course I became a professional academic teacher, I remained acutely aware of the need to find ways of bridging the gap. *The Political Quarterly* was conceived as a device for this purpose. It was to provide a bridge between the world of thought and the world of action, between the writer, the thinker and the teacher on the one hand and the statesman, the politician and the official on the other.

My drive to launch this review was also motivated at the intellectual level by a desire to improve the condition of Britain by injecting new ideas, new proposals, new ways of looking at the problems confronting the nation, the Empire and the world. The conduct of affairs since 1918 had been highly unsatisfactory. The postwar governments of Lloyd George and his 'hard-faced businessmen', Bonar Law (1922), Baldwin (1923 and 1924) and Ramsay MacDonald (1924) had been uninspiring and unconstructive. At home, the General Strike of 1926 was a reflection on the attitudes of the coal owners, the trade unions and the government; unemployment was rife; little progress had been made in education, public health, social security, the position of women, or better opportunities for the underprivileged. Abroad, Lloyd George had almost got us involved in another war with Kemal Attaturk; our government had backed the anti-Bolshevik forces of Kolchak and Dennikin, thereby poisoning our relations with the USSR for years; we had demanded very heavy reparations from Germany regardless of the consequences against which Keynes had warned us; and there had been no serious attempt to disarm Germany or to adopt a genuine disarmament policy ourselves.

The Fabian Society, which I had joined hopefully under the spell of Bernard Shaw, the Webbs and other founding fathers, was moribund in the extreme. 'The story of the Fabian Society proper' during the 1930s, Margaret Cole has written, 'can be very briefly told, for it is one of inertia amounting to almost complete stagnation.'[1] It was not until 1932 that the New Fabian Research Bureau was formed as a breakaway movement from the parent society.

In these circumstances there was a clear and urgent need for great deal of new and vigorous thinking in every aspect of public affairs, and this demanded new channels of communication, a focusing point for vigorous and progressive minds. The new political review was intended to respond to this need.

In launching *The Political Quarterly* I was guided by a theory I held (and still hold) about the structure of public opinion in Britain. This theory rests on the belief that all or nearly all new ideas or progressive policies begin with discussions or writing among a very restricted circle of persons of exceptional ability and concentrated interests. This applies not only to bodies interested in political reform like the Fabian Society or PEP, but also to those interested in particular spheres of public policy, such as the Howard League for Penal Reform or the Town and Country Planning Association. The membership of these elites, and the circulation of their publications, is very restricted, and perhaps numbers only two or three thousand persons. After intensive discussion in these narrow circles, ideas or proposals which survive and win acceptance are presented to a wider audience through the weekly papers. By means of such journals as the *New Statesman*, the *Spectator*, the *Economist*, *Time and Tide*, *The Statist* and *New Society*, and now through some of the more sophisticated radio and television broadcasts, new ideas reach a larger section of the public, including that elusive and ill-defined person the general intelligent reader. The number of this wider circle is probably between 250,000 and 350,000 persons. After this second level of discussion, ideas or proposals which survive criticism and offer promise of desirable change then break through to the mass audience in the national daily and Sunday newspapers.

We never expected *The Political Quarterly* to attain a large circulation, but we did believe that it could exercise a wide influence through the weekly and daily Press, through broadcasting and television, through its impact on political leaders. This belief has been realised to my own knowledge on a number of occasions.

Before a new quarterly could be started it was necessary to obtain the support of a wider circle of persons of much greater reputation and influence than Kingsley Martin or I possessed. We accordingly enlisted the interest of about 40 or 50 leading intellectuals whom we invited to a private meeting at the London School of Economics to discuss the project. It was very favourably received. Soon afterwards we were able to issue the following printed prospectus. The signatories included adherents of both the Labour and Liberal parties, and some were not known to belong to any party. All were persons of intellectual distinction with a keen interest in public affairs. The prospectus read as follows:

A POLITICAL QUARTERLY

It is proposed to establish a Quarterly Review, which will have as its special object the discussion of social policy, public administration and questions of industrial and political organisation, primarily in Great Britain, but also, from time to time, in other countries. Its aim should be to do for these matters what the *Round Table* has attempted to do for imperial politics. While treating them in a scientific spirit, it would have as its subject current political and social problems, not political science in the abstract. It would differ from the existing reviews, partly because the space at its command would enable it to aim at a standard of thoroughness impossible in a short article, and partly because it would be planned by a group of writers holding certain general political ideas in common.

While its intellectual basis would be an acceptance of the view of the necessity of industrial and social reconstruction it will not be mortgaged to any one political party, nor be committed in advance to any particular programme. To discover truth and promote social well-being will be its only definite loyalties; and as a journal it will know no other allegiance. Thus it would welcome contributions from persons of different political connections, provided that they were of the necessary quality. It should be realistic and critical in spirit, and should attempt to handle its subject with sufficient authority to attract the attention of all persons seriously interested in political and social questions, whatever their political views. While it would naturally be mainly concerned with questions of topical interest, it should endeavour to treat them in a broad and philosophical manner, and should aim at diffusing knowledge and stimulating thought, rather than at presenting a case. It should draw on the experience of the Continent, the USA, and the British Dominions, as freely as on that of this country, and should appeal not only to English readers but to all serious students of political, economic and social questions.

The reasons for thinking that such a journal would meet a demand are as follows:

1. There is no journal in England today which attempts to deal authoritatively with questions of social policy and political organisation. The whole tenor of political discussion in England is at the present time in a profoundly unsatisfactory condition. The national daily newspapers, with scarcely more than one exception, are either controlled by a handful of millionaires who definitely prevent the effective expression

of opinions from which they differ, or else are harnessed to the yoke of a particular political party. The weekly sixpenny journals, excellent though they are as commentaries on current events, are unable to devote the necessary space required for the adequate discussion of the larger political and social questions; while the monthly reviews, attempting, as they do, to cover every field of human activity, necessarily do so in a superficial manner. It is a serious matter at the present juncture, obviously a critical period in English history, that there should be no recognised avenue through which new ideas on social and political affairs can emerge for intelligent printed discussion.

2. Political and social questions are occupying an ever-increasing amount of public attention and will continue to do so more and more in the future. Apart from pamphlets and books, the great development of experience and thought in these fields, both in Great Britain and in other countries, has never been made accessible to the man in the street. He will not read a quarterly journal, but he will read the daily Press, and the journal would influence him by supplying the materials upon which the more reputable newspapers could draw.

3. The discussion of all political and economic questions suffers because there is no organ in which they are treated thoroughly, with reasoned arguments and a candid presentation of the available evidence. The result is that the general public is at the mercy of catchwords. There is also a growing number of persons who are not committed to any programme but who are nevertheless interested in a serious discussion of social and economic policy. Consider, in the light of these demands, the almost entire absence of any serious discussion in the Press of the real nature of the coal problem, or of unemployment, or of the problems of combinations and monopolies, or of trade unionism, or of the experience of our own and other countries regarding the possible methods of organising industries under public ownership and of their advantages and defects. There has probably never been a period in which so many political and economic experiments have been made in Europe as in the last ten years. Yet hardly any serious attempt has been made to estimate their significance and value.

Whatever views may be held as to questions of policy, in the sphere of political or economic organisation, it will be agreed that the first condition of a sane treatment of difficult questions is that the relevant facts should be known and should be discussed with candour and impartiality. A quarterly, such as is suggested, would do valuable work in helping to spread an understanding of the real nature of the problems with which the country is confronted. The probability that within five or ten years a government will be returned which is pledged to large measures of economic and social reconstruction makes the diffusion of such an understanding all the more important.

The size and format of the proposed journal would be so arranged as to include, among other regular features, reviews of current English and foreign literature and relevant official publications, and a digest of judicial and administrative decisions of public significance. But the main value of its contents will lie in its special articles.

We believe that it will be possible to form a group of contributors sufficient to ensure a continuous supply of matter of adequate quality, and it is believed that the editor contemplated is one who will command general and cordial approval.

The main difficulty to be overcome is the question of finance. It is estimated that an initial guaranteed sum of £2,000 will secure the journal for a period of at least two years. It is hoped that afterwards it may become self-supporting.

P. J. NOEL BAKER	HENRY CLAY
ERNEST BARKER	G. D. H. COLE
C. DELISLE BURNS	G. LOWES DICKINSON
A. M. CARR-SAUNDERS	P. SARGANT FLORENCE
MARGERY FRY	T. H. MARSHALL
T. E. GREGORY	KINGSLEY MARTIN
LYNDA GRIER	C. S. MYERS
FREDA HAWTREY	PERCY NUNN
L. T. HOBHOUSE	OLIVIER
J. A. HOBSON	W. A. ROBSON
EVA HUBBACK	C. P. SCOTT
H. J. LASKI	R. H. TAWNEY
F. LAVINGTON	BEATRICE WEBB
A. D. LINDSAY	SIDNEY WEBB
C. M. LLOYD	LEONARD WOOLF
J. J. MALLON	BARBARA WOOTTON

The next step was to raise money. The minimum amount considered necessary to ensure a trial run of three years was £2,000, allowing for substantial deficits during this period. This proved to be an arduous, time-consuming and exhausting task. Few of the signatories were able to contribute anything substantial. Eventually we persuaded a number of our friends and acquaintances to contribute sums varying from £5 to £150, but the total came to less than half the amount needed. I have related elsewhere in some detail how I succeeded in inducing Bernard Shaw to give me £1,000 for *The Political Quarterly*, and it is certain that without his help we should never have got the review started.[2] I had known G. B. S. well for several years and he had shown me much kindness and encouragement. But it took me 18 months to overcome his reluctance and scepticism, though some of it was possibly assumed in order to test our keenness and persistence. He insisted on his donation being kept a secret, and that the finances should be handled in the most businesslike manner. This was very typical of G. B. S., who perfectly understood that the quarterly was not intended to be a commercial enterprise—he was, of course, quite right. Then with the help of a colleague in the Law Department of LSE I formed a small company called The Political Quarterly Publishing Company Limited. The cost of doing so must have been the lowest since joint stock companies were invented!

Meanwhile, we had set up a small committee to take responsibility for launching the quarterly. This consisted of Leonard Woolf, A. M. Carr-Saunders,[3] Harold Laski, J. M. Keynes, T. E. Gregory,[4] Kingsley Martin and myself.

It was agreed among us privately that J. L. Hammond should be invited to be the editor. He was a brilliant and experienced journalist, a social historian of great eminence, and a man of high political ideals and moral purpose. We somewhat rashly mentioned his name to actual or potential supporters as the person 'we hoped to get' as editor regardless of the fact that he had not finally decided to act. He had written to Laski on July 4, 1927, saying: 'It is a great honour to be considered in such a light and you may be sure that if the project comes off I should not turn it down unless I really thought I should not do it satisfactorily.' However, as the project began to take shape and our expectations of realising it rose, he decided he could not accept. On November 27, 1928, he wrote to me saying that he had had a talk with Tawney about the proposed quarterly and 'I am afraid that my mind is quite made up on the problem of the editorship.' He expressed a willingness to serve on any committee we might set up to advance the project. He added: 'I wish I could have given you a more satisfactory answer to the question of the editorship but the first condition of success in any such undertaking is that the editor should believe that he can make a good job of it and in this case the conviction is unfortunately lacking.' Hammond was shortly afterwards elected a member of the Executive Committee.

We then tried to persuade Hammond to become joint editor with Leonard Woolf but again he refused. Woolf was unwilling to become sole editor but was prepared to be joint editor with someone he could agree to work with. Unknown to me, he wrote to Martin saying that he thought I would be the most suitable person to act as joint editor with him.[5] When the matter came before the Committee, they decided to appoint Kingsley Martin and me as joint editors.

The appointment of Kingsley had not been entirely free of doubt, partly because some members of the Committee thought that his living in Manchester might cause difficulties of personal contact with me, and partly because others, as Keynes put it in a letter to me of June 28, 1929, were 'a little afraid of Martin's alleged rashness'. Kingsley wrote afterwards to Leonard saying he felt badly about the matter and received a characteristically generous reply from him:

Thére is no need for you to feel bad. I always tell the truth unless there is a very good reason for telling a lie, and in this case there was no need for me to do so. The Quarterly interests me and I like having a finger in interesting pies, but as I said (truthfully) I have not really the time for it and was glad to get out of it for that reason. My position at the moment was however not entirely easy, as I had talked to so many people on the Committee about all the possible candidates. I did not therefore feel it was quite fair to the Committee to withdraw absolutely at once until I had seen that the Committee definitely did not think that your being in Manchester was a ground for not having you. That was why I thought it best to let them discuss us.

His attitude was confirmed by Keynes in his letter to me, in which he said that Woolf's only reason for not withdrawing was to remain available in the event of the Committee feeling that they were a little afraid of appointing Martin. He did not in the least want the job for himself. On July 4, 1929, I explained in a letter to Bernard Shaw that following Hammond's refusal 'What we have decided to do in default of an editor of equal standing and maturity to him, is to have an Editorial Board consisting of the members of the Committee . . . together possibly with one or two other similar individuals. These names will be presented to the world on the cover of the Quarterly and the actual work of editing will be done jointly by Kingsley Martin and myself. Kingsley Martin, whom you met when you dined with me at Princes Gate, is a very able and energetic young man who is now one of the chief leader writers on the *Manchester Guardian*, where he was called to replace C. E. Montague. Prior to that he was on the staff of the School of Economics. He has written two or three books including one on Lord Palmerston, *The British Public and the General Strike* and a recent volume on *French Political Thought in the Eighteenth Century*. As far as I am concerned, I did not at all desire to have any share in the editorship but the Committee unanimously insisted on my lending a hand, mainly on the score, I imagine, that there is no one else to cover the field of Local Government, Labour Legislation, Administrative Law, and Law Reform generally with which I am more or less familiar. I don't think that the choice is a good one but it was difficult for me to refuse.' G. B. S. raised no objection to this arrangement and shortly afterwards sent me a cheque for £1,000.

During the first year of publication, which began in January 1930, only the names of the Editorial Board were printed without any indication that Kingsley and I were in charge of the editing, but thereafter this was changed. All the members but one of the Editorial Board became directors of the company, and each was issued with a £1 ordinary share, of which there are one hundred authorised. All the financial supporters received Mortgage Debentures for their contributions. The idea was to separate the proprietary interest from control, which was to rest with the members of the Editorial Board as holders of one ordinary share each.

A practical matter which had to be settled well in advance of publication was the question of a publisher. I decided to approach Macmillans, partly because they had recently published one of my books, and partly because I felt it would be an advantage for a periodical of progressive outlook to be published by a firm of impeccable respectability and of high repute. I accordingly went to see Mr Harold Macmillan in the firm's beautiful country-house style of offices in St Martin's Street, and asked him if Macmillans would be willing, to publish *The Political Quarterly*. I showed him the prospectus, explained the editorial arrangements, and emphasised that the new periodical would have a frankly progressive and left of centre approach. Mr Macmillan said that this would not matter if the contents were of high quality. I assured him we intended to aim at the highest possible quality of contribution. He then said that Macmillans would be willing to publish the new periodical, subject to satisfactory financial conditions and the agreement of his partners. On July 18, 1929, he wrote to me confirming that Macmillans would be glad to undertake publication on a commission basis, and outlining the terms.

Mr Harold Macmillan took a personal interest in launching the new quarterly and gave us much useful advice—for instance, I have in front of me a long handwritten letter which he wrote from Bolton Abbey in August 1929 dealing with practical details. We were published for many years by

Macmillans and left them only because we thought it would be better to be handled by a periodical publisher rather than a book publisher.

I recall one incident at the end of my visit to Mr Macmillan. He had not yet published *The Middle Way* but it was already clear that he was at odds with right-wing elements in the Tory party. I said: 'I sometimes wonder why you are where you are in political life.' He looked at me hard and replied: 'I regard the Conservative party as the only means of achieving reform by general consent in this country.'

The first number was issued on January 28, 1930. It was well received by the kind of people whose opinions we valued. Tawney, Laski and Lowes Dickinson expressed very favourable opinions. Walter Lippmann wrote from New York (where he was editing *The World* at the time) saying he thought the first issue excellent. Philip Noel Baker wrote that the second number was 'awfully good, a real improvement on the first number which is saying a lot'. Macmillans wrote that: 'the impression we have here is that *The Political Quarterly* has made a rather effective start. To have obtained a subscribers' list of over 500 before the second number appears is a distinct achievement.' H. G. Wells wrote belatedly regretting that the new quarterly should have appeared when *The Realist* was struggling to survive. *The Realist* was intended to be a journal of scientific humanism, and contained articles on art and science as well as politics. It was published monthly and came to an end after scarcely a year of life.

From a journalistic point of view we had made an encouraging start. Politically we could scarcely have chosen a better time. The futility and lack of direction of the second Labour government of 1929, the foolish and suicidal policy of the Liberal party in assuming the role of a balancing power cramping almost every Labour measure; the disastrous disruption of the Labour party by the defection of MacDonald, Thomas and Snowden in 1931; the impotent and short-sighted attitude towards unemployment and the great depression of the government, the Treasury, the Bank of England and official circles generally; the plight of several of our major industries and the misery of the depressed areas; the threatening international situation: all these causes produced a widespread state of frustration and dissatisfaction. The political intelligentsia with a progressive outlook to whom we hoped to appeal were very willing to listen to any voices and views which might help to raise the country from the slough of despond into which it had fallen.

From an economic standpoint the beginning of 1930 was a most unfavourable moment at which to launch a new periodical. We had scarcely been going for a year before the financial crisis of 1931 caused a serious and widespread curtailment of both public and private expenditure. Keynes had made no impact with his revolutionary theory of the causes and cure of unemployment and slump, and his most important work *The General Theory of Employment, Interest and Money* was not published until 1936. There was thus little effective opposition to the traditional wisdom, advocated by the government and the establishment, of meeting the great depression by reducing expenditure all round. Public libraries cut down their subscriptions, and private subscribers followed suit in the pathetic belief that the patriotic duty of every good citizen in the economic blizzard was to reduce his personal expenditure to the greatest possible extent.

The consequences were serious for a newly founded periodical striving for a footing. Our losses in 1930, 1931 and 1932 exceeded our expectations and made heavy inroads on our modest capital. However, we managed to survive, and among those who helped us through our difficulties was Sir Stafford Cripps.

It must have been in the latter part of 1933 that I ventured to seek further help from Bernard Shaw and this gave rise to some very lively and hard-hitting correspondence between us.[6] Bernard Shaw's letter of refusal was as follows:

R. M. S. Rangitane, outward bound London to New Zealand,
at present roasting near the Equator.

February 24, 1934

Dear Robson,

At last I have a moment's leisure to write to you about the P.Q., and to give more than a glance at the figures you supplied me with. They seem to me quite conclusive: the experiment has failed. The receipts are dwindling; the sales are dwindling. I shall not throw the handle after the hatchet by pensioning it: I cannot afford such games (the popular impression that my settled income is boundless is a delusion: I can finance an experiment occasionally out of the windfalls that occasionally happen in the theatre even to me; but I cannot keep lame ducks from year to year; and my last two plays have flopped just as badly as the P.Q. and for much the same causes).

Derelict magazines are hard to kill; or rather they are hard to bury. Their ghosts keep walking often for years and years. I think it shocking to bleed Cripps personally to keep the wreck afloat; but if I were the editor I should offer to make the paper the organ of all the dictators; of Kemal, Hitler, Mussolini, Roosevelt, Pilsudski, Doumergue, De Valera, Mosley, and of Cripps too, if he cares to give a final kick to 'the putrefying corpse of Democracy'. The blazing fact that nobody mentions is that of late years every political adventurer who promises to suppress or sidetrack parliament instantly gets an overwhelming vote of confidence from his nation. If the P.Q. were to make itself the mouthpiece of this movement, a modest subvention from each of these heroes, accompanied by an occasional article from their pens, might keep the rag afloat; but if it sticks to the Labour party, or to any parliamentary party whatever, it will succumb to the general nausea which the words parliament, liberty, democracy, etc., etc., now set up. The nausea may not be intelligent; but it is a reaction that must be catered for; and one of its symptoms is a curious appetite for bad language. But as blackguardism without artistry is mere commonplace, all the political notes should be written by Virginia Woolf. The old politico-literary stodge is no use now. I return the balance-sheet, etc., as you may want it to persuade some millionaire who doesn't understand figures that the P.Q. offers him the chance of a lifetime.

Faithfully,
G. Bernard Shaw

The reference to Cripps arose from my having explained to Shaw that Sir Stafford Cripps had recently given some financial support to assist the review through this difficult initial period, and in doing so had expressed to me his warm appreciation of *The Political Quarterly*.

Shaw's blistering letter was more than I could swallow. I had for some time regarded with apprehension and regret his growing acceptance of dictatorship and his readiness to reject and destroy democratic institutions. I sent the following answer:

June 9, 1934.

Dear G. B. S.,

I waited to answer your letter of February 26th until you had time to get off the Equator and to return to a more temperate zone.

Your letter raises two quite separate matters. One relates to the financial position of *The Political Quarterly*, and perhaps I should deal with that first.

It is quite true that we had a falling off in sales, and therefore in revenue, during the last six months of 1932 and the first half of 1933; but this was scarcely a matter for surprise in view of the financial stringency which had occurred the preceding year, and which invariably hits an enterprise such as *The Political Quarterly* about a year later. Why you should suggest that the paper should throw up the sponge because of a temporary set back I cannot imagine. It would be as reasonable to suggest that you should stop writing plays because (as you tell me) your last two have flopped, As a matter of fact, the really important thing about *The Political Quarterly* is that although we raised the price last April to 5s, the circulation has scarcely fallen at all, and we have as a result a very large increase in revenue. In consequence, the financial position has enormously improved, and I have every reason to believe that the stability of the paper will be assured.

I come now to the quite separate matter, namely, your statement that any journal which stands for parliamentary methods is completely doomed, and that the only hope is to sell out to the dictators. Incidentally, I note with interest that the eight whom you mention does not include the name of Stalin, the only Socialist among the lot. I am amazed—and so is everyone else—at the way in which you seem to be willing to be led astray by the nonsense which is talked by all these anti-parliamentary gentlemen. If they were Socialists I could understand and forgive your delusions, but in view of the fact that they are one and all violent anti-Socialists and therefore opposed to all the doctrines which you have advocated for the past fifty years, I cannot imagine why you should expect those of us who are still Socialists to follow their cries. Do you seriously imagine that Italy, Germany, Turkey, or Poland are one atom nearer a socialistic régime today than they were ten years ago before they had these Dictatorships, or than we in this country are under representative institutions? If I may say so without disrespect, it is you who have been deceived by talk—despite all your contempt for the endless talking of the parliamentary regime. The only difference is that you have been deceived by the ridiculous pretensions of the Dictators, Personally, if I am to be deceived by talk, I prefer it to be the talk of someone whom I have elected or can at least throw out without being myself chucked into a concentration camp. There is just one question I want to ask you in conclusion: how much of your work do you think you would have been allowed to do if instead of living in this country under these despised institutions you had been born under one of the dictatorships? If I remember correctly, you made an enormous fight even against the Censor of Plays.

Of course, I and every other intelligent person knows that the Parliamentary machine is absolutely archaic, but I prefer to follow Cripps, who wants to reform it and make it effective, rather than you, who want to abolish it. In any case, I do not intend to desert Socialism merely because reactionary dictatorships happen to be popular at the moment.

Shaw did not resent in the slightest degree my spirited reply to his onslaught: his good temper in controversy was one of his most amiable traits. A few days later I received a laconic postcard from him:

> June 16, 1934.
>
> I have received a letter signed W. A. R., but evidently written by the Duchess of Atholl.
>
> Anyhow I have done my share for the P.Q., and will waste no more money on it. You had better get somebody to review my last two prefaces for it seriously, especially the reply to Chesterton.[7]
>
> G. B. S.

G. B. S. was adamant in refusing to give us a farthing more, and looking back I can understand his feeling that he had done enough. He nonetheless remained well disposed towards *The Political Quarterly* in other respects, and contributed several articles to its pages.

The editorial structure has remained unchanged throughout the past 40 years. There has always been an Editorial Board, whose members were directors of the company, and except during the war editorial responsibility has been shared by two joint editors. I have already related how Kingsley Martin and I were the first joint editors. In the autumn of 1930 Martin was sacked by the *Manchester Guardian* as a leader writer and came south to London. Soon afterwards he was appointed editor of *The New Statesman and Nation* to which be devoted the next thirty years of his life. It was obvious to both of us that no one could edit a weekly review and a quarterly periodical simultaneously: one or the other would suffer, and in this instance *The New Statesman* had a much greater claim on Kingsley's time and attention. So in the summer of 1931 he retired as joint editor and was succeeded by Leonard Woolf. Martin remained a member of the Editorial Board until his death in 1969 and he took a continuing interest in the paper he helped to found. For many years he contributed regularly both articles and surveys.

Leonard Woolf and I were joint editors from 1931 to 1958, except during the years 1941 to 1945 when he was in sole charge. I was then engaged on war work in the Civil Service and had no time or energy to spare for anything else, quite apart from the propriety of even a temporary civil servant editing a periodical such as this. After he withdrew from the post of joint editor in 1958, Leonard Woolf acted as Literary Editor until 1962 when he was succeeded by Richard Greaves. He continued to be an active member of the Editorial Board until his death last August.

I worked with Leonard Woolf in complete harmony and friendship for the 23 years of our association as joint editors. I can remember only one serious difference of opinion which arose over the abdication of Edward VIII. He wanted to support the King in an editorial and I did not agree to this because I was not in favour of a republic which I felt certain would be brought about if Mrs Simpson became either Queen or a morganatic wife. Leonard took a rationalist and libertarian view of the situation, whereas I believed and still believe that popular support for the monarchy is not based on either rational or libertarian grounds. In the end we did not publish an editorial on the subject. Apart from this episode we collaborated perfectly. Our judgements about contributors and articles were almost always in agreement and our special interests were complementary. Leonard had an exceptional knowledge and understanding of foreign policy, international affairs, the League of Nations and the United Nations, disarmament, Imperial and Commonwealth matters. My social interests concerned British and foreign government, public administration, constitutional and civil service questions, public law, law reform, nationalised industry, local government, and so forth. We both had very wide interests outside our special fields.

Leonard was a completely reliable man in every way. If he said he would do something he invariably did it. Articles were quickly read and letters promptly answered. He was extremely generous in looking after the quarterly when I went abroad from time to time as visiting professor. He was also very generous financially, and for many years refused to take the small honorarium the editors received for their labours.

My appreciation of Leonard's great contribution to *The Political Quarterly* and his personal qualities has not been evoked only by his recent death. In a letter I sent to him on July 22, 1940, explaining that I had accepted a temporary appointment in a Government Department and could not continue to act as joint editor while in the Civil Service, I wrote:

I would like to tell you how immensely I have enjoyed and appreciated our association together in the review. I scarcely think it would be possible to have a more sympathetic understanding and common sharing of outlook than we have had in these past years. Your generosity in every way has been remarkable.

I do think it *most* important to keep *The Political Quarterly* going at all costs so long as it is humanly possible. Long-distance thinking has become more necessary than ever since the war. I will, of course, do anything I can to help as an ordinary member of the Board, consistently with the obligations of my official status.

I received a warm reply.

After his resignation in 1958 as joint editor Leonard Woolf's place was taken by T. E. M. McKitterick, who served in that capacity until 1966, when Bernard Crick was appointed in his place.

The Editorial Board remained relatively stable although a good many changes have occurred during the past 40 years. Of the original nine members John Maynard Keynes, G. Lowes Dickinson, Harold Laski, Kingsley Martin and Leonard Woolf continued to serve until they died. J. L. Hammond withdrew in 1933 owing to ill-health. The late Sir Alexander Carr-Saunders resigned in July 1938 on becoming Director of the London School of Economics, which he felt was incompatible with any political commitment. Sir Theodore Gregory, who lived abroad a great deal, resigned in 1940. Sir Arthur Salter (now Lord Salter) joined the Board in 1932 and resigned in January 1940 when he became a minister. He rejoined in 1948 but left in 1951 on becoming a member of Winston Churchill's Caretaker Government. Sir Ernest Simon (later Lord Simon of Wythenshawe) joined the Board in 1935 and played an active and valuable part until his death in 1960. G. D. H. Cole served from 1946 until his death in 1959 and gave us much help and advice. Barbara Wootton (Baroness Wootton) was a member from 1951 until 1966, when she withdrew owing to pressure of parliamentary and other obligations. R. H. S. Crossman was a colleague from 1940 to 1960. Professor B. C. Roberts was on the Board for ten years from 1957. A. L. Rowse was a member of the Board for a short time between 1943 and 1946. All the other members of the Editorial Board are still serving.

This concludes my brief history of the founding of *The Political Quarterly* and the part played by the people who gave it their help and support. I will show in a separate article the problems which confronted the editors in the early years of its existence.

Notes

1 Margaret Cole, *The Story of Fabian Socialism*, p. 218.

2 See my article 'Bernard Shaw and *The Political Quarterly*' in *The Political Quarterly* for July–September 1951. This was reprinted in my recent book of essays entitled *Politics and Government at Home and Abroad*, Allen and Unwin, 1967.

3 Then Professor of Social Science at Liverpool University.

4 Then Professor of Banking at LSE.

5 In a letter dated February 23, 1929, of which I was unaware until a copy came into my hands after Leonard Woolf's recent death.

6 I have given a fuller account of my relations with G. B. S. in my essay 'Bernard Shaw and *The Political Quarterly*' in *The Political Quarterly*, July–September 1951. Reprinted in my collection of essays, *Politics and Government at Home and Abroad*.

7 I reviewed the collected volume of his prefaces in the issue of *The Political Quarterly* for October–December 1934.

In the course of the review I examined Shaw's attitude towards democracy and dictatorship, and remarked that 'in spite of all his scepticism and raillery Mr. Shaw is philosophically a democrat. . . For him the fundamental problem is how to make the machinery of democratic government fool-proof.' He had advocated in turn anthropometric tests, the formation of panels of tested persons, and finally vocational election, as methods of discovering the persons qualified by nature to be rulers. The impracticability of all these methods was obvious; and, as I pointed out, the essential weakness of Shaw's position was that he wanted to make the democratic process fool-proof instead of eliminating the danger by educating people our of their political foolishness. He recognised that we are 'dangerously uneducated' but did not seem to realise that if we want people to be sufficiently enlightened to be able to select intelligently leaders freely, we must use the educational machine to enlighten and instruct them in their functions as citizens.

Further reflection led Bernard Shaw to modify considerably the adulation of dictatorship he had shown in the 1930s; and he must have been influenced by the suicidal madness, wickedness and folly of Hitler and Mussolini. For his final position we may turn to *Everybody's Political What's What*, published in 1944.

Here he explicitly declared we must reject the Hitler plan of government because '. . . it gives one man more authority and responsibility than one man can bear'.

The Dilemma of Modern Socialism

J. M. KEYNES

Vol. 3, no. 3, July–September 1932

BESIDES two arms and two legs for oratory, gesticulation and movement, Socialism has two heads and two hearts which are always at war with one another. The one is ardent to do things because they are economically sound. The other is no less ardent to do things which are admitted to be economically unsound. I mean by economically sound, improvements in organisation and so forth which are desired because they will increase the production of wealth; and by economically unsound things which will, or may, have the opposite effect.

And there is a further distinction to make. Things which are economically unsound are advocated for two widely different sorts of reasons. The first set are in pursuance of the ideal. Those who are influenced by them are ready to sacrifice economic wealth for the attainment of higher goods—justice, equality, beauty, or the greater glory of the republic. The second set are political—to get up steam, to bribe political supporters, to stir up the embers of the class war, to irritate and exasperate the powers that be and to make their task more difficult and perhaps impossible, so that the mere force of events may compel their deposition and replacement. Thus some things may be advocated *in spite of* their being economically unsound, and other things may be advocated *because of* their being economically unsound.

These three *motifs* exist, variously compounded, in the breast of every socialist. They are seen magnified, and therefore clearer, in the *politik* of the Bolshevists, the changes and vacillations in which are due to the fluctuating preponderance of one or the other *motif*. The Marxian creed, I take it, is that the third *motif*, the revolutionary, should preponderate in the first phase, the phase of attaining power; that the first, the practical, should preponderate in the second phase, when power has been used to prepare the way; and that the second, the ideal, should preponderate when the socialist republic emerges out of the blood and dust and travail, fully fledged. The Revolution, the Five-Year Plan, the Ideal—that is the progression. But the distinction between the phases is not clear cut—all three *motifs* are present in some degree all the time. For English purposes one might perhaps sum the *motifs* up as the political, the practical and the ideal.

Now it is, I suggest, enormously important to know what one is doing, in what phase one is dwelling and in what proportions the *motifs* are mixed.

For my part I should like to define the socialist programme as aiming at political power, with a view to doing in the first instance what is economically sound, in order that, later on, the community may become rich enough to afford what is economically unsound.

Published by Blackwell Publishing Ltd, 9600 Garsington Road, Oxford OX4 2DQ, UK and 350 Main Street, Malden, MA 02148, USA

My goal is the ideal; my object is to put economic considerations into a back seat; but my method at this moment of economic and social evolution would be to advance towards the goal by concentrating on doing what is economically sound. But there are others, I know, who would prefer, even today, to advocate what is economically unsound, because they believe that this is the best way to gain political power (which in any case is the first step), and that to render the existing system unworkable is the only means of reaching a new system. In my judgement both these notions are false; because the ruin of the old system, so far from making the construction of the new technically easier, may, on the contrary, make it impossible. For it will have to be on the basis of increased resources, not on the basis of poverty, that the grand experiment of the ideal republic will have to be made. I do not overlook the difficulty of getting up steam when things are going reasonably well. But I consider that precisely *that* is the problem to be solved. To be sufficiently deep-founded on the best intelligences and finest and strongest emotions of the community, to be able to keep up steam when things are going reasonably well; to thrive, not on the vapours of misery and discontent, but on the living energy of the passion for right construction and the right building up of a worthy society—that is the task.

This leads me to the daily perplexity of British socialism, and perhaps of socialism everywhere, as I see it. The practical problem, the problem of how to do what is economically sound, is mainly an intellectual problem and, as it happens, a very difficult intellectual problem, about which there is much disagreement. But intellectually a large element, probably the predominant element, of the Labour party is old fashioned and even anti-intellectual. It has been the trouble for years past that the leaders of the Labour party have differed from the leaders of the other parties chiefly in being more willing to do or to risk things which in their hearts they have believed to be economically unsound. They have not fundamentally disagreed with the other parties as to what is economically sound or unsound. Mr Thomas's ideas, for example, of what is economically sound are, and always have been, almost exactly the same as those of the Tory Nationalists, Mr Neville Chamberlain or Mr Amery; and Viscount Snowden's ideas have been just the same as those of liberal economists and deflationists such as Mr Runciman or Sir Herbert Samuel or Lord Grey. They have been totally out of sympathy with those who have had new notions of what is economically sound, whether the innovator has been right or wrong. And this condition of affairs goes deep into the bowels of the Labour party. For the same is true, on the whole, of many others of the party's most respected pillars.

Now this puts the Labour party into a feeble position when—as it happened last summer as a result of the deflation—the country has got into such a pickle that there is an overwhelming and universal demand for a practical solution, when everyone is determined that, for the time being at least, we must ensue what is economically sound. For it means that in such a conjuncture most of the Labour leaders agree at heart with their opponents; so that having a bad conscience, they become exceedingly ineffective for the practical purposes of government. The Labour Cabinet was in a hopeless position last August, because most of them conscientiously believed in the Gold Standard and in deflation by economy, and were not prepared to throw these things overboard. Yet at the same time they were equally unprepared to sacrifice the political and the ideal *motifs* in which they had been brought up.

Therefore the first task of the Labour party, if it is to be effective is, as I see it, to become intellectually emancipated as to what is economically sound, without losing either its political strength and its political organisation, which goes so deep into the social and economic life of England, or its ideals and ultimate goals. For in the modern world it has to be one thing or the other. Either the revolutionary *motif* must prevail or the practical *motif*. Nothing lands you in a sillier position or one which will draw down more certainly or more justly the contempt of the British people than not to know, when you propose something, whether the object of proposing it is because it is economically sound or because it is economically unsound. No one knew at the last election which leg the Labour party was standing on, least of all the party itself.

For my own part I would urge that we stand at a point in economic evolution when it is desirable to concentrate on what is economically sound. There are two good and sufficient reasons for this. In the first place it happens that the most pressing reforms which are economically sound do not, as perhaps they did in earlier days, point away from the ideal. On the contrary they point towards it. I am convinced that those things which are urgently called for on practical grounds, such as the central control of investment and the distribution of income in such a way as to provide purchasing power for the enormous potential output of modern productive technique, will also tend to produce a better kind of society on ideal grounds. There is probably less opposition today between the practical aim and the ideal than there has been hitherto.

In the second place there is so much to be hoped today from doing what is economically sound, that it is our duty to give this *motif* its opportunity. For it may be capable of solving once and for all the problem of poverty. At present the world is being held back by something which would have surprised our fathers—by a failure of economic technique to exploit the possibilities of engineering and distributive technique; or, rather, engineering technique has reached a degree of perfection which is making obvious defects in economic technique which have always existed, though unnoticed, and have doubtless impoverished mankind since the days of Abraham. I mean by economic technique the means of solving the problem of the *general* organisation of resources as distinct from the *particular* problems of production and distribution which are the province of the individual business technician and engineer. For the next twenty-five years in my belief, economists, at present the most incompetent, will be nevertheless the most important, group of scientists in the world. And it is to be hoped—if they are successful—that after that they will never be important again. But during this horrid interval, when these creatures matter, it is of vast importance that they should be free to pursue their problem in an environment—for they, with their mixed subject-matter, are, of all men, the least independent, as the history of their theory shows, of the surrounding atmosphere—uninfluenced, as far as possible, by the bias of the other *motifs*.

All this has been brought to a head, or at least brought to notice, by the radical changes in modern technique, especially in the last ten years, which are so brilliantly described in Mr Fred Henderson's *Economic Consequences of Power Production*. Immemorially man's muscles have been, for the vast majority of purposes and operations, the source of power, sometimes aided by wind, water and domestic beasts. *Labour*, in the literal sense, has been the prime factor of production. It made a vast difference when, for transport and for certain limited operations, other sources of power were added. But even the addition of steam and electricity and petrol have not made, in themselves, so radical a change, as has the character of the new processes of production which have, in latter years, grown up with them. For until these latter years, the chief effort of new machines was to render *labour*, i.e. man's muscles, more efficient. Economists could plausibly argue that machinery was cooperative, not competitive with labour. But the effect of the latest types of machinery is increasingly, not to make man's muscles more efficient, but to render them *obsolete*. And the effect is twofold, first to furnish us with the ability to produce consumption goods, as distinct from services, almost without limit; and secondly to use so little labour in the process that an ever-increasing proportion of human employment must be occupied either in the field of supplying human services or in meeting the demand for durable goods which, if the rate of interest were low enough, would be still far from satisfied.

Thus the apparatus of economic organisation is faced with a problem of readjustment of unusual difficulty in itself. If it is true that this apparatus has always been misunderstood and badly operated, if the supposed inner harmony and self-balancing characters of the economic system, in reliance on which our fathers were ready to surrender the system to *laissez-faire*, are an illusion, it is a natural result that events should be finding out where our intellectual weakness lies. Our prime task, therefore, is to discover, and then to do, what is economically sound. This temporary concentration on the practical is the best contribution which we of today can make towards the attainment of the ideal.

The Choice before the Labour Party

R. H. TAWNEY

Vol. 3, no. 3, July–September 1932

I

Now THAT the dust has settled, it is possible to examine the landscape left by the earthquake. The election of 1931 was, by general consent, a considerable sensation. But neither the preliminary manoeuvres described by Lord Passfield, nor the methods adopted during the contest itself, are the phenomena on which today it is most profitable for a member of the Labour party to reflect. Political coroners may sit on the corpse of the late Cabinet, but the ordinary citizen is more concerned with its behaviour before life was extinct. What matters to him, and what is likely to determine his attitude when next the Labour party appeals for his support, is less the question of the circumstances in which the last government went out, than that of what it did, attempted, and neither did nor attempted to do, when it was in. It is possible that his verdict on its death, if at this time of day he paused to consider it, would be, neither murder nor misadventure, but pernicious anæmia producing general futility.

For the events of the late summer of 1931 were the occasion, rather than the cause, of the debacle of the Labour party. In spite of the dramatic episodes which heralded its collapse, the government did not fall with a crash, in a tornado from the blue. It crawled slowly to its doom, deflated by inches, partly by its opponents, partly by circumstances beyond its control, but partly also by itself. The gunpowder was running out of it from the moment it assumed office, and was discovered, on inspection, to be surprisingly like sawdust. Due allowance must be made, no doubt, for the cruel chance which condemned it to face the worst collapse in prices of modern history; and due credit must be given for the measures which it introduced, but failed, through no fault of its own, to pass into law. But, granted the inexorable limits, can it seriously be argued that it was audacious in working up to them?

The commonest answer to that question was given in two words: minority government. To the writer it appeared at the time, and appears today, unconvincing. When the Cabinet took office, two alternatives were open to it. It could decide to live dangerously, or to play for safety. It could choose a short life, and—if the expression be not too harsh—an honest one; or it could proceed on the assumption that, once a Labour government is in office, its primary duty is to find means of remaining there. If it acted on its principles, it could not hope to survive for more than twelve months. It could postpone its execution, but only at the cost of making its opponents the censors of its policy. It would invite them, in effect, to decide the character of the measures

Published by Blackwell Publishing Ltd, 9600 Garsington Road, Oxford OX4 2DQ, UK and 350 Main Street, Malden, MA 02148, USA

which it should be permitted to introduce, and to determine the issues of the next election.

The late government chose the second course. It chose it, it must in fairness be admitted, with the tacit approval of the great majority of the party, including, as far as is known, those trade union elements in it which afterwards revolted against the results of the decision. The effects of its choice were, however, serious. Parts in life, once adopted, develop their consequences with a logic of their own, overriding the volition of the actors cast for them; however repulsive, if played at all, they must be played with gusto. Once convinced that discretion was their cue, ministers brought to the practice of the golden mean a conscientious assiduity almost painful to contemplate. They threw themselves into the role of The Obsequious Apprentice, or Prudence Rewarded, as though bent on proving that, so far from being different from other governments, His Majesty's Labour government could rival the most respectable of them in cautious conventionality.

Industrial and social reconstruction, the favourite theme of Labour orators, owed little to the existence of a Labour Cabinet. It doubtless felt itself precluded, till the Macmillan Committee had reported, from making up its mind on the questions of currency and credit which were to prove its undoing. Even in matters, however, where delay was not imposed by circumstances, its action did not err on the side of trenchancy. It found coal, cotton and steel with one foot in the nineteenth century; it left them there. What passed in its inner councils is, of course, unknown; but it gave few outward symptoms of realising that, if the modernisation of the major industries is to be handled at all, it must be planned as a whole, or of grasping the necessity of creating a permanent organ to press it steadily forward, or of appreciating the importance of devoting attention to the long-range aspects of unemployment, as distinct from monthly fluctuations in the number of unemployed. It had even to be stimulated by the protests of its followers in the House into proceeding—too late—with its little Education Bill. In one sphere, indeed, that of international policy, it achieved, in the opinion of good judges, solid and genuine successes. Apart from that important exception, and from the fact that, if King Log was bad, King Stork would be worse, what strong reason could be advanced for desiring its survival?

The degeneration of socialist parties on assuming office is now an old story. If it is worthwhile to recall the latest British version of it, it is not in order to visit on individuals' collective shortcomings. It is because, till its lessons are learned, the wretched business will go on. If the laments of some ex-ministers at the 'conspiracy', which 'stabbed them in the back'—as though a Titan, all energy and ardour, had been felled at his forge by the hand of assassins—were merely undignified, they would properly be ignored. Unfortunately, they are worse. What Labour most needs is not self-commiseration, but a little cold realism. These plaintive romancers would dry its tears with a tale of Red Riding Hood and the wicked wolf. They retard the recovery of the party by concealing its malady. They perpetuate the mentality which requires to be overcome before recovery can take place. The sole cure for its disease is sincerity. They offer it scapegoats.

If it is sincere, it will not be drugged by these opiates. It will not soothe the pain of defeat with the flattering illusion that it is the innocent victim of faults not its own. It is nothing of the kind. It is the author, the unintending and pitiable author, of its own misfortunes. It made a government in its own image; and the collapse of that government was the result neither of accident—though that played its part—nor of unfavourable circumstances—though luck was against it—nor, least of all, it must be repeated, of merely personal failings. It was in the logic of history; for 1929–31 repeated 1924. It sprang from within, not without; for it had begun within six months of the government's return, and the flight from principles was both earlier and more precipitate than the flight from the pound. It was the consequence, not of individual defects, but of a general habit of mind and outlook on affairs which ministers had acquired long before they could anticipate that power would be their lot. What was tried, and found wanting, in short, in 1929–31, was, not merely two years of a Labour Cabinet, but a decade of Labour politics.

Such, and not merely the events of a few weeks last summer, were the cause of the debacle. If these are the realities, to make the conduct of individuals, however odious in itself, the main target of criticism is to exaggerate their importance. To expel a person is not to exorcise a spirit. The truth is simpler and more serious. In the swift growth of the movement since 1918, its inner flaws had been concealed. But they had not disappeared; indeed, some of them had deepened. At the moment when the reality of power seemed almost within its grasp, its old faults found it out. It now has an interval in which to meditate its errors.

II

The gravest weakness of British Labour is one which it shares with the greater part of the world, outside Russia, including British capitalists. It is its lack of a creed. The Labour party is hesitant in action, because divided in mind. It does not achieve what it could, because it does not know what it wants. It frets out of office and fumbles in it, because it lacks the assurance either to wait or to strike. Being without clear convictions as to its own meaning and purpose, it is deprived of the dynamic which only convictions supply. If it neither acts with decision nor inspires others so to act, the principal reason is that it is itself undecided.

This weakness is fundamental. If it continues uncorrected, there neither is, nor ought to be, a future for the Labour party. A political creed, it need hardly be said, is neither a system of transcendental doctrine nor a code of rigid formulæ. It is a common conception of the ends of political action, and of the means of achieving them, based on a common view of the life proper to human beings, and of the steps required at any moment more nearly to attain it. A movement, like an individual, cannot build its existence round an internal vacuum. Till the void in the mind of the Labour party is filled—till interests are hammered by principles into a serviceable tool, which is what interests should be, and a steady will for a new social order takes the place of mild yearnings to make somewhat more comfortable terms with the social order of today—mere repairs to the engines will produce little but disillusionment.

There is much criticism at the moment of organisation and programmes. Some of it, like that which ascribes the troubles of the party to its trade union connections, is misconceived. It is obvious that the unions, like other elements in English society, including the intelligentsia, are most imperfectly socialised. It is obvious that the weight which is given them at party conferences by the card vote is an anomaly, which has a historical justification, but is not permanently defensible. The picture, however, of torpid and rapacious trade unionists impeding bold schemes of constructive statesmanship is a caricature; it cannot truly be said that the late government was harassed by recurrent pressure to sacrifice the larger aims of the movement to the sectional interests of one element in it. Some of the criticism, again, like the recoil of some members of the party from the social services—as though to recognise unemployment pay for the sorry makeshift it is involved repudiating the communism of Public Health, Housing and Education—is a mood of reaction, engendered by defeat, which in time will pass. But much of it is justified. The only comment to be made on it is that it does not go far enough.

Of course the programme of the party needs to be modernised; of course its organisation requires to be overhauled. No one who knows how the former is made and the latter works is likely to remain long on his knees before either. But, granted the obvious weaknesses of both— granted the intellectual timidity, conservatism, conventionality, which keeps policy trailing tardily in the rear of realities, and over which, if one's taste is for brilliance on the cheap, it is so easy to make merry—the root of the matter is elsewhere. These defects are the symptoms, not the source, of the trouble. They are, not causes, but effects.

The characteristic vice of the programmes of the party, as set out in conference resolutions, is that too often they are not programmes. They sweep together great things and small; nationalise land, mines and banking in one sentence, and abolish fox-hunting in the next; and, by touching on everything, commit ministers to nothing. The characteristic defect of its practical procedure is its tendency to rely for success on the mass support of societies, and the mass vote of constituencies, of whom neither have been genuinely converted to its principles. It requires an army. It collects a mob. The mob disperses. That is the nature of mobs. But why are Labour programmes less programmes than miscellanies—a glittering forest of Christmas trees, with presents for everyone, instead of a plan of campaign for what must be, on any showing, a pretty desperate business? Because the party is at present without any ordered conception of its task. Because it possesses in its own mind nothing analogous to what used to be called, in the days when it was necessary to put jobs through to time, a Scheme of Priorities. Because it has no stable standard of political values, such as would teach it to discriminate between the relative urgencies of different objectives. Because, lacking such a standard, it lacks also the ability to subordinate the claims of this section of the movement or that to the progress of the whole, and to throw its whole weight against the central positions, where success means something, and failure itself is not wholly a disaster, instead of frittering away its *moral* in inconclusive skirmishes.

And why is the Labour party's organisation, in spite of its admirable *personnel*, stronger in numbers than in quality? For precisely the same reason. Because the finest individuals are nothing till mastered by a cause. Because the party, being itself not too certain what that cause is, has found it difficult to present it in a form convincing to plain men, of whom the majority, in England as elsewhere, are not politicians. Because, instead of stating its faith, undiluted and unqualified, and waiting for their support till, with the teaching of experience, which today teaches pretty fast, they come to share it, it tried to buy their votes with promises, whether they shared that faith or not. Because it appealed to them, on the ground, not that a Labour government would be different from other governments, but that it would be a worthy successor to all British governments that had ever been. Because, when it ought to have called them to a long and arduous struggle, it too often did the opposite. It courted them with hopes of cheaply won benefits, and, if it did not despise them, sometimes addressed them as though it did. It demanded too little, and offered too much. It assured them that its aim was the supersession of capitalism, but that, in the meantime, the two-hooped pot should have four hoops. Is it surprising if they concluded that, since capitalism was the order of the day, it had better continue to be administered by capitalists, who, at any rate—so, poor innocents, they supposed—knew how to make the thing work?

These, it will be replied, are hard sayings. They are; but, unfortunately, they are true. The inner state of the movement has been concealed from itself by the glamour of a word. That word is Socialism. In 1918 the Labour party finally declared itself to be a Socialist party. It supposed, and supposes, that it thereby became one. It is mistaken. It recorded a wish, that is all; the wish has not been fulfilled. If it now disciplines itself for a decade, it may become a Socialist party. It is not one at present. Until it recognises that it is not Socialist, it is not likely to become Socialist. Like any other creed, socialism has two aspects. It implies a personal attitude and a collective effort. The quality of the latter depends on the sincerity of the former. The collective effort involves three essentials: agreement as to the kind of society which it is desired to establish; agreement as to the nature of the resistance to be overcome in establishing it; agreement as to the technique, the methods and machinery, required for its establishment. The history of British socialism, during the present century, is largely the story of the concentration of attention on the third requirement, to the neglect of the two first.

The effort devoted to questions of method has, in itself, been admirable. But expedients require, in order that they may be applied, and produce, when applied, the results intended, a situation in which their application, their continuous application on a large scale, is possible. Such a situation can exist only if socialists come to power, not as diffident agents of policies not their own, but as socialists, and, having done so, are prepared to deal with the opposition which they will encounter. They must have created behind them, before they assume office, a strong body of opinion, which 'knows what it fights for, and loves what it knows'. They must have measured coolly the forces which will be mobilised against them. The Labour party has done neither.

The reasons are partly historical. The British Labour movement was offered in its youth a foreign, and peculiarly arid, version of Marxian socialism. It very sensibly rejected it—very sensibly, not because the doctrine was Marxian, but because, in its pedantry and lack of historical realism, it was anything but Marxian. Then the unexpected happened. The seed sown by the pioneers began to bear fruit. The movement became a political power. Whole battalions were shepherded into it, much as the troops of Feng-husiang, 'the Christian general', were baptised with a hose. Thanks to the judges, the unions were the first wave. The war brought another; the election of 1923 a third; the events of 1926 a fourth. By that time a generation had grown up to which it seemed as easy to be a socialist—as easy, if you please!—as it had seemed difficult in 1900.

The result was that the British Labour party, like British industry, was for a time too prosperous. It behaved, as the latter had behaved, as though summer would last for ever. It had inherited from the nineteenth century the economic psychology of an age of expansion. In the flush of success, its political psychology assumed for a time the same florid complexion. It deceived itself both as to its own condition, and as to the character of the forces on its side and against it. It mistook luck for merit; treated votes, which were clearly indispensable, as equivalent to convictions, as to the practical value of which it was not equally certain; and drugged itself with the illusion that, by adding one to one, it would achieve the millennium, without the painful necessity of clarifying its mind, disciplining its appetites, and training for a tough wrestle with established power and property. It touched lightly on its objectives, or veiled them in the radiant ambiguity of the word socialism, which each hearer could interpret to his taste. So it ended by forgetting the reason for its existence. It has now to rediscover it.

Yet the objective of a socialist party, and of the Labour party in so far as it deserves the name, is simplicity itself. The fundamental question, as always, is: Who is to be master? Is the reality behind the decorous drapery of political democracy to continue to be the economic power wielded by a few thousand—or, if that be preferred, a few hundred thousand—bankers, industrialists and landowners? Or shall a serious effort be made—as serious, for example, as was made, for other purposes, during the war—to create organs through which the nation can control, in cooperation with other nations, its own economic destinies; plan its business as it deems most conducive to the general well-being; override, for the sake of economic efficiency, the obstruction of vested interests; and distribute the product of its labours in accordance with some generally recognised principles of justice? Capitalist parties presumably accept the first alternative. A socialist party chooses the second. The nature of its business is determined by its choice.

That business is not the passage of a series of reforms in the interests of different sections of the working classes. It is to abolish all advantages and disabilities which have their source, not in differences of personal quality, but in disparities of wealth, opportunity, social position and economic power. It is, in short—it is absurd that at this time of day the statement should be necessary—a classless society. It is not a question, of course, either of merely improving the distribution of wealth, or of merely increasing its production, but of doing both together. Naturally the methods required to attain that objective are various, complex and tedious. Naturally, those who accept it may do so for more than one reason—because they think it more conducive to economic efficiency than a capitalism which no longer, as in its prime, delivers the goods; or merely because they have an eccentric prejudice in favour of treating men as men; or, since the reasons are not necessarily inconsistent, for both reasons at once. In either case, they are socialists, though on matters of technique and procedure they may be uninstructed socialists. Those who do not accept it are not socialists, though they may be as wise as Solon and as virtuous as Aristides. Socialism, thus defined, will be unpleasant, of course, to some persons professing it. Who promised them pleasure?

The elements composing the Labour party are extremely miscellaneous. If variety of educational experience and economic condition among its active supporters be the test, it is, whether fortunately or not, as a mere matter of fact, less of a class party than any other British party. That variety means that the bond of common experience is weaker than in parties whose members have been taught at school and college to hang together. Hence it makes the cohesion which springs from common intellectual convictions all the more indispensable. There is room for workers of all types in it, but on one condition. It is that, in their public capacity, they put their personal idiosyncrasies second, and their allegiance to the objectives of the party first. If they accept titles and such toys, without a clear duty to the movement to do so; or think that their main business is not fundamental reconstruction, but more money for the unemployed; or suppose that such reconstruction, instead of being specially urgent in the circumstances of today, must be kept in cold storage till the automatic occurrence of a hypothetical trade revival; or, like thirty-six Labour members in the last House of Commons, regard the defence of the interests, or fancied interests, of denominational schools as more important than to strike a small blow at class privilege in education, they may be virtuous individuals, but they are not socialists. To the Labour party they are a source, not of strength, but of weakness. They widen the rift between its principles and its practice.

The programme of the party, again, covers a wide range. Nor need that be regretted, but, again, on one condition. It is that the different proposals contained in it should be rigorously subordinated to the main objective. Clearly, class-privilege takes more than one form. It is both economic and social. It rests on functionless property, on the control of key positions in finance and industry, on educational inequalities, on the mere precariousness of proletarian existence, which prevents its victims looking before and after. Clearly, therefore, a movement seeking to end class privilege must use more than one weapon; and clearly, also, the Labour party's programme, like all socialist programmes, from the *Communist Manifesto* to the present day, must include measures which are secondary as well as measures which are primary. The essential thing is that it should discriminate between them. What will not do is that a programme should be built up by a process of half-unconscious log-rolling, this measure being offered to one section of workers, and that, because no one must be left in the cold, being promised to another.

The Labour party can either be a political agent, pressing in Parliament the claims of different groups of wage-earners; or it can be an instrument for the establishment of a socialist commonwealth, which alone, on its own principles, would meet those claims effectively, but would not meet them at once. What it cannot be is to be both at the same time in the same measure. It ought to tell its supporters that obvious truth. It ought to inform them that its business is to be the organ of a peaceful revolution, and that other interests must be subordinated to that primary duty. It is objected that, by taking that course, it will alienate many of them. It may, for the time being; new models are not made by being all things to all men. But it will keep those worth keeping. And those retained will gather others, of a kind who will not turn back in the day of battle.

To formulate from time to time, amid swiftly changing complexities, international and domestic, a Labour policy which is relevant and up-to-date, is a task for the best brains that politics can command. But, when policy has been determined, two facts are as certain as political facts can be. The first is that, if a Labour government, when it gets the opportunity, proceeds to act on it, it will encounter at once determined resistance. The second is that it will not overcome that resistance, unless it has explained its aims with complete openness and candour. It cannot avoid the struggle, except by compromising its principles; it must, therefore, prepare for it. In order to prepare for it, it must create in advance a temper and mentality of a kind to carry it through, not one crisis, but a series of crises, to which the Zinovieff letter and the press campaign of last year will prove, it is to be expected, to have been mere skirmishes of outposts. Onions can be eaten leaf by leaf, but you cannot skin a live tiger paw by paw; vivisection is its trade, and it does the skinning first. If the Labour party is to tackle its job with some hope of success, it must

© 2011 The Author. The Political Quarterly © 2011 The Political Quarterly Publishing Co. Ltd

mobilise behind it a body of conviction as resolute and informed as the opposition in front of it.

To say this is not at all to lend countenance to a sterile propaganda of class hatred, or to forget that both duty and prudence require that necessary changes should be effected without a breakdown, or to ignore the truism that the possibility of effecting them is conditioned by international, as much as by domestic, factors. It is curious, in view of the historical origins of the Liberal movement, and, indeed, of such recent history as the campaign of 1909 against 'the peers and their litter', that Liberals, of all people, should find a rock of offence in the class connections of the Labour party. The reason for facing with candour the obvious and regrettable fact of the existence of a class struggle is not, of course, to idolise class, but to make it less of an idol than in England it is. It is to dissolve a morbid complex in the only way in which complexes can be dissolved, not by suppressing, but by admitting it. It is to emphasise that the dynamic of any living movement is to be found, not merely in interests, but in principles, which unite men whose personal interests may be poles asunder, and that, if principles are to exercise their appeal, they must be frankly stated. The form which the effort to apply them assumes necessarily varies, of course, from one society to another. Any realist view of the future of British socialism must obviously take account of the political maturity and dependence on a world economy of the people of Great Britain. It does not follow, however, that the struggle to be faced is less severe on that account. Intellectually and morally it may be more exacting.

If there is any country where the privileged classes are simpletons, it is certainly not England. The idea that tact and amiability in presenting the Labour party's case—the 'statesmanship' of the last government—can hood-wink them into the belief that it is also theirs is as hopeful as an attempt to bluff a sharp solicitor out of a property of which he holds the title deeds. The plutocracy consists of agreeable, astute, forcible, self-confident, and, when hard-pressed, unscrupulous people, who know pretty well which side their bread is buttered, and intend that the supply of butter shall not run short. They respect success, the man or movement that 'brings it off'. But they have, very properly, no use for cajolery, and laugh in their sleeves—and not always in their sleeves—at attempts to wheedle them. If their position is seriously threatened, they will use every piece on the board, political and economic— the House of Lords, the Crown, the press, disaffection in the army, financial crises, international difficulties, and even, as newspaper attacks on the pound last summer showed, the émigré trick of injuring one's country to protect one's pocket—in the honest conviction that they are saving civilisation. The way to deal with them is not to pretend, as some Labour leaders do, that, because many of them are pleasant creatures, they can be talked into the belief that they want what the Labour movement wants, and differ only as to methods. It is, except for the necessary contacts of political warfare, to leave them alone till one can talk with effect, when less talking will be needed, and, in the meantime, to seize every opportunity of forcing a battle on fundamental questions, When they have been knocked out in a straight fight on a major economic issue, they will proceed, in the words of Walt Whitman, to 're-examine philosophies and religions'. They will open their eyes and mend their manners. They will not do so before. Why should they?

III

If such are the objectives of the Labour party, and such the forces against it, what are the practical conclusions? They are four, relating respectively to programmes, propaganda, discipline, and tactics.

The conclusion of an article is not the proper place for even the outline of a policy, which, with the world sliding as it is, may be out of date in six months. But certain points are clear. The business of making programmes by including in them an assortment of measures appealing to different sections of the movement must stop. The function of the party is not to offer the largest possible number of carrots to the largest possible number of donkeys. It is, while working for international peace and cooperation abroad, to carry through at home the large measures of economic and social reconstruction which, to the grave injury of the nation, have been too long postponed, and with that object to secure that the key positions of the economic system are under public control.

That task must, of course, be interpreted in a broad sense. It is not for Labour to relapse into the Philistinism of the May Report, with its assumption that all but economic interests, and those interpreted à la capitalist, are of secondary importance. Side by side with action of a strictly economic character, such as the transference to public ownership of foundation services, including the banks; the establishment of machinery to bring the supply of capital to industry under public control; the creation of a permanent Industrial Development Commission to press steadily forward the modern-isation of industrial organisation; and such other measures of the same order as may be adopted, must go a policy for the improvement of education, health, and the system of local government, which themselves, it may be remarked, are matters not irrelevant to economic prosperity. It is monstrous that services vital to the welfare of the great majority of the population, and especially to that of the young, should be crippled or curtailed, while the *rentier* takes an actually larger percentage than in the past of the national income. If that income is too small to permit of our ensuring that all children have proper opportunities of health and education, it is clearly too small to allow us other luxuries, including the continued payment of £300,000,000 odd a year to holders of war debt. A Labour government should not wait till circumstances are favourable to a voluntary conversion, nor should it deal with war debt alone. It should follow the example set by Australia and other countries, and, indeed, as far as a disregard for the sanctity of contractual obligations is concerned, by the highly respectable Cabinet at present in power. It should compulsorily reduce fixed interest charges.

Of the general considerations which arise in planning a programme, the most important are three. The essentials must be put first, and sectional claims must not be permitted to conflict with them. The transference of economic power to public hands must take precedence over the mere alleviation of distress. It must be recognised that any serious attempt to give effect to such a policy will provoke a counter-attack, including action to cause economic embarrassment to the government of the day, and measures to meet it must be prepared in advance. The present government has shown that wealth can be redistributed and existing contracts broken, by the convenient procedure of Orders in Council. The precedent should be remembered. An Emergency Powers Act is on the statute book. Labour must be prepared to use it, and, if the powers which it confers are insufficient, to pass another.

What a Labour government can do depends on what, when in opposition, it has taught its supporters to believe will be done. 'Never office again without a majority' is the formula of the moment. But quality of support is as important as quantity. The Labour party deceives itself, if it supposes that the mere achievement of a majority will enable it to carry out fundamental measures, unless it has previously created in the country the temper to stand behind it when the real struggle begins. Much of its propaganda appears to the writer—himself the least effective of propagandists—to ignore that truism. What is needed is not merely the advocacy of particular measures of socialist reconstruction, indispensable though that is. It is the creation of a body of men and women who, whether trade unionists or intellectuals, put socialism first, and whose creed carries conviction, because they live in accordance with it.

The impressive feature of Russia is not that, apart from agriculture, the items in its policy are particularly novel. It is that, whether novel or not, they are being carried out. The force which causes them to be carried out is, not material, but spiritual. It is the presence of such a body, at once dynamic and antiseptic, the energumens, the zealots, the Puritans, the Jacobins, the religious order, the Communist party—call it what you please—which possesses, not merely opinions, but convictions, and acts as it believes. Its existence does not depend on political forms; it is as compatible with parliamentary, as with any other, machinery. Till something analogous to it develops in England, Labour will be plaintive, not formidable, and its business will not march.

The way to create it, and the way, when created, for it is to set about its task, is not to prophecy smooth things; support won by such methods is a reed shaken by every wind. It is not to encourage adherents to ask what they will get from a Labour government, as though a campaign were a picnic, all beer and sunshine. It is to ask them what they will give. It is to make them understand that the return of a Labour government is merely the first phase of a struggle the issue of which depends on themselves. It is objected that such methods involve surrendering for a decade the prospect of office. It may be replied that, if so, impotence out of office is preferable, at any rate, to impotence in it. It does not prejudice the future, or leave a record to be lived down. But is it certain that, had the late government spoken in that sense before coming to power, and then fallen in 1930 in the attempt to carry a measure of first-class importance, it would have been less likely to supply an alternative government in 1936?

Talk is nauseous without practice. Who will believe that the Labour party means business as long as some of its stalwarts sit up and beg for social sugar plums, like poodles in a drawing room? On this matter there is at the moment a good deal of cant. The only test is the practical one; what behaviour is most conducive to getting on with the job? A distinction may be drawn, no doubt, between compliance with public conventions and conduct in matters of purely personal choice. If one is a postman, one can wear a postman's uniform, without thereby being turned into a pillar of sealing-wax. And, if Privy Councillors make up for the part, when duty requires it, by hiring official clothes from a theatrical costume-maker, who will let them for the day at not unreasonable rates, there is nothing to shed tears over, except their discomfort. The thing, all the same, though a trifle, is insincere and undignified. Livery and an independent mind go ill together. Labour has no need to imitate an etiquette. It can make its own.

It is one thing to bow down in the House of Rimmon, for practical reasons, when necessity requires it. It is quite another to press, all credulity and adoration, into the inner circle of his votaries. But the criticism on the snobbery of some pillars of the party, though just as far as it goes, does not go far enough. Those who live in glass houses should not throw stones. The truth is that, though the ways of some of the big fish are bad, those of some of the smaller fry are not much better. Five-pounders and fingerlings, we insist on rising, and—shades of Walton!—to what flies!

It will not do. To kick over an idol, you must first get off your knees. To say that snobbery is inevitable in the Labour party, because all Englishmen are snobs, is to throw up the sponge. Either the Labour party means to end the tyranny of money, or it does not. If it does, it must not fawn on the owners and symbols of money. If there are members of it—a small minority no doubt, but one would be too many—who angle for notice in the capitalist press; accept, or even beg for, 'honours'; are flattered by invitations from fashionable hostesses; suppose that their financial betters are endowed with intellects more dazzling and characters more sublime than those of common men; and succumb to convivial sociabilities, like Red Indians to fire-water, they have mistaken their vocation. They would be happier as footmen. It may be answered, of course, that it is sufficient to leave them to the ridicule of the world which they are so anxious to enter, and which may be trusted in time— its favourites change pretty quickly—to let them know what it thinks of them. But, in the meantime, there are such places as colliery villages and cotton towns. How can followers be Ironsides if leaders are flunkies?

One cannot legislate for sycophancy; one can only expose it, and hope that one's acquaintances will expose it in oneself. The silly business of 'honours' is a different story. For Labour knighthoods and the rest of it (except when, as in the case of civil servants and municipal officers, such as mayors and town clerks, they are recognised steps in an official career) there is no excuse. Cruel boys tie tin cans to the tails of dogs; but even a mad dog does not tie a can to its own tail. Why on earth should a Labour member? He has already all the honour a man wants in the respect of his own people. He can afford to tell the tempter to take his wares to a market which will pay for them and himself to the devil. While the House of Lords lasts, the party must have spokesmen in it. Peerages, therefore, have very properly been undergone, as an unpleasant duty, by men who disliked them. It should in future, be made clear, beyond possibility of doubt, that that reason, and no other, is the ground for accepting them. When it is necessary that a Labour peer should be made, the victim required to play the part of Jephtha's daughter should be designated by a formal vote of the parliamentary party meeting. It is not actually essential that the next Annual Conference should pass a resolution of sympathy with him and his wife, but it would be a graceful act for it to do so. What odious Puritanism! Yes, but the Puritans, though unpleasant people, had one trifling merit. They did the job, or, at any rate, their job. Is the Labour party doing it?

If there is the right spirit in the movement, there will not be any question of the next Labour government repeating the policy of office at all costs which was followed by the last. Whether it takes office without an independent majority is a matter of secondary importance compared with its conduct when it gets there. Its proper course is clear. The only sound policy for a minority government is to act like a majority government. It is not to attempt to enact the less controversial parts of its programme; for its opponents give nothing away, and will resist a small measure of educational reform as remorselessly as a bill for the nationalisation of the land. It is to fight on large issues, and to fight at once. It is to introduce in the first three months, while its prestige is high and its *moral* unimpared, the measures of economic reconstruction which it regards as essential. It will, of course, be defeated; if it is in a minority, in the Commons, if it is in a majority, in the Lords. In the second case, it can use the Parliament Act, supposing it to be still law, and go to the country on the abolition of the House of Lords; in the first, it must demand a dissolution. In either, it will do better for the nation and itself by forcing the issue, than by earning as its epitaph the answer which Sièyes gave to the question what he had done during the Terror: 'j'ai vécu': 'I kept alive'.

It is objected that such a policy involves sacrificing opportunities for useful work, particularly in the field of international affairs. It may—for the time being; had the late government acted on it, Sir John Simon would have succeeded Mr. Henderson after one year, instead of after two. On a long view, however, the dilemma is less absolute than that argument suggests. The League is what the rulers of the Great Powers, and the interests behind them, permit it to be. In the light of the history of the last thirteen years, and not least of 1931–32—in the light, for example, of their attitude in the test case of Manchuria and of the tragic farce of the Disarmament Conference—can it seriously be argued that they are eager that it should itself be a power, or that even a Labour government, if it holds office at the mercy of its opponents and the League's, can succeed, during a brief spell of precarious authority, in making it one? It is obvious that, as the world is today, no nation can save itself by itself; we must cooperate, or decline. But is it probable that international cooperation can be built on a foundation of states dominated, in their internal lives, by ideals antithetic to it? Those who cannot practise their creed under their own roof can practise it nowhere, and one contribution, at least, which a Labour government can make to that cause is to be made at home. It is to apply to the affairs of its own country the principles which, it believes, should govern those of the world. It is to extend the area of economic life controlled by some rational conception of the common good, not by a scramble, whether of persons, classes, or nations, for individual power and profit.

Sir Arthur Salter, in contrasting the frank individualism of the nineteenth century with the improvised, half-conscious experiments in collective control of the postwar world, observes that 'we have, in our present intermediate position between these two systems, lost many of the advantages of both, and failed to secure the full benefits of either'. In the sphere of international, as of domestic, policy, the attempt to give a social bias to capitalism, while leaving it master of the house, appears to have failed. If capitalism is to be our future, then capitalists, who believe in it, are most likely to make it work, though at the moment they seem to have some difficulty in doing so. The Labour party will serve the world best, not by doing half-heartedly what they do with conviction, but by clarifying its own principles and acting in accordance with them.

Economics in the Modern World

G. D. H. COLE

Vol. 4, no. 2, April–June 1933

THE CLASSICAL theories of Economics and Politics, on which the university students of today are still being brought up, were constructed by and for an age of successful individualism. They grew up amid, and were largely based upon, that rapid and uncontrolled expansion of man's power over nature which lies at the root of modern Capitalism, and above all of that phase of it we call the 'Industrial Revolution'. In face of this swift onrush of productive power, the system which men had built up in the past for the collective control of their economic lives came to appear petty and obstructive; and the first duty of the reformer seemed to lie in the clearing away of a mass of ancient rubbish which still impeded the course of economic and political advancement. Bentham, with his sweeping doctrine of Utilitarianism, was the foremost prophet of this destruction. The 'greatest happiness' principle became the powerful solvent of ancient institutions that had turned into current abuses; and in calling upon all men's traditions to justify their life or perish, Bentham and his followers hewed the path for economic and political thought into the nineteenth-century world. Nineteenth-century theory, in both politics and economics, based itself on Bentham; and, though his own work was mainly political, the triumph of his ideas was most complete in the economic field, because there the new forces of which he was the interpreter had their foundations.

In the circumstances of the time, Utilitarianism was bound to take on an individualistic form, though there is nothing essentially individualistic about the Utilitarian principle. The new economic forces were being wielded by individuals, and such collective forces as existed were for the most part antagonistic to their growth. The struggle for progress appeared as a struggle to escape from the bondage of the old collective controls; and it seemed natural not only to back the individuals who were contending for the power to make full use of the new productive powers, but also to set out to remould political institutions in harmony with the new economic individualism. In economics, the human being was conceived as an individual agent of production, making his impression upon a 'free market' in accordance with the quality of his productive powers. Every man's natural ambition was to become an *entrepreneur*, and no obstacles of law or custom ought to be allowed to stand in his way if he had the requisite personal qualities. Landlords were out of favour, because their power rested on monopoly, and not upon individual initiative. Wage-earners were those who lacked the right to exact monopolistic tribute, or the personal qualities needed for becoming *entrepreneurs*. The *entrepreneur* alone was the self-realising indi-

Published by Blackwell Publishing Ltd, 9600 Garsington Road, Oxford OX4 2DQ, UK and 350 Main Street, Malden, MA 02148, USA

vidual—the self-made man—in the fullest sense; and on his enterprise rested the progress of mankind.

A political theory was needed to complement this theory of the economic world. All aristocratic theories were ruled out, because they all involved a foundation of monopolistic privilege. There remained only democracy; and the Benthamites were thorough-going democrats in their theoretical outlook. 'One man, one vote', was the only sound political principle, even though such 'fantastic notions' as that of 'natural rights' were flung overboard; for 'one man, one vote' corresponded in politics to the equal right of all to exploit the powers of production to the height of their capacity. It alone would secure that the persons of most political enterprise would get most weight in shaping the affairs of nations.

Parliamentary democracy thus appeared as the logical complement of Capitalism in the economic field, and it became necessary to square the economic survival of the fittest with the political principle of the greatest happiness of the greatest number. Adam Smith made smooth the way for the conception of an 'economic harmony', whereby each man in pursuing his own interest would be somehow guided to secure that of society as a whole. On the one hand, it was contended that the freedom of enterprise and trade from all forms of restriction would lead to the maximum total production of wealth, and that higher production would necessarily enlarge the funds available for the remuneration of labour—the famous Wages Fund of the classical economists; and on the other hand, when the Wages Fund was given up, its place was taken by the notion that the higher the productivity of labour the higher would its wages also be. But in addition, as Jevons and other writers hit on the notion that value depended on utility, measured by consumers' demand, rather than on labour or cost or price of production, the conception of the underlying economic harmony was reconstructed in a new form. Each consumer, it was urged, would be as a rule the best judge of what he wanted; and the unfettered freedom of the market, by allowing him to exercise free choice among all the goods and services offered for sale, would automatically maximise satisfactions, in that each consumer would spend his income on what he wanted most, and the scarcity of goods would cut off only the less urgent demands.

This view, of course, rested on an assumption. The Austrians, who were its chief exponents, delighted to show that any individual consumer, having a given income, would clearly spend it to the best advantage he could, and thus tend to get the maximum of satisfaction; and they then proceeded to assume that what was true of any individual consumer must be true of all, and therefore of the market as a whole. This, however, was to ignore the fact that different consumers possessed very different incomes and were, therefore, by no means equally placed for making their several demands effective. Goods in a market tend to sell at a uniform price for any two like products of equal quality; and one shilling in the hands of the poor man has only the same purchasing power over goods as one shilling in the hands of the rich. It is doubtless true that, as men satisfy first their most urgent needs, the poor man tends to get a higher average satisfaction out of each shilling of his income than the rich; but, if he has far less shillings to spend, he also gets far less total satisfaction, though there is no evidence that his needs or capacity for satisfaction are any less. Accordingly, there is always a presumption that, the nearer the distribution of income in a society approaches to equality, the higher is the total satisfaction likely to be derived from the goods this income is used to buy. Inequality is therefore defensible on Benthamite principles only to the extent to which it can be shown to be necessary in order to maximise the total of wealth produced. It can be at best only a necessary evil; and maximum production with unequal distribution *may* result in less total welfare than a smaller product more evenly distributed.

Nor is this all. Many economists have recognised the unequal marginal utility of money to different purchasers, and yet have clung to the opinion that the 'free market' is somehow a guarantee of maximum welfare. But it is evident that this view, if it is put forward *a priori*, depends on an unwarrantable identification of want with demand, whereas the economic system in fact takes no cognisance of wants unless they appear in the market in the form of effective demand. The theory, favoured by Jevons and the Austrians, and by the *laissez-faire* revivalists of our own day, that prices depend on demand conditions, which are then identified with 'utility', is doubly false. It is false because there is no necessary coincidence of utility with demand, and it is false because it assumes the independent existence of incomes apart from the productive process.

If once the economist is allowed to begin by assuming this independent existence of incomes, he will find no difficulty in building upon this assumption a perfectly logical case in support of the view that prices depend upon demand, though even so he will not be able to prove that the satisfaction of the highest price offers is any guarantee of the highest possible total of human welfare or satisfaction. But it is preposterous to grant him this assumption, in face of the fact that incomes are actually generated in the productive process. It is easy enough to demonstrate the logical priority of want over supply; for it is clearly absurd to produce goods unless they are wanted. But this in no way shows that demand is prior to, or governs, supply; for want and demand are not the same thing. Wants are—just wants, whereas demand is want armed with an income—with a supply of purchasing power.

It cannot therefore be legitimate to assume the existence of demand as starting point of economic analysis, unless the conditions which create demand are assumed as well. And it cannot be irrelevant, if we are to take account of demand, to enquire into the origin of the incomes which convert want into demand. But as soon as we do embark on this enquiry, the beautiful simplicity of the Austrian doctrine is destroyed; for it has to be admitted that demand, so far from being itself the sole cause of production, is itself produced in the course of production, and that the magnitude and the direction of the demand existing at any time depend alike on the scale on which production is being carried on, and on the proportions in which incomes are being distributed in the productive system, or redistributed subsequently by levies upon the incomes generated in the course of production.

This is, of course, admitted up to a point; but, having admitted it, the adherents of the 'demand' school fall back on their second line of defence. Within the productive system, each factor of production is paid for in accordance with its 'marginal productivity', that is to say, broadly, at a price corresponding to the value contributed by the last unit of it that is actually employed. The location of the marginal point for each factor is set, we are told, by the conditions of consumers' demand; for the intermediate demand for all the factors of production is derived from the demand for consumers' goods and services. The consumers are willing to pay so much or so much, according to the quantity placed on the market, and in accordance with the varying marginal utility of the commodity to themselves. What they are willing to pay has to be divided out among the factors of production; and the division will be decided by the competition between the factors to secure employment, on terms which will inexorably make the remuneration of each factor coincide with its marginal productivity.

Now, this looks very like a true picture of what happens. For, if we look at the economic world at any particular moment, incomes do exist, and do make up a total of composite demand in accordance with the preferences of buyers; and the demands of final consumers are reacting upon the productive system so as to cause changes in the demand for, and the prices offered for, every factor of production, from the various kinds of labour and materials to machines, insurances, and borrowed or invested capital. If we once assume the incomes, or even take them as we find them in the market at a particular time, all the rest seems to follow logically.

But we cannot do this; for it is equally true and relevant that the production, and the distribution of incomes which goes with it, is the source of the demand. The incomes cannot exist until production has taken place, any more than production can go on in the absence of incomes to purchase the product. In effect, the abstract method of starting with a single aspect of the economic system, and then deriving the rest from it, will not do. The system hangs together, as a system. All its aspects exist together, and the relation between them is one not of cause and effect, but of mutual determination.

This, however, may be held to have nothing to do with individualism. In my view, it has a great deal. The abstract method is essentially atomistic. It tries to lead us to an understanding of the economic world by a separate analysis of its parts, and above all by basing this analysis on a supposedly typical sample. We are asked to begin by studying the behaviour of a typical businessman reacting to the typical consumer's demand. That the consumer and the business man, and the behaviour of both, are correctly described does not mean, unhappily, that we have been brought any nearer to an understanding of the system within which they both exist. For their behaviour is a reaction to the system, and would be quite different in many respects if the system were changed.

The object of the advocates of *laissez-faire* is to show that there exists, in any organised economic society, a possibility of equilibrium, and a tendency for equilibrium to be actually realised if economic forces are left 'free'. Thus, it is assumed that, if the consumers possess a certain income, and distribute that income in accordance with the principles of utility, there follows inexorably a certain set of prices at which all the available factors of production will be able to be fully employed. If, then, unemployment of any factor actually exists, this is a sign of disequilibrium, which must be the result (unless it is a mere passing result of friction due to economic change) of obstructive forces which are somehow keeping the prices of certain things unduly high. The high prices may arise from *entrepreneur* monopoly, Trade Union pressure, or social legislation, or other forms of interference with the law of the free market; but it is assumed that there must be for everything an equilibrium price, at which the available stock will be fully absorbed.

This would be perfectly true, if incomes and their distribution were unaffected by changes in the prices of the factors of production. But in reality these prices are incomes, or constituents of incomes, and no change can take place in any of them without affecting the character of demand. There *may* be a level of prices for all the factors of production at which all these factors will be employed to the full. But there may be no such level, within the existing industrial system. For if high wages or interest rates can cause unemployment by making production unprofitable to the *entrepreneur*, low interest rates can so check the accumulation of capital, and low wages so depress the level of consumers' demand for ordinary consumption goods, as to have the same result. Nor is there necessarily a right wage or interest rate between these two at which full employment of resources will be secured. For the system of prices which will enable *entrepreneurs* to employ all the resources at the existing level, and with the existing distribution of incomes, may introduce such changes into the level and distribution of incomes as again to upset the balance.

The presumption in favour of *laissez-faire* as a means of preventing unemployment and ensuring maximum production cannot therefore be sustained. If we want to establish a balance involving the full use of productive resources, we shall have to establish it by the coordinated control of the factors concerned, and not by allowing prices (and therefore incomes) to find their own level. This is not because there is, as some people have supposed, any inherent tendency in the present economic system towards a deficiency of purchasing power in relation to the actual volume of current production; for, save as an occasional accompaniment of banking deflation, no such tendency exists. It is rather because the distribution of incomes, rather than their aggregate amount, constitutes the vital factor. In order to secure full employment, incomes must be so distributed that the demand arising from them coincides with the power of the productive system to supply the various types of goods and services, and equally the productive system must be constantly adjusted to fit in with the demands arising out of the actual distribution of incomes. If the double adjustment could be successfully made, unemployment as more than a matter of friction would disappear. But we cannot rely on the adjustment being made automatically, when the factors are left uncontrolled. For the attempt to get equilibrium in one field will always tend to upset equilibrium elsewhere.

In plain fact, the mechanism of modern capitalist society is not self-adjusting. But the truth goes deeper than this; for in economics, as in politics, the forces upon which it rests are not isolated individuals exchanging goods in a market which is simply a place of meeting for many individual buyers and sellers, but groups, institutions, associations and classes which cohere in varying degrees, and by their cohesion shape the conditions of exchange. What is called monopoly is not an occasional and exceptional interference with the working of a market normally 'free', but an omnipresent condition varying in strength and degree from case to case. Production is not, in such a system, a mere response to demand, though it is limited by what consumers can be persuaded to buy; for the persuasion of consumers by suggestion and advertisement forms an integral part of the productive system, and the *entrepreneurs*, by their control of prices, fix the limits of demand fully as often as they leave the conditions of demand to fix the price. Consumers' demand, again, is not a thing existing absolutely, but rather a response to an existing structure of prices constantly modified by changes in the distribution of incomes through production, as well as by the acts of the producers in devising new goods and new methods of production, and in influencing the direction of demand through various forms of propaganda. The trader, mediating between producers and consumers, is influenced fully as much by changes in the conditions of supply as by the changing tastes of the consumers. And finally, though consumers' purchases are still for the most part made individually, or by households, demand tends to go by groups and classes, according to social fashions and conventions of living, rather than by the personal valuations of individual consumers. The producer standardises supply in order to lower costs by mass production; and the consumer is led to standardise demand, not only as a means to cheapness, but also as a response to the producers' suggestions and the traders' stocking of standard lines.

This collectivisation of the market, on the sides of production and consumption alike, progressively restricts the range of individual action, and makes obsolete all analyses of the economic situation conceived in *laissez-faire* terms. In these circumstances, the hankering after *laissez-faire* is mere inverted Utopianism—a wish for a different economic system belonging to the past, and not for an improvement in the working of the productive system of today. For it is not *laissez-faire* to be governed by the contentions of a large number of imperfect and sectional monopolies; but this is the only possible consequence in the world of today of a refusal to use the state as an instrument of economic regulation. The source of our present troubles is not that states interfere too much, but that their interference remains external and mainly negative. Being external and negative, this interference is as liable as any other sectional and limited control to lead to a disequilibrium; for it lacks the power to balance one act of intervention by others designed to bring the rest of the system into the right adjustment. States, when they have interfered of late years, have so often made a mess of things that it is tempting to conclude that they should not interfere at all. But they have interfered for the most part, not because their governments wished to do so—on the contrary most governments have a strong theoretical bias in favour of letting industry alone—but because they have been irresistibly driven to interfere, in order to correct maladjustments which have arisen out of the working of the system itself.

The most profound of these maladjustments arise from the present transitional organisation of the productive process. In a simple society of individual producers, goods are brought to market and sold for what they will fetch, and their prices in terms of other goods determine the standards of life of the various producers, All incomes are the direct outcome of selling goods in the market, and every expectation of earning an income acts directly as an incentive to production. But in the modern system, based on the hire of capital and labour by a special class of *entrepreneurs* acting on behalf of a wider body of shareholders, this is not the case. Only *entrepreneurs'* and shareholders' expectations of income act as incentives to production in an unqualified sense: other incomes, those of creditors and wage- and salary-earners, act also as deterrents, because they appear as costs reducing the net expectations of the *entrepreneurs* and the shareholders. It is true that these latter incomes are essential for the purchase of the product, and do serve as incentives to that extent. But the sums paid out in wages and salaries can only be recovered by the sale of the product, whereas the sums paid out as profits represent a demand not balanced by outgoings, and to maximise these is accordingly the object of the *entrepreneur*. Wages, interest and profits are all alike incomes, forms of purchasing power to be received by the sale of the products of industry. But wages and interest (and also rents) are balanced by outgoings, and appear as deterrents to production because any rise in them threatens to reduce the margin between cost and selling price.

Thus, whereas a community of independent producers would be in no wise tempted to reduce production because of a fall in prices, a capitalist community is at once tempted to react in this way, in order to escape the burden of wages and interest. And, if once production is reduced in this fashion, the result is to cancel incomes as well as products, and to cause supply and demand again to approach a balance at a lower level. There is accordingly no necessary reason why a factor of production once disemployed should ever be re-employed, or why depression should not be self-perpetuating. In fact, if reliance were placed solely on the internal rhythm of the economic system itself, apart from forces arising outside the circle of depression or from deliberate reflationary action within it, there is no necessary reason why any slump should ever end. Production and consumption can balance, subject to secondary friction, at any level of activity. The most perfect balance would be achieved if production stopped altogether, and all the consumers were dead.

This being so, our analysis of the modern economic system must take full account, not only of the relation of incomes as a whole to production as well as to consumption, or of the effects of varying distributions of incomes on consumers' demand, but also of the differences between those incomes which constitute costs, and therefore deterrents to production, and those which, arising out of a surplus of price over cost, constitute incentives to production. It matters to the determination of the level of productive activity, not only in what relative magnitudes incomes are distributed, but also in what forms. And any society in which some incomes are also costs, whereas others are not, is bound to be liable to that kind of disequilibrium which appears in the unemployment of productive resources.

The remedy is to convert all incomes back to the form which they possessed when the economic system was carried on by independent producers, but to do this in a new way based on the collective character of the modern process of production. It is to make the national income a national dividend, that is to say a claim on the part of every citizen to a certain share in the total supply of goods and services that can be made available for consumption. This is compatible with the existence of fixed money claims, such as wages and salaries or interest or rents, only if the community, by a collective control over prices, is in a position to adjust the purchasing value of these fixed money claims so as to equate them to the supply of goods and services that can be made available. In the alternative, if prices are to be left free to vary uncontrolled, all forms of income must be variable too, or else the balance of production and demand will be lost. But variable prices and variable incomes together are not consistent with any effective planning of the use of productive resources: so we are compelled to rely, as a means of maximising the utilisation of these resources, on a careful and coordinated adjustment of incomes and selling prices at the levels necessary to secure this result.

Thus, in the economic sphere, the partial monopolies characteristic of modern production lead on to socialisation; and the tendencies to disequilibrium arising from the unequal pulls of conflicting groups and classes can be overcome only by the supersession of these sectional forces by an inclusive public monopoly. Similarly, in the political sphere, it is futile to analyse the forces of today in terms of individual citizens, or voters, or as if the candidate appeared before the electors simply as an individual political *entrepreneur*, appealing on the strength of his personal qualities. For in fact the electors are arranged in groups, classes, interests, acting together under the stress of collective incentives and desires; and candidates stand for parties, which are the embodiment of wider or narrower collections of policies based on these same divisions among men. Any political theory which ignores these collective realities is utterly meaningless and unrealistic; and, once again, the only way in which the conflict of sectional interests can be transcended is by merging the rival groups in a wider collective unity. Politics, as well as economics, stands in need of socialisation; but, as political groups are mainly, though not wholly, the reflection of economic classes and interests, the transformation of politics can in fact only follow, and not precede, the socialisation of the economic life of the community.

Meanwhile, to study realistically the facts of today and the tendencies which are shaping the future, we must think in terms, not of typical individuals, but of the strength and influence of the contending collective forces. For economic and political analyses are alike in value only if they are at once truly descriptive of current facts, and—what is really the same thing— revealing of the tendencies which are driving us forward to the next stage of social development. For tendencies are facts, more really and fundamentally matters of fact than abstractions which are conceived in static terms. If there is such a thing as equilibrium, in either politics or economics, it must be a dynamic and not a static equilibrium. Finally, we must above all avoid abstract reasonings based on the conception of the individual citizen, or consumer or producer, as the determining force in political or economic affairs, and must learn to think rather in terms of constantly developing and interrelated groups as giving form and substance to the activities of the individual. Economics and politics, in these dynamic forms, may be harder both to teach and to learn than the hallowed formulæ of the individualist schools. But a science is not the better for being easy, if in order to simplify its problems it consents to distort the truth.

Utopia and Reality

LEONARD WOOLF

Vol. 11, no. 2, April–June 1940

WE ARE living through a period in which the use of power, force, or violence is playing a predominant part in human society. The phenomenon is not confined to the relations between states; it can be observed within states in the relation between government and individuals and between individual and individual. Societies and historical periods have differed widely in their organisation of power and in the way in which force or violence has been applied to human relations. Until comparatively recent times it was commonly held that the communal control of power and the elimination of force or violence from human and social relations were important elements in civilisation. It was even believed that these views were not merely utopian aspirations, but had in many cases been translated into historical facts. In the nineteenth century the potential power of a physically strong man to impose his will upon a physically weak man had in most places been rendered inoperative by social organisation. By similar methods the potential power of the man with a club, an axe, or an automatic pistol had also been rendered inoperative. The power of kings over their subjects, of aristocrats over commoners, of men over women, of governments over citizens, of employers over employed had often, it seemed, been eliminated or modified. Most people believed that it was possible not only to control or modify the use of power, but also that of violence, and to do so effectively for an intelligent purpose. It seemed to be undeniable that the use of torture and flogging as methods of 'doing justice' had been abolished in some places, that in others it was no longer possible for a man to be hanged for stealing a sheep or a few pence, and that in others the utopian idea of abolishing the death penalty had been adopted without apparently increasing the number of murderers or of their victims.

In the nineteenth century the control of the use of power and the efforts to eliminate force and violence from the relations between states, governments, and individuals were closely associated with the practice and theory of liberalism, democracy, and humanitarianism. The war of 1914–1918 for four years reversed this process of controlling, sublimating, and eliminating the use of power or violence. War between states is not only the logical result of 'power politics', it is power politics reduced to their simplest terms. It also entails the adoption of force and violence as primary elements in determining a vast number of human and social relations which at other times are regulated by discussion, compromise, 'law', or other non-violent methods. Few people will deny that this four-year period of power and violence had a considerable effect upon European society and the minds of Europeans. The simplest and most direct effects of historical events are often soon forgotten or underestimated by historians and politicians. It is a simple fact that an enormous majority of those Europeans who were not killed in what they then called the Great War did not like it; in fact, they disliked it so intensely that enormous numbers of ordinary persons said: 'Never again', by which they meant that in their humble opinion everything should be done which was possible to eliminate war from European society. Their aspiration may or may not have been utopian—we shall consider this question later—but their convictions, the state of their minds were a political reality which was having profound effects all over Europe and which not even the most realist statesman, general, or historian could afford to neglect.

One effect of this conviction was the founding of the League of Nations. The disillusionment of ordinary men and women in 1918, their feeling that war was in the twentieth century not a tolerable way of life, or even of death, their dim doubts as to whether it had proved to be an effective method of 'settling anything'—these things were not the only cause of the birth of the League of Nations, but they had a good deal to do with it. The statesmen—other than Wilson—who established the League did not believe in it; they thought themselves to be realists and the League utopia. The statesmen who 'worked' for the League for fifteen years or so did not believe in it; they thought themselves to be realists and the League either utopia or a convenient or inconvenient instrument—it depended upon circumstances—of national policy. The main impetus which had brought the League into being and prevented it from being completely scrapped by realists or reality was another reality, the voice of common people who had said and might perhaps still say: 'Never again'.

The League failed. As it failed, ordinary people could no longer be heard saying: 'Never again'; you heard them saying clearly, often bitterly, always helplessly, in the streets of cities, in fields, and villages, 'It is coming again'. The two realities were not unconnected. The failure of the League may have been due to its having been utopian, but it was not an isolated historical incident, the casual failure of an academic dream brought up with a jolt against the hard facts of life. It was only part of a general historical process or movement which can be clearly discerned in the period between November 1918 and September 1939. It gradually became clear that the postwar Europe was not going to return to the nineteenth-century attitude towards power, force, and violence. In many countries governments allowed private armies to fight one another in the streets of great cities. Dictatorships took the place of democracies. Pogroms became a recognised method of administration; change of government or even of the government's programme or policy were effected or prevented by 'massacres', 'purges', executions, or political assassinations.

Fascism in Italy—national socialism in Germany—Stalinism in the USSR—Pilsudski or a government of generals or colonels or majors in Poland—little dictators in the little countries—Manchuria, Abyssinia, the destruction of the republican government of Spain, the destruction of the democratic republic of Czechoslovakia, the invasion and partition of Poland—thus we have reached the second great war. These facts can only be stated and interpreted in terms of power, force, and violence. They are the negation of another series of terms which had previously seemed to have some meaning to human beings: peace, law, order, common interests, compromise, liberty and democracy. Human beings are never content just to accept the facts, their miseries, savagery, and stupidities. They have an itch to explain and interpret them, to find some fig leaf of a theory or philosophy to cover the nakedness of their own folly or cruelty. Politicians and professors of politics and history are always ready to supply fig leaves, theories, and philosophies, to comfort the dead, the dying, the disappointed, and the crucified with the assurance that nothing could possibly have happened except in the way in which it did happen and is happening and that everything is for the best in the worst of all possible worlds.

So today you will find any number of people offering us fig leaves to cover fascism, communism, and war, theories which prove the inevitable failure of democracy and the League of Nations, philosophies which discover the seeds of a new world in the most ancient forms of violence and slavery. There is a family likeness in all these *ex post facto* consolatory explanations, they rely upon a distinction between illusions, shams, or utopias and realities. Democracy was a 'sham'; dictatorship is a 'reality'. The common interests of nations and peace are an illusion; conflict of national interests and war are 'real'. The League of Nations was 'utopian'; power politics are 'reality'. The validity of these theories and of the practical policies, based upon them, which we are exhorted to pursue must depend upon what is meant by this distinction between political or historical utopia and political or historical reality. To understand the distinction is, therefore, not an academic, but a highly practical question, for it is clearly politically imbecile to ignore realities or to pursue policies which are impossible of attainment—only we must know what is a reality and what is 'impossible of attainment'.

Our search for enlightenment may well start from a book by Professor E. Carr which has recently attracted much attention.[1] Mr Carr is Professor of International Politics and has an intimate knowledge of his subject. His book on Bakunin proved him to be a man of intelligence with an unusual capacity for historical impartiality. His new book is an attempt to lay the foundations of a science of international relations and at the same time to 'analyse the underlying and significant, rather than the immediate and personal, causes' in the history of the last twenty years which have brought us once more into war. The whole of Professor Carr's analysis is based upon a distinction between utopia and reality, and if anyone should be capable of making us understand what it is it should be he. There are, as one would expect, very good things in the book, acute analysis of particular situations or processes, illuminating comments on particular events, and trenchant and often salutary criticism of things, theories, and persons with whom Professor Carr is out of sympathy or out of understanding. And yet the book fails in its purpose. It does not give us the beginnings of a science of international relations, because its method is unscientific. It attempts to interpret the events of the last twenty years by means of a distinction between what is utopian and what is real in policy. But, although the whole of his argument depends upon the difference between 'utopia' and 'realism', he never makes clear the distinction between them either to himself or to his reader. The reason is that he had not pushed his analysis either of terms or of events or of causes—particularly psychological causes—far enough.

Let us begin with terms. The term utopia is commonly used in two different ways. We speak of a dream or a polity being utopian in the sense that it contains a purpose or is based upon a hope or ideal which is incapable of fulfilment, and in this sense we oppose it to 'realism'. But it is also used in the sense of 'unreal' as opposed to 'reality'. The two senses are not the same, but they are continually confused with disastrous results to truth and clear thinking in political controversy and in Professor Carr's book. This can best be shown by examples. Professor Carr's thesis is that the beliefs, objectives, and policies of nineteenth-century liberal democrats and of the supporters of the League of Nations in the international field were utopian. He means by that that their beliefs were false and that their objectives and policies were impossible of attainment—not by any means, it will be observed, the same thing. He has a good deal to say about the falseness of their beliefs, but he never clearly demonstrates to us why their objectives and policies were impossible of attainment. He often implies that the failure of the League and of the attempt to reconstruct a peaceful Europe was 'inevitable' merely because it was a failure. This attitude can be seen in the emotional colour of his adjectives in such a sentence as 'The first and most obvious tragedy of this utopia was its ignominious collapse.' Here you have the vulgar and false view that failure is 'ignominious' and proves somehow or other that the attempt itself was discreditable and unattainable. These superficial judgements are characteristic of contemporaries: in 1790, 1830, 1848, 1900 and 1918, if Professor Carr had been a Frenchman, he would have talked about the 'triumph' of democracy and the democratic ideals of the 'Revolution', but in 1800, 1828, 1851 and 1939 he would have talked about their 'ignominious collapse' and utopianism.

As a matter of fact, Professor Carr is himself really well aware of all this. Where he approves of a policy which has failed, as for instance Mr Chamberlain's appeasement policy, he sees that the failure does not prove its utopianism or its ignominy, and in his other book he writes: 'There is a common inclination in politics to take the deterministic view that any policy which fails was bound to fail and should, therefore, never have been tried. The charge that British Ministers were the dupes of the Axis Powers should not be too lightly made.' If the collapse of the policy of appeasement does not prove that it was utopian, the collapse of the League does not prove that it was utopian, and if Mr Chamberlain's failure was not ignominious, why should Professor Carr see ignominy in the failure of the League?

The answer to this question is that Professor Carr is unconsciously infected with the temporary social psychology of the time, the acceptance of power and force and conflict as the primary (and therefore best) elements in social organisation and human relations, and that he feels the necessity to provide the fig leaf of a theory to cover the results of this psychology. He does this by assuming that policies and social objectives inconsistent with *existing* facts or with the psychology of power, violence and conflict are utopian, and his theory or proof is based upon a confusion between the two senses of 'utopian' and upon the common, but completely unscientific, assumption that power, violence and conflict are more 'real' elements in society than, e.g., beliefs, law and cooperation for a common end or common interests.

The League was a political and social organisation of states. It was established in answer to a demand, and in this sense it had an objective or ideal—the elimination of war, the resolution of international conflict and the promotion of the common interests of states or nations. The ideal or objective was not in the League, but in the heads of those who established it or caused it to be established. The League is utopian only if those ideals or objectives are impossible of attainment. The policy of the League, which aimed at organising the relations of states upon the basis of their common rather than their conflicting interests, is not utopian merely because it aimed at an unattained ideal or objective, as Professor Carr and many other people frequently assume. All policies, even of the most realist statesmen, aim at unattained ideals or objectives. The policy of Hitler aims at the as yet unattained ideal or objective of organising the relations of states in Europe on the basis of force and conflicting interest, with Germany having an overwhelming superiority of power and therefore able to promote her interests at the expense of other states. In Professor Carr's sense his policy is 'realist'; in fact, it is highly probable that his objective will not be attained and is unattainable, and is therefore really utopian. Again, Mr Chamberlain's policy had as its ideal or objective peace with Hitler by abandoning any common resistance to aggression, any obligation to aid victims of aggression, and by placating Hitler and yielding to his demands. The objective was certainly not attained and was probably unattainable, and the policy was abandoned for its exact opposite. If the criterion of utopianism is attainability, the policies of Hitler and Mr Chamberlain are no less utopian than the League policy.

Professor Carr's dealing with utopianism and reality in connection with policy is unsatisfactory because he does not carry his analysis of the psychology of political objective or ideal far enough. But it also breaks down in another important way: it accepts the vulgar delusion about the 'reality' of some political concepts and the 'unreality' of others, and then illicitly argues that a policy concerned with the former is 'utopian' and a policy concerned with the latter 'realist'. For instance, Professor Carr maintains that the international policy of nineteenth-century liberalism and of the League both broke down because they were based on the promotion of the common interests of states and not on the conflict of state interests. They ignored the problem of power, which is the instrument of conflicting interests. Conflicting interests and power are 'real'; harmony of interests is unreal or non-existent and political instruments of cooperation in common international interests are therefore also 'unreal'. Hence power politics are real and the League and the liberal policy of free trade and international cooperation 'utopian'.

This kind of attitude towards 'interests' and 'power' is very common at the present moment, but it is rooted in muddled thinking. The idea that there is some 'reality' in a conflicting interest which does not exist in a common interest is an illusion. It springs from the obvious fact that most people are more *conscious* of their own immediate interests than of common interests and that the pursuit of common interests almost always entails the abandonment of some immediate individual interests. But the political reality of interests does not depend upon people's consciousness of them, but on the relative effects of different actions and different forms of social organisation. In private life and national politics we have learnt this by bitter experience, and no one believes that the interest of men with knives to commit murder and robbery is more 'real' than the interest of men with knives to refrain and be restrained from committing murder and robbery. International psychology is still, however, so crude that even a man like Professor Carr can believe that the interest of Germany in cutting the throat of Czechoslovakia is more real than the interest of both Germany and Czechoslovakia in living peacefully together and composing conflicting interests by compromise, merely because Herr Hitler has a very large army, a very large air force, and a very loud and rasping voice.

The question what interests are real, or to put it in another way what is really the interest of an individual, a group, a class, or a nation, cannot be settled in this cavalier way. A study of the history of human society and of international relations, not to speak of one's own life, will make one very careful not to dogmatise about real or unreal interests *in any particular case*. But it also teaches this lesson: that *generally and in the long run* common interests are more real than conflicting interests politically. Nearly every one would agree that this is true with regard to the internal organisation of the national state; in the long run and generally every one gains by the pursuit of a common interest even at the expense of individual interests; even the potential murderer is better off in the end if he refrains or is restrained from cutting the rich man's throat; a class which ruthlessly pursues what it considers its own interest at the expense of other classes nine times out of ten digs its own economic grave. But there is reason for thinking that what is true of national is also true of international society. For many centuries now the relations of states have been determined by acceptance of the hypothesis that their conflicting interests are so exclusively real that they must form the basis of national policy. I cannot believe that, if Professor Carr and others who agree with him examine impartially the results, they can maintain that they are encouraging. It would be interesting to learn which of the 'Great Powers' had really gained by their ruthless pursuit of conflicting interests in the years

LEONARD WOOLF

1790, 1815, 1870, 1914 and 1939, and which had lost by pursuing utopian common interests. And *realpolitik*? If reality is to be judged by success, what is the judgement of history upon the work of such realists as Napoleon I, Napoleon III, Bismarck, Wilhelm II, the Russian Tsars, not to speak of British imperialists? The fact is that nothing is more 'utopian' than the idea that you can create a stable and permanent society by power and the pursuit of conflicting interests; the ideal is unattainable because it involves an attempt to use two of the most unstable and disintegrating of all social forces, violence in the service of cupidity, as the primary ingredients in that cement which is to hold society together.

The question whether cooperation of states in common interests is possible, whether the power of individual states can be controlled internationally as the power of individuals, groups, and classes have been controlled nationally, and whether these objectives and the preservation of peace can be attained through some such international organisation as the League is at the same time much simpler and more complicated than it appears in the books of those who see some peculiar reality in power and conflict and are therefore continually reading the burial service over democracy, the nineteenth century, and internationalism. It has little or nothing to do with 'morality', 'reality', 'liberalism' or 'reason'. Whether the policy of organising European states pacifically and of eliminating the *probability* of war is or is not utopian depends solely upon whether that objective is or is not attainable. It has nothing whatsoever to do with some imaginary quality of 'reality' attaching to power or violence and to 'conflicting interests', but not attaching to law, cooperation and common interests. The attainability of a political objective almost always depends mainly upon three elements: facts, psychology and the creation of social machinery or organisation appropriate to the object or purpose of the policy and to the psychology. For instance, the attainability of the purpose of Zionists depends first upon such facts as the size of Palestine and the climate of its several districts. It would be utopian to ignore these facts and to put into Palestine more Jews than could exist there or to put a million Jews suddenly into a district of Palestine which is a waterless desert. Another element which has to be considered is the power of the Arabs to shoot Jewish immigrants, and yet another is the conflicting and the common interests of Jews and Arabs. Here it is partly a question of fact and partly of psychology; there is no question of some mystic element of reality attaching to some of the facts and not to others. It is a fact that the Arab has or may have the power to shoot the Jew; it is also a fact that he has or may have the power to cooperate with the Jew. It may be his immediate interest, i.e., he may gain at the moment, by shooting the Jew, but on the other hand it may be his 'real' interest, i.e., he might gain more, by refraining from shooting and by cooperating with the Jew. The power to shoot is no more and no less 'real' than the power to cooperate, and the conflicting interest which is served by shooting is no more and no less 'real' than the common interest which is served by cooperation. Here the most important element is really psycho-

© 2011 The Author. The Political Quarterly © 2011 The Political Quarterly Publishing Co. Ltd

logical. The attainability of the Zionist policy will depend upon whether Arabs and Jews pursue their separate interests by conflict or whether they pursue their common interests by cooperation. Lastly, provided that facts and psychology did not make the purpose of Zionism impossible, it would still be necessary to create a form of government appropriate to the peculiar purpose, the peculiar facts, and the peculiar psychology.

This analysis applies no less to the problem of war and peace and international relations than to that of Zionism. Five hundred years of European history have proved that the 'realist' system of power politics, war and the conflict of interests is grotesquely utopian. Its purpose is to ensure stability of national power, glory, prosperity and peace; its result has been a kaleidoscope of loud-voiced jingoism and national glory alternating with war, defeat, misery and impoverishment. The reason why power policy and the attempt to establish a stable European society upon it always fails and always must fail is that it ignores both the reality of facts and the reality of psychology. That of course does not mean that the opposite policy, which was embodied in the League idea, is attainable. Whether a pacific international system, based upon cooperation in common interests, is possible in Europe will depend primarily upon facts and upon psychology. But I am inclined to think that the main difficulty, the real cause of the League's failure, is not to be looked for in facts and in 'reality' but in psychology.

The international relations of France and Britain between 1895 and 1939 throw light upon the general problem of international relations and upon the effect of psychology. In 1895 France and Britain had a large number of conflicting and a large number of common interests. In the autumn of 1903 when Lansdowne and Delcassé sat down to discuss Anglo–French relations, nothing had happened to alter the objective reality of those interests. The conflict of some and the community of other interests still persisted; both series were 'real'. This fact blows up the whole of Professor Carr's argument about utopianism and reality in international relations. For in 1903 a revolution in Anglo–French policy and relations took place and it was determined mainly by psychology, not by power, realism, or utopianism. Before 1903 the governments of the two countries conducted their foreign policy on the basis and hypothesis that the most important, the 'real', interests of France and Britain were in conflict, and that their common interests were illusory, the utopian hallucinations of little Englanders and pacifists. What benefited France harmed Britain, and vice versa twice over. The basis of their international relations was therefore assumed to be conflict of interests, and the main instrument of policy was power. Cooperation, compromise, political machinery for composing differences or pursuing common interests were ruled out; on both sides of the channel statesmen thought of the use (or threat of using) power, economic or military, to promote the interests of their own country at the expense of the other as the proper and inevitable instrument of policy.

In 1903 the relations between the two countries were completely and permanently changed, not owing to any change in their existing interests or in their relative power, but by a decision of their governments, and this decision was caused by a psychological change. Lansdowne and Delcassé did not suddenly see that the conflicting interests had suddenly become 'unreal' and the common interests 'real'; they came to the conclusion that in general and in the long run the two countries would gain more by pursuing common interests and attempting to compose conflicting interests by compromise than by continuing the pursuit by each of its own interests at the expense of the other. As soon as this psychological change took place, it had a devastating effect upon the importance of power as an element in the relations between the two states. In 1895, the relative power of the two countries had been an element of primary importance in their relations and policy; after 1904 it became negligible. The reason was that once the objective of policy had been changed by the Entente, power became a negligible and inappropriate instrument of that policy. This shows the absurdity of ascribing some peculiar quality of reality to power in international relations. Power is a very real element in human society, just as are law, cooperation, ideas, beliefs and ideals; its importance at any particular moment depends to a large extent upon the social or political objective which at that moment individuals are pursuing.

There is absolutely no reason to believe that the change which took place in 1904 in the national policies and international relations of France and Britain could not also take place in the policies and international relations of all the Great Powers, or all the states, of Europe. It is no answer to say that it was only fear of Germany which made France and Britain cooperate instead of fighting one another and that their cooperation was directed *against* another Power. To say that is to admit that psychology and not reality, power or utopianism is the primary determinant in the international situation. If fear of Germany was sufficient to turn France and Britain away from the pursuit of their 'real' conflicting interests into the pursuit of their 'utopian' harmony of interests and to eliminate the probability—one might almost say possibility— of war between them for half a century there is no reason, except psychological, why fear of mutual destruction should not effect a similar change in the policies of all European states.

That is the real international problem which confronts Europe and civilisation today. It is not a choice between utopia and reality, but between the psychology of conflicting interests and the organisation of power politics on the one hand and the psychology of common interests and the organisation of international cooperation on the other. The psychology of common interests and of cooperation and peace are there; it is, no doubt, weak, particularly among statesmen, generals, and perhaps professors, but it is there, and has widened and deepened in the last century. Its weakness is largely due to two causes. The first is the universal obstacle to civilisation in all spheres of human society, the fact that pursuit of common interests almost always means the abandonment of some conflicting, individual, immediate interests. The immediate appeal of the individual, conflicting interest is immensely strong, and it requires intelligence and restraint to see or learn that in the long run the individual may gain by abandoning it in the pursuit of common interests. Secondly, the international organisation of power is itself a tremendous obstacle in the growth and influence of the psychology of cooperation. It breeds fear, and fear is the greatest fomenter of conflict among human beings and the most potent destroyer of cooperation.

No sensible man will pretend that establishment of international peace is an easy thing. Whether it is possible depends upon whether the international organisation of power, as it exists today, can be altered and whether the psychology of common interests and cooperation can be made an active determinant of national policies. These things may not prove possible, but they are not impossible because conflict and conflicting interests are real, and cooperation and common interests are utopian. To believe that is merely to try to rationalise one's own and other people's primitive psychology.

Note

1. E. H. Carr, *The Twenty Years' Crisis, 1919–1939*, Macmillan. It should also be read together with a smaller book which Professor Carr published about the same time: *The Foreign Policy of Britain from 1918 to 1939*, Longman.

Notes on the Anglo–Saxon Character

KINGSLEY MARTIN

Vol. 11, no. 3, July–September 1940

I

HITLER has expressed a special detestation for British and American journalists. He holds them responsible for the war. In a madly inverted sense he is right. If the world had not been told what Hitler's plans were and what his régime was like, his piecemeal conquests might have succeeded without any but isolated wars. During the early days of the Nazi régime the most strenuous opponents of Hitler were the foreign journalists in Berlin. First under the leadership of Edgar Mowrer and then under William Ebbutt of *The Times* the international journalists insisted on sending truthful dispatches and maintained for several years a considerable degree of independence. Gradually Goebbels got rid of these stubborn tellers of the truth. Excuses were found for expelling them; they were harried and threatened and forbidden official information. Gradually editors who wanted up-to-date news from Berlin substituted 'yes-men'. Even so, there were always a number of journalists, mainly Americans with world reputations, who were too important to be easily kept out of Germany and who filled the world's newspapers with accounts of the persecution of the Jews, Hitler's military plans and the horrors of the concentration camps. To tell the truth about these matters was necessarily to make war more likely. Only if Hitler had been able to keep the world as ignorant as Germany could he have succeeded without rousing the British and American peoples.

These journalists have lived an extraordinary life during the last ten years. I know no race of men so independent, so tough, so realistic, and so fundamentally humane. Ask them what God they served and they would tell you that they were newshounds and nothing more. They were observers, and if what they saw and reported roused decent people to righteous anger, that was the fault of Fascism and not theirs. They have told their story in cables, articles and books from every country where violence has sought either to impose or remedy injustice. They have demonstrated that peace is not compatible with justice and that in this epoch the price of liberty is often death. They have tried hard not to take sides. They have been news reporters, not politicians, and yet, since facts are the most effective propaganda, they have been the most powerful of anti-Fascist propagandists. Nor in their lives have they always been able to resist the logic of their own reports. Often they have been compelled to drop the role of observers and take part in the struggle itself. Some of them were more than reporters in the Spanish Civil War. Others became deeply involved in the war in China and risked their

Published by Blackwell Publishing Ltd, 9600 Garsington Road, Oxford OX4 2DQ, UK and 350 Main Street, Malden, MA 02148, USA

own lives and jobs in helping to save the lives of refugees. Because they could not escape the logic of Hitlerism and knew its methods and purposes at first hand they became, when they advocated no policy, the most fervent protagonists of the policy of resistance to Nazi Germany. Observers first, they could not help being men and moralists.

In a remarkable play called *Thunder Rock* by Robert Ardrey, acted this summer in Kensington, we are shown two such journalists who are no longer able to maintain their pose of neutrality. They agree that they have no message for the world; things have gone too far. Civilisation is crashing. They want to put a message in a bottle and throw it into the sea, so that sometime their words may mean something to posterity. But what is the message? One of them, an airman, wearing the American reporter's conventional garment of tough cynicism, decides that he must throw himself into the struggle somewhere. It does not matter what he does; he cannot remain an observer. He is on his way to China to fight against the Japanese bombers. Has he really no faith or ideals left? asks his friend. Would he fight for the Japanese? He is furious. What! Bomb Chinese civilians instead of dying in battle against the Japanese? . . . He breaks off, realising that he has given himself away. His cynicism is only skin deep; he is under a compulsion to take an active part in helping the victims of violence even though he has little hope of good coming from it. He is contemptuous of his friend, Charleston's, solution. Charleston has found an ivory tower, a lighthouse, where he works alone in the middle of Lake Michigan. He too has lost his 'objectivity', as he explains, and has had to get out of journalism. He too is a moral being, he is still trying to resist the impulse to throw himself into a struggle too complex to understand. He seeks a personal solution in a past epoch, only to find that the characters he recreates in his mind were themselves confronted with problems similar to his. They too believed that civilisation was ended and they failed to make their contribution to its salvation because they too acted as immigrants, paralysed by catastrophe. Fortified by a rational hope that he may be mistaken, even as they were, and that it may still be possible to aid the growth of the good, he too abandons his ivory tower.

I ask myself whether one can imagine such a play being written by anyone but an American or a Briton. This type of moral conflict is almost an Anglo–Saxon speciality. The Englishman and the American are sure in their hearts that it is their duty to put the world to rights. They may withdraw from obligations as the Americans did in 1919 or as British governments have done consistently since the last war. But it has been with an intense sense of moral discomfort and it is this moral preoccupation as much as fear for their own safety that has in the end led them into war with Germany. Confronted with the agonising choice of surrender to the Nazis or devastating war, men and women in France, Czechoslovakia, Norway, Holland and Belgium have all hesitated and been overwhelmed. But the choice was to them, far more than to us, a choice of evils, consciously realised. They weighed the chances of survival. The British and Americans never doubted their survival until the

Germans were actually in the Low Countries and Channel ports. Always they argued on the basis of morality. Was war ever right and, if so, was this war justifiable or necessary? They thought not in terms of power, but in terms of ethics.

II

To generalise about the innate character of so-called 'races' and nations is the temptation of fools and historians. There are no pure races and we know nothing of the psychological attributes of the national germ cell. We know that governments act differently and that people at various epochs behave according to national patterns. Beyond that, generalisations about national character are usually superficial and misleading. The French, according to my mother's geography book, were 'a gay people, fond of light wine and dancing'. The Germans were dreamy, wore spectacles and drank beer. The Russians were mystics, living close to the soil and worshipping the Tsar. The Americans were Shylocks and the British called by Providence to rule the world. You had only to cross the seas or change your generation to get all these ideas reversed. The Germans were called to rule the world; so were the French not so long ago. In the eighteenth century the English were regarded as a revolutionary and unstable people, who made a habit of cutting off the heads of their kings. After the French Revolution these roles were precisely reversed. It would not be difficult to compile a list from the writers of every country claiming exactly those qualities we deny them and denying us the qualities we claim. There is always evidence for all such generalisations. I have known Russians more phlegmatic than any Englishman and English-men more excitable than any character in Dostoevsky. Germany makes the most interesting study of all. It is safest not to say that the Germans are a 'race of carnivorous sheep', well though that phrase summarises the predatory and disciplined behaviour that is so familiar to us. One may learn more but reach no satisfying conclusion by a more materialistic approach; one notes that Germany was never conquered by Rome, that the peasant upheavals that brought in the West of Europe an increase of popular power resulted in Germany in a more oppressive feudalism, that the development of Germany was thrown back by centuries through the destruction of the religious wars and that when Germany was unified the task was done, not through the democratic urge everywhere alive to the early nineteenth century, but through the conquering power of the poorest, most militant and racially the least Germanic part of Germany.

I believe that the characteristics of which the British have so often boasted—the courage (an almost universal human characteristic), the individualism, tolerance, sportsmanship and the rest—are mainly to be attributed to Britain's insular position and to the confidence resulting from freedom from invasion for nearly nine hundred years.

In the nineteenth century, we were so much the dominant empire and so much stronger than anyone else that we learnt to extol lack of foresight as a virtue. From our insular security, it was easy and attractive to support the underdog; the observer always tends to take the part of the weaker side in a scrap, and Britain had the practical incentive that it was always to our interest to prevent any great power from becoming dominant on the continent. Palmerston, John Russell and Gladstone gave us a generous notion of ourselves in foreign affairs. Interest and sportsmanship coincided. Unafraid ourselves, the public enjoyed it when the government sent stern letters of protest to despots, urged on them the virtues of the British Constitution and more or less openly supported the agitations of oppressed minorities. No one has yet attempted a careful survey of the effects of our intervention on behalf of the Greeks, the Italians, the Poles, the Hungarians, the Bulgarians, and the Armenians. We certainly helped the Italians and the Greeks, but it must be admitted that our help was offset by the expectations of help that we roused, but did not always fulfil. No historian has yet worked out the full influence of men like Kossuth, Mazzini, Garibaldi, and Kropotkin, on the minds of British intelligentsia and the working class. John Bull, we were brought up to believe, was a friend of the weak and the oppressed, and since he was often oblivious to the real meaning of British imperialism in India, Egypt and elsewhere, he easily won the reputation of hypocrisy. He accepted as axiomatic that foreign empires were tyrannical and oppressive, and that Britain must have an Empire and must somehow or other not be tyrannical and oppressive. He was willing on occasion to punish his servants if they shot down natives; the one thing he never did was to admit that empires cannot exist without shooting or the threat of shooting.

In the eighteenth century, the British middle class was swept by a Puritan Revolution, which coincided with and was partly derived from the needs of industrialism. During the nineteenth century, the Puritan mentality dominated British Liberal opinion and was surprisingly successful in imposing itself on the quite un-Puritan landed aristocracy, which indeed maintained a full share of power by itself profiting by the industrial possibilities of the age and learning to govern in partnership with the middle class. Peel and Melbourne could succeed one another; Derbys and Greys were still among the rulers of England in 1914. The essential craving of this mentality is to be at ease with its own conscience; it cannot admit what every man of affairs knew to be the case—that government is always a more or less ugly thing, that consent is never more than partial, and that force conquers an Empire and plays a large part in maintaining it. Above all, a Puritan democracy can never go into a war without a moral excuse; a moral excuse by itself will not be sufficient, but nor will a reason of state or call of self-interest. The two must coincide. The foreigner noted with grim amusement the British genius for finding a moral reason to coincide with a political necessity or an economic advantage.

Brought up in a Puritan middle-class home, I cannot ever remember hearing politics discussed except in terms of right and wrong. Trade was good. Tariff Reform was wicked, and there were excellent economic arguments in favour of the first and against the second. Those arguments would scarcely have counted if Free Trade had not also been a peace doctrine making for cooperation among nations, in opposition to the immorality of tariffs which were associated with class and national selfishness and the war mentality. We were fighting in the army of the good, for progress and social reform; the Conservatives, who opposed us, had themselves to accept these criteria. The Utilitarian creed of Bentham, the view, that is, that policy must be decided by the happiness and prosperity of the masses, was not the real creed of the Conservatives, who believed (and could have quoted good arguments from Coleridge and others for their belief) in authority and government by a ruling class with experience and a tradition. But they were shamed out of their real creed; they argued on their opponents' premises and were forced bit by bit to give way to a democratic philosophy.

In the realm of foreign affairs, the results of this moral preoccupation among the population have been constant and profound. It has been impossible for our rulers, even if clear-sighted themselves, to be honest with the public. The man who is responsible for the policy of a great Empire has to do innumerable things that do not square with the teachings of Christianity. A simple-minded ruler like Queen Victoria saw no ethical problem; to her, Christian duty was always that which suited the interests of the British ruling class. An honest Christian like Bright found it impossible to remain in a Cabinet, while a gigantic and complicated intellect like Gladstone's was constantly driven into the most involved and, as it often seems to us, disingenuous arguments to justify actions which a Disraeli, who was not a Christian in any sense we need worry about, would have done simply on the ground that they were expedient. This does not mean that Gladstone was not a man of principle; on the contrary he risked his career by his book on 'Church and State', and again, as a freelance, he behaved with the greatest courage in exposing the nauseous evils of Neapolitan prisons. But in office the gap between principle and practicability had somehow to be bridged. The public had to believe that justice and right were being done, just as certainly as it had to be satisfied that British interest and prestige were being upheld. Hence, in examining our pre-war history, we have to disentangle at every point what our statesmen were doing to maintain and extend the Empire from the reasons they gave for doing it. Often, no doubt, they convinced themselves of these reasons, but their success or failure depended rather on their capacity to convince the public that what they were doing was morally justified.

England's last aggressive war was fought in South Africa. During the Boer War, the Fabian Society published a manifesto supporting the war on the intelligent ground that backward nations should be developed and that it was the duty of conscious socialists to see that the resources of the earth were fully exploited in the interests of the whole population. This was to state in socialistic terms substantially the same doctrine of responsible imperialism which was held by Milner, Grey, Haldane and Asquith. Amongst the upper class, the individualism which had been dominant when all Oxford men 'went through the Mill', had given way to the neo-Hegelian philosophy of T. H. Green. Historically, we may trace this change from the mid-nineteenth-century period, when British capital still found its outlet in the home market, through the second industrial revolution in the 'seventies with the same middle-class people who had returned Bright to Parliament for Birmingham and who now found a more fitting representative in an imperialist like Joseph Chamberlain. The new Liberal imperialists occupied most of the key positions in the Liberal cabinets which ruled England between 1906 and 1914, but the mass of the Liberal public remained unconscious of the change. In the reaction after the Boer War, they maintained a good conscience as followers of Campbell Bannerman, the anti-imperialist in South Africa, and of Lloyd George, who was dubbed pro-Boer and had been forced to escape from Birmingham Town Hall in a policeman's uniform.

In the reaction after the Boer War, the mood of Britain reverted to Liberalism; Campbell Bannerman's settlement in South Africa was generally regarded as a wise piece of statesmanship which showed that we had given up being bullies and aggressors and wanted to live on good terms with our neighbours. It has been generally true in English history that a generation that has known one war is slow to face another; it is only when a younger generation has arisen which has only heard about the last war through the romantic eyes of historians and retired generals that the country becomes ready to light again. That is one reason why Lord Roberts, who tried to rouse us to a belief in the German menace, so completely failed to meet any response to his national campaign. And that is one reason why Britain was psychologically and militarily, so unprepared when war came in the summer of 1914. Lord Grey is commonly accused, and with some justice, of having failed to let the British people know of its commitments to France and Russia, and of having failed even at the last minute to make that unequivocal declaration of our solidarity with France which might have deterred the Kaiser or at least deterred the German General Staff from invading Belgium. But justice is not always done to Lord Grey's difficulty. Grey and Asquith and Haldane were conscious imperialists—that is to say, as students of foreign affairs brought up in the Oxford not of John Stuart Mill but of T. H. Green and Jowett, they conceived it to be their business to maintain the supremacy of the British Empire and preserve the balance of power on the continent. Involved in foreign complications all over the world, it was not possible to maintain isolation. But pacific England in a Liberal phase was turning its back on imperialism and was becoming intensely interested in the social reform programme of Mr Lloyd George; it would not have supported any open commitments to foreign countries. Joseph Chamberlain had tried to make an alliance with Germany just before the Boer War, and it was probably because

Germany had lost the wise guidance of a Bismarck that the chance was thrown away under the mistaken belief that Britain could never make up her imperial squabbles with France, which the *Daily Mail* had wanted to 'roll in blood and mud' as recently as 1899. Because of that mistake on Germany's part, Britain and France became allies, and, in consequence, Britain became also an ally of Tsarist Russia while Germany found herself with enemies on both fronts. But those immensely complicated and important decisions were quite outside the ordinary man's knowledge. He was pleased when Germany was checked in 1906, scarcely alarmed when Hungary seized Bosnia in 1908, and glad when a strong speech by Mr Lloyd George at the Mansion House warned off the Kaiser in 1911.

It was indeed only in 1911, during the Agadir crisis, that the country came to realise that war was still a likely possibility. For Lord Grey to have come out with an honest statement about our position would certainly have split the Liberal party, with internal and external consequences which he would certainly have regarded as disastrous. It seemed better to keep foreign politics as the prerogative of a small inner cabinet. Those who are interested in the technique of government can most easily gain an insight into the way this was managed by reading the fascinating memoirs of Lord Esher. Here one watches astute brains working behind the scenes. New Cabinet Ministers are carefully weighed. Has So-and-so risen to fame because of his success with the common people? If so, he must be watched, but not told too much. Or is he a quiet reliable member of one of the old families who can be trusted not to confuse government with politics, and trained for eventual service in that supreme body, the Committee of Imperial Defence, which Lord Esher devoted his life to building? Lloyd George and John Burns had their uses; they spoke in the moral language which the people understood. They did it all the better no doubt for believing themselves high-minded anti-imperialists. But they were not men to let into the Committee of Imperial Defence.

The more one reads of pre-war history, the more clearly one sees this sharp distinction between the governing men, concerned with empire, and the politicians concerned with social reform and popular favour. A man like Asquith was the natural Premier since he belonged to both worlds and it was his business to adjust their relations. The first group, the governing imperialists, were mainly permanent officials, many of them unknown to the public. Lord Esher was asked to be Viceroy of India, but said 'he would rather break stones'; he was offered the post of Secretary of State for War by Balfour and refused, only to be approached by Asquith for the same position when the Liberals came into power. He was perhaps the most influential man in England, but he was scarcely known to the public except as a name in a list of those who attended the King. In the same way, the real heads of the great Service Departments were usually hidden from the public gaze. It is worth while remembering that the personnel of the Diplomatic Service and the Foreign Office was almost exclusively recruited from a few public schools with the governing tradition. Lord Esher and his friends would have been happy if this division between politics to please the public and government to maintain British interests could have been complete. It was not difficult to maintain continuity when new governments came in, because the ambitious politician was not much interested in questions of defence and imperial policy, and there were always quieter men like Haldane, who were interested rather in the substance of power than in political popularity. But the two spheres could not be kept wholly distinct. The immense energy of a man like Mr Lloyd George, for instance, had a pervasive influence. One may trace in Lord Esher's diaries, the alarm that was felt when the reforming Chancellor's taxation proposals brought on a conflict with the House of Lords, a situation, as Lord Esher put it, 'too perilously' like 'that of 1640 for my taste'. Lord Esher advised the Crown throughout the struggle over the Lords, the Budget and Ireland: he was the shrewd intimate of Balfour and the King; he was always on the side of the Tories, but anxious above all to avoid the sort of conflict that would bring the King into politics and rouse democracy too much to assert itself. Esher and his friends knew well that in the last resort this subtle game of maintaining two incompatibles, an Empire, which is ultimately governed by force in the interests of a ruling class, and a democracy which may indirectly profit by the Empire but which is founded on ideas of consent and morality, depended on the existence of safeguards which would prevent the electorate from damaging the institution of private property.

To the Committee of Imperial Defence and the Inner Cabinet, the European crisis of 1914 did not come as a surprise. They had hoped that it would not come at all, but they had feared that it might, and were at least partially prepared for it. They were not fully prepared, partly because Service departments usually prepare for the last war rather than for the next one, and partly because eight years of Liberal government, mainly occupied with social reform, had not provided liberally for the fighting services. But their naval and military agreements with Russia and France were fully developed; after Haldane's vain effort to come to an understanding with Germany in 1911, he had been put in charge of the organisation of an expeditionary force and had accomplished his task with great efficiency. The problem lay in the fact that the public, Parliament and indeed the majority of the Cabinet did not know of these preparations or of our obligations to France and Russia. The governing men knew well that if Austria invaded Serbia, Russia must help Serbia, and that France would be obliged to help Russia, and we should have to dispose of our fleet in a manner prearranged with France and Russia, and likely to bring us into conflict with Germany. Moreover, a German victory on the continent would be fatal to Britain's position. Almost inevitably, if war began, we should be involved. But this would not be enough for the public who would want a moral as well as a strategic and imperial reason for fighting. It would be necessary, for instance, to satisfy Mr Lloyd George, who was the most popular radical politician and who was opposed to our entry into a war on account of a quarrel in Eastern Europe. The invasion of Belgium solved the government's dilemma.

III

The war of 1914–1919 was an immense drain on the manhood and vitality of all classes in Britain and in France. A few far-seeing imperialists knew that they could not permanently maintain their ascendancy on the old self-regarding basis. The French understood this well; they saw the problem simply in terms of a revived German menace, and they sought to build up the League of Nations as a permanent guarantee of the status quo in Europe. In the idealistic reaction from the war, that Puritan middle class which had played so large a part in British politics in the nineteenth century took a very different view of the League. If they had been accustomed to view politics in terms of power, as the French were they might still have believed in the League. They could have looked at it as Norman Angell did, as a means whereby the security of Britain and France could be obtained during an intermediate period required for the building of an international system which would render aggression impossible and great armaments unnecessary. Unfortunately their morality came into headlong collision with what was called French realism. The conflict wrecked the League. Germany was neither effectively suppressed not intelligently conciliated. To the French, British behaviour was inexcusable. We entered the war; directly it was over we assumed that we could step out again and view Europe from our superior isolation. But I am not again about to tell the story of how Britain and France supported each other and threw away mankind's opportunity. Nor am I going to examine the fundamental contradictions of British capitalism which lie behind the confusions of our foreign policy. I want only once more to point out the chasm that existed between the governing men and the vocal groups of British opinion.

The governing men were groping blindly in a new world in which their traditional behaviour no longer brought the expected results. They could not for a moment adjust their minds to the ideal of an international society. They were dimly conscious that their word was no longer law in the world and they were terrified of explosions from the underworld such as that which had led to communism in Russia. They lived by expedients, and because they could think out no consistent policy they were unable to rule effectively and only just able to resist the demand for idealistic policies which seemed to them to bear no relation to British interests. Meanwhile no one attempted any honest reply to those idealists who were as much as ever set upon following a moral path and as little as ever in a position realistically to calculate its cost. The idealistic element in the British public was certainly right in holding that British and France through the League could have done anything they liked in Europe up to 1935; they were probably right in thinking that Japan could have been checked without war in 1931. But the moral way of looking at the matter, which was the only way the public, particularly the Left public, had learnt, gave those who governed a continuous excuse for avoiding actions which they did not wish to take. The one sentiment that united the entire country was the desire to avoid war. For the first time in history a ruling class feared war even more than the 'intellectuals'. Hence it was always possible to plead lack of power and lack of armaments and to throw confusion into the ranks of those who wished to build a world in which aggression should be impossible.

The 'Left' throughout this controversy has an excellent case, because it was obvious throughout the Manchurian, Abyssinian and Spanish wars that the primary reasons for the inaction of the British and French governments was sympathy with the ruling class of Japan and Italy. But it should in fairness be admitted that there was deep confusion in the minds of many who asked for strong action by Britain and France. The idealistic public still lived unconsciously in the nineteenth-century world in which we believed that in foreign affairs we acted from moral motives, and the Communists, who believed nothing of the sort, deliberately exploited British morality and humanitarianism. And the fact that the League existed and represented the power of fifty-two nations, on paper at least, gave good ground for retaining the notion that righteousness rather than self-interest should dictate policy. Some of us certainly argued that loyalty to the Covenant was Britain's best defence and the only alternative to monstrous rearmament. But I recall as a vivid instance of a state of mind expressed in countless meetings over a period of years, a particular 'united front' gathering in the Town Hall of a provincial city to discuss sanctions against Italy. The first speaker vigorously demanded economic sanctions and as vigorously denounced a war as the betrayal of the working classes. The next supported economic sanctions, but pointed out that they might lead to war, and that in that case we should be committed to it. The third said that since war was possible there must be no sanctions. The fourth said of course there must be no war, but that we should block the Suez Canal at once, and the fifth took the entire discussion away into the lofty realms of Christian pacifism. All the speeches dealt with the problem in terms of morality; the difficulty lay in the conflict of two moralities, the moral feeling against war, and the moral desire to prevent the triumphant progress of organised brutality.

It was this deep and general confusion between hatred of war and desire to put the world to rights that gave Mr Chamberlain his peculiar hold. Mr Chamberlain represented Big Business and City interests; he thought in terms of trade. But his loathing of war was shared by everyone in Britain and it was for that reason that he was able to maintain office until the time when, nine months after war had been declared, it became obvious that there was no way out of it and also that there was a grave danger of losing it without the leadership of those who were prepared to carry through the reorganisation necessary to wage it.

Singularly unresponsive to the undercurrents, and unusually aloof from the main current of popular British tradition, Mr Chamberlain was the very man to put international politics on a business footing. At last and at the wrong epoch we had a Prime Minister who was converted, not by the doctrines of the postwar League of Nations Norman Angell, but by the Norman Angell of

1912 who taught that war could never be anything but disastrous to economic interests. Mr Chamberlain saw clearly the immense dangers of the old nationalist feeling, of that moral attitude which is part of the Puritan tradition of Britain. The old cries, the rights of small nations, the fight of right against might, international law and the rest, had become to him as unreal as it had to many socialists. The socialist believed that he saw beyond them to the day of popular international government; Mr Chamberlain believed that he saw through them to the political possibility of successful cooperation between capitalist governments. Thus when Mr Chamberlain went to Munich his umbrella became a symbol. It was the symbol of business and respectability in contrast to romance and adventure: the symbol of the substitution of the commonsense weapons of peace for the weapons of war. It was the financier's shelter against bombs; it was an appeal for moderation, comfort and decency made in the heart of a nation led by ruthless, warlike and revolutionary men.

But it is only partly true that Mr Chamberlain took the traditional morality out of British politics. He had his own moral standards and in a world in which every sane person regarded war as a wicked and loathsome anachronism, to stand as a peacemaker, or even as the man who kept his country out of war, was in itself to make a moral appeal. I know that after Munich Mr Chamberlain sincerely believed that he had indeed been the instrument of Providence in saving his country from war. Mr Chamberlain's biographers and friends have all borne testimony to the influence of Mrs Chamberlain on the Prime Minister; she is, I believe, if not a member, at least a close sympathiser with the Oxford Group Movement. Sir Horace Wilson, now head of the British Civil Service and Mr Chamberlain's close adviser, is, I hear, also an adherent of Dr Buchman. It must be remembered that Dr Buchman publicly thanked God for Hitler, because Hitler had saved Europe from Communism. Now, I don't for a moment suggest that Mr or Mrs Chamberlain ever liked Hitler or the Nazi régime; indeed, as a British businessman, accustomed to the give and take of commercial intercourse and humanely averse to cruelty and persecution, I am sure that Mr Chamberlain loathed the Nazis and all their works. But I think he too assumed that Hitler was a bulwark against Soviet Russia, thanked God for the delivery of Europe from Communism, and approached the problem of Nazi Germany in the spirit of a good Buchmanite, who is guided to eschew cut-throat competition and come to terms with his business rival whatever his morals or methods. It is certain that he saw, when he came to office, that Europe was heading for war and that he knew that the one power that seriously threatened Britain was Germany. It is known that in 1935, when the question of Abyssinia arose, that the experts reported the British Navy would be in a position to deal, if necessary, with two of the aggressive powers, but it would be highly dangerous to engage in war with more. They reported that the only serious danger came from Germany. The natural Foreign Office reply to such a diagnosis was that we needed allies in the east of Europe in order to maintain a balance of power and keep Germany in check. That was to state the matter from a purely British national angle. It was also possible to state this policy idealistically and to urge that through the doctrine of collective security we could build up a system in which all the nations would stand together against aggression and which Germany could enter if she would. But Mr Chamberlain, the realist, was convinced that whether in its Foreign Office or its idealistic form the doctrine of the firm stand against the aggressor would lead us into war.

As a business man, he assumed that the new Germany would need, as all great industrial enterprises did need, more *Lebensraum*, more room to expand, and as he explained on more than one occasion, Germany's natural field for expansion was in eastern and southern Europe. Therefore, it seemed to him that the way to peace was to persuade this new Nazi Germany rationally to expand its economic power without making war on its neighbours; to assure Hitler, who seemed obsessed with the fear of encirclement, that we were not his enemies, but his willing collaborators; that we had no objection, provided he left the West alone, to his domination of eastern Europe. The Left described this as the policy of war against the Soviet Union. The matter is not so simple. Hitler had announced in *Mein Kampf* a determination to colonise the Ukraine, and if he had a free hand in the East, it was obvious that a Russian–German war was probable. That, Mr Chamberlain would have said, was not his business. If it happened we should at once be immune from the danger of Bolshevism and from the aggression of Hitler. It might or might not happen. His concern was to disinterest Britain in eastern Europe, to prevent the absurdity, as he felt it, of Britain once again becoming involved in the age-long struggle between Slav and Teuton, and to heal, if he could, the rivalry between France and Germany and between British and German imperialism. The decisive factor was that British and German capital could both gain by collaboration and would both be destroyed by war. Hence he evolved a simple policy that appealed to his instincts and, he believed, to British interests. He would make direct personal contact with the dictators whose *entourage* he distrusted, he would override the traditions of British policy and discard the usual advisers, and attempt the personal task of winning the friendship and collaboration both of the Italian and German dictators. Mr Chamberlain assumed, as the stricter Marxists assumed, that Hitler's Germany was subject to the usual appeals of capitalism. Munich would have worked if Hitler too had been a disciple of Norman Angell. One assumes that Mr Chamberlain has not read *Mein Kampf*.

It is difficult to tell just what is happening to the character of Britain today. We remain even in war surprisingly tolerant and decent. If there are bitter feelings beneath the surface because we have been disastrously led and because out soldiers have been killed by inefficiency, stupidity, routine and half-heartedness, these feelings are repressed in face of the common danger. These feelings will find expression, I venture to prophecy, in new and strange ways at a later stage. For the moment many English people are proud of being left alone to fight and relieved as well as anxious at the defeat of their allies. All the islander's pride is aroused. Mr Baldwin and many others had told us that we could no longer rely on our insular security. But it is one thing to know intellectually that a blow has been struck at the foundations of your faith and another actually to discard that faith. Still instinctively the British think of Britain as 'a fortress built by Nature for herself, against infestation and the hand of war, a precious stone set in a silver sea which serves it in the office of a wall, or as a moat defensive to a house against the envy of less happier lands'. Today we are wondering how good a defence this moat will prove against the envy of less happier lands, and we know in our hearts that whatever happens in this war we are now and for ever irrevocably part of Europe. We shall no longer decide on moral grounds nicely balanced with those of interest whether to help this nation or that; we shall never again preach sermons from a bomb-proof pulpit—that is now an American prerogative. We shall suffer with Europe as part of Europe and have to learn like other frightened people to use our brains. Muddling through was no sign of genius; it just meant that we had more money, more security and a bigger fleet than other people and so could more easily afford our mistakes. A knock-out blow has been dealt to British morality. We shall calculate in future not from the mountain heights of security, but from the common levels of expediency which have dictated the policies of other European nations. We shall perforce become realists. Britain must develop a new 'national character'.

A Plague on All Your Isms[1]

BARBARA WOOTTON

Vol. 13, no. 1, January–March 1942

I

A WORD that ends in ism should be a kind of shorthand. Shorthand notes are useful when they can be read back. When they cannot they are useless.

Unhappily the vocabulary of politics and social affairs is littered with ism-words which are quite as useless, and considerably more dangerous, than illegible shorthand. Sometimes the writer or speaker of these words seems to have no clear idea in his own mind of what his particular ism is supposed to stand for: sometimes it is used, consciously or unconsciously, to convey a false picture of reality. In these cases speech (or writing) fails to perform its primary function as a means of communication. It is reduced to a series of laryngeal noises (or inkspots). When that happens, the time has come for a revision of vocabularies, since intelligent and cooperative thinking is impossible, unless there can be communication between the thinkers. Unfortunately, however, such revisions are apt to be bitterly resisted. For the very words that are due to be thrown away are often charged with violent feeling; and we are not willing to make the emotional adjustments necessary to discard them.

In this context we may classify the political isms into three classes: the terms of indiscriminate abuse; the sacred dogmas; and the terms of visionary escape. The word Fascism was, before the war, rapidly establishing itself as an example of the first variety. It was applied to Mussolini's Italy, to Hitler's Germany and, from time to time, by the Left in this country, to Mr Chamberlain's government. According to the definitions collected by Stuart Chase[2] its meaning to the politically unsophisticated in the United States ranged from 'A large Florida rattlesnake in summer' via 'the equivalent of the National Recovery Act' to 'what Hitler's trying to put over'. One might, I suppose, reasonably denounce Mr Chamberlain for some of the things for which one denounces Hitler or Mussolini (and particularly for the fact that he himself did not denounce these two as he should have done). But effective political thinking could only be frustrated by the attempt to comprise the policies of all three governments, or their 1938 heads, under a single term. If 'Fascist' is merely a synonym for 'objectionable', why not use this word instead, and avoid implications as to the grounds, as distinct from the fact, of the objection?

To the Left wing sympathiser, the most obstinately obstructive example of the dogma type of ism is Marxism. To the question: 'Are you a Marxist?' there really is only one adequate answer—'What a silly question!' It has been

Published by Blackwell Publishing Ltd, 9600 Garsington Road, Oxford OX4 2DQ, UK and 350 Main Street, Malden, MA 02148, USA

pointed out hundreds of times that Marx made some very illuminating contributions to the interpretation of social phenomena. These may well be comparable to the contributions made in other fields by Darwin, Faraday, or Pasteur. But it is noteworthy that the tendency to erect the discoveries of these various pioneers into a school, an ism, or a dogma is in inverse proportion to their connection with social affairs. I have never heard the word Faradayist. Pasteurist had, I believe, a brief reign, and Darwinist a considerable one. Faraday died in 1867, Pasteur in 1895, Darwin in 1881, and Marx in 1883. But only in the case of Marx, has the ism survived to block further advances in knowledge and understanding, sixty years after the death of the Master. In all the other instances we have assimilated the true and shaken out the false in what these great men left behind them, so that we can get on unhampered with the job of trying to add something of our own: with the result that much has, in fact, been added.

It is, no doubt, legitimate to hold the opinion that Marx was more often, and more importantly, right, and less often and less importantly, wrong, than anybody else who has written about social affairs in the past century—or twenty centuries, if you prefer. If so, let us by all means pay tribute to his genius. By labelling yourself a Marxist you do not, it is true, *necessarily* commit yourself to more than the view that Marx was a wiser man than anybody else whose name you might alternatively adopt. But even so you are laying up difficulties in the event of subsequent knowledge demanding a revision (as presumably *some* day it must) of even this opinion. For then you will have to disown your label; and that, as experience shows, involves a certain loss of prestige, and so creates a serious temptation to ignore such knowledge when it comes along. The label implies a declared bias in favour of stopping where somebody else stopped. Why on earth should anybody wish to do this? To judge from the look of the world around us, we get along slowly enough, in all conscience, with the business of adding to our *effective* knowledge, that is, with enlarging our ability to control social relations satisfactorily. The last thing that we want is an unnecessary brake.

The visionary-escape type of ism is best illustrated by that most sorely abused of all ism-terms—socialism. Because of its wide influence, and because of its tendency to inhibit thinking just where thinking is most needed and potentially most fruitful, this is now one of the most dangerous of all political abstractions. It is, therefore, about this that I wish particularly to write.

Now socialism to the socialist means something very nice. That much is agreed. What exactly that nice thing is, is not so much a matter of agreement. The fact that professing socialists are not even of one mind as to whether the USSR is, or is not, a socialist state seems to suggest a fairly fundamental state of confusion. It is moreover a common experience for any socialist speaker who does attempt to give some sort of realistic body to his conception of the socialist society to meet the criticism: 'That is not socialism at all.' The obvious answer to that criticism is that it is entirely irrelevant. If a plan is a good plan, it does not matter two hoots what you label it. It should be judged on merits, and those who are interested should attempt to find some common and definable criterion of merits, and apply this to the particular proposal under discussion. But it is remarkable how seldom the criticism is dismissed on this ground. The fact that it can be made, and that, when made, it is not thus disposed of is evidence that the term socialism conveys no common meaning to the parties concerned, that it actually obstructs communication between them, and should, therefore, be dropped. Fundamentally this type of argument (e.g. the endless discussions as to whether the Soviet Union is or is not a socialist state) are not arguments about socialism at all. They are arguments about the (very important) subject of people's conception of desirable and undesirable ways of dealing with social problems; and they are *frustrated* by the intrusion of the socialist phantom. 'Socialism' has here degenerated into a term of general approbation in just the same way as Fascism was at one time emptied of all but abusive significance.

Further, the habit of thinking in terms of two, and only two, sharply contrasted and mutually exclusive 'systems', corresponding respectively to the Platonic ideas of socialism and capitalism, and of attempting to judge concrete proposals in terms of these ideas, is disastrously out of touch with reality. From Washington to Moscow, from Stockholm to Ankara, the twentieth-century world exhibits a vast variety of economic and social experiments, customs, institutions, ways of behaving; and the results produced, in terms of the everyday life of ordinary people, are not less varied. It is true that some common elements can be traced in all this confusion. But the attempt to fit everything into one or other of our two systems simply distracts attention away from differences that are significant towards similarities which are often imaginary. The only things that matter are the answers to such questions as: How do people live? Are they free to speak their minds? Do they have enough to eat? What sort of houses do they live in? Do they have fun and gaiety in childhood, adventure and opportunity in youth, ease of mind and body in old age? In these respects there were, before the war, great differences between the Danish peasantry and the slum populations of Chicago, between the sharecroppers of the American South and the miners of the Donetz basin. The system classification rides roughshod over these differences, or pretends that they do not exist. Such make-believe will not get us anywhere.

Use of mechanical formulæ about system-changing as a means of evading serious thought on real problems is the most deplorable vice of all. How many hundred times have not discussions about minimum wages or family allowances or the League of Nations or a capital levy been swept aside by the retort that it is no use talking about any of this till you have changed the system? It happens in Labour Parties, in Co-operative Guilds, in undergraduate societies, among the WEA. The retort is, of course, perfectly legitimate provided that the critic is prepared to consider *concretely* what he is proposing to change into what, and what are the best methods of changing it. But how often is this the case? The point at issue here is not, as is often represented, a difference between reformists and revolutionaries. Revolution is quite as capable of being expressed concretely as is any reformist proposal. It is very concrete when it happens! The revolutionary can advocate a general confiscation of all industrial property, or the suspension of suitable persons from lamp posts. These are *intelligible* policies, on the merits of which intelligent opinions can be formed. But a policy of changing one indefinable into another indefinable lies in the realm, not of intelligibility, not (alas!) of works, but of faith and faith alone.

The change-the-system attitude is, in fact, an example (to borrow another ism-word) of the dangerous variety of utopianism. It is pure fantasy: a method of escape from a situation which is felt to be intolerably difficult. Since one does not solve real problems by running away from them, or by the incantation of magical formulæ, the prevalence of this attitude (and among the Left public generally it is prevalent) is extremely dangerous. To say this is not to admit that the label 'utopian' is necessarily pejorative. There are in fact two forms of utopianism. The bad form is that just illustrated. But the admirable and useful form is the utopianism of those who advocate policies which appear to the promoters to be in themselves desirable, but are unattainable so long as other people do not share this opinion. J. S. Mill was utopian in this sense when he demanded equality of the sexes in 1869. So are many who advocate a federal political system in Europe after this war. But the fact that other people do not already agree with an opinion is the silliest possible reason for keeping quiet about it. If your view is right, how can others accept it, if they are not to hear of it? If it is wrong, how can you see what is wrong with it, if they never have a chance to tell you? Moreover, particularly in circumstances where public opinion has some influence in shaping events, it is the plain lesson of experience that desirable reforms begin as paradoxes and end as commonplaces. No doubt Mill's essay was ridiculous at the time when he wrote it. That was a reason for writing it. If the charge of utopianism is used to inhibit the expression of opinions that are still at the ridiculous stage, they will all, sensible and silly alike, remain permanently at that stage.

II

In view of the immense prestige of socialism, it is worth while trying to sort out a little more carefully the various strands that are tangled up in contemporary usage of the word: in order to see whether something reasonably precise and coherent can be made of them; and whether, if so, that something is a suitable subject for political campaigning.

I have found that among professing socialists three ideas are associated with the word more frequently than any others. These are (1) social equality; (2) the full utilisation of resources under a system of 'production for use and not for profit'; and (3) public ownership or socialisation of industry. Possibly the most widely acceptable definition of socialism is that it is a state of society in which all these objectives have been attained.

If so, the use of a single ism to cover the lot begs a number of questions. For these three aims stand on quite different levels. In particular there is a confusion of ends and means; and it is very dangerous to wrap up your ends and means in one bundle and stamp the lot with the socialist seal. For to do this is to beg the question of whether the means proposed will in fact promote the ends desired. And that implies that, if you should ever come to think that they will not, you will be unable to say so without raising doubts as to the sincerity of your socialist faith.

For example: social equality is desired, when it is desired, for its own sake; or at most as a direct constituent in human happiness and dignity. It is, I think definable with fair precision.[3] At all events it is clear that large differences in wealth, opportunity, or prestige unrelated to function, militate against it. So, if we wish for an equalitarian society, let us get on with the job of tackling these.

The 'fullest available use of resources' is also an intelligible end, at least if it is read to mean the abolition of avoidable poverty. But economists have legitimately pointed out that, in view of the great variety covered by the omnibus word 'resources', and the fact that these can be used in thousands of different ways, maximum production is an extremely elusive goal to define in theory, or to recognise in practice. Are four vacuum cleaners and six bicycles more or less than six vacuum cleaners and four bicycles? This is not just the hair-splitting of the sequestered academic. It is a real problem that arises in real practice. It puzzles the heads of the Soviet planners in the actual business of plan-making. Every elaborate modern community must have some method of deciding how much of what is to be produced. And the choice of that method calls for hard thinking. Recently, some of that thinking has been undertaken by economists who are also professing socialists.[4] Some of these economists have argued that the most reliable method will, in general, be to work upon the principle of producing the things that show a profit and stopping the production of those that are not, in the strict commercial sense, profitable. This is a highly technical matter and cannot be argued here. These economists may be wrong; but at least they have called attention to a practical problem, and have shown up the void covered by the production-for-use-and-not-for-profit formula. That formula cannot tell you when or where to open a railway or a mine, to build or demolish a house in your socialist society. No doubt, if you spent thousands of pounds on a branch line which only served a village of three hundred people, and these people already had access to another railway a mile or so away, somebody would *use* the new line. But does it follow that you ought therefore to build it?

The third strand in the socialist bundle is unmistakably means rather than end. A nationalised industry is not an element in happiness and dignity in the way that living on terms of fellowship and equality with your neighbours is. Socialisation is desirable, if it is desirable, because it is expected that it will enable people to live better, or to have more freedom, not because it is a Good-

Thing-in-Itself. Here there are several points to be noted. First, it is plain that socialisation of industry *can* be used to promote ends that are in flat contradiction to the freedom and equalitarian abundance which are also tied up in the same socialist bundle. It can, for instance, be used to promote the domination of a bureaucratic hierarchy; and it certainly seems to be an essential element in totalitarian war-making. So we had better reserve judgement about the socialisation business until we know what we are socialising for. It is not a matter of principle: it is a matter of method or expediency.

Second, it is by no means certain that socialisation is always and in all circumstances the ideal road to equality and abundance. Economic and administrative inventiveness has not been idle in the past half-century, and one might as well keep abreast of it. There are a hundred and one weapons beside formal transfer of ownership to public authorities in the armoury of those who know what they want, and are prepared to be intelligently opportunist about getting it. There is for instance the limitation of profit, the ceiling income, the deliberate adjustment of controlled prices, the free distribution at the taxpayer's expense, the compulsory delivery. Most of these are very modern inventions. It is absurd to dismiss out of hand their possibilities in the creation of a society in which people live well and on terms of equality with one another—merely because they are not traditionally included under the term socialism, which was itself invented before they were. It would be no more absurd to refuse to listen, even experimentally, to a broadcast concert, merely because, traditionally, prior to the invention of radio and gramophone, music could only be enjoyed if the listener was within earshot of the actual performers.

And, third, it is the final absurdity to suppose that, because socialisation is itself a traditional element in socialism, therefore it can, in and by itself, eliminate *all* that is objectionable in capitalist industry. It is true that a worker in a publicly owned enterprise cannot be embittered by the thought that one result of his day's work is to make a particular rich man richer still. That is important. But that is not everything. That does not mean that when the alarm clock rouses the Soviet factory worker he is never tempted to steal another hour's sleep; or that he never wishes his wage packet was larger or his annual holiday longer. There are some things about going to work for *any* employer, which are the same yesterday, today and tomorrow.

In any complex and specialised society there must, in fact, always be conflicts of group interest. One of the most persistent of these is the employer–worker conflict—in one or other of its many forms. The Soviet authorities know that very well; though their uncritical admirers in this country frequently do them ill service by pretending that they do not. In the Soviet Union elaborate machinery is provided for dealing with these conflicts in the form of agreements between enterprises and their employees, regulating the conditions of employment. Whether these agreements are, in fact, freely negotiated or duly observed is not, in this connection, of significance. The fact that they are made at all is an admission that employer and employee cannot be expected to see eye to eye on all points, and that their mutual relations must be adjusted somehow.

In a well-ordered community these conflicts would of course be reduced to a minimum; but the well-ordered state will, equally, be alive to the need to provide smooth-working machinery for settling those that must remain. Certainly such conflicts need not always be the same, still less need they be as exacerbated, as those that disfigure contemporary England or America. But they cannot all be charmed away by the fact that in a socialist state we should all, in some general sense, be working for the community. Working for the community for four hundred roubles is not the *same thing* as doing the same work for the same community for six hundred.

III

The moral of all this is, I think, that we must be as concrete as possible in our ends, and intelligently empirical in our choice of means. Rather than embark upon a full-blooded campaign for 'socialism' or the 'socialist faith', we should draw up a list of some half-dozen specific objectives that must take front place in any reconstruction programme. Such a list might include (1) the essential personal freedoms that have been traditional in this country: these do not need much definition because we have been familiar with them in actual practice; (2) a nutrition standard expressed in terms of the minimum constituents of a physiologically satisfactory diet; (3) a housing standard expressed in terms of space-plus-amenities (e.g. a bathroom for every family); (4) an educational standard in terms of the duration of school life and the provision of so many places in such and such types of post-elementary schools and colleges; (5) a leisure standard expressed as so many hours a week to do what you like with; and (6) a limit on inequality expressed as nobody's income to be more than x times anybody else's.

This is not intended as a considered or final list. The items are chosen merely to illustrate the *degrees of concreteness* necessary, and the fact that if specific ends of this kind were in fact achieved, it would not matter at all whether you called the result socialism or not. (If we pitched the standards high enough and wide enough, there would not be much else to bother about for a good while to come!) Whatever the list contains, the point is that it must be concrete; and the next step must be to draft considered plans for getting from here to there.

These plans will certainly necessitate the nationalisation of some industries; the establishment of drastic controls in others; the manipulation of prices so as to provide satisfactory incentives in yet others. The choice of means will demand much knowledge and much unprejudiced thinking. Never mind. All that matters is to find, and to follow, the particular road which will get us to the particular destination in view. Then we can tick off the items on our list one by one as actually accomplished. And then add others, of course.

There is another reason for taking this very earthy view of the task before us. That reason derives from a particular diagnosis of the causes of our present discontents. The essence of that diagnosis is that more is at fault with our heads than with our hearts. This is not a popular view with the Left at present. On the contrary, a remarkable retreat into ethics is already in progress. Victor Gollancz has written a plea for a new political morality: John Strachey has spoken to the undergraduates of Oxford (or was it Cambridge?) of the virtue of love: and the Fabian Society is sponsoring a new campaign for socialism with a special stress on the ethical.

But are the implications of all this in keeping with the facts of experience? The fundamental ethical drives of most people, most of the time, seem to me sufficiently admirable to be capable of sustaining a world which would be absolute heaven by comparison with that in which we now live—*if only those drives had a chance to express themselves efficiently*. Kindliness and generosity are notoriously widespread virtues. The number of perverts who derive pleasure from the infliction of serious injury upon their neighbours is still, in ordinary experience, very small. No doubt it can be increased by suitable education, as has been done in Nazi Germany; but for this purpose a pretty deliberate and rigorous training seems to be necessary.

And *yet* the most amiable people are perpetrating the most revolting cruelties upon one another. That is the essential tragedy of our present plight. And only those who can out-Vansittart Vansittart deny that this is true of many millions now fighting on both sides. Does not this tragedy suggest that what is at fault is not so much a breakdown of morality as a failure to provide the channels through which good moral sentiments can make themselves effective in public affairs? Thousands of Englishmen, Frenchmen, Czechs, Dutch are today convinced that it is only by the perpetration of these cruelties, by killing, maiming and blinding their fellow creatures that they can safeguard the survival of ordinary toleration and kindliness. They never ought to have got into a position in which such a proposition would make sense. They *have* got into it, not because they like it, not because of their own viciousness, not even because of the viciousness of the Germans. They have got into it because of their own and the Germans' failure to think through, and to bring into being, the social institutions which, in our bewilderingly complex world, would enable their decent feelings to find efficient social expression. In a simple orderly community, like a village, it is easy to be friendly to your neighbour if you happen to feel like it. In our complicated anarchic world, whatever you may feel, it is impossible.

It is useless to tell people to be good when they (and you) are good already. Those who do so lay themselves open to the suspicion of trying to be good because they have failed to be clever—the more so when the call for goodness comes from those whose political morality has been as irreproachable as that of the leaders of our ethical drive. Indeed it is worse than useless. It is dangerous. For if the channels along which ethical fervour can discharge itself in effectively promoting its own ends are blocked, one or other of two things will happen. Either there will be frustration and disastrous disillusion; or the emotion will be diverted into courses leading to ends utterly opposed to those which it was intended to realise. The first is what happened here in the reconstruction period after the last war. The second is what made Germany Nazi.

IV

The whole of the above is an attempted application of a more general proposition: that is the proposition that the future of civilisation—perhaps one should rather say the creation of civilisation—depends, not upon a change of heart or upon greater moral fervour, but upon the application to social and political problems of the scientific method which has accomplished such marvels in other fields. That method implies patient and accurate observation of the facts, and choice of means, not for the satisfaction which their use gives to the user, but for the likelihood that they will, in fact, promote the ends in view. It is the attitude which cleans the carburettor, instead of kicking it, when the car will not go. Above all, it is an attitude which is innocent of the loathsome art of propaganda, in every sense except that of the effective publication of verifiable statements.

The faint marks of that attitude are just beginning to make themselves visible in social and political life: but only just. The volume of precise knowledge of social conditions is slowly growing. Mass Observation, for all its crudities and imperfections, has taught us a *little* about the actual facts of our own behaviour. Gallup Surveys have made it a *little* more difficult for every politician to claim that 'the whole country is behind' his every dictum.

In this astonishing age we have learnt to fly above the earth and to voyage beneath the deeps of the ocean. Our stockings are made from coal and air, our spectacle frames from milk. We make love without conceiving and have our teeth removed without pain. And all this has been accomplished, not by campaigning for isms, but by the unfettered exercise of the human intelligence. A nationwide campaign under the slogan 'Rise above it' never put a single aeroplane into the air. Already the nineteenth century has gone down in history as the age of discovery in the non-human sciences. The opportunity is open to write the history of the century that lies before us as the age of science in human affairs. If that opportunity is lost, there may well be no history at all.

Notes

1 The substance of a lecture given to the Fabian Summer School, 1941.
2 *The Tyranny of Words*, p. 132.
3 I have tried to define it in *End Social Inequality* (New Democratic Order Series).
4 E.g. Dickinson, *The Economics of Socialism* and Hall, *The Economic System in a Socialist State*.

The Economic Aims of the Labour Party

HUGH GAITSKELL, MP*

Vol. 24, no. 1, January–March 1953

THE BRITISH Labour party has never been encumbered by a precise and rigid collection of dogmas set out in the works of the socialist Fathers. If in discussing socialism we refer to Karl Marx or Robert Owen it is usually for historical interest rather than to produce a quotation which clinches the philosophical argument.

Nor have we ever been much interested in the disputes about 'scientific' and 'utopian' socialism. To tell the truth, we were never much impressed with either. Marxism we looked on as an interesting sociological theory which like most such theories contained a lot of half truths, which its exponents insisted on promoting to the status of the one and only true Gospel. In any case the Marxist hostility to idealism and its emphasis on inevitability—which was claimed to be so scientific—did not somehow suit a practical and rather unimaginative people like ourselves. Moreover, those fierce footnotes, exploding with hatred and oddly at variance with all the scientific jargon, made little appeal to men and women nurtured in the traditions of Christianity as expounded in Non-Conformist chapels.

As for utopianism—whose influence on the British labour movement has certainly been greater than that of Marx—its weakness in our eyes was not idealism but the remoteness of some of the ideals, the unreal assumptions about human behaviour and the lack of common sense applied in trying to achieve them.

For the last fifty years at least socialist thought here has been for the most part practical and positive, concentrating on the two questions, 'What do we want?' and 'How do we get it?' The answers to the questions have of course changed from time to time as some of the things we want have been achieved and others no longer seem relevant. For example, in the early days the repayment of the national debt figured high in the list: nobody feels the same about this now. But basically our economic aims spring from a desire to get rid of certain evils which exist under what we call capitalism and which, we believe, must continue to exist under capitalism. Hence our conclusion that we must change from a capitalist to a socialist society.

The major economic evils—for so they seem to us—are insecurity, inefficiency and injustice. Correspondingly our major economic aims are full employment, high productivity and social justice. We want in short a classless

*Chancellor of the Exchequer in the late Labour government.

Published by Blackwell Publishing Ltd, 9600 Garsington Road, Oxford OX4 2DQ, UK and 350 Main Street, Malden, MA 02148, USA

society, where such differences in income—or wealth—as exist are based on genuinely acknowledged merit or need and not on the accident of birth, where there are more jobs going than people seeking them and where our economic activities are so organised as to give us the best results for the efforts we put in. I fully realise that the economic philosophers could start punching holes in this statement of aims. But this is not a philosophical essay, and I believe that what I have said does correspond pretty well with what most labour people would like to see.

I realise too that one and perhaps two of these aims are shared by Conservatives. Certainly the Tory party would claim to be as keen on high productivity as we are and some of them, though not always convincingly, would protest their acceptance of the need for full employment. That leaves however two major differences between the parties—and in the economic field these are the two major differences. First the Tories do not share our enthusiasm for social justice, equality, the classless society—call it what you will. It is not surprising that this should be the great divide. For in all socialist theory in every country and in every century, the one common feature has been the indictment of injustice and unfairness in capitalist society. Secondly, apart from this fundamental difference in aims, there is a disagreement about means to the other two aims—full employment and high productivity— which is so important and so mixed up with what are really different emotional attitudes that it comes near to being, itself, a difference over ends.

This second difference is broadly that we believe that the achievement of these aims requires a very substantial degree of public intervention, control and ownership too, whereas the Tories, though they now accept some of our arguments, still hope and work for a predominantly *laisser faire* economy.

It may appear surprising that apart from a reference to public ownership in the previous sentence, I have not so far included 'the nationalisation of the means of production, distribution and exchange' in the fundamental aims of the Labour party. The difference between means and ends is, as I have just implied, not always clear, but it seems to me that nationalisation—even in a comprehensive form—falls into the former rather than the latter category. Nationalisation should not be looked on as something which is good in itself, but as something which contributes to the economic aims which I have already put forward. It is true that at an earlier stage in socialist thought nationalisation was regarded as the one supremely important means to achieve these aims. Today it still is important as a means, but its relationship to socialism is by no means the same.

The reason for the change is that the full implications of parliamentary democracy are now understood and accepted and that these include the necessity both for a gradual extension of public ownership and for the payment of fair compensation to existing owners. There is little doubt that in the nineteenth century, socialism and wholesale nationalisation were looked on as almost, if not quite, identical because the transfer to public ownership was assumed to take place more or less simultaneously in every industry, and without payment of full compensation. The chief evil of capitalism was, as I have said, always injustice, and injustice in turn was regarded as due to the payments of profits, dividends, and interest—unearned income. Therefore, the argument ran, take over the means of production, stop this flow of unearned income altogether (save perhaps for compassionate allowances), pay the worker the full product of his labour and introduce the just society all at once.

But if the transfer to public ownership is gradual and full compensation is paid, this argument falls to pieces. Full compensation implies that the owners of the industry to be taken over should not be penalised as compared with other capitalists; hence the transfer to public ownership does not stop the flow of unearned income: all that happens is that it takes the form of a rather smaller and more certain flow of interest payments instead of a larger but much less certain profit income.

The case for paying compensation in full need not be argued here. Apart from any moral objection to the confiscation of property without regard to the wealth of the individual, there is the practical difficulty that private firms in other industries not yet, but due to be, taken over would retaliate in face of the threat of confiscation by reducing investment and getting out as much as they could while they could, And this simply does not square with the efficient operation of the private sector which is obviously to be desired throughout the long period of transition, inevitable under democratic conditions.

Does the case for nationalisation, then fall? By no means, though it needs to be thought out and restated. It is still a necessary means to the achievement of socialist ideals, because it contributes in various ways to all three of the aims l have mentioned. It helps the move towards greater equality because it prevents people from making any more private fortunes in the industries taken over, because the flow of interest is smaller than the corresponding profit incomes, because on the whole, via the pressure of public opinion, it puts a brake on the payment of very high salaries (though the need to compete with private industry sets a limit to what can be done here). It helps the maintenance of full employment and higher productivity because of the greater control over investment which it places in the hands of the government. It assists the government to determine the direction of investment and so to carry out more easily specific plans for economic development. It leads to greater efficiency because it makes possible the economies of large-scale administration and production—especially important in some industries—without the establishment of a private monopoly. It thus avoids the evil of a great concentration of private power without responsibility to the community and escapes the danger of restrictive policies being followed because of the desire to maximise profits. It leads to the enforcement of higher standards of safety, health and welfare for employees, and it creates at least a framework for the development of industrial democracy.

Thus, although nationalisation is certainly not the be all and end all of socialism, the extension of public ownership yet plays an essential part in the strategy of the Labour party. But how far should it go? The answer surely must be—as far as is necessary to achieve our major objectives. Exactly where the line should be drawn is a matter which will depend partly on how far we use other means to get to our goal, and partly just on experience.

Certainly the frontier will have to be pushed out further than at present; and in deciding where to push it out we should clearly select those industries where the case on merit is strongest —as indeed we have done so far. But on the other hand we ought to consider whether there are not some parts of the economy which we shall always in the foreseeable future prefer to leave in private or co-operative ownership—such as retail distribution, farming (as apart from land owning), the small builder, garages, etc. And if we so decide, it would be very much better to say so and to make it plain that we wish to encourage small businesses of this kind. Politically one of our dangers at the moment is that we tend to be regarded as a party opposed to the energetic enterprising small man who wants to get on, whereas in fact through our policy of full employment, better education, training schemes, and in many other ways we are all the time providing far wider opportunities for the individual than ever before.[1]

So much for the fundamental economic aims which we, all the time, set before us. But a government does not govern in a vacuum. When it comes into power it inherits a particular set of historical circumstances and a host of problems which have to be dealt with; and throughout its life it will have to spend a large part of its time and energies in coping with new developments which probably could not have been foreseen. This is particularly true in the field of foreign and economic affairs, especially in a country so much affected by overseas events as Britain.

For this reason policy must also be fashioned as we go along; and in meeting new situations new aims come to be accepted. The most obvious instance of this at the present time is the balance of payments, both the overall UK balance and the dollar–sterling balance. Although even before the war this was a problem, it has recently come to dominate the whole economic situation. Thus a solution to the balance of payments problem must be added to the list of our economic aims. Indeed, we know perfectly well that without a solution the other aims cannot all be achieved.

To take this analysis through the next stage and to study in detail the problem of how we reach our objective—the aims within the aims—is impossible in the scope of this article. If I try to deal with them all, there will be no room to say anything useful about any of them. I therefore propose to concentrate on two only—full employment and equality and to leave out, except in passing, productivity and the balance of payments. The choice is arbitrary, but the subjects I propose to pursue happen to be the more distinctively socialist of the four. Even so I can do little more than present an outline to indicate the way the mind of the Labour party seems to me to be shaping. There is fortunately much thought and discussion taking place within the party at present. Several books by leading labour economists are being written and there is a prospect that the 1950s will see a renaissance of British socialist thought comparable to the blossoming of ideas which occurred before, during and just after the First World War.

Our attitude to the problem of full employment has been greatly influenced by the 'Keynesian revolution'. Indeed one might almost say that just as the early Fabians were influenced by the Ricardian theory of rent and its development by John Stuart Mill, so their successors today have been influenced by the 'General Theory of Employment' and subsequent academic thought based upon it. By this I mean not that the Labour party talks in Keynesian jargon of 'marginal propensities' and 'liquidity preferences', but that it believes that the problem of unemployment in a closed economy can be solved at least to a large extent by regulating total demand.

It would, for example, be agreed that the general level of spending can easily be increased by budgetary investment and credit policy, and that by a combination of these policies it would be possible to prevent a depression internally. But it so happens that this was not the problem the Labour government had to face. In the immediate postwar situation our problem was how to prevent inflation and avoid a balance of payments deficit while at the same time maintaining full employment.

The general principle of our policy in these circumstances was to continue both monetary and physical controls—the former to be used to keep the level of home demand high enough to ensure full employment, the latter to prevent this developing into inflation and upsetting the balance of payments. Thus while imports were for the most part controlled by state purchase and quotas, private investment was regulated by building licensing, public investment by direct government decision, the prices of essentials were held down by controls and subsidies—with the concomitant of rationing to ensure 'fair shares'—and industry was guided to some extent by raw material controls and again by building licensing. This apparatus of controls achieved, in effect, two objects—first, by protecting the economy from inflationary pressure naturally set up by a very high level of employment, it made that high level possible; and secondly by holding back supplies of luxuries from the home market (the austerity policy) in order that there should be a greater supply of essentials—it involved some redistribution of real income in favour of lower incomes. Thus we had council houses before expensive flats, imported timber before American clothes, cars exported to buy essential imports instead of being delivered for motoring at home.

Looking back on all this, I see no reason to modify the general principles of our policy. Quite apart from humanitarian motives it is hard to believe that we should have achieved such a remarkable increase in production and productivity without the full employment policy. And it is, I think, quite certain that if we had not had the controls we should have been obliged—in order to protect our balance of payments and check the rise in prices internally—to hold back production by our credit and budgetary policy and deliberately to create a higher level of unemployment.

Just how much higher it is hard to estimate. Some would say that with 3% out of work (600,000) the economy could run without controls; others that we should have to approach or even go beyond the 5% (1 million) mark.

This does not mean, however, that the problem of maintaining full employment without inflation is solved. There were undoubtedly weaknesses in our policy, and some difficult questions will have to be answered. Before turning to these, however, I must make some further reference to the balance of payments problem.

The deflationist school paints a picture of Britain in chronic deficit because of a too high level of employment and its inflationary accompaniment. But the facts do not bear this out. To begin with it is quite unreasonable to assume that we ought to have been in balance in 1946 and 1947. In view of the position we were left in at the end of the war when lease-lend stopped so suddenly, it was perfectly natural that for a time we should run a deficit while we were both restocking (filling up the pipeline) and building up our export trade. And it was in order to enable us to do this that we obtained the postwar loans from the USA and Canada. In the years 1948 and 1949 we had in the one case a small deficit and in the other a small surplus. In 1950 we had a surplus of £240 million. In 1951 this became a deficit of £500 million. In 1952 we shall probably have a small surplus. This can hardly be described as a picture of chronic deficit. It is true that the surplus of 1950 was partly due to the running down of stocks and work in progress that year, the correction of which was one of the causes of the deficit of 1951. But the main cause of the deficit of that latter year was the quite extraordinary change in the terms of trade against us—a change which was all the more difficult to handle because of the extreme suddenness with which it took place. I can understand the criticism that we were too slow in adjusting our plans to meet a new situation. But what I cannot understand is the notion that it would have been easier to deal with the situation if we had no import controls and had relied solely on monetary policy. All that can be said for this chronic inflation doctrine is that if we had deflated more and had more unemployment and less production, and if consumption had been reduced by this as well as by lower imports or higher exports, then we should have had an even larger surplus in 1950 and a larger cushion to take the strain of 1951. But I cannot agree that this justifies the sweeping generalisation, so often made in some quarters, that our system of full employment plus controls has failed and that we must return to pre-war orthodoxy and rely on monetary policies only.[2]

And now for some of the real weaknesses in our policy and some, as yet, unsolved problems. In the first place the experience of these last years shows clearly, I think, that while it is possible through monetary policy and physical controls to prevent excessive inflationary pressure from the demand side, it is more difficult to stop a 'cost' inflation. If wages rise faster than productivity, then, except in so far as the advance is at the expense of profits, it is inevitable that prices will rise too. Much has been said and written on this subject in recent years. Sometimes the danger is exaggerated. But few people would be so bold as to say that there was no problem. It is partly a question of education, partly a matter of institutions. There is no simple solution, but I believe it can be handled, given real cooperation between the trade unions, the employers, and the government.

Another rather more difficult problem arises in connection with controls. The last Labour government took over a complete set of wartime controls, gradually discarded those which were not needed, and retained the others. When the next Labour government comes into power, most of the controls may have been swept away; setting them up again will not be so easy as merely maintaining them. Moreover, in some cases the public may not take kindly to the idea at all. Are we, for example, to reintroduce food rationing, if this has meanwhile been abolished? Of course the need for it would not arise unless and until the rise in incomes (together possibly with the revival of subsidies) caused shortages at the prevailing prices. But if we do not favour the idea—because of the political disadvantages—we shall have to be careful not to create the conditions in which it becomes necessary.

We ought also to examine more closely the relationship of negative controls to efficiency. There is no doubt that raw material shortages, carried beyond a certain point, have a very bad effect on production. Again, whenever quotas have to be fixed in relation to past records, they tend to militate against the young, enterprising firm. Can we find some better system of deciding allocations between firms?

I would be inclined, myself, to the view that the key physical controls in the private sector, without which we could not carry out a full employment policy, were foreign exchange, import and building licensing and price controls, but that we should aim at normally confining ourselves to these. This means that we should try to adjust our monetary and credit policy so as to make it unnecessary to have many other physical controls—except occasionally the allocation of a scarce raw material.

This brings me to the third question on which more thought is needed—the part to be played by credit policy generally and the rate of interest in particular in the planned economy. This is an extraordinarily complex matter on which economists have written a vast amount. Perhaps the prevailing view among the left wingers today is that credit policy is of vital importance, that there should be more direct control of the size and character of the assets held by the banks, but that the use of the bank rate is both too crude and too expensive a weapon to be relied on; we should therefore do best to rely on selective credit policy, encouraging bank lending in the case of one industry and discouraging it in the case of another. In general, I share these views, though I have doubts on two points—the capacity of the branch bank managers to administer the selective credit controls and whether the level of stocks and work in progress can be effectively controlled in this manner.

For there can be no doubt—and this is really my fourth problem—that one of the weak parts in our whole planning machine was our inability to watch sufficiently closely the movements of business inventories and to influence them in the way we wanted. Partly this is just a matter of adequate statistical returns, but it is also a question of what instruments of control can be used. It can be argued that had we had the knowledge and the controls, we should have had neither such a large trade surplus in 1950 nor such a large trade deficit in 1951.

Finally there is one general limitation on the kind of controlled economy I have been describing—the controls are almost all *negative*. They are designed to steer the economy the way the government wishes by stopping people from doing things. This is, up to a point, the natural type of control in the private sector for the simple reason that you cannot force people to lose their money. It provides, as I have already suggested, one of the arguments for nationalisation. But more attention needs to be paid to the question of what positive inducements can be provided for the private sector. The two most obvious are subsidies and guaranteed purchases. Both of course have been used— especially in agriculture. Initial allowances at different levels for different industries have also been suggested. The difficulties of using these in a big way as instruments of planning are primarily political. There is a danger that the pressure of vested interests rather than the needs of the economy will decide how and where and for how long they will be used. This, however, is part of a wider problem which emerges in one way or another if you attempt to go beyond a plan to keep the general level of demand at an adequate level.

It will not be denied, even by those who dislike official statistics, that in the last twelve years there has been a substantial advance towards greater economic equality. This has come about, I suggest, in at least four different ways. First and most familiar has been the striking increase in the taxation of high and middle incomes. This was introduced during the war but has broadly been continued in the postwar period. The income tax concessions made by the Labour Government since 1945 were designed, as far as possible, to benefit the lower taxable incomes. Secondly, there has been the substantial increase in free social services which though available to all are, for various reasons, not always used by better off people. In this respect the expenditure on education has been relatively more valuable to the cause of equality, because the middle classes still tend to pay for their own education, while in the case of the health services, for example, they have themselves been perhaps the greatest beneficiaries.

Thirdly, there has been a steady rise in the share of wages and salaries in the nation's income. Between 1946 and 1951 the rise in total wages and salaries *before* tax was 60%, the rise in farm incomes 50%, professional earnings 33%, small businesses 9%, and rent, dividend, and interest received only 5%. Even allowing for a small increase in the working population, and the fact that these figures relate to personal income and therefore exclude undistributed profits, the change is sufficiently remarkable.[3]

Fourthly—but much less important—there is the point made earlier in this article that real incomes of the better off have been held back by such measures as rationing and import and building licenses.

But though there is undoubtedly much more equality today, the process of breaking down class barriers and introducing equality of opportunity has certainly not gone as far as socialists desire. What, then, are the next steps to be taken towards this end?

There is, I think, a growing feeling that techniques of simply increasing taxation on incomes still further and expanding social services with the proceeds is not an adequate answer to our problem. Much nonsense, to be sure, is talked about the harmful effects of taxation on incentives to work. The more serious economic objection to still higher taxation lies, more in the difficulty that beyond a certain point it causes people to reduce saving or to dissave instead of to cut their consumption. But it is the political difficulty which seems to me the most important one. For the amount which can still be transferred from higher incomes, i.e. those paying surtax, is now relatively small. If by some fiscal device, all incomes in excess of £2,000 a year were taken by the revenue, the additional yield was estimated in 1951 to be only a little over £50 million compared with a total budget of over £4,000 million. Any attempt to raise large additional sums by income tax on the usual lines, over and above the increase of revenue at existing rates which may be expected as the national income grows, must involve higher taxation on middle incomes—say £500 to £2,000 a year. Moreover we must face the fact that people do not like having too much of their money being spent for them on free communal services and too little being left to them to spend as they like. While none of us would deny the practical necessity for free communal services in some spheres, and while, because of the redistribution effect, they have up to now undoubtedly contributed to greater equality, beyond this there is in my view no special reason why socialists should favour all such services as against a fair distribution of the money involved which the recipients can spend as they wish.

And here we come up against the problem of how far it is desirable to equalise post-tax *earned* incomes still further. How much more, for example, should a chairman or managing director receive in 'take home money' as compared with the lowest paid labourer in the industry? No doubt this is in part dependent on public opinion—and, as opinion changes, so the differential can change. But it would be worth while enquiring what sort of standards would be considered appropriate today. The present range, apart from a few exceptions, is of the order of 7 or 8 to 1. Should we try and narrow it?

For my part I would say that our strategy in the next stage towards greater equality ought to be directed not to narrowing still further the differences in earned income so much as at three other matters—'expenses', education, and the distribution of unearned income and the property from which it is derived. For I believe that these are three of the major causes of inequality today and that in tackling them we should enjoy a good deal more popular support than by proceeding along the more familiar road of higher taxation on incomes—earned and unearned alike.

The extent to which people can claim and be granted 'expenses'—especially for entertainment—has been the subject of comment for a long time, and, though its quantitative significance may not be very great, it gives rise to irritation and cynicism among the vast majority who do not enjoy these privileges. The problem is not at all an easy one. It is difficult to decide where to draw the line and it is almost impossible to check in every case whether it has been drawn in the right place. But some idea of the way in which the more excessive allowances could be stopped was given in one of the amendments which the opposition put down to the 1952 Finance Bill.

The education ladder is, of course, very much wider than it used to be. But the fact remains that differences in education are still a major cause of differences in economic and social status and that these differences in education are to a too great extent still related to the position of the child's parents. There are those who go to the secondary modern schools and leave at 15, there are those who go to the secondary grammar schools and leave at 17 or 18, there are those who go from the grammar schools to the universities—and there are those who go to the 'public' schools and may or may not go on to the universities.

I am no educational expert, but it seems to me that if we really want equal educational opportunity for every child, then we need two major changes—one within the state education system and one about the relationship of private to state education. As regards the former, we ought surely to try to eliminate the kind of class structure that often exists between the secondary modern and the secondary grammar schools, and we ought more and more to try and ensure, in so far as there have to be differences in the amount of education given, that, throughout, these are determined solely by the ability of the child.

On the second point, we have to face the fact that the desire 'to do the best for your child' is a very powerful and natural emotion which it would be foolish to ignore or suppress. But it is also true that this desire operating in our present educational system does produce great inequalities of opportunity. It seems to me that if we are not to prohibit 'private' schools—to which there are objections—the only course is to improve the quality of state education until it becomes mere foolishness for people to pay to have their children educated privately. The expense of 'private' education is so high today in relation to post-tax incomes that parents can often only afford it by drawing on their capital—capital which the vast majority of the population do not possess except in very small amounts. Thus to some extent the question of greater equality in education is bound up with our third major problem—that of the distribution of property.

It is important to tackle this, in the first place because the distribution of property is much more uneven than the distribution of income and because, as far as is known, the move to greater equality seems to be going more slowly here. But it is also important because without doubt the capacity to spend capital is an important cause today of inequality of living standards. It is important, finally, because, in so far as it is mostly based on inheritance or luck, the unequal distribution of property is all the less justifiable. How then should it be tackled? I can only briefly record my general views. I believe that there is still everything to be said for concentrating on the point at which wealth is inherited. It seems to me that public opinion which would react against a capital levy, except in very special circumstances, does not really support the handing over of large accumulations of wealth from one generation to another. Exactly how our present system of death duties should be reformed so as to make it more effective, I cannot discuss here.

But it is quite certain that any really vigorous effort to attack the problem in this way would encounter one very serious obstacle—avoidance by gifts *inter vivos* and by spending out of capital. It would therefore be essential to anticipate this by counter measures. As I have indicated, the problem of dissaving is already a serious one for those who wish to preserve full employment without inflation and also press on to greater equality. And gifts *inter vivos* are today already a frequent method of avoiding death duties. It is therefore necessary to find some method—possibly through fiscal reform by which we can effectively put a stop to both practices. If we can find this and overcome the administrative and political difficulties which its introduction would involve, we should then be able to maintain a sufficiently high rate of saving in the community and so provide ourselves with a secure base from which to make another great advance towards the just society.

Notes

1 I have sketched here the case for nationalisation today. Of course there are also difficulties and problems. One of the most serious—which many in the Labour party do not full appreciate—is the difficulty of finding people who are good enough and also willing to take on the colossal jobs of large-scale business administration.

2 I cannot deal here with the long and tangled story of the dollar balance of the Sterling area since the war. There were in my view serious weaknesses in the management of the Sterling area at this time, but that does not affect the conclusion of this paragraph.

3 The fact that the index of share values shows no significant rise in this period suggests that the ploughing back of undistributed profits did not offset the sharp relative fall in property incomes.

The Future of British Politics: an American View

SAMUEL H. BEER*

Vol. 26, no. 1, January–March 1955

IN THE coming months there will be a crescendo of electioneering, and politicians in their clipped, straight-faced British way will misrepresent one another almost as absurdly as partisans in the noisy battles of American politics commonly do. But as between the two major parties, what is the real 'differential'—to use Sir Winston Churchill's expression? The Tories have not attacked the welfare state, but have preserved and extended it. Labour, on the other hand, even when freed from the responsibilities of power, carries less and less conviction in its role as the radical party. An American is bound to miss many nuances of British politics but he will, I think, find a great many British observers who will agree that today the main lines of British policy at home would be much the same no matter which party was in power and that if Labour is returned to power in the next election we may expect as much continuity with present Tory policy as there has been with Labour policy under the present government.

Virtual bipartisanship in foreign affairs, although no less important, is less surprising. But what is the meaning of this convergence of party policy in domestic affairs? Perhaps it is only temporary. Perhaps the Left will soon gather its forces and its thoughts and the next few years will be a time of bitter partisan strife and radical social reform. But this seems almost as unlikely as an equivalent onslaught by the Right. Barring undue interference by outside forces—such as a slump in the west or a war in the east—Britain seems to have entered a long period of political peace. What reasons are there for thinking that the present moderation may continue? What is likely to be the substance and shape of politics if it does?

To ask what is the real 'differential' between the parties—that is, how their actual policies would differ if they had power in similar circumstances—is a speculative question. But since it is in a sense a question which every voter must attempt, a foreign student of British politics may be excused for suggesting some tentative answers. From them we may get some idea of the nature of the issues of the future and of the kind of politics in which they will be fought out.

At one time, public ownership was the distinctive doctrine of Labour. What else separated it from the radical reformers of the Liberal party? Today, as everyone knows, this doctrine is the subject of a profound *crise de conscience* in

* Professor of Government, Harvard University, Mr Beer spent last year in England studying British politics and government.

© 2011 The Author. The Political Quarterly © 2011 The Political Quarterly Publishing Co. Ltd
Published by Blackwell Publishing Ltd, 9600 Garsington Road, Oxford OX4 2DQ, UK and 350 Main Street, Malden, MA 02148, USA

the party, reminiscent in some ways of the crises of belief in the churches when in the nineteenth century they were obliged to bring their dogmas up to date. In Bevanism we have a fundamentalist reaction, but as regards the bulk of the party and most of its leaders it is highly doubtful whether Labour is still committed to public ownership as a means of controlling the economy or remaking society.

There is a clear conflict between the parties over steel, although even on this issue the differential is much less than that suggested by the slogans of 'public ownership' and 'free enterprise', Perhaps also the list included in *Challenge to Britain* will stand. Or will the Morrisonian opposition to 'lists' and preference for general criteria and a free hand for governments prevail? In any case, how urgent will be the priority which a future Labour government will assign to further measures of public ownership? The inner doubts of the party and the lack of a clear sense of direction on these questions make it no hazardous guess to expect that political pressures and calculations of electoral expediency will considerably influence how they are answered.

A major work of the Tory government has been the lifting of controls and whether one agrees with the policy or not, it would be niggardly to deny them credit for having done what they set out to do. Yet in this sphere it is even more difficult than in that of public ownership to find a radical differential. One reason is that opinion in Britain—in particular the opinion of the professional classes—has a way of moving in unison and independently of party philosophies. With regard to economic planning and control there has been since the war such a movement of opinion which government policy in general has followed, regardless of the party in power, and which party opinion itself has tended simply to reflect. Toward the end of the war and immediately after it, great store was put in the peacetime future of central economic planning and control. Sir Oliver Franks's lectures[1] were typical and the Industrial Charter showed that official Tory policy itself was much influenced. But criticism rose and disillusionment soon set in, and during the later years of the Labour government—Harold Wilson began his 'bonfires of controls' in 1948—civil servants and ministers, as well as economists generally, turned strongly against physical controls and detailed planning. Upon the change of government, the relaxation of controls set in motion by Labour was continued by the Conservatives, although it must be emphasised, at a more rapid rate.

The task of separating the effect of party policy from that of the movement of informed opinion is made even harder by Tory flexibility. When the Conservatives took power at the height of the economic crisis following on Korea and rearmament, they vigorously tightened up and added to the controls which Labour had already imposed to meet the emergency. Even today, although the work of dismantling has been carried out on a large scale, a Tory government still retains and operates no inconsiderable number of controls, and the budget, as in the days of Cripps, is boldly used not only to maintain economic equilibrium, but also to promote productivity and to accomplish particular purposes, such as the encouragement of certain exports. Mr Butskell and Mr Gaitler speak the same language, even if they do not have exactly the same ideas.

Labour's policy statements by no means support a doctrinaire position on planning and controls and some leading socialists will say that their political belief has nothing to do with control, but is entirely concerned with equality. What a future Labour government would do, however, would probably depend less on social philosophy than on the compulsions of the situation. In particular, if Labour seriously intends to carry out rapidly and fully its promises of huge additional expenditure on social services, then its next government will be obliged to impose a tight system of planning and control and to maintain it indefinitely. In itself and in its consequences, such expenditure would seem to be the source of an important differential between the parties.

Yet if Labour has receded on the questions of public ownership and economic control, the Tories have expanded their notion of what can and ought to be spent on the social services. The Tories justly claim to have had a major part in founding the welfare state; not been the party of *laissez-faire*. But their conceptions of welfare expenditure at the end of the war were modest as compared with Labour's and the internal struggle by which the party was brought around to accepting the revolution of 1945 centred less on nationalisation and planning than on the scale of welfare expenditure. Tory budgets have continued the steady increase in the amounts spent on the social services and if central government expenditure on housing and education is added, the trend is the same, whether we take absolute figures or percentages of total expenditure. Only as a percentage of national product does this expenditure show a slight decline—a matter of less than 1 per cent. Nor have the Tories chosen to alter the method of financing the welfare state and to reverse the redistributory effects of heavy income taxation. Butler's principal reduction was essentially a return to the rates prevailing before Gaitskell's budget of 1951, which was designed to meet the special circumstances created by the increase in the arms programme. Other changes, such as the raising of the point at which liability to pay standard rate of income tax begins, clearly benefit the less well-to-do, while the benefits to the professional classes, such as raising the earned income relief from £400 to £450, have been modest. Even if we reckon in the reduction of food subsidies, it is doubtful if any of the less well-to-do have suffered an appreciable loss and some—e.g. single persons— have clearly gained on balance.

Policy may be reflected in the method of expenditure as well as the amount. In the increase of the amount spent on family allowances, for instance, one might trace the influence of not only the Tories' special concern with the family, but also their general 'net and ladder' theory of the social services— that is, aid particularly for those in need—which they oppose to Labour's concept of them as 'a levelling instrument'. In how many spheres of activity, however, do we actually find such a special Tory emphasis? One might well expect, for instance, that under Conservatives subsidised houses would be built only for those who cannot afford an economic rent and that the swelling figures of the housing programme would represent a boom in private building. In fact, the proportion of houses built by private enterprise has risen only from one in five to one in four and today more houses carrying a subsidy—which amounts to something like 40 per cent of the economic rent—are being built under the Tories than were built under Labour. Macmillan has done better than Bevan, but he has done much the same thing. Indeed, a simple continuation of the present trend, given enough time, is likely to end in that municipalisation of rented dwellings which Labour half-heartedly proposed as an alternative to the Rent and Repairs Acts.

Since the war, the political pressures behind the housing programme have been irresistible, compelling governments to give it perhaps the highest priority even as against defence and also producing that unique scene when a Tory conference revolted against its platform and forced the party to proclaim a target of 300,000 houses a year. But hardly less powerful and surely more lasting are those pressures which gather around the social security programme. The old-age pensioners in particular are a large and growing body who, although not well organised as a pressure group, are sharply aware of their interests, of which the competition between the parties continually serves to remind them. If in the field of social security the Tories were to follow the 'net and ladder' approach, they might well prefer to put additional funds into an increase in public assistance, rather than spread them among various types of benefits, some of which are inevitably paid out to persons not greatly in need. They have chosen, however, to meet Labour's promise to restore all benefits to the level of purchasing power which they had in 1948, proposing indeed to make good the rise in prices since 1946. As an election year draws near, both party conferences put the raising of old age pensions in the forefront, 'and', tartly commented the *Manchester Guardian*, 'on the domestic side, not much else besides'.

Outside the realm of economic reform and income redistribution lies what might prove to be the most explosive issue of all: Labour's commitment to comprehensive schools. An American may be pardoned if he wonders why British egalitarians have not taken up this cause long ago and if he believes that such schools, if generally established, would do more to destroy social inequality and the remnants of the class system than sweeping measures of nationalisation. In any case, such a step would constitute a great structural reform and would excite the bitterest party and class feelings. Adding to this pledge the immense redistributory proposals of Labour's welfare programme and the tight system of planning which these in turn would entail, we may be satisfied, even without reckoning on the shadowy possibilities of further nationalisation, that Labour is still potentially as radical a party as ever. But actually what is likely to happen? Will not the forces of moderation which have so greatly helped to keep the Tories from straying into reaction and Labour from making even more extravagant promises continue to operate?

These forces are in the first place electoral. 'As each party is supported by twelve million voters', said Sir Winston at Blackpool, 'they must have a great deal in common.' In a sense the evenness of the division of the electorate itself induces caution in party tactics. The opposing armies are not composed of single-minded partisans, but include on each side a margin of waverers who might have chosen the other cause. Perhaps in the right circumstances a bold programme of reaction or radicalism might remake the bases of opinion on which this division rests. But for the time being, the dictates of prudence are to avoid pitched battles of opposing social philosophies and to fight through small raids, designed to capture votes from particular groups.

Such a tactic is difficult for a party based on class in ideas or in membership, since it means that the party may have to appeal to groups in the 'other' class and also that in so far as the tactic succeeds such class basis as the party may have will be worn away as a coalition of interest groups takes the place of the organisation of a class. These considerations, however, do not greatly affect British parties, since they are class parties in only a limited sense, their social bases, indeed, being not much different from those of the Democratic and Republican parties. Labour, no more than the Democrats, wins the whole vote of the working class—the proportions are almost exactly the same in the two cases—while the Tories like the Republicans draw support from all classes and income groups.

The tactic of the small raid on the particular interest group is not only compatible with the social bases of British parties. It is also encouraged and shaped by the structure of the welfare state. To establish such a system of benefits stimulates recipients to political activity and gives that activity a focus. An interest group which was previously apathetic may turn into a strong political force when its members become clients of a welfare pro-gramme. The National Farmers' Union, for instance, grew most rapidly in numbers and influence not during the depressed twenties and thirties, but as farmers prospered and enjoyed government favour during and after the war.

From this tactic and these shaping forces results not a politics of class or of social philosophy, but a kind of pressure politics. The term is inexact as applied to British politics today if it suggests that policy is made simply by groups pushing an inert government or party this way and that, for it is often the government or party which in the competition for electoral support teaches the group what its rights and interests are and excites it to demand them. The term also may not be taken to mean that the political activity of the pressure group involves noisy threats and loud, demanding claims. The day of mass demonstrations in Whitehall or the lobbies of Westminster is pretty well past. The civil servants of the organised interest groups of the British Legion, the Farmers' Union, the National Union of Teachers, the Federation of British Industries, the Transport Workers and countless trade unions, trade associations, and professional organisations—deal directly and continually with civil servants in government; occasionally they or their chiefs have recourse to ministers, less often to MPs. While the outright corporatism of the war period, when organised bodies were in whole or in part taken directly into administration, has been dismantled, a quasi-corporatism remains which leaves no important group without a channel of influence. It is a rare and serious charge—as at the time of the Anglo–Japanese trade agreement of last year—to accuse the government of making public policy without first consulting the special interests concerned. Above all, the whole process is orderly and quiet; there seems almost to be an understanding on the order in which claimants may raise their demands. A group may not, as was said of MPs when they proposed a rise in their pay, 'put themselves at the head of the queue'.

One of the best illustrations of this pattern of politics and of how it tends to produce 'bipartisanship' is provided by the farmers who, under the leadership of the National Farmers' Union, have enjoyed the favour of government under both Labour and Conservatives, during war and peace, in times of world food shortage and world food surplus. Tightly organised, brilliantly led, and including some 90 per cent of their potential membership, the NFU could teach lessons to the American farmers, of whom only about a third are organised and who are divided among three main organisations. Most interesting, however, among the things illustrated by their relations with the parties is the tendency of the present political situation sometimes to produce a 'reversal of alliances', as party leaders, taking for granted the votes of traditional supporters, sacrifice or skimp the interests of these for the sake of winning votes normally attached to the other party. More than a trace of this appears in the Conservative policy towards trade unions, as is suggested by complaints on the Tory right wing that for a Conservative government they have been exceedingly free with employers' money in their attitude toward wage claims. But the relations of the farmers with Labour are an even better example, for here we have a capitalist class who nevertheless have found, as E. G. Gooch put it at the Margate conference, that 'Labour in office proved to be their best friend'. Among the grounds for such a policy is the calculation that, as he pointed out, 'you cannot have a Labour government again with overwhelming power until you win many rural seats'. But to make a play for rural seats, of which some two dozen are marginal, probably means some skimping of urban interests. The parliamentary Labour party made this hard choice when not long after the Margate conference it decided to support the increase in horticultural duties proposed by the Conservative government, even though at that time, as one might expect of a party which has its main strength among the less well-to-do urban consumers, Labour was making the cost of living a principal issue, and although the consumption of fresh fruit in Britain had not yet regained its pre-war level.

Strengthening the moderating tendencies of this balance of electoral forces is a certain balance of social forces. That balance consists in the fact that many groups in the society hold what is almost a veto over public policy in their power to refuse their work, their talents, their capital, or simply their hearty cooperation in worrying out public policy. John Strachey squarely stated the problem for a future Labour government when he observed that if such a government came to power pledged to a radical redistributionist policy there might well be a flight of capital. Of course, the threatening possibilities are not all on one side. An equally serious disturbance would face any Tory government which attacked the welfare state. Trade unions as well as financiers and managers have a veto power and in the years before 1951 the chances of widespread, industrial unrest if a Tory government came to power were held up as a warning to voters. In the event, these dangers did not materialise simply because the Tories yielded all along the line, even to the point of dropping the demands of their 1950 manifesto that 'a final settlement' be arranged concerning contracting out and compulsory union-ism. We can expect a future Labour government to show a similar respect for realities.

As regards the proposal that the aircraft industry be nationalised, for instance, this veto power means that such a step would very probably lead the team of designers upon whom the industry depends for progress to pack up and go to the United States. But it need not take so drastic a form. Consider what will be the feelings of grammar school teachers if they are transferred *en masse* to comprehensive schools in which their old schools with their distinct-ive traditions have been submerged. Would they be capable of offering that warm and whole-hearted cooperation which any school must have from its teachers if it is to work well?

If radical reform is to succeed in a democracy—and the same would hold of equivalent action on the Conservative side—not only must a majority have voted for it, but the minds of all must have been prepared. Even opponents must to some extent be ready to accept the change and to obey not merely the letter, but the spirit of the law. Such a general spirit of reform was abroad in Britain after the war and provided an atmosphere in which radical structural reforms and extensive economic planning and control could succeed. This is not the case today. On the contrary, even in the heart of the Labour move-ment, among the trade unions and the co-operatives, both public ownership and economic controls meet with no enthusiasm and often with outright hostility.

Perhaps in an individualist society where groups were less highly organ-ised and less aware of their interests, mere majority support might suffice as a basis for large-scale reform. But today the extent of group power, nurtured by the welfare state and the quasi-corporatism of the relations of government and the economy, means that Britain is close to the point at which a society must move with near unanimity or not at all.

As applied to Britain, however, this way of looking at things, while true, puts the matter too much in negatives. A modern society may indeed reach a condition of 'pluralistic stagnation' —to use a phrase applied to the later years of the Weimar Republic—but this is hardly the impression which the visitor brings back from Britain today. The powers which are in balance there are not 'have-not' powers, straining against frustration. They are rather 'satisfied' powers very much content with their spheres of influence and with the general economic and social settlement which guarantees them. No visitor who remembers the Britain of the thirties can fail to mark today's contentment, the relaxation of tension, the return of consensus. Something of importance has happened in social standards and ideals.

In one sense, it is curious that the great reforms of social and economic structure and of material conditions have not resulted in more striking changes in the realm of standards and ideals. One might reasonably expect that the two spheres of the economy and culture would change together. It was a belief of the early socialists—Sydney Olivier, for instance—that the reform of material conditions would produce a new and higher social ethic. At the 1954 meeting of the TUC, Herbert Morrison spoke of the need for such a new ethic—a 'new morality' based on 'the public service' motive. But what has actually happened? Certainly there has been no outburst of what Olivier called 'the social instinct' or of that collectivist devotion and enthusiasm which actually governed large sectors of personal conduct during the war. As members of the working class have come to enjoy better material conditions they have neither retained their old, nor created a new mode of life, but, as Donald Chapman wrote in these pages last summer,[2] they have simply adopted that of the lower middle class. The British workman can hardly be brought to live in an apartment house, even though such collectivist habitations are more economical of land and might sometimes even be cheaper to build. He will have his own semi-detached villa, preferably with a stout fence in front and a separate garden behind, where he works for his personal benefit.

But neither is the spirit of British society today individualist, if by that you mean the spirit of unbounded individual aggrandisement and of capitalist enterprise. A sociologist friend of mine touched on this point while summarising the results of a survey he had just concluded. The working classes generally, he said, as they improve their material conditions, adopt the consumption habits of the lower middle classes. They do not, however, adopt the familiar middle class aspiration to own a shop or business. On the contrary, according to his observations, they prefer to remain wage-earners, rather look down on the small shopkeeper and use their surplus energies to ensure that they get the maximum possible benefits from the welfare state. When Donald Chapman finds a likeness between the new Britain and the United States except 'in the case of personal acquisitiveness', this is a major exception. In all classes, if my experience is a fair guide, the profit motive is under such a cloud as would be inconceivable in the United States.

It would seem as if motives and ideals have in some degree developed with material conditions and that some sort of 'mixed ethic' had emerged to match the mixed economy and to support the present moderate polity. Its precise shape deserves study, as do its origins. I should like to conclude by asking the question: to what extent is this social ethic new?

'In Europe at the present time', Bertrand de Jouvenel has written, 'great discredit weighs upon the notion of personal interest. History and ideology unite in a single condemnation, the socialist dream reviving in minds the deeply etched images of knight and monk. European opinion has only to go back to its origins in order again to call "ignoble"—that is not noble—that activity which has profit for its motive.' In Britain, even at the height of Victorian *laissez-faire*, powerful remnants of the pre-Victorian age, monarchy and aristocracy, did indeed, as Bagehot observed, restrain the rule of money. Today the Toryism which derives not from Victorian capitalism, but from an earlier time, Tudor and mercantilist, can without undue strain join with the anglicised socialism of Mr Attlee in support of the welfare state. The forces which have overthrown liberal, capitalist England have roots deep in the past. Is it not strange that there should be a new enthusiasm for monarchy. A king or queen is a symbol of the fact that the state is not just a night-watchman.

Notes

1 *Central Planning and Control*, by O. S. Franks.
2 'What prospect for the Labour party?' *The Political Quarterly*, vol. xxv, No. 3, p. 205 (July–September 1954).

Parties, Pressure Groups and the British Political Process

R. T. McKENZIE*

Vol. 29, no. 1, January–March 1958

SAMUEL BEER, perhaps the ablest American student of British politics, commented recently: 'If we had some way of measuring political power, we could possibly demonstrate that at the present time pressure groups are more powerful in Britain than in the United States.'[1] The realisation that this may be the case appears to have grown rapidly in Britain in recent years and, in most quarters, the reaction to it has been gloomy;[2] indeed, among many publicists the gloom has given way to outright despair. Thus, according to Paul Johnson, assistant editor of the *New Statesman*, 'Acts of policy are now decided by the interplay of thousands of conflicting interest groups, and cabinet ministers are little more than chairmen of arbitration committees. Their opinions play virtually no part in shaping decisions which they subsequently defend with passion . . . When everyone's wishes count, nobody's opinions matter.'[3]

There are no doubt many explanations of this despairing (and, I would argue, belated) recognition of the powerful role played by interest groups in Britain. There can be no question that their activities and their influence have increased in recent decades. This surely was inevitable; once it had been largely agreed by all parties that the governments (national and local) should collect and spend over a third of the national income, tremendous pressures were bound to be brought to bear to influence the distribution of the burdens and benefits of public spending on this scale. And further: a new and powerful factor was injected into the equation when the trade unions, since the Second World War, won recognition (in Sir Winston Churchill's phrase) as an 'estate of the realm'. The highly articulate middle class (by whom, and for whom, so many of our journals of opinion are written) developed an acute sense of claustrophobia as they watched the giants around them, organised business, labour, the farmers, and the rest, struggling among themselves (and often with the government of the day) for an ever larger share of the national income.

* The author is Reader in Sociology in the University of London (London School of Economics and Political Science). He is the author of *British Political Parties: The Distribution of Power within the Conservatives and Labour Parties*.

An unexplored field

These developments since the Second World War provide reason enough for the new and acute awareness of the role of pressure groups in Britain. But in addition it must be noted that the standard accounts of the British political system (whether in the school texts, or in the academic journals) have done little or nothing to inform even the comparatively well-educated section of the British community about the realities of the sort of pressure politics which has always been a major factor in political life in this country. An American writer on this subject quotes a British information officer lecturing in America in 1954 as saying that there is 'a complete absence of pressure groups and lobbies in Britain'.[4] Unfortunately such a remark cannot be dismissed as a misguided effort in national propaganda; it was no doubt an honest expression of a widely accepted myth about the British political system.

Twenty years ago Sir Ivor Jennings demonstrated the vitally important part played by pressure groups in the parliamentary arena: 'much legislation,' he wrote, 'is derived from organised interests . . . most of it is amended on the representation of such interests, and . . . often parliamentary opposition is in truth the opposition of interests' (*Parliament*, p. 503). But, strangely, no scholar in twenty years has taken the cue; as yet, there has been no full-dress study of the role of pressure groups in the political process (although the first book on the subject in America appeared in 1908).[5] Indeed, it is only in the past three years that learned articles have begun to appear on the problems of definition and methodology and on the activities of particular interest groups. If the scholars and serious publicists have been so remiss, perhaps even the well-informed citizen can be forgiven for harbouring the illusion that pressure groups are a uniquely foreign political phenomenon accounting for the 'pathological state of American democracy' and the *immobilisme* of France.

The respective roles of pressure groups and parties

A starting point in clarifying the situation in this country, is to examine the respective roles in the British political process of political parties and of pressure groups. One source of confusion about the role of party has arisen from Burke's much quoted observation that a party is 'a body of men united for promoting by their joint endeavours the national interest upon some particular principle in which they are all agreed'.[6] This remark has been leaned on much too heavily; it provides no explanation at all of the function of party in a democratic society; and even as a *description* of parties it is misleading because it places far too great a stress on the role of principle (and by implication, on the role of ideology and programme).

Yet some exponents of democratic theory, starting, it would appear, from Burke's definition, have implied that political parties serve (or ideally ought to serve) as the sole 'transmission belts' on which political ideas and programmes are conveyed from the citizens to the legislature and the executive. According to their ideal political model, a group of citizens first organise themselves into a political party on the basis of some principle or set of principles; they then deduce a political programme from these principles and their candidates proceed to lay this programme before the electorate; if the party secures a majority in Parliament it then implements the 'mandate' given it by the electors. If issues arise not covered by the 'mandate', then it is for the MPs to use their own judgement in deciding what to do; they are to deliberate, one gathers, in a kind of vacuum in which no external pressures (either from the constituencies or from organised interests) play upon them.

According to this ideal democratic model, it is the exclusive function of the parties to canalise and to transmit the will of the citizenry to their elected representatives who then proceed to transmute it into positive law. The existence of organised groups of citizens, standing outside the party system and pressing the legislature and the executive to adopt certain specific policies, is either ignored or treated as an unfortunate aberration from the democratic ideal.

This conception of the democratic process is, in fact, completely inadequate and grossly misleading even if one applies it in this country, where parties are based on rather more specific sets of principles than they are in many other countries. (Although even in Britain it would not be easy to list the respective 'sets of principles' on which the members of the Conservative, Labour, and Liberal parties 'are all agreed'.) Max Weber offered a better working definition of parties when he described them as 'voluntary associations for propaganda and agitation seeking to acquire power in order to . . . realise objective aims or personal advantages or both'. The 'objective aims' may be of greater or lesser importance in providing the basis of association and the motive force for the activity of a particular party. But there is little doubt that it is the 'collective pursuit of power' which is of overriding importance. It is obvious too that during the pursuit of power, and after it has been achieved, parties mould and) adapt their principles under the innumerable pressures brought to bear by organised groups of citizens which operate for the most part outside the party system.

I would argue that the basic functions of parties in the British political system are to select, organise, and sustain teams of parliamentarians, between whom the general body of citizens may choose at elections. The 'selection' and 'sustaining' of the teams is mainly the job of the party outside Parliament; the 'organisation' of the teams (and the allocations of roles, including the key role of party leader and potential Prime Minister) is the function of the party within Parliament. It does not matter whether the party is organised on the basis of a set of principles on which all its members are agreed, or whether, alternatively, it represents merely an organised appetite for power. In either case parties play an indispensable role in the democratic system by offering the electorate a free choice between competing teams of potential rulers. In Britain, the parties do profess their loyalty to differing sets of principles and these help to provide an element of cohesion for the parties themselves, and they have the further advantage of offering the electorate a choice, in very broad terms, between differing approaches to the social and economic problems with which governments must deal.

None the less, elections in this country are primarily rough-and-ready devices for choosing between rival parliamentary teams. Under our electoral system (with its disdain for the principles of proportional representation and its penalisation of minor parties) the winning team of parliamentarians rarely obtains half the votes cast. (Indeed only two governments since 1910 have managed to do so.) And even when, as in 1951, the winning party, the Conservatives, obtained fewer votes than their Labour opponents, no one challenges their right to rule the country.

Pressure groups as a corrective to electoral anomalies

It is, in part, one suspects, because of the tacit recognition of the enormous and legitimate role played by organised interests that the public acquiesces in the apparent anomalies of our electoral system. It did not much matter that a Conservative government took office in 1951, having obtained fewer votes than the Labour party which it ousted; the Conservatives would be less sympathetic to the aspirations of the principal supporters of the Labour party (the trade unions), but the new government were bound to be aware that they could not administer the economic affairs of the country unless they paid very close attention to the demands and the opinions of the trade unions. The trade unions for their part showed no disposition to sulk in their tents when the party of their choice was defeated in the election (although it had obtained more votes than the victors). The trade unions could not expect to play a dominant role in determining the policies of the new government; but they could be confident that most of the channels of communication between the trade unions and the newly elected executive would remain open and that their views would carry great weight with the new administration.

I have suggested that any explanation of the democratic process which ignores the role of organised interests is grossly misleading; I would add that it is also hopelessly inadequate and sterile in that it leaves out of account the principal channels through which the mass of the citizenry brings influence to bear on the decision-makers whom they have elected. In practice, in every democratic society, the voters undertake to do far more than select their elected representatives; they also insist on their right to advise, cajole, and warn them regarding the policies they should adopt. They do this, for the most part, through the pressure-group system. Bentley, in the first trail-blazing analysis of pressure groups written fifty years ago, no doubt over-stated his case when he argued that individuals cannot affect governments except through groups; therefore, Bentley claimed, the 'process of government' must be studied as 'wholly a group process'. But there can be no doubt that pressure groups, taken together, are a far more important channel of communication than parties for the transmission of political ideas from the mass of the citizenry to their rulers. It is true that a larger proportion of the electorate 'belongs to' political parties in this country than in any other democracy. (The Conservative and Labour parties together claim a membership of over nine million, rather more than one in every four of the voters.) But the number of *active* members who do the work of the parties in the constituencies, who draft the resolutions debated in party conferences and so forth, is not more than a few hundred per constituency. This stage army of the politically active, numbering a hundred thousand or so in each party, invariably claims to speak in the name of the millions of inactive members of the party and, indeed, on behalf of the twelve or thirteen million who normally vote for each party at an election. Further, they alone choose the candidates for their respective parties, and this is of course a vitally important function, since nomination is tantamount to election in two-thirds or three-quarters of the constituencies in Britain. But it is perfectly clear that when most citizens attempt to influence the decision-making process of their elected representatives, they do so through organised groups which we call 'interest groups' or 'pressure groups'.

The articulation of group demands

David Truman, in the most recent full-dress analysis of interest groups, defines them as 'shared-attitude groups that make certain claims upon other groups in the society'. [7] And he adds that when they make their claims through or upon any of the institutions of government, they may be called *'political interest groups'*. In popular parlance they become *'pressure groups'*, which is an acceptable enough term, so long as the word 'pressure' is not permitted to carry a too pejorative connotation. Pressure groups differ from parties in that they seek to influence the policy decisions of politicians (and administrators) without themselves seeking to assume direct responsibility for governing the country.[8] And the *pressure group system*, in the language of the sociologists, is the set of institutional arrangements in any society which provides for the 'aggregation, articulation, and transmission' of group demands, when these demands are made through or upon governments.

Three categories of pressure groups

Many attempts, some of them very elaborate, have been made to classify pressure groups. But a very simple and workable threefold classification is possible: first there are the *sectional groups*, which include all those whose basis of association is the common economic interest or vocation of their members (e.g., the Federation of British Industries, the National Farmers Union, the Trades Union Congress, the National Union of Teachers, etc.).

Their principal function is to advance the interests of their members and to provide them with a variety of services; but inevitably, in the course of their work, they spend a great deal of their time attempting to influence the decisions of elected representatives in one or another of the organs of government.[9] Secondly, there are the *promotional groups*; they are not usually organised on the basis of a common economic or vocational interest, but are devoted to the advancement of a particular cause such as prison reform, the abolition of capital punishment, the defence of animal welfare, the strengthening of Sabbatarian legislation, etc. These first two categories include almost all groups which are of major political significance within the pressure-group system. But it is possible to designate a third category: *all other groups* which are not included within the first two. This may seem an odd method of classification, but it is very nearly true that every group within a society, however non-political its purpose occasionally attempts to influence public policy. For example, a Ramblers Association 'comes alive politically' on the rare occasion on which Parliament discusses Bills dealing with land use or national parks. The philatelists' associations admittedly would rarely be classified as pressure groups, yet they too no doubt occasionally make representations to governments with respect to the policies pursued in issuing stamps. It is difficult indeed to think of any groups which would not under certain circumstances attempt to bring pressure to bear on the elected decision-makers.

David Truman and others have devised another category to which they attach considerable importance: *potential interest groups*. An example of what they have in mind is the category of people, largely unorganised, who are deeply devoted to maintaining the 'rules of the game' by which political democracy is sustained. When interest groups or political parties seriously transgress these (largely unwritten) rules, then this potential interest group is likely to spring into life. The first indications of its existence might take the form of letters to *The Times* drawing attention to certain dangerous developments in the eyes of the letter writers. Subsequently, if the situation is considered serious enough, *ad hoc* organisations would no doubt be set up to recruit support for those who shared the anxieties of the founders. We have recently seen such a potential interest group taking tangible form as a result of the BBC's decision to reduce the hours of broadcasting on the Third Programme. It soon became apparent that we had amongst us, perhaps without realising it, a potential pressure group devoted to the defence of high standards in sound broadcasting. Indeed, the more one contemplates the British political scene, the more extraordinary it seems that students of the political process in this country should have so largely ignored the role of pressure groups. There can be few countries in the world in which the inhabitants so readily and so frequently organise themselves into groups for the purpose of influencing or changing the minds of their elected representatives.

Political affiliation or neutrality?

Certain of the great sectional groups choose to work through one or other of the great political parties in addition to bringing external pressure to bear on them. Thus, a large proportion of the trade unions are directly affiliated to the Labour party and a number of unions also sponsor Labour candidates. But, as was noted above, the Trades Union Congress as well as individual unions reserve the right to deal directly with governments, whether Labour or Conservative. The relations between the business community and the Conservative party are more obscure, in part because the conservatives do not permit direct affiliation of organised groups, and also because they do not publish their accounts. It can be taken for granted, however, that businessmen, as individuals and in groups, provide the greater part of the Conservative party's revenue.[10] Yet the great associations representing the business community, such as the Federation of British Industries, expect to be and are intimately consulted by Labour governments. The Federation explains its own purpose in these words: *'whatever the government in power*, [the Federation] seeks to create conditions in which each firm has the maximum opportunity to turn its own ideas and resources to the best account in its own and the national interest'.[11]

Certain other associations, such as the National Union of Teachers, have also sponsored individual candidates for one or other or both parties. But, as the experience of the National Farmers Union suggests, most interest groups in recent years have tended to avoid a too close association with a particular party. This is partly no doubt because both parties, during their terms of office since the Second World War, have shown their willingness to serve, up to a point, as brokers reconciling the interests of rival pressure groups.

There is no doubt widespread fear that parties will in fact degenerate into nothing more than brokers serving competing interest groups; and it is this fear which underlies much of the hostile comment on the activities of pressure groups, and which inhibits a realistic evaluation of the positive and legitimate function of these groups in the political process. It may well be that much writing on pressure groups too casually assumes a happy state of equilibrium. (Bentley argued that 'the balance of group pressures is the existing state of society'.) There is no doubt that governments which indulge in 'piecemeal surrender to interest groups' become incapable of devising a coherent social policy. In the extremity, of course, government action could become merely the resultant of the forces that play upon the decision-makers.

The experience of Sweden

But the danger can easily be exaggerated. Sweden can be described even more aptly than this country as 'a pluralist society' yet it is far from the 'pluralist stagnation' which some critics of the interest-group system fear. Gunnar

Heckscher (who is both a professor of politics and a Conservative member of the Swedish parliament) recently commented that 'It is now regarded as more or less inevitable' in Sweden that certain of the powerful interest groups 'should exercise a power almost equal to that of Parliament and definitely superior to that of the parliamentary parties'.[12] Yet he does not see in this situation any really serious ground for concern; nor is there, he says, any demand in Sweden that action should be taken to curb the powerful organisations. Heckscher attributes the comparatively good health of the Swedish body politic to the 'strong sense of responsibility among group leaders' and the 'politics of compromise' which govern the relations between the great groups themselves, as well as their relations with governments.

Despite the political and social tensions in contemporary Britain, surely much the same comment can be made about the situation in this country? Vague as the phrase may be, the concept of the 'national interest' is still to the forefront in the course of almost every big sectional dispute in this country. Business, Labour, the farmers, the professors, still consider it expedient to argue their case, at least in part, in the terms of the national interest. Governments may from time to time give in to one or other of the great pressure groups, also in the name of the 'national interest'. But they also on occasion stand out boldly against the claim of pressure groups on the ground that to give way would be to *betray* the national interest.

The effect of pressure groups on government

If governments may have appeared in recent years to be more pusillanimous than heretofore, it may be in part because since 1950 we have been living in an unusual period of knife-edge parliamentary majorities; and during such periods governments are bound to spend a good deal of time peering over their own shoulders. It is too often forgotten that a uniform 1 per cent shift from one party to another means a turnover of eighteen seats, and hence a drop of thirty-six in the ruling party's majority. (Thus if at the next election the Conservatives suffer a net loss of two in every hundred of those who supported them in 1955 then their government will be defeated.) One of the most effective ways of minimising the influence on governments of at least some pressure groups, if this is considered urgently necessary, would be to provide one party or another with a sweeping parliamentary majority.

There are of course other grounds or concern, quite apart from the possibly inhibiting effect of the pressure-group system on governmental decision-making. Many fear that the powerful groups are becoming more powerful and the less well-organised groups relatively weaker. Samuel Eldersveld, writing of the situation in the United States, discussed the possibility that the interest-group system is resulting, not in increased political competition, but in imperfect competition, leading to oligopoly.[13] And he adds that the 'diversification of power sources [in America] means that the decision-making process is more indirect, non-public, and obscure'. The same fears are often expressed in Britain. Are there not a very few great interest groups, it is suggested, whose leaders form a kind of inner circle of 'oligarchs' which deals frequently and intimately with senior ministers? And is it not the case that this handful of people decide the fate of the whole community, which is, for the most part, unaware even of the issues they are deciding? Again, it would be foolish to ignore evidence of the trend in this direction; equally foolish to ignore the countervailing forces. Certainly it is true that the leaders of big business, big labour, and the farmers have greater ease of 'access' to senior ministers, whichever party is in office. But it would be inaccurate automatically to equate 'access' with 'influence'. (To take a slightly frivolous example it seems likely that a Conservative government would be more willing to defy the trade unions and a Labour government the business organisations, than either of them would be likely to defy the Sabbatarian groups, which are not thought to have very ready access to ministers.) And further, it must be remembered that intimacy of contact involves the recognition of mutual responsibilities. Ministers may explain the situation to interest-group leaders frankly and then ask their cooperation 'in the national interest'.

The unorganised, inarticulate sections

There remains, however, the problem of the ill-organised (or even unorganisable) section of the community. Is there not danger that they will be either ignored or trampled upon by the really powerful interest groups? Certainly the danger is real. But it is the politicians' ultimate worry to see to it that the 'little men' (each of whom has as much political influence in the polling booth, at least, as anyone in the land) do not revolt against their policies in such numbers as to bring about their electoral ruin. This surely is one ultimate safeguard of the ill-organised. Indeed, it is arguable that in the long run governments are at least as frightened of the unorganised consumers (in their capacity as voters) as they are of the highly organised economic interests. None the less there is an area of public policy in which the absence of organised groups represents a serious problem. Thus, for example, governments under pressure from shop employees and certain categories of shop-owners, may contemplate further restricting shop hours; there is no one to speak for the shoppers. Or again, governments may be fearful of liberalising licensing hours because of the pressures they would set in motion against themselves from the highly organised temperance forces; there is no organised body to speak for the drinkers. Here, it seems to me, the public opinion polls have a legitimate and important role to play. The evidence they can produce of the shoppers' attitude to proposals for restricting shop hours, or the drinkers' attitude to licensing laws, should be *one* of the factors taken into account by the decision-makers, in addition to the views of the organised interests, in arriving at their policy decisions.

But with reservations such as these, it seems to me reasonable to conclude that the pressure-group system, with all its dangers, is both an inevitable and an indispensable concomitant of the party system. It provides an invaluable set of multiple channels through which the mass of the citizenry can influence the decision-making process at the highest levels. Is it possible that the widespread uneasiness about pressure groups in Britain today is really a result of the shift in the balance of power between the classes? In the paper quoted above, Eldersveld remarked that in 'the fluid politics' of America there is no longer 'a decisive ruling class' but rather a set of 'multiple elites'. The same development has obviously occurred in this country; and it is clear that the new elites are struggling to assert their strength in part through the pressure-group system.

Notes

1 S. H. Beer, 'Pressure Groups and Parties in Britain', *The American Political Society Review*, March 1956, p. 3.
2 Thus even so well informed an observer as W. J. M. Mackenzie concludes that the dominant role of organised groups in British public life means: 'We are gradually shifting back into a situation in which a man is socially important only as a holder of standard qualifications and as a member of authorised groups, in fact into the new medievalism which was the promised land in the days from the younger Pugin to William Morris.' W. J. M. Mackenzie, 'Pressure Groups in British Government', *British Journal of Sociology*, June 1955, p. 146.
3 P. Johnson, 'The Amiable Monster', the *New Statesman*, October 12, 1957, p. 468. In the same vein, Bernard Hollowood has remarked that 'Parliament has become the abused referee of the big power game and . . . the unhappy millions on the terraces are powerless, almost voiceless spectators' in 'The Influence of Business and the City', *Twentieth Century*, October 1957, p. 253.
4 Cited in F. C. Newman, 'Reflections on Money and Party Politics in Britain', *Parliamentary Affairs*, Summer 1957, p. 309.
5 A. F. Bentley's *The Process of Government*.
6 *Thoughts on the Present Discontents*, World's Classics edition, vol. II, p. 82.
7 D. B. Truman, *The Governmental Process*, p. 37.
8 It is admittedly comparatively easy to make this distinction into a preponderantly two-party system of the sort that exists in Britain and the United States; but it is more difficult in certain Continental countries, where minor parties, which would elsewhere be content to function as pressure groups, offer candidates at elections even though they have no prospect, or even expectation, of winning full responsibility for governing the country. And of course it is arguable that in this country the Scottish and Welsh Nationalists are little more than pressure groups seeking to publicise their cause by offering candidates at elections. For a further discussion of this question see Allen Potter, 'British Pressure Groups', *Parliamentary Affairs*, Autumn 1956, pp. 418–419.
9 These sectional interest groups are the organisations, in Franz Neumann's phrase, 'by which [social] power is translated into political power'. *The Democratic and the Authoritarian State*.

10 It is important to remember, however, as F. C. Newman has pointed out, that in the case of both parties 'it is the programme that attracts the money; the money does not structure the programme', in 'Reflections on Money and Party Politics in Britain', *Parliamentary Affairs*, Summer 1957, p. 316.
11 *The FBI, what it is, what it does*, p. 1 (italics mine). For a very valuable examination of the structure and functioning of the FBI, see S. E. Finer, 'The Federation of British Industries', *Political Studies*, February 1956, pp. 61–84
12 G. Hecksher, 'Interest Groups and Sweden', a paper presented to the *International Political Science Round Table* , Pittsburgh, September 7–14 1957 (duplicated), p. 8. See also his 'Pluralist Democracy; the Swedish Experience', *Social Research*, December 1948, pp. 417–461. It should be noted, in connection with Hecksher's remark quoted above, that there are five parties in the Swedish parliament, and in such circumstances it is perhaps less surprising than it would be here to remark that certain of the great sectional groups are more powerful than the parliamentary parties.
13 S. J. Eldersveld, 'American Interest Groups', a paper presented to the *International Political Science Round Table*, Pittsburgh, September 7–14, 1957 (duplicated).

Democracy and Ideology

BERNARD WILLIAMS*

Vol. 32, no. 4, October–December 1961

I

THE TERM 'ideology' is not in very good odour in serious political discussion in this country, except in purely historical or descriptive connections. The grounds of the distaste for the term centre round the feeling, perhaps, that an ideology is something inherently totalitarian in tendency, or at least involves an uncompromising fanaticism inappropriate to liberal democracy of the British type. This feeling is fortified, on the whole, by experience of the outlooks and methods of argument of those who have proclaimed either the existence of, or (more characteristically) the need for, 'an ideology of Western values' and so forth; in their case, from MRA upwards, the aim of the discussion is often patently that of finding an emotional or intellectual engine that can be neatly fitted into the pre-existing capitalist chassis.

However, it may well be that these qualms attach to the term because it is narrowly or superficially understood. In its broadest sense, I take the term 'ideology' to stand for a system of political and social beliefs that does two things. First, it embodies some set of values or ideals, and, consequently, some principles of action: though such principles will be out of necessity very general, and in some cases mainly negative, being concerned more with limitations on political action, for instance, rather than with an overall aim of it. Secondly, an ideology connects with its values and principles of action some set of very general theoretical beliefs which give the values and principles some sort of backing or justification. The generality of these beliefs must, moreover, be of a special kind, if we are to speak of 'an ideology': they must, I think, be general beliefs about man, society, and the state, and not merely about some aspect of man in society. For instance, a belief in Free Trade or federalism, even though supported by general economic or political reasons, could not by itself constitute an ideology. The distinguishing mark of an ideology is that its general beliefs concern man and society as such, and hence concern things that are presupposed in any political or social situation whatsoever.

If this represents fairly accurately what is involved in the notion of an ideology, it will be clear that a totalitarian ideology will be only one sort of ideology; on this account, there can as well be ideologies of liberalism as of totalitarianism, just as there can be conservative as well as revolutionary ideologies, democratic as well as absolutist ones. It may be, also, that

* The author is a Lecturer in Philosophy at University College, London.

ideologies differ in their degree of explicitness. One's normal picture of an ideology, it is true, is of a body of fairly well-articulated beliefs, explicitly formulated and constituting in the limiting case a form of creed, inculcated by authorities and developed by casuists. But once again, this may be one sort of ideology, to be found at one end of the scale; at the other end, there may be systems of beliefs far less explicitly formulated, correspondingly less openly inculcated, but which may nevertheless exist implicitly or in a society or group, and perform much the same function as the noisier form of ideology, directing and shaping political discussion and action. That they do perform the same action will be the justification for applying to such systems of belief the term 'ideology'; an application which may have the merit of encouraging the search for such tacit systems of presuppositions, and the attempt to make them more explicit. It must be worthwhile to make them more explicit, if they exist: for one thing, that which is less openly inculcated is more liable to evade criticism.

It seems, then, at least worth asking whether such tacit ideologies exist in cases of political beliefs that lack the more explicit or creed-like ideology; and I shall attempt to do in this article—I am afraid, very sketchily—in respect of liberal democracy. First, however, I shall make some remarks about the most obvious and important example of an explicit ideology current at the present time, Marxism.

II

These remarks are merely meant to bring out one or two features of Marxist beliefs that significantly illustrate the nature of explicit ideologies.

(1) Marxism exhibits the dual nature of ideologies very clearly, by having both a very developed and comprehensive theoretical superstructure, and a great deal of practical content. How closely the two are linked in the case of the government of the USSR is, of course, a matter that is constantly being debated: but even in that case, it would clearly be unwise to suppose the linkage to be purely factitious, and the role of the theory to be merely that of a dressing for policies of straightforward nationalism or expediency, arrived at by other means. In any case, in so far as there is a debate on that issue, it is rather a debate about how far the Soviet government is Marxist, and not a debate about the practical content of Marxism.

(2) It is typical that Marxism was not the invention of professional philosophers; not merely in the trivial sense that Marx himself, and most important Marxist thinkers did not hold chairs of philosophy, but in the sense that its ideals and aims were not merely formulated by reflection and made effective by teaching, but were grounded, to various degrees, in the actual political and social situation that people found themselves in. It is a feature of well-based ideologies that what they tell people to do is *to some extent* what they would do without being conscious of the ideology; this does not mean that ideologies are in fact ineffective, but only that the theoretical part of an

effective ideology gives a picture of man and society which is to some extent correct. There is no real paradox here, though there may seem to be. An ideology may have an effect, in shaping, coordinating and making conscious political and social ends, even though these ends are to some extent pursued independently of any explicit appeal to the ideology. Indeed, that this should be so is evidence that the theory of the ideology is well-based.

(3) There is, however, a real paradox nearby, in which Marxism, because of its notable consciousness of these issues, is notoriously involved. The fully self-conscious and reflective ideologue is bound to recognise the existence, contemporary and past, of ideologies different from his own, with differing practical recommendations. So far there is no difficulty: he may suppose rival ideologies to be the product of error, ignorance, insincerity, etc. If, however, his ideology is of the type, like Marxism, which offers in its theoretical part a general explanation of ideologies themselves, and sees them as themselves historical social products, a well-known difficulty will arise, since it will require a sustained psychological dissociation to prevent such theoretical explanation from getting hold of his own ideology, with a consequent lessening of confidence in its absolute truth. Ideologies whose structure subjects them to this difficulty have tended to provide a transcendentalist escape hatch, which allows the ideology itself not to be subject to social or historical determination in the same sense as others; there are resemblances in this respect, not surprisingly, between the Marxist and the Hegelian philosophies. A particular form of this sort of difficulty arises over the interpretation of the historical development of the Communist Party of the Soviet Union; the attempt to explain this development in Marxist terms is a particularly serious form of deviation, known (I believe) as *bourgeois objectivism*.

These difficulties of *over-explanation*, which arise with any ideology which can explain the existence and nature of all ideologies including, eventually, itself, are well known. It may be added that there is a corresponding weakness of *under-explanation* which arises with some less ambitious ideologies, the theoretical part of which may be such as to leave it a complete mystery why there should ever have been any ideology other than themselves. Most forms of political rationalism or simple utilitarianism are likely to encounter this difficulty; the picture they give of man is of a being who should be expected to have unanimously accepted that picture centuries ago.

(4) It is also a familiar feature of Marxism that it belongs to a group of revolutionary ideologies that may broadly be called *millennialist*. Not only are its efforts directed, by the theory of revolution, to a recognisable end, but this end is supposed to be followed, at some interval, by the suspension of the historical processes which are largely the subject of the theoretical part of the ideology. There follows from this a rather curious unbalance in the relations between the theoretical and practical parts of the ideology. Up to the millennial point, they are closely integrated, the class theory of history closely supporting the aim of class revolution; after the millennial point, the theory ceases to apply altogether, and no ideological signposts are offered for the

directions that life should take then. It is not a criticism of Marx that he should not have said more about the classless society; but it is a very noticeable incompleteness in the ideology that it should devote men's efforts to the achievement of a state of affairs, the character of which it is, by the nature of its theory, virtually incapable of determining.

No doubt further political and social changes will continuously arise to occupy the millennium, which will accordingly contain more than patriotism, consumer goods, and space travel; but those changes the ideology it stands cannot pronounce on. This limitation is obviously a structural feature of any millennialist ideology; and in all cases this feature must present a paradox— that the theory can tell us a great deal about the necessity of travelling, but practically nothing about the consequences of arriving. The only millennialist ideology that can escape a paradox here will be one in which the millennium is genuinely transcendental, which transfers everything at the millennial point from the hands of man to those of a supernatural agency: in such a case it is entirely consistent that the ideology should tell men how to travel, but not what they will be doing on arrival, for that will be out of their hands. For Marxism, however, the point of travelling is precisely to arrive at a point where everything will be in our hands.

III

We may now ask whether we can identify any system of beliefs, however tacit and latent, which might be called an ideology of liberal democracy. By 'liberal democracy' I mean a system of government characterised by a universal and secret suffrage, for a choice of different rulers; an independent press and freedom of expression; and by what may generally be called the rule of law, which includes the requirement of a fair trial for any alleged offence, limitations on the powers of the police, etc. It is as well, I think, to mention the provisions of the rule of law separately from the others normally collected under the title 'liberal democracy', since they do not follow merely from the notion of democracy, in the sense of a genuine popular choice of representatives, by itself, but further require the existence of an active public opinion concerned with justice. It would be possible to have all the institutions of democracy genuinely working, and yet the rule of law be flouted, if the electorate were indifferent to its being flouted.

The very rough characterisation of liberal democracy just given is given in primarily institutional terms; but it must, of course, be understood that the actual existence and functioning of such a system implies the existence of more than a set of institutions. For institutions of this type will in fact function only if they have certain kinds of social foundation, e.g., of an electorate not too radically and violently divided on vital issues; so that in thinking of liberal democracy as a going concern, one must think not only of certain institutions, but of certain attitudes which are the precondition of those institutions functioning.

One attitude that is, in this sense, a precondition of the institutions functioning, is a measure of *toleration*. To be more precise, one has to add one further condition of toleration being necessary, namely, that there should be attitudes and groups to which people need to be tolerant; for presumably if a people were spontaneously entirely unanimous on important issues, the democratic machine would function excellently without any need for toleration. However, this condition scarcely needs, for any real situation, to be spelled out; and indeed, even at the theoretical level, one might well wonder whether, if there were no need for toleration, there would really be much need for democracy, since there be no requirement of choice between policies or social attitudes, but only between persons to administer the state. This might be sufficient to keep the democratic machine going, but certainly not in any very full-blooded way.

We may say, then, that one precondition of liberal democracy's working is toleration: sufficient toleration of rival groups, with different attitudes, to allow one to foresee—if not with equanimity, at least without fundamental despair—their coming to power, or otherwise influencing the governmental process. However, this kind of toleration, the kind which is a precondition of the democratic machine working at all, is toleration directed only towards certain groups: namely, those groups who are, in effect, the alternative government, or potentially alternative government. This we may call *essential* toleration: essential, that is to say, to the working of the democratic machine. It is essential toleration that is directed in this country at the moment by the Conservative and Labour parties towards each other.

There is, however, another kind of toleration that is always, and rightly, regarded as part of the liberal democratic outlook, and for which, perhaps, the word 'toleration' is most characteristically used: this is the toleration of minorities, racial, religious, and so on. Such toleration is not essential to the working of the machine in the way that the sort just discussed is. For if all the major power groups were united, say, in anti-Semitism, anti-Semitic persecution could flourish without jeopardy to the actual workings of the democratic process. This we may call non-essential toleration; where 'non-essential' is to be understood, of course, in the technical sense just discussed, and not as meaning that such toleration can be dispensed with if convenient.

Much needs to be said about this distinction between essential and non-essential toleration, if it is to be properly worked out. In particular, it is clear that the characterisation of the two sorts of toleration merely in terms of what sorts of groups they are directed towards is too crude. If, for instance, one has a healthy public opinion passionately engaged in the defence of minorities, what seems to be non-essential toleration might turn out to be essential; for persecution of a minority might have the effect of so incensing public opinion that the government was overthrown by force, and the democratic process brought to a halt. Of such a case, however, it can be noted that in describing it, one has to posit a public *belief in* non-essential toleration, so that it does not really break down the distinction. Again, there is the perpetual problem for liberal democracies of parties which do not themselves subscribe to the system. In terms of the distinction, it would seem that toleration of such parties would necessarily be non-essential; since it could scarcely be essential to the workings of democracy that alternative government be countenanced which would bring those workings to an end. On the other hand, if such a party is the only real alternative to the existing regime, it will then be the case that there is no field for the operation of essential toleration at all. This unhappy result seems merely to constitute the correct description of an unhappy situation.

However it should be refined, the distinction between two sorts of, or two operations of, toleration seems to correspond to something real. Corresponding to it, there is a possible distinction between the general attitudes that underlie toleration. For essential toleration will be underwritten by any belief that underwrites the democratic system itself: this follows merely from its being essential. But of non-essential toleration this will not necessarily be true, since I might have the firmest belief in the democratic process, and hence in the toleration of anything necessary to its workings, but no *general* belief in toleration at all.

This, at least, is a theoretical possibility; and one may be able to find actual examples of such attitudes. For instance, it may be that there are in the United States at the present time at least some groups whose attitudes are a genuine combination of a belief in the operation of the democratic, two-party, machine, and a strong desire for general conformity—and, indeed, the enforcement of conformity—in all matters that do not directly abut on the political struggle. However, it must be said that such a combination is at least not very common. More common, of course, is the combination of a belief in the democratic system with a lack of tolerance for some particular groups; but this is really a different matter, since the persons who have such attitudes usually accept, or claim to accept, the principles of non-essential toleration in general, but make a particular exception to them against certain groups, on special grounds or merely irrationally. What would be interesting from the ideological point of view would be the combination of a belief in democracy with no belief in non-essential toleration at all; and this combination certainly seems to be at least rare.

It is not hard to see why such a combination should be rare. For it seems that there could only be two sorts of grounds on which an opposition to non-essential toleration in general can rest. Either the opponent of such toleration believes that he possesses *certainty* on the matters of belief, conduct, etc., on which the minority groups hold divergent views, and moreover thinks that it is the right or duty of the state to impose the truth in such matters; or else, while he does not claim certainty on such matters, he thinks that society should be strongly unified round some set of beliefs or other, and so will not tolerate the divergent opinions—not, like the first man, because he believes them to be false, but merely because he sees them to be divergent. Any opposition to non-essential toleration will, I think, be found in the end to rest on one of these two sorts of grounds. But either of these grounds is also a sufficient ground for being opposed to essential toleration, and so to liberal democracy itself. The first man cannot be in favour of free competition at the governmental level of policies and social views, at least one of which he must regard as absolutely false; while the second man will obviously recognise an opposition between liberal democracy and the highly unified and closed society which is his aim.

If this line of argument is correct, it would seem that the grounds of belief in liberal democracy are closely bound up with the grounds of belief in toleration in general; and both involve the rejection of both of the attitudes just described as grounds of opposition to non-essential toleration. The liberal democrat cannot put a very high price, at least, on the ideal of a community highly unified in belief; and he must be one who either does not claim certainty in the matters about which divergent views are to be found in society, or, if he does claim such certainty, must believe that the state has no right to impose what he regards as the truth on those who do not believe in it.

Corresponding to these last two alternatives, two strains of democratic thought can be identified. Corresponding to the first, there is the strain of *scepticism*; corresponding to the second, the strain of belief in *individual rights*. The first broadly takes the line that since we do not, and perhaps cannot, possess any certainty about political, moral, and religious matters, the safest course for society is to allow a free competition of opinions and attitudes. There tends to go with this a sceptical or at least minimalist attitude to democracy itself: namely, that it is the best system yet devised for running a society, though no more absolute claim can be made for it. The second, individual rights, type of thought is slightly more ambitious. This would claim that it was certain that democracy was the ideal form of government, since it is the only form that truly represents the relations of man to the state; which are, that the state is an instrument for maintaining the rights and the welfare of an assemblage of individual men. If this is what a state is, then it is certain that the correct way of running a state must be that which allows the translation of the views and preferences of individual men into political action; while preserving, however, the rights of those involved in society who do not agree with the majority of it.

Neither of these strains of democratic thought can, of course, be taken quite by itself. On the one hand, scepticism alone could not constitute a basis for any political outlook: it has to be fortified by some view on what is worth pursuing or avoiding. Indeed, the sceptical argument implies that there are some things that we know ought to be prevented if possible, such as suffering and tyranny, and directs its scepticism rather against any larger pretensions to discern a programme for man's fulfilment or improvement. But even scepticism fortified like this will not lead all the way to democracy; it could lead just as readily to a Burkean position, which takes man to be poised so insecurely over the darkness that all he can do is to hold on to whatever well-tried ropes of tradition happen to surround him. The scepticism that leads to democracy has to be supplemented by some elements of the individual rights doctrine: it has to start with a presumption in favour of individual men choosing their own way. It has to be a scepticism which is at least as suspicious of any inherited authority or caste privilege as it is of Utopian or millennialist aspirations.

Just as the sceptical approach needs some help from the individual rights doctrine, if it is to lead to democracy, so conversely. The curious dialectic of Rousseau's *Social Contract*, and still more of the uses to which that work was put after its author's death, illustrates the possibility of moving from an individualist position, which regards democracy as certainly the only justified form of government, to an interpretation of democracy in which a mystical General Will, or the glorification of a *Gemeinschaft* society, perversely take the place of the original liberal conception of individual rights. Here it seems that it is some measure of the scepticism of the first approach that is needed to discourage the excessive detachment of the rights of man from what men would normally and unmetaphysically regard as their rights.

IV

Does this set of ideas that has very roughly been sketched constitute any sort of tacit ideology of liberal democracy? Two obvious objections occur to one against using the term 'ideology' here: first, that what has been sketched is too tenuous, and secondly, that it is insufficiently dynamic.

As to the first point, it can fairly be replied that what has been sketched, besides being only sketched, is incomplete: and this in two ways. For one thing, the theorist of democracy would not stop at mere assertions of scepticism or of individual rights such as have just been discussed. The scepticism would itself be rooted in a general doctrine about human knowledge; as has, of course, been the case in the British tradition, in the connection between liberalism and empiricism. The individualist doctrine of the relations of man to the state would, again, be argued for on philosophical grounds. So in this respect, the tenuousness of what has been sketched just follows from the fact that, necessarily, not enough has been sketched. A second way in which the sketch is incomplete is that, even if it were enough as a theory of liberal democracy, there will be few political thinkers who will be content with an ideology which was an ideology *only* of liberal democracy; they will characteristically add to this some further ideals to be realised *in* liberal democracy, which will themselves have some further ideological basis. I take this to be characteristically the case with ideals of *social* democracy. As I have defined liberal democracy, social democracy is to be regarded as a species of it, not as something opposed to it; and the characteristic situation of the social democrat is to take the sort of basis of liberal democracy that has been discussed, with special emphasis on the individual rights side, and raise a more elaborate structure on it, particularly by pressing the concept of *equality* inherent in it, and giving it an economic foundation. This, at least, will be the case with social democracy of the liberal kind most familiar in this country; this is not to say that there are not also other bases of social democracy, for instance, of more Marxist character. But it is not to the point here to pursue the possible bases of social democracy; but merely to illustrate by this example how the notions of liberal democracy may be part of a more substantial set of beliefs.

On the second question, of whether the notions of liberal democracy are sufficiently dynamic to constitute anything that could be called an ideology, I can make here only two points. First, the question of how dynamic the ideals of liberal democracy are as a motive to political action gets a different answer depending on where you are. In the face of colonial or totalitarian regimes, they have been and still are intensely dynamic. In a régime which is itself liberal democratic, they are naturally less so, save in respect of guarding the system against abuse or attack. But this is, of course, a necessary consequence of the whole structure, since the whole idea of the thing is that what men choose to pursue in the context of a free society is not itself ideologically determined. Here we meet again the point, suggested above (section II), that Marxism is in this respect in exactly the same situation when it gets to its post-millennial point—that this is a situation for which the ideology, by its very nature, does not provide for. The chief difference is that Marxism contains the suggestion that this state will be of quite a different nature from what has gone before, and that one need not worry what it will be like, since it will be in some ideal way self-regulating; while the liberal democratic outlook does not include such an illusion.

Secondly, it may be felt that the ideas of liberal democracy are less dynamic than, say, Marxism, in the weaker sense that they are just less exciting, because they offer a less thorough-going explanation of political life and human action. It is of course true that they offer fewer explanations; the explanatory element in this set of beliefs is very low indeed. But this is, of course, for a special reason: that the sceptical and empiricist elements in the outlook embody the belief that such explanations are not to be reached at the ideological level at all, but are the business of positive science, for the findings of which the liberal democratic outlook leaves an infinitely extensible hole. I think it is true that the views of man and society embodied in this outlook do to some extent make an *a priori* trespass on this scientific field—the outlook would have no content at all if it did not. In various ways, the outlook does determine the shape that such scientific explanations might be expected to take; but it remains true that it is extremely and self-consciously unambitious in producing explanations as part of the outlook itself.

In general, I think it might be said that the liberal democratic outlook does constitute a tacit ideology, but that it is a peculiar example of that species, in being the *smallest* ideology that can actually survive. It offers some practical proposals, and backs them up with some views on man, society, and the state. Where, however, its larger relatives offer large-scale explanations of history and human life, it offers for the most part a programme of empirical inquiry;

and where they offer large-scale predictions and hopes, it offers few predictions and a good number of warnings. This small-scaleness may not be entirely a disadvantage. It may be that ideologies are like dinosaurs; the small ones no doubt came off worst in a contest of roaring or clawing, but when the big ones started to collapse under their own weight, the small ones turned out to have been better endowed for survival.

The Woman's Vote: What Has it Achieved?

MARGARET COLE*

Vol. 33, no. 1, January–March 1962

LAST November there died, aged seventy-odd, the lady who in her youth made headlines by cutting up the Rokeby Venus in the name of *Votes for Women*. I do not know whether it was that item of news which prompted the Editors of *The Political Quarterly* to invite me to write this article; but I should certainly have been glad of the opportunity to ask that militant heroine of fifty years ago what she made of it all in the end.

For Votes for Women, in those far-off days, was a panacea—a word of power, like Reform of Parliament a hundred years before. In one of the more flamboyant passages of the *Political Register* William Cobbett asked himself whether parliamentary reform would remedy a whole list of grievances and produce a vast number of desirable changes, and in his best italic capitals answered: '*IT WOULD DO THEM ALL!!*' In similar style, suffragists and suffragettes alike claimed that the enfranchisement of women would not merely remove the stigma of equating them with infants, felons, and idiots in an evaluation so insulting that even today one reads of it with astonishment, but would also raise up women to positions of high authority in Parliament and the professions, would lift the status of the downtrodden, and generally humanise and improve all round the condition of society. Moreover, their opponents, while not precisely sharing this view of the probable results, seemed, judging by the language they used, at least to agree that the results would be revolutionary. 'Women's rights', as readers of Queen Victoria's letters will recall, 'is a subject which makes the Queen so *furious* that she cannot contain herself.' Nor could a good number of her subjects.

The vote conceded

Before the end of the First World War the risk was taken, and the vote conceded, though the male legislators in their wisdom decided that ten years must pass before women under thirty years old could be regarded as sufficiently educated to be entrusted with it—how oddly that reads today, when we have almost reached the point where women of thirty, having borne their children and tended their infancy, will be urged to come back to 'gainful employment'.

* The author is an Alderman of the LCC and chairman of its Further Education Committee. Author of *Beatrice Webb, the Story of Fabian Socialism*, etc., and many works jointly with G. D. H. Cole.

In 1919 came the lavish promises of the Sex Disqualification (Removal) Act, which declared explicitly that neither sex nor marriage should be a bar to 'the exercise of any public function, the holding of civil or judicial office, the carrying on of any profession, or membership in any professional institution'. True, there was in the Act a little section allowing for revisions giving power to regulate the admission of women to the civil service and the conditions of their service and to reserve to men posts in the colonial, diplomatic, and consular services; true, also, that the Act had not been in force very long before the House of Lords decided that its provisions did not apply to their own august ranks and slammed the door of their Chamber in Lady Rhondda's face. Still, the two Acts were there; and the editors have asked me to produce an estimate of their results, of what has happened in the forty-two years during which the flag of freedom has been at the masthead. This, of course, can be but sketchily done, both for reasons of time and space, and because some of the information which one would particularly like to have is missing or not recorded; but perhaps an impressionist picture can be given.

Women in Parliament and government

Since the vote is primarily a political instrument, and since political information is more easily come by, let us begin with politics proper. Immediately after emancipation, three women were elected to Parliament. Two 'inherited' seats vacated by their husbands—one Liberal and one Tory; the third, the Sinn Fein Countess Markiewicz, had no intention of taking her seat. Since then the number of women MPs has fluctuated; today there are twenty-five of them. There have been three women Cabinet Ministers, two Labour and one Tory, two of these three being Ministers of Education; today there is none. Fourteen women have held minor government office, a few of them more than once: six women are now peeresses. This is not a very impressive record. I have heard it argued that *in relation to their numbers in the House of Commons*, women have had quite their fair share of office. I have not worked out—nor has anyone to my knowledge—the statistical facts about this contention; but even if it were true, what is much more important is the commonplace that in both major parties (the Labour record being rather better than that of the Tories) agents and selection committees boggle at putting forward women for safe or winnable seats. Whether the belief on which this is based, that a woman candidate is an electoral liability, is correct is neither proved nor capable of proof; there is no controlled experiment.

Local government councillors

In local government there is rather more gain to show, though this is due very largely to the remarkable record of the London County Council. The LCC has had five women Chairmen since Labour took control in 1934, five women

Vice-Chairmen (Labour), and nine Deputy Chairmen (appointment made by the opposition party). Of the councillors (including aldermen) of today forty-one out of 146 are women, and twenty-nine others have been co-opted to standing committees. Six out of the fifteen main committees, including the Education Committee, are chaired by women, and no fewer than five of the six sub-committees of the Education Committee.

Outside London the position is very different. It was not until 1958, for example, that the County of Middlesex nerved itself to appoint a woman to the chair of its Education Committee. *Whitaker's Almanack* showed, in 1961, three women chairmen of county councils, and in the eight closely printed pages of its Municipal Directory of England and Wales only fifty-two women who were mayor or chairman of council, of all the hundreds of towns and cities listed therein. Perhaps one should add in, as curiosities, the two women who, two years earlier, were high sheriffs of Welsh counties, one being the wife of the Lord Lieutenant; but by and large it is only London county which shows anything like the result which the pioneers expected—perhaps that is one reason why the males of the Royal Commission decided to destroy the LCC. So much, then, for those elected to govern. What about those who are paid by them to do the actual governing?

The Civil Service

In the civil service, as is common knowledge, the little proviso about 'regulating the admission and the conditions of employment' worked very nicely for a long while, particularly through the operation of the marriage bar. Infiltration into the higher ranks was very slow. But now there are two women Permanent Secretaries with salaries of £7,000 per annum (both Dames[1]), and two other civil servants at top rates. According to the records of the Fawcett Society, there are four women Under-Secretaries and thirty-four Assistant Secretaries. There is (by statute) a woman Prison Commissioner, and some women Chief Inspectors of Police. The Senior Medical Inspector of Factories is a woman; there is a woman Parliamentary Counsel, and over sixty women in posts whose starting salary is £2,000 and upwards. The number of women in the administrative class ranges round about 9 per cent of the number of men. This is not enormous, but sizeable, when the 'conditions of employment' are taken into account. (The BBC has women governors, and has had women in fairly high positions, but none in the top rank.)

The Foreign Office, and the Diplomatic Service, preserved their virgin purity much longer than the home departments did theirs; it was not until 1946, after the Labour government had set up the Gowers Committee to report, that the door was forced to open an inch or two, and in December of that year a woman slipped through it—she did not stay long. Three years later there were three women inside; since then there has been a very thin trickle of others into A Branch. Some appointments drew Press attention: a woman was consul at Copenhagen in 1954, and another deputy consul-general in New York from 1955 to 1959; the woman proconsul at Geneva died in 1956. There has never been a woman ambassador—no Englishwoman has cried 'Call Me Madam'; therein we lag well behind several other countries.

Local government officers

The picture presented by local government is not unlike that in the home civil service, except that London is not here in the van. None of the chief officers of the LCC, nor their deputies, is a woman (not even the Children's Officer); the highest point reached is that of Assistant Education Officer. There have been women Medical Officers of Health, though for a long time there were none, partly because local authorities were very slow to appoint women to posts, such as Tuberculosis Officer, which were generally regarded as essential steps to the heights. In 1956 a woman was appointed Director of Education for Wiltshire; another in 1959 became Town Clerk of St Albans. There may be one or two other comparable cases which I have missed, but in general the tale is of women in lowly and middling posts, with only a handful of exceptions.

The legal profession

Turning now to the professions, one must admit that the proportion of women who have risen really high would greatly have disappointed the pioneers. The two most publicised professions—apart from teaching, which is in a different category—are law and medicine. In law, despite the 1919 Act, no woman is a judge nor, as far as one can see, likely to become one, though a woman was last year appointed 'temporary judge' to the Manchester Crown Court. The sole woman stipendiary magistrate retired recently—after a reasonably long run, it is true; there is one woman recorder, and in 1960 there were five women QCs. (There are, of course, women JPs in large numbers, some of whom, like the late Madeleine Robinson, have chaired courts with distinction; but they should be reckoned as social workers, not in the legal category.) The census of 1951 showed 151 women barristers as against 3,084 men; I do not know how many of these were actually practising, nor what the 1961 figures will be, but I should be surprised if they showed any great advance.

The medical profession

It is really surprising, after the long and well-publicised struggle of women to get into the medical profession, which has resulted in a steady increase of women doctors—in no way, however, comparable with the 3:1 ratio of women to men in the Soviet medical service, which seems to be a fact—that so few women appear to have attained the commanding heights. The most distinguished woman doctor has probably been Dame Hilda Lloyd, who was President of the Royal College of Obstetricians, and in 1958 a woman entered the General Medical Council. The position of women MOHs has already been mentioned; and as late as August 1961 Dr Janet Aitkin was drily commenting that 'teaching hospitals don't often give jobs to women'.

Other professions

It is clearly impossible in a single article to traverse the list of the professions, even were information less scanty. There has certainly been some increase in women's professional employment; but it provokes some thought that in engineering, where Dame Caroline Haslett worked so long and so persistently in the women's cause, there were, in 1960, only 107 women members of the various Institutes, out of a total of 113,000, and that the Chartered Association of Secretaries had seventy-nine women out of over 6,000. As to business, the Institute of Directors has 852 women members out of more than 35,000, about one-third of them, it is calculated, having got there 'through family connections'—as have the men, of course. It is mildly interesting to observe that last autumn a medical research unit of that Institute, having studied 350 of the monstrous regiment, reported that physically the women compared favourably and that it would be a good thing to have more of them—even if it is also a little disconcerting to learn that one of their physical advantages is longevity. 'Red-Hot Grandmas Run Industry' may yet be the headline. In 1956 the Birmingham Stock Exchange returned a flat NO to a woman applicant—so much for the Sex Disqualification (Removal) Act.

There are plenty of women, of course, holding high place in the teaching profession; but this has been the case for many years. Besides the heads of girls' schools and women's colleges, there are women professors—one in Oxford, two in Cambridge, over a dozen in London, and more at other universities. But not many women are encouraged to sit on the governing bodies of public schools. There are also women high up, some paid, some unpaid, in the social services, those traditional Cinderellas of the salary system—was it not Beatrice Webb who advised the writer, in the matter of filling a post, to decide first what ultimate salary could be afforded, and if that were £1,000 a year, to look for an Oxbridge male graduate, if £500, for 'a non-university man', and if £250, for 'a competent woman'? It is impossible even to estimate the number of these, but all must have had experience of the extremely competent (or extremely formidable!) secretary or chairman of a 'voluntary society'.

Files of cuttings in libraries will add little drips of achievement, sometimes to one's surprise—'1958, Edinburgh University appoints first woman Professor'—goodness, what has Edinburgh been doing all these years?—but when they all are added together it does not seem to amount to very much—the tired waves gaining only a painful centimetre; and it does at least suggest the conclusion that the people who count in Britain are not clamouring to see women in high executive positions.

In this article I am gathering facts, not seeking to find reasons or to draw morals; but one must observe that the facts as gathered seem a trifle discouraging to the advocates of higher education for women. Headmistresses, faced with reproachful statements that women are not playing their rightful part in a technological society and told that only ten out of 675 Diplomas in Technology[2] have been gained by women, might well ask what the women are supposed to do when they have got them.

Equal pay

The mention of equal pay, however, brings one to the second of the old high claims for emancipation—the great legislative and administrative changes it was supposed to bring about. Here it is much more difficult to be precise, for many factors besides the women's vote influence Parliament and the establishment, and nobody, so far as I am aware, has made even a half-study of the desires and opinions of women as elicited by candidates and canvassers at election time—or even embarked on a comparison of social conditions in Switzerland, the country of the still-disfranchised woman, with those obtaining in Britain. On a very strict interpretation it would be possible to argue that the only reform which can with certainty be credited to the vote is the removal of turnstiles from the LADIES.

One need not, however, be quite as scrupulous as that; one can, I think, credit certain changes without much fear of contradiction. And one of these is Equal Pay. I feel no doubt that equal pay in the civil service, teaching, and for administrative staff in local government and the nationalised industries, which is a solid fact and not, like the phrases in the 1919 Act, a symbolic gesture which may in practice mean almost nothing at all, was a very great gain, and one which would not have been made had women not been voters. It was not the case, seven years ago, that women were leaving the teaching profession, or failing to enter it, in numbers so startling that there was a clear *economic* argument for raising their salaries to the men's level; it was the triumph of a principle, and the Fawcett Society was quite right to stage a large celebration at the completion of the process.

Furthermore, the granting of equal pay to so large a number of women—to which must obviously be added the numbers of those who had previously enjoyed it, such as doctors and employees of the BBC—had the result of considerably narrowing the gap outside the favoured occupations. We do not have equal pay in Britain—far from it. Therein we are well behind others: the arguments so cogently presented in Beatrice Webb's evidence to the 1918 Committee on Equal Pay[3] and reiterated by the present writer to the Royal Commission on Equal Pay of thirty years later, could do with restatement today—will anyone take on the job? But at least the gap is far less wide, even in industry, and outside it more and more bodies are ceasing to discriminate sexually in the remuneration they offer—even if they occasionally achieve the same end by proposing a salary which only a female church-mouse could afford to accept.[4]

I should also unhesitatingly include family allowances, so long opposed or at best cold-shouldered by organised male trade unionists as well as by others, and brought into being largely by the pressure of women, canalised and led by Eleanor Rathbone and Eva Hubback. I am not quite so sure about the inclusion of non-gainfully employed wives and mothers, as of right, in the national health service; though it was of great benefit to them and greatly appreciated, only Lord Beveridge can tell us whose arguments chiefly moved him to include it in the Beveridge Report.

Social legislation

Of direct cause-and-effect relationship in other social services, if we take the women's vote *as a whole*, I am very much less sure. One would have expected enfranchised women to press effectively for reform of the marriage, divorce, and bastardy laws, for example, for very much better housing, for more and better education; but though women's societies of all complexions, and of course individual women, have advocated and agitated for all these steadfastly over the years, I cannot find any real evidence to show that women have striven hard *en masse*—or harder than many men—to bring them about. Any really heavy pressure by the woman voter on the question of housing, to take one instance only, would, I should have ought, have left us in less of a mess than seems the case in the winter of 1961. Some of the causes once ardently advocated, such as pensions for spinsters of fifty-five, seem to have faded for lack of support, while at least one, the separate assessment of the incomes of husbands and wives, in which women, one would think, would be increasingly interested as their paid employment grows and the standard of earnings rises, seems as far off as ever.

I conclude, then, that in this field the improvements arising more or less directly from the enfranchisement of women, though perceptible, are much less than its protagonists believed or hoped, many changes arising from alterations in 'the climate of opinion' generally; and I must in honesty admit that there are occasions when the effect has been quite the other way. My husband, a strong supporter of votes for women, was frequently heard to say that while women ought to have the vote as a matter of socialist principle, the result of giving it to them would be disastrous, because the bulk of women were (a) unintelligent, (b) reactionary, and would immediately vote the wrong way and hold back advance instead of promoting it. I do not myself think that such a sweeping generalisation can be proved; but I cannot forget, for example, Conservative party conferences at which embattled Tory ladies screamed for immediate increase in floggings, birchings, and hangings, or other less-publicised occasions on which 'representative'(?) women did not show themselves, to put it mildly, strong champions of the right to life, liberty, and the pursuit of happiness. Is the Mothers' Union a force making for the increase in Christian charity? Can one, in sum, really say more than that there are *some* changes which do appear to have owed a good deal to the political influence of women voters, but that, as regards the rest of the field, the fact of emancipation has given women's voices the chance of being heard equally with those of men, and that where those voices have sounded on the 'right' side, that side has thereby been strengthened? I do not think one can.

Women in society

I do not wish, however, to end this article without some reference to the wider scene, to the immense change which has taken place *socially*, in the appearance, manners, and general attitude of women in society—and of society towards women—since Edwardian days. This can be dated pretty closely from the First World War, when 'war work' did away, of necessity, with so many of the restrictions, physical and social, which had bound women of the upper and middle classes, and put money of their own into the pockets of their working-class sisters. This new freedom did not vanish after the war was over and the working women streamed back out of the war factories, and the 'limpets', to use the attractive mixed metaphor then current, were 'combed out' of the civil service; and it has gone on growing rapidly. Thanks largely to better food, physical training, better health services and medical care, better education, better clothes, the ordinary woman of today would scarcely be recognised by her suffrage sister; and the woman sportsman, the woman Olympic champion, the woman mountain-climber, is now so common an object as scarcely to rate newspaper notice as such. Moreover, public opinion is clearly with this aspect of emancipation; it is fairly safe to say that in ordinary life there is hardly any obstacle to a woman doing what she likes, provided she wants to do it, and can.

This cannot, as I said, be attributed straightforwardly to the vote; it began before 1918. But there may be some doubt whether, if women had not been voters, the process would have proceeded so smoothly during the interwar years. Hitler and Goering, for a time, were pretty successful in reversing the process in Germany, in pushing German women back into the subjection of the 'five Ks' (*Küche, Keller, Kinderstube, Krankenstube, Kirche*); and there were not a few who would like to have seen it happen here. This is, of course, entirely a matter of conjecture; what can be confidently said is that the *economic* power of women as consumers—not the lavish consumer only or mainly, but the ordinary consumer—has enormously increased. The women's magazines, so often randomly abused, have done a very great deal to improve the living standards, not only of women themselves, but of their houses and families in the matter of furnishing and elimination of drudgery as well as of food and clothes; and whatever view electors and politicians may take of the importance of women, there is no doubt about the view of the Press and the advertisers. Perhaps it is they whom we should ask for the final judgement.

Notes

1 The number of women who have been 'decorated' is not, I fear available; it would be interesting to see to what extent an 'honour' is used as compensation for underpaid employment.

2 *The Times*, November 20, 1961.

3 *The Wages of Men and Women—Should they be Equal?* The argument did not affect Mrs Webb's realistic appreciation of the actual situation in the twenties, which has been mentioned earlier. See also *The Rate for the Job*, by Margaret Cole (1946).

4 While this article was in press the British government once more refused to implement the ILO Convention on equal pay. According to Ministry of Labour figures only one woman in a hundred working in industry, as against fifty men, takes home more than £14 a week.

The Reform of Government

WILLIAM A. ROBSON*

Vol. 35, no. 1, April–June 1964

THERE has recently taken place an immense amount of talk and writing about our system of government and the need to improve it. This sudden awareness of the necessity for change is a welcome sign; for during the past thirty years it has been almost impossible to arouse the slightest public interest in governmental reform. Complacency and indifference have been the watchwords not only of ministers and politicians of all parties, but also of civil servants and newspaper editors. There have, it is true, been many changes in the structure of the Cabinet, Departments and public administration in the past three or four decades; but they have been adventitious, arising out of this or that event, and without any attempt to consider the present and emerging needs of the country from a broader standpoint.

Parliamentary indifference

Parliament in particular has been extraordinarily supine about questions concerning the system of government. What is almost contemptuously referred to as 'a machinery Bill'—that is, a Bill creating a new Ministry or introducing some important change in the responsibilities or organisation of Departments—is usually passed with little or no scrutiny, criticism, or opposition. Parliament very rarely concerns itself with the Civil Service, unless there is a major scandal with political implications like Crichel Down. Administrative tribunals have been persistently ignored by the House of Commons; while regional planning and local government reform have been shamefully neglected subjects during the whole of the present century. Indeed, I know of no other country where the legislature takes so little interest in the political, administrative, and judicial system; and where so little curiosity about its working is evinced.

There is virtually no difference between the parties in this respect. All of them have concentrated on policies and programmes, while neglecting means and processes.

Now at last there is a realisation that we need to catch up with the modern world not only in science and technology, industrial management, and marketing methods, but also in the way we govern ourselves, the methods by which we plan for the future, the effectiveness with which public policy is formed, ministerial decisions are made, and government programmes carried out.

* The author is Professor Emeritus of Public Administration in the University of London. He has written many well-known books on British government and politics.

While this change of public attitude is a welcome one, a great many half-baked ideas have been flying around in recent months, and there is a distinct risk that instead of a comprehensive examination of the governmental system we shall get a number of remedies with fancy names applied here and there, while the more serious defects of the system go untouched. I would remind those readers who find the notion of a general inquiry into the public service strange and unacceptable that the Canadian government appointed in 1960 a Royal Commission on Government Organisation 'to inquire into and report upon the organisation and methods of operation of the departments and agencies of the Government of Canada and to recommend the changes therein which they consider would best promote efficiency, economy, and improved service in the dispatch of public business'. This Commission had a substantial research staff and was also authorised to engage outside research teams. The five volumes of its reports throw a great deal of light on defects in the Government of Canada and contain a mass of useful recommendations. In the United States the two Hoover Commissions carried out elaborate inquiries into the Executive Departments of the Federal Government, the first reporting in 1949 and the second in 1955.

Whether or not the government which comes to power after the next general election is willing to appoint a Royal Commission with broad terms of reference—and this would certainly involve delay in introducing changes which are urgently needed—there are a number of matters which should unquestionably be placed on the agenda of a reform programme.

The status of Parliament

The most fundamental question is the position of Parliament, and particularly its relations with the Executive. It is generally recognised that the status of Parliament has declined to a serious extent during the postwar era; and if this tendency is to be reversed the House of Commons must be prepared to assert its rights and authority more forcibly than it has done in recent decades. After all, the *power* of Parliament is intact: it is the will to exercise it which is lacking. No government, whatever its political complexion, is going to make the first move towards enhancing the status of Parliament: the initiative must come from the House of Commons.

The notion that every issue before the House shall be treated as a question of confidence in the government is thoroughly pernicious. A defeat in the House of Commons should not cause the Prime Minister and his Cabinet to resign unless it involves a major issue of policy or the conduct of a minister or the government as a whole. If this change of attitude were brought about, the independence and freedom of Parliament would greatly be enhanced.

In a recent House of Lords debate on the structure of government, Lord Boothby complained that the House of Commons has lost its status as an electoral college, and become no more than a forum of debate between two well-disciplined political armies. He alleged that the real debates nowadays take place in the private meetings of the parliamentary parties; and it is here that the crucial decisions on party policy are made.[1] This is certainly not always true, especially as regards the party in power. Nevertheless, the primary responsibility of an MP today is to the party machine rather than to his constituency or his conscience. The dependence of MPs and candidates on the support of their party is due to objective causes, such as universal adult suffrage, the large size of constituencies and the consequent importance of organisation, expensive publicity, etc., at elections; but the degree to which members subordinate themselves to party decisions in the day-to-day work of Parliament is a matter which is within their collective control.

During the past twenty years, the House of Commons has succeeded in obtaining two instruments for increasing its knowledge and influence. One is the Select Committee on Statutory Instruments, the other is the Select Committee on Nationalised Industries. Both these committees were set up as a result of back-bench pressure, in which Lord Molson played a leading part as a Conservative MP; and in each instance a reluctant government eventually gave way. On each occasion the argument was between back-bench MPs and ministers or ex-ministers, irrespective of party.

One of the most necessary changes is for Parliament to take a close and continuing interest in the Civil Service and central government organisation. This aim would begin to be realised if the House of Commons were to set up select committees on these twin subjects; and I believe that any government would find it hard to resist the proposal on rational grounds. But ultimately, if the legislature cannot get its way by other means, it must be prepared to go ahead in the face of government disapproval. The notion that this will lead to a dissolution is, I believe, one of our constitutional myths which is debilitating the parliamentary regime.

One can, of course, easily think of any number of functional committees which Parliament might establish: on defence, foreign policy, Commonwealth affairs, social services, education, etc. These would be basically different in kind from any which now exist in this country, and are likely to meet with much greater opposition from the government. I doubt whether it would be possible to confide frankly to a Select Committee all the considerations which influence defence policy.

One matter which deeply affects both MPs and ministers is the question of salaries. The present position is profoundly unsatisfactory. MPs receive the quite inadequate stipend of £1,750; and they are placed in the highly invidious position of having to determine their own salaries, with the political implications which that involves. The remuneration of ministers is equally unsatisfactory. A minister in charge of a major Department receives £5,000 a year—a figure which dates from Victorian days—while his Permanent Secretary will be paid £7,000 or more. The remuneration of ministers is far below judicial salaries and the salaries paid to full-time members of the boards of nationalised industries. If we wish to maintain the attractions of a political career for able and ambitious men, we cannot allow these anomalies to continue. Not only must the remuneration of both MPs and ministers be brought into relation with the levels prevailing elsewhere in the public service, but the determination of parliamentary and ministerial salaries should be entrusted to a small independent body or alternatively linked with those of the higher civil service or the judiciary. By this means the matter could be taken out of politics, and the hardship at present suffered by politicians without other sources of income relieved. The main object of this reform, however, is to prevent the progressive deterioration of the material attractions of political life. We do not want people going into politics for the sake of money; but on the other hand we do not want people deterred from entering or remaining in politics because of the low level of salaries paid to MPs or ministers. Britain compares very unfavourably with a number of countries in this respect.

Lord Shawcross and others have called for a revision of parliamentary procedure, whereby there would be only one debate on the principle of a Bill; and the Committee stage would be conducted on a non-partisan basis. He wants more standing committees, with frequent private sessions. Certainly the present procedure is highly repetitive; and when a Bill is opposed tooth and nail, as happened with the London Government Bill, it could scarcely have passed through the parliamentary machine at all if the guillotine had not been applied—despite loud protests from the Opposition. On the face of it, there is much to be said for omitting the debate on the report stage or on third reading.

How effective is the Cabinet?

The Cabinet remains in theory the supreme authority in the government. Is it so in fact? Lord Boothby, who has never been a Cabinet Minister, asserts that the Cabinet as such is no longer an effective instrument of government and that there has been a sharp decline in the system of Cabinet government. The Cabinet, he says, 'has become a rubber stamp for giving formal sanction to the decisions and actions of ministers' about which in the complexities of the modern world the Cabinet cannot be expected to have more than superficial knowledge. He attributes the decline in part to the increased size of the Cabinet.[2]

The size of a committee is always an important factor in the success of its functioning. Before the Second World War Britain had the largest Cabinet of any country; it included all ministers except one or two holding offices which were regarded as of subordinate status, such as the Postmaster-General. At the end of the Second World War the number of ministers had increased but the Cabinet was reduced in size by excluding a substantial number of ministers.

In the past twenty years, however, there has been a steady increase in the number of ministers[3] in the Cabinet and a decline in the number who are not members, as the following table[4] shows:

	Churchill June 1945	Attlee Dec 1946	Attlee March 1950	Churchill Nov 1951	Churchill Jan 1955	Eden Jan 1956	Macmillan Jan 1957	Macmillan July 1962	Douglas-Home Oct 1963
Cabinet ministers	16	18	18	16	18	18	18 (19)+	21	23
Non-Cabinet ministers	19	13	13	14	11	10 (11)*	10 (9)+	8	14

* The Office of Paymaster-General was not filled from December 1955 to October 1956
+ Mr. Maudling was included in the Cabinet in September 1957

The trend is a curious one in view of the exclusion from the Cabinet of the Secretaries of State for War and Air and the First Lord of the Admiralty *after* the Churchill Caretaker government of 1945, in which they were Cabinet Ministers; the disappearance of the Secretary of State for India after India became independent in 1947; and the fact that the Commonwealth Relations Office and the Colonial Office, which were formerly represented by separate Secretaries of State in the Cabinet, are now headed by a single minister (Mr Duncan Sandys) instead of by two Secretaries of State. The presumption is that Prime Ministers have been under great pressure to enlarge their Cabinets during the postwar years—only Sir Winston Churchill has resisted the tendency.

The result is that we now have a Cabinet as large as or larger than almost all those which existed from 1901 to 1939 apart from Lloyd George's famous War Cabinet of five members.[5] It is probable, to say the least, that this has reduced the effectiveness of the Cabinet as an organ for deciding the most important issues. What we do not know is how efficiently the system of Cabinet Committees (in which non-members are included) operates; but it may well be that the Cabinet is tending to become a report-receiving body or that the centre of gravity has shifted to the Cabinet Committees. Lord Boothby cites as examples of peacetime decisions made without the knowledge of the full Cabinet, Lord Attlee's decision to manufacture atomic weapons and Lord Eden's decision to make plans and to issue directions for the attack on Port Said in the Suez crisis. Such ignorance, however, was by no means unknown in earlier Cabinets, as Earl Loreburn, Lord Chancellor in Mr Asquith's Cabinet, showed in *How the War Came*.

On general grounds there can be little doubt that the present Cabinet is too large for effective participation by all its members and that a reduction in its size would lead to fuller and more concentrated discussion of major questions of policy.

Aids to policy formation

A matter of the greatest moment is to ensure that ministers have access to the best possible advice in deciding policy questions. Britain is about to enter a period of rapid and extensive economic, technological, and social change, and it is essential that the government's policies should be correctly formulated with the advice of people who are capable of understanding the basic issues involved. One aspect of this is that much greater use should be made throughout the public service of advisory councils to Departments. The Ministry of Education has derived immense benefit from its Central Advisory Council, whose reports have had a profound influence on policy. The National Insurance Advisory Committee has, within its special field, been of great value in advising the Minister of Pensions and National Insurance both on regulations and on matters of policy. But there are no Standing Councils to advise the Board of Trade on location of industry policy; or the Ministry of Housing and Local Government on town and country planning. Nor does the Treasury have any Standing Council to advise it on matters concerning the Civil Service. There can be no doubt that a more widespread use of bodies of leading experts and well-informed laymen by the central government could be of great help to ministers both in helping to formulate policy and in improving the standard of administration.

Other aspects of this subject were touched on by several speakers in the House of Lords debate referred to above. Lord Todd, an eminent man of science, wished to ensure that scientists should be able to play a larger part in helping to solve the problems confronting ministers. He urged that there should be in every Executive Department a Scientific Secretary, aided by an Advisory Council, whose task would be to keep in touch with scientific developments likely to be of value to the Ministry, whether occurring inside or outside government agencies. He would be on a similar level to that of the Permanent Secretary. He would have a staff which could carry out operational research and deal with the day-to-day scientific and technological problems of the Department. Men suited for such important posts might be recruited both from inside and outside the Scientific Civil Service. They would be scientist-administrators of a special type, possessing practical judgement as well as an understanding of scientific advances. Lord Todd included in the term scientist those versed in natural sciences, engineering, and social sciences. The scientific and administrative secretaries would advise the minister jointly on appropriate matters.[6]

Lord Taylor declared that most of the serious mistakes governments have made in the postwar years have been due to poor intelligence work; to a failure to assemble the facts; and to basing decisions on political preconceptions rather than on a dispassionate analysis of the available data.[7] He gave examples drawn from housing, higher education, the supply of doctors, unemployment, and other fields.

There are several other ways in which ministers could obtain more aid than they now get in the formation of policy. They might, for example, make much more use of research institutes or university departments than at present. They might have closer and more systematic relations on particular matters with small groups of intellectuals such as the Fabian Society, the Bow Group, or PEP. They might invite such bodies, or specialised societies like the Town and Country Planning Association or the Howard League for Penal Reform to carry out investigations in particular fields as a prelude to policy-making.

All governments rely on royal commissions and official committees, and these bodies have a long and honourable history of public service to their credit. But a difficulty which most royal commissions and official committees face is that they seldom have any research staff of their own or money with which to engage the services of outside bodies to carry out investigations on their behalf. In the United States, official committees are always given either a qualified staff of researchers or sufficient funds to get work done by outside bodies. Here the usual practice is to appoint men and women who know nothing about the subject and hence are 'uncommitted' and 'open-minded'; and they are expected to obtain all the information they need by questioning witnesses who very often represent special interests, pressure groups, and similar bodies whose desire to reveal the truth is not usually their predominant characteristic. This method is antiquated and unsatisfactory.

It is worth noticing that the Robbins Committee owes part of its success to the exceptional fact that it was a body whose members possessed a considerable knowledge of education; and that they had ample funds to enable them to employ a highly qualified research staff. Both these conditions should normally be observed in appointing royal commissions or committees.

Another reform which is needed is the strengthening of each minister's private office. This at present consists only of a principal private secretary and one or two assistant private secretaries together with a few shorthand typists. While I would not advocate a full-blown *Cabinet du Ministre* such as one finds in France, it would be a great advantage to a minister if he could bring two or three trusted advisers into his private office on a salaried basis to help in the formation of departmental policy. They would not be established civil servants and would expect to leave when a change of government, or even a change of minister, occurs.

The Prime Minister's office

We can turn now to the organisation of the Executive. The first need is to give institutional expression to the changed position of the Prime Minister, who is no longer merely *primus inter pares* but the working head of the government, responsible for its successful operation as a whole. There has been a great growth in the functions of overall policy-making and management in recent decades, but except for the Cabinet Secretariat and the Central Statistical Office they have all gone to the Treasury. In addition to economic and fiscal policy, the Budget, monetary and balance of payments matters, taxation and control of expenditure, the Treasury has been made responsible—or has made itself responsible—for practically all civil service and establishment matters (apart from recruitment), O and M, the machinery of government, the economic section, economic planning, the capital investment programme, and much else. Such a vast concentration of power in a Ministry of Finance would never have been tolerated but for the fact that the Prime Minister is also First Lord of the Treasury and thus throws his protective mantle over the Great Leviathan. But the Prime Minister's relation with the Treasury is very sporadic and tenuous except in regard to a few specific matters where his consent is explicitly required, such as the appointment of permanent secretaries, deputy secretaries, and other chief officials in all Departments.

The Treasury is grossly overloaded; and the appointment of a Chief Secretary, an Economic Secretary, and two or three Joint Permanent Secretaries can neither conceal nor remedy that state of affairs. The prolonged failure of the Treasury as an economic planning agency; the frequent financial crises of the postwar era; the stagnation of the economy; the poor performance of the Education and Training Division; the negligent handling of the Anglo–French Concorde supersonic aircraft project[8]—all these indicate not only defects of ministerial policy but also shortcomings in the administrative and technical work of the Treasury in its role as the Central Department. The National Economic Development Council is a belated attempt to set up a more effective instrument of planned economic growth than the Treasury has shown itself to be under Conservative ministers.

Meanwhile, the Prime Minister has no instrumentality with which to carry out his coordinating, policy-devising, overriding, and supervising functions. One possible way of increasing his effectiveness would be to transfer several of the 'central' functions of the Treasury to the Cabinet Office, which is under the direct control of the Prime Minister. Among them might be the regulation of the Civil Service, establishment and training, O. and M., and the new functions envisaged by the Plowden Report. Alternatively, these functions might go into an enlarged Prime Minister's Office under the immediate care of a Minister of State.

The organisation of Departments

A great many proposals were made, at the 1963 political party conferences, regarding government Departments. Some are sensible, others foolish. Merely changing the name plates on the Whitehall buildings does not by itself alter anything. The suggestion put forward by Mr Christopher Layton at the Liberal Assembly for a Ministry of Expansion is mere word-spinning, for while economic growth may be an aim it is not brought nearer by setting up a Department which is labelled with the aim. The new Ministry, according to Mr Layton, would absorb *inter alia* the development functions of the Ministry of Labour and of the Board of Trade. One should look with suspicion on all proposals to concentrate development functions in a single Ministry, because it is highly unrealistic to separate current administration from development in any sphere of activity.

Mr Harold Wilson's proposal of a Minister for Disarmament is based on a similar fallacy. Disarmament is a policy objective; responsibility for its achievement must rest partly with the Foreign Office and partly with the Ministry of Defence. In what way is such a policy advanced by naming a Department or a minister after it?

Mr Wilson also proposed the appointment of a Minister of Production or Economic Planning—the name is apparently not decided. Economic planning is a function which has been badly handled and neglected by the Treasury, and there is everything to be said for making it the chief preoccupation of a new Department. It is generally assumed that NEDC will remain in existence whatever the result of the general election; and the Council's terms of reference include the examination of the economic performance of the nation 'with particular concern for plans for the future in both the private and the public sectors of industry'. But it is not really a planning body, but rather an organ of ascertainment, calculation, coordination, and persuasion.[9] The work of NEDC does, however, immensely increase the need for planning both in the private and the public sectors of the economy. The responsibility for planning should form part of the machinery of government much more definitely than does NEDC. There would be substantial advantages in giving the task to a new Minister of Planning or Production, or a Planning Commission forming part of the government.

The new minister or Commission should take over the functions of the Board of Trade regarding the location of industry, the responsibility for regional development now borne by Mr Heath, and possibly the town and country planning powers of the Ministry of Housing and Local Government. The dichotomy between the Board of Trade as the Department which controls the location of industry, and the Ministry of Housing and Local Government, which is the central authority for town and country planning, is thoroughly unsatisfactory. The Board of Trade's policy on industrial location has veered in many different directions since 1945; and no one knows what it is at any given moment—or why. There has, indeed, been no public thinking on this subject by the Board, apart from the building up and diversification of the Development Areas. The Ministry of Housing and Local Government, for its part, has failed miserably to foresee the need for regional planning, and is only now beginning to address itself to the task, which it regards—wrongly in my opinion—as a central government function.

The new minister would thus be concerned with both economic planning and with physical or land use planning. In town and country planning social purposes are at least as important as economic aims, and it is essential that the former should not be subordinated to the latter. There is much to be said for integration at the centre, provided that the two kinds of planning are given an equal standing. But even so, we shall never achieve an effective system of planning until we establish regional councils to be responsible or planning at the regional level.

Education

The need for strengthening ministerial responsibility for higher education has been manifest for several years. The Robbins Committee has recommended a Minister of Arts and Science for Higher Education, and other autonomous bodies concerned with Science or the Arts, such as the Research Councils, the Arts Council, and the Standing Commission on Museums and Galleries. Mr Wilson had forestalled their report with a similar proposal at a Fabian Society meeting at Scarborough.

The case for a separate Department derives basically from the need for a more concentrated attention on the expansion and development of higher education at the governmental level. The Robbins Committee considered the advantages and disadvantages of placing universities within the jurisdiction of the Ministry of Education, and rejected the proposal on two grounds. First, that the autonomy of the universities and certain other institutions is so important and distinctive a feature of their existence that they must not be subject to a Department dealing with non-autonomous schools or colleges. The second ground was that research is as important a function of universities as teaching, and this again demands an association with research organisations in a separate Ministry. The Committee may have been influenced by the widespread opposition of the universities to any tutelage by the Ministry of Education.

In this country we have never, at any time or at any level, been accustomed to looking at the educational system as a whole. So it is not surprising that neither the Robbins Committee nor most university teachers or administrators should give this objective a high priority in their thinking. Its importance has generally been seriously underestimated. For this reason there is much to be said in favour of the proposal which the government has adopted—and which the Labour party put forward at a much earlier date—for a Secretary of State for Education and Civil Science, with under him a Minister of Education (much like the present one) and a Minister for Higher Education and Science with a separate administrative organisation somewhat on the lines of the Robbins recommendation. Only the Secretary of State would normally be in the Cabinet, though Sir Alec Douglas-Home has invited Sir Edward Boyle to remain in the Cabinet although only a Minister of State.

This solution should ensure coordination in planning and the allocation of resources. It should enable the universities to continue as autonomous bodies; and it should bring them into an organic relation with the scientific research councils. It is very much better than two entirely separate Ministries each struggling for power, money, and prestige.

WILLIAM A. ROBSON

Scientific research

This brings me to research, which for the first time in the history of this country has become a major political issue. In his address to the Labour party conference Mr Wilson stated his intention to establish 'a full Ministry of Science', which he contrasted with the present office of the Minister for Science, 'with no powers, no staff, no scientists, no clear direction of what he is about'.

The Department of Scientific and Industrial Research is not a Ministry of Science, but an unsatisfactory substitute for one. It is unique in that it is controlled by a Research Council with executive powers, composed of leading scientists, industrialists, and trade union officials. The Minister for Science appoints the Council and its Secretary, who is also the Permanent Secretary of the Department. But the minister is not in charge of DSIR in the usual sense of the term.

The Trend Report—whose recommendations have been accepted by the Conservative government—proposed to abolish DSIR and to set up in its place a new autonomous Industrial Research and Development Authority, to be responsible for the support of industrial research, and to take over many of the research stations now under DSIR. The Report advocated the transfer to a new Science Research Council of most of the functions of DSIR in relation to universities. The minister would have some important new responsibilities for promoting civil research and development; and on him would fall the task of deciding the allocation of resources among the various Research Councils, the new Industrial Research and Development Authority, and the several international agencies in which Britain is participating. To assist him an advisory body would be appointed.

The Trend Report did not appear to envisage a Ministry of Science; but rather a minister with considerably enlarged powers of influencing, mainly through finance, a number of independent agencies. The Report was signed before the publication of the Robbins Report; but the Trend Committee went so far as to say that there would be obvious advantages in one and the same minister being responsible for higher education and civil scientific policy.

In a letter to *The Times*, Mr R. H. S. Crossman propounded the Labour party's view of a Cabinet Minister responsible for higher education and research; and this accords with the view strongly held in academic circles that the twin functions of teaching and research are indissoluble components of university work. A minister concerned solely with distributing money among a series of independent Research Councils or similar bodies is unlikely to occupy a position of much power; and the support of a properly staffed Ministry appears to be essential for effective action. The Trend Committee appears to have overlooked the possibility of the minister becoming a mere mouthpiece for expressing views which have been pressed on to him by the various scientific bodies with which he will be surrounded.

A weakness of the Trend Report is that the existing gulf between the universities and industry in this country is likely to be increased by the sharp distinction which the Report draws between academic research, which will be the preoccupation of the Science Research Council, and industrial research, which will be the concern of the new Industrial Research and Development Authority. The relation between industry and the universities is far closer in the United States or Western Germany than it is in this country; and there is ground for saying that we have suffered substantial disadvantages from the remoteness which persists here. The establishment of a Ministry of Technology, which the Labour party favours, might increase this remoteness unless great care were taken to guard against it.

DSIR has many shortcomings; but it does have important links with the Universities. Thus it awards postgraduate studentships to enable young scientists and technologists to receive full-time training in research methods, and also research fellowships to help young research workers to develop their abilities. It makes grants to investigators of established reputation in universities or technical colleges to assist their work in new or existing fields by acquiring expensive apparatus and materials, or engaging additional assistants.

DSIR also has close relations with industry through the research associations which it supports with annual grants; and through its research stations, many of which, like the Building Research Station, are providing services to particular industries. If DSIR were merged or associated with the Ministry for Higher Education one advantage could be to bring the Universities and Colleges of Advanced Technology into closer relation with industry—a highly desirable object in the applied sciences. It might also broaden the outlook of DSIR which has only very recently begun to take a limited interest in a few selected aspects of the human sciences which have a close bearing on industrial needs. This, too, is a desirable aim.

Mr Harold Wilson, however, speaking in the House of Commons on the Address in reply to the Queen's Speech, said that the Ministry of Aviation provided a ready-made nucleus for a Ministry of Research and Technology— 'whether or not it had responsibility for pure science'.[10] He appears to contemplate pure science going to the Minister for Higher Education (under the Secretary of State for Education) while applied research and technology would go to a separate Ministry. This would exacerbate the existing separation between the universities and industry to which I have already referred.

In any reform of the central government a high place should be given to the role of research in the civil departments. The differences of attitude among them are striking. A few, such as the Home Office and the Post Office, may be called research-minded, although their research programmes do not extend to all their interests and should be widened in scope. At the other end of the spectrum are certain departments which are positively hostile to research. In between these extremes are a large number which are in varying degrees apathetic or indifferent. The subject is too large to pursue in detail here, but one can say that every civil department should be required to have a Director of Research and Development, a research programme, and at least the nucleus of a research staff. It should also have an advisory or executive Research Council containing persons of distinction from outside the Civil Service as well as a proportion of official members. This is the minimal requirement needed to give research a footing in every department.

The Civil Service

We can turn now to the Civil Service. I do not share the opinion of those who blame the Administrative Class for all or most of the shortcomings, failures, and disappointments which Britain has experience in the postwar years. This is a most unfair and distorted view. The Civil Service, in my opinion, is one of our greatest national assets; and the Administrative Class has many virtues as well as some defects.

What are those defects? The worst is—or has been hitherto—a profound disbelief in training at the centre, by which I mean the Treasury. The higher command at the Treasury has for long clung to its traditional belief that public administration can be learned only by doing; that it is an art which can best be acquired by a system of apprenticeship—that is, 'by watching Nellie'. A large proportion of the most senior members of the Service still believe that a good classics degree—meaning Greats, of course—is the finest preparation for the highest positions. The Education and Training Division has been the Cinder-ella of the Treasury—starved of resources, talent, and status, and with frequent changes of personnel. (Some of the training schemes run by other departments are excellent. I do not for a moment intend to criticise the whole mass of training activities which take place in the Civil Service.)

This lack of interest in, and facilities for, training has been a continuous theme of criticism during the past twenty years. The Assheton Committee on the Training of Civil Servants declared in 1944 that the service as a whole, and individual members of it, had suffered in respect of efficiency, morale, and the spirit of public service through the absence of a general system of training for all civil servants, aiming both 'to increase the competence of the individual and to give the whole profession a higher conception of the contribution it can make to the welfare, happiness, and good government of the community'. The deficiency in training schemes, they reported, was particularly marked in respect of the Administrative Class. Many political scientists and other competent observers have enlarged on this theme. Yet the impact of informed criticism on the Treasury has been slight. The junior administrative course for Assistant Principals has until this year consisted of three weeks of isolated talks. It has taken nineteen years for the Assheton Committee's recommenda-tions to blossom forth into a fourteen-week course for Assistant Principals (with an extension of a further seven weeks for those from economic departments) very recently started at the new Administrative Study Centre.

This is a promising beginning of what one hopes will be a new and less outmoded outlook in the Treasury towards training. We still have a long way to in this field if the Civil Service is to be properly trained for tasks of today and tomorrow.

One of the greatest needs is for a central Staff Training College, which would preferably be open to local government officers and officials in the nationalised industries as well as civil servants. But the Treasury has turned this down repeatedly. Here again we are lagging behind the achievements of several other countries. Is it too much to hope that the Administrative Study Centre may evolve from its present modest scope to become such a Staff Training College?

A second serious defect in the Civil Service is the reluctance of members of the Administrative Class to appoint members of the Professional Class to the highest positions. The Professional, Scientific, and Technical Class, as it is called, includes the physicists, scientists, engineers, statisticians, actuaries, lawyers, architects, economists, doctors, psychologists, planners, and so forth. These men, with their professional qualifications and special skills, are a large group and their work and knowledge is of mounting importance in the modern state. Yet apart from exceptional cases, such as the Permanent Secretary of the Department of Scientific and Industrial Research, these men are seldom, if ever, appointed to the highest administrative positions, even if they have outstanding administrative ability.

The opinion is widely held among competent observers that the Civil Service would benefit from a regular intake of men and women from other walks of life to the senior and middle-range administrative posts. In the House of Lords debate there was virtual unanimity on this point. Lord Melchett advocated a fairly large number of addition posts at these levels to be filled largely from the professions, industry, trade unions, the City and universities.[11] Lord Strang dissociated himself from the view that an arts degree is a better qualification for a civil servant than any other kind of degree. It would be better, he said, if more established civil servants had an economic or scientific or technological background. The injection of men from outside with specialised knowledge or wide experience can be refreshing and fruitful.[12] Lord Selkirk said that what is wanted is not scientific service men but scientific men in the administrative departments, on the same footing as any other administrative officer.[13] He wanted to see one type of entrant taken in at about thirty-five years of age. Lord Morrison of Lambeth recommended more interchange between the Civil Service, local government, and the public corporations.[14] Viscount Caldecote thought that about a third of the Civil Service above the rank of principal, and in the executive class, should be recruited from industry.

Several of the best civil servants in the higher positions during the postwar period entered the service on a temporary basis during the Second World War. This demonstrates the advantage of bringing in an infusion of outside talent from other walks of life. The Civil Service should undoubtedly remain a career service, at least to the extent it is now. But for some years past there has been a substantial stream of senior administrative and professional civil servants resigning in order to go into commerce or industry. It is time that a reverse flow of recruits from both private and public enterprise and local government was started.

*   *   *

These, then, are the main matters which should receive immediate attention if we wish to create a more vigorous, far-sighted, and efficient political and administrative system. The changes which have been outlined are designed to enhance the role of Parliament and raise the status of MPs and of ministers; to improve the effectiveness of the Cabinet; to reduce the excessive concentration of power in the Treasury; to provide the Prime Minister with the necessary organs of overall control which his position demands; to provide more effective means of planning within the government; to supplement and improve the existing aids to policy formation available to ministers; to make departmental provision for research and development both within and without the government; and to improve the training of civil servants. Without a programme of reform of this kind, it is unlikely, to say the least, that we shall be able to respond quickly and effectively to the need for change in the technological age in which we live.

There is, in my opinion, too much denigration about the past and pessimism concerning the future of this country to be found in current discussions about almost every aspect of our national life. The complacency, the refusal to face blatant facts, the escapism, the triviality of the popular Press, the foolish incantations about affluence—these influences have been highly damaging to public morale and have evoked a high degree of nonchalance in many strata of society.

There is now, at long last, unmistakable evidence of profound changes in public opinion. People are disturbed; they are more realistic; and they want change. They have acquired positive attitudes to education, to science, and to planning. They are dissatisfied with Britain's position in the world and want to make it better. From these discontents a new dynamic could arise. It must be guided and harnessed by government; but this can be done only if the government itself is more dynamic. This should be the object of the Age of Reform.

Notes

1 254 H.L. Deb. (January 15, 1964), cols. 639–640.
2 *Ibid*. col. 642.
3 The total number of ministers has also greatly increased. In July 1939 there were sixty-four ministers of all ranks, including Parliamentary Secretaries and Government Whips. In 1946 the number was seventy-seven; in July 1950, eighty-three; in December 1963, ninety. 254 H.L. Deb., No. 23, Lord Morrison at cols. 624–625.

4 1 am indebted for this table to Hans Daalder, *Cabinet Reform in Britain 1914-1963*, Stanford University Press, pp. 134–135.

5 See D. N. Chester, *Development of the Cabinet in British Government* since 1918, p. 32.

6 254 H. L. Deb. No. 23, cols. 672–674.

7 *Ibid.* cols. 679–680.

8 See the severe criticism of the Select Committee on Estimates, Second Report, Session 1963–64, Transport Aircraft, B.P.P. 42, H.M.S.O., paras. 79–90.

9 See 'The Functions of the National Economic Development Council', by Dr Joan Mitchell, *The Political Quarterly*. October–December 1963.

10 November 19, 1963.

11 254 H.L. Deb. (January 15, 1964), col. 596.

12 *Ibid.* col. 608.

13 *Ibid.* col. 622.

14 *Ibid.* col. 634.

Socialism or Social Democracy?
The Choice for the Labour Party

JOHN P. MACKINTOSH, MP*

Vol. 43, no. 4, October–December 1972

THERE has never been a time in the history of the Labour party when it would not have been appropriate to write an article on 'the current crisis', but there are features of the present situation which are both more peculiar and more serious than the old recurrent crises over leadership, doctrine and tactics.

A brief summary of the situation is that, for the first time since the early 1930s, a combination of forces including the left has won the support of the non-doctrinal centre of the Party, but the peculiarity is that this has happened when the left (and, as a result of its commanding position, the Party as a whole) stands for nothing except hostility to the measures of the present Conservative government. Yet those normally labelled as the right, who have provided most of the ideas since the late 1950s, have been so upset and thrown off balance by their recent defeats that they appear to be divided and somewhat demoralised and have managed only to fight rear-guard actions.

The oddity of the situation is brought out, for example, by looking at the Twelfth Annual Congress of the Second Socialist International held this July in Vienna. If the programmes and achievements of the many socialist parties represented at the Congress are examined, there is a great degree of similarity. All the parties have become reformist, in the sense that they accept the democratic system and free elections and, while all are prepared to intervene in economic affairs to promote social justice, none of them intend to replace capitalism by a totally different or 'socialist' economic system. Once in power these parties have followed similar policies introducing increased welfare benefits, a public housing programme, a health service, and they have all attempted to plan the economy of their own country, including taking control of certain industries. The principal objective has been greater social equality within each community. The Germans, being very conscious of theory, spelt this out in their Bad Godesberg Programme of 1959. Hugh Gaitskell tried to do the same in the Clause Four controversy, but because the Labour party is a non-theoretical and somewhat backward-looking or sentimental party, he lost, though his policies were adopted in practice both then and in the subsequent period in office under Harold Wilson. It is significant that, having won a large majority in 1966, Harold Wilson only completed the last remnant of the old nationalisation programmes by taking over the iron

* The author is Labour MP for Berwickshire and East Lothian, and author of *The British Cabinet* and other works. He last wrote for *The Political Quarterly* on 'The Problem of the Labour Party' in the January–March issue of this year.

and steel industry. Though he shared a pragmatic readiness to take over docks or special industries that were failing, there was no nationalisation 'shopping list' of the kind the Labour party had had in its manifesto in 1945, 1950 or 1951 each of which was intended as a step towards further, virtually total public ownership.

Fundamental Socialism or Reformism

The peculiarity of current British politics is that at a time when all the socialist parties in the world are clearly reformist and even the French Communist party has joined the French Socialists in an alliance based on a reformist programme, the left are in a strong position in the Labour party and have managed to suggest that to be a 'social democrat' is something undesirable and that a return to a purer, more fundamental socialism is possible.

It is hard to discover what is meant by this. In fact, the left do not appear to want a return to the old Clause Four type of total public ownership. Although one or two Labour MPs still talk in this way and although there are elements in the constituency parties still moving resolutions on these lines at branch meetings (one such resolution is carried *nem con* every year at the conference of the Scottish Regional Council of the Labour Party), there are few who do in fact believe that this is the correct course for the Party. Most people realise that nationalisation was never an end in itself; it was always a means to several ends. The old theory was that by ending the payment of profits to rentiers in these industries, the class system would be weakened (the manager who took over from the former owners was just a better paid, specialised worker). Also, by removing those with an interest in exploitation, nationalisation was supposed to bring harmony into labour relations. In addition, by imposing public control, these industries could be fitted into a national plan and it was thought that with no profit motive, production could be designed to meet social needs rather than simply the demands of those with money.

Broadly speaking, nationalisation has not had any of these specifically socialistic effects here or in other countries, though it has permitted increased investment and concern about the impact of policy changes on the workers and on the public. But these improvements could equally well be achieved by other methods. As a result, few people think the Labour party would recover its relevance and idealism if it simply proposed to take over one major industry after another in its next period of office.

So what is this more authentic socialism which is being proposed as an alternative to the social democracy of recent years? It cannot be a serious list of policy proposals because this is just what the Labour party is lacking at the moment. (The recent Green Paper published by the NEC does not come into this category.) No one could enumerate a series of positive commitments for change with which the Labour party or any section of it, from the Tribune Group to the extreme right, is presently identified.

The new socialist fundamentalism currently being advocated is more a mood or an approach to politics. It may be hard to pin down in policy terms, but it can be smelt. John Gyford and Stephen Haseler have made a serious attempt to identify it in their Fabian pamphlet, *Social Democracy: beyond revisionism*. They call it 'working class populism'. It derives from 'a mild, tolerant yet real class war' and 'has always had a feeling of the grass roots about it'. This populist–socialist approach, they say, has been a 'channel for the unwealthy, the uneducated and the unmetropolitan'. They accept that many of the socialists of this kind are well-off workers but the resentments are relative; what is taking place is 'a movement of the marginally well-heeled, the provincial, the regional, the unfashionable and the unimportant'.

The alternative group identified by Gyford and Haseler are the social democrats or 'left-wing liberals' as the 'true socialists' often call them. It is alleged that they are preponderantly middle class, impressed by technology and 'élitist' in their outlook. They do not respect working-class culture and prefer to emphasise *classlessness*; group rights do not seem as important to them as *individual* rights.

This analysis has clearly fastened on to some of the current divisions in the Labour party and has some relevance to recent social developments. Many on the traditional left, from Michael Foot to Stan Orme, support populist class-orientated demands not because they derive from a socialist philosophy but because they come from 'their people'. This means that they can support car workers or dockers demanding wage increases far above national increases in productivity simply because they are made by a group of organised workers acting in a class-conscious way and united by a common feeling of alienation, boredom and resentment at the standards enjoyed by the university-trained, white collar managerial staff. On the other hand, the social democrat is culpable of elitism and intellectualism because he looks at the consequences of granting such demands, sees that the result is to push up prices and thus cut the living standards of those who cannot win above average pay awards; in other words, that the result is to increase inequality whereas he wants a criterion by which to support only those demands that do not damage other workers or those living on social security benefits. Gyford and Haseler point out that the difference of outlook highlighted by this example spreads far beyond the central issue of wages and equality. Because the social democrats are interested in individual rights and social justice, they will accept liberal legislation legalising homosexual relations or abortion when much of this is alien to working-class group feeling which thinks of liberty more in terms of what groups can do and of what status they have in society. For much the same reasons, the social democrats are keen to pay out money to the Arts Council and favour the BBC while the populist/socialists would prefer to help provide facilities for football clubs and watch commercial TV since it talks their language. The social democrat is bothered about economic growth producing pollution and damaging 'natural ecological systems' while the populist/socialist wants rapid growth since it will provide more jobs, higher pay and better conditions in physical terms.

If this contrast is developed and widened to cover the full spectrum of current political issues, social democrats are internationalist and pro-Common Market while the populist/socialist is suspicious of foreigners and uninterested in foreign policy. For much the same motives, the former try to be liberal on immigration laws while the latter group is suspicious of coloured workers. Underlying all these specific reactions, the social democrat wants to end the class system (and can therefore be accused of wanting to make everyone middle class) while the socialist by instinct expects the class system to continue and this is comforting as he can then continue to resent the system. This kind of socialism is a deeply conservative outlook based upon fear of change; it expects that the inevitable burden of adjusting to modern methods will fall predominantly on the workers so that the first priority is to defend the positions already won by the Labour Movement.

It is obvious that to characterise these two approaches is at once to caricature, to impose a coherence which does not fully exist. It is easy to think of people who, though mainly in one category, have some opinions shared by the other side. For instance, some who are clearly 'socialist' by this set of criteria nevertheless are deeply involved in race issues, that is, in ensuring fair treatment for coloured immigrants and in getting immigration quotas relaxed. The left in the House of Commons played a major and honourable part in resisting the Commonwealth Immigration (Kenyan Asians) Bill in 1968. On the other hand, there are those, of whom Tony Crosland is the most conspicuous example, who are archetypal social democrats, yet are strongly in favour of economic growth and regard most of the ecology-doomwatch case as alarmist nonsense whose practical effect, if implemented, would be to perpetuate inequality.

Aspects of the division

Yet it would appear to be true that this division between a populist/socialism ready to back all demands from the working class and a perhaps older desire to pursue reformist left-wing principles on the merits of each case, does indeed exist. The division came out quite clearly on two occasions in the Dick Taverne case. The first was revealed on television, when it became clear that some of the activists in the Lincoln constituency party did not merely object to Taverne's pro-European views; they objected to his lack of a class-conscious approach to politics. It came out again when the NEC turned down his appeal on a twelve to eight vote which fell almost directly along the lines suggested. This decision set aside the recommendation of the organisation subcommittee of the NEC that Taverne's appeal should be upheld on the grounds that the rules of natural justice had not been fully observed by the Lincoln party.

This division also explains how former right-wingers, such as James Callaghan, Fred Peart and Willie Ross, have been able to work in an easy and comfortable alliance on the Shadow Cabinet with left-wingers such as Michael Foot and Peter Shore; they are united not just by hostility to the Common Market but by their common willingness to back all opposition to redundancies, to back all strikes and to reject all aspects of Conservative legislation, indeed all change of any kind. In this sense, the populist/socialist approach has moved away from what used to be known as Bevanism. The latter was a doctrinaire position ready to advocate new measures and ready to oppose working-class group demands if these, on analysis, proved to be contrary to socialist principles. Viewed in this way, Barbara Castle was the last of the Bevanites because, when she became convinced, as Minister of Employment, that certain aspects of trade union activity were contrary to the interests of the working class as a whole, she was prepared to argue this case and to introduce legislation to prevent such actions. Whether her proposals would have been effective or not, the point is that her whole approach was to judge the results of social actions according to her political principles, whereas the current populist/socialist approach is quite different; the major unions want to retain the 1968 legal status quo in industrial relations and that is enough. For them, to discuss the legislative framework surrounding British industrial relations and to examine the effects of certain types of group actions on other sections of the community is half-way to becoming a Tory; none of the present 'genuine socialists' would contemplate such behaviour.

It is true that some of this reluctance springs from one of the traditional approaches to opposition; that the opposition should not make constructive suggestions but just oppose. It is far easier to offer a blanket opposition. Nevertheless, there is a gap between this position and that of the more old-fashioned socialists who believed they were creating a new fairer society and that the abuse of power by any group just because it had a stranglehold on a section of the economy was both anti-social and anti-socialist. The present populist/socialist position is not to raise such questions but simply to ask who is making the demand? If it is a group of workers, they must be supported and only those who are intellectuals, elitists and middle-class social democrats would pause to consider the effects of the conduct in question.

Difficulties of populism

There are, however, some intractable difficulties for those taking the populist/socialist position. The first is that there is no method of solving conflicts between one group of workers and another. If dockers claim the right to 'strip and stuff' containers and thus threaten the jobs of packers dispersed around a number of factories, who is right? The support of the populist/socialist tends to go to the best organised and most defiant group, presumably because they are showing most working-class vigour, but this has no obvious relationship to socialism or to justice. Put in another way, to back those who shout loudest or press hardest is to neglect the weakest and worst paid groups who are often incapable of making a strong case. Another aspect of the problem is that the large general unions, realising that the worst paid workers excite public sympathy, often frame their demands in this light; but if they then also insist on keeping differentials, they are not in fact doing anything to decrease relative poverty. Yet, once again, the socialists who are pledged to support every trade union position have nothing to say about this.

These difficulties come to a head over the question of an incomes policy. Part of the doctrine of the socialists is that any incomes policy is undesirable simply because it is unacceptable to the larger, more powerful unions. But if all union demands are permitted, the result is to increase inequality in two ways. The first occurs simply because the better paid are the best organised. A recent analysis found that between January 1 and January 31, 1970, the top ten working-class groups had wage settlements on average every ten months and had rises on average of 18 per cent. The ten poorest paid workers groups had settlements on average every twenty months of an average of 7.7 per cent. This shows that the result of leaving the unions to battle for themselves is to increase inequality.

The second effect of extravagant wage increases on income differentials comes through the effect on prices. Professor Beckerman, in his book on *The Economic Record of the Labour Government, 1964–70*, concludes that while the improved cash benefits provided by the Labour government did reduce inequality, this narrowing of the gaps ceased in 1969–70 because excessive wage demands led to inflation, which in turn reduced the standard of living of the poor and those living on fixed incomes or social security benefits. He concludes that inflation damaged the position of the working class as a whole and that those union leaders responsible for the excessive wage demands are 'either incapable of understanding this or are guilty of cynical betrayal of the interests of their members'.

The point of raising these issues is that if the Labour party has any purpose, whether under 'socialist' or 'social democratic' leadership, a major part of the purpose must be to promote social justice. And it is impossible to have social justice in a society where there are gross inequalities in income and in personal wealth. In other words, one of the fundamental purposes of the Labour party is to reduce inequality. Yet there is irrefutable evidence that to permit free collective bargaining and to encourage inflationary wage demands runs directly counter to this basic objective. Thus a socialist party without an incomes policy is a contradiction in terms.

There is no 'real socialist' country in the world, from Yugoslavia to Sweden, from China to Rumania, that leaves wage bargaining to the free play of the power groups concerned. Those of the populist-socialist left who are prepared to discuss the issue, will feel embarrassed at this point and take refuge in the argument that they are prepared to contemplate an incomes policy, but only when all other social and taxation policies are entirely acceptable. This is a perfect get out, as the condition will never be fulfilled. It is clearly true that a government which was actively taxing the rich and helping to reduce poverty would be more acceptable to the unions, but it is quite another matter to suggest that all unions would voluntarily ask only for non-inflationary increases.

Certain things cannot be denied. The first is that it is the task of trade union leaders to seek the maximum benefit for their members and this may easily exceed the amount which would prevent further price rises and thus safeguard the interests of the weaker sections of the community. Secondly, a socially just policy nowadays may involve taxing the upper groups among the weekly wage-earners to help those who are at the bottom of the scale and this is bound to be unpopular with at least some of those affected. But thirdly, and even more to the point, it is surely wrong to argue that, given a government which redistributes income in a socialist way, this would have enough impact upon rank and file trade unionists to persuade them in all cases to moderate their own demands in such a way as to make a voluntary incomes policy feasible. After all, doctors and school teachers are no less socially responsible than miners or railway workers and most of these professional groups are quite uninterested in or positively opposed to a wealth tax or higher family allowances; and they have been putting in wage claims of the 22 per cent to 30 per cent level. The point is that organised groups seek their own interests and, as such groups have become more powerful in modern societies, there is more and more difficulty in persuading them to consider the well-being either of their class or of the community as a whole, whether or not the government is, in its other policies, pursuing socially equitable policies.

The central defect in the current populist-socialist position is that they will not consider the overall principles involved. They are not far from the position of Enoch Powell who argues that the degree of intervention and paternalism involved in an incomes policy makes it inherently unworkable in a democracy. Powell would regulate total consumption (that is, he would have an incomes policy) by overall control of the money supply and a floating exchange rate. To devalue (or float downwards) is, after all, just a method of cutting everyone's standard of living by putting up prices. But, once again, it is grossly inequitable and it is amazing to find people who regard themselves as being on the left in politics advocating what amounts to a right-wing laissez-faire policy on wages. Yet to refuse to set out criteria for wage increases and to destroy machinery for enforcing such criteria is to admit that there is no way of pressing the case of the weakest, most poorly paid elements in the community.

Another problem for populist-socialism is that, being suspicious of any reservations about working-class demands and of any talk of reconciling interests among workers, there is a tendency among the left to imagine and to say that the answers to current political problems are easy and obvious; that rank and file activists have solutions to policy problems at their finger tips, or rather in their instinctive responses, so that any failures by Labour governments must be due to the pernicious refusal of social democratic leaders to enact these obvious policies. In fact, nothing could be further from the case.

There is, for example, no issue which the Labour party would like to solve more than the present rapid escalation in land prices. The inhibiting factor is not lack of 'socialist will power' but lack of a viable solution. Two solutions have been tried, one being the development charges introduced by the Attlee government and abandoned soon after the Conservatives took office in 1951 and the other being the Land Commission set up by Harold Wilson. Both solutions failed and, at present, no one in the Labour party has produced a workable and equitable alternative. One thing is certain; there is no easy answer, much less one which is obvious to most party members. The same is true of such complex questions as a reduction of regional differentials or the abolition of poverty in a way which neither destroys incentives nor antagonises the section of the working class who are earning incomes which are just above the benefit level.

Negativism

Anti-internationalism marks the populist-socialists, springing in part from the arguments of the anti-marketeers and in part from the mild but definite xenophobia which can easily be aroused among the working class. Yet it is clearly important for the next Labour government to avoid the difficulties which the Wilson administration encountered because it kept trying to operate as a world power capable of standing on its own. It will be necessary to work with the European powers of much the same international standing as Britain to prevent more currency crises, to devise an industrial policy which will allow multinational companies to develop in Europe while keeping them under proper supervision and to see that one country's regional policies do not undercut those of its neighbours. Yet it is still convenient for the left to pretend that cooperation, particularly with the most relevant powers in Europe who are joined in the EEC, is either unnecessary or too geographically restricted, too ineffective or too dangerous to be accepted as a permanent feature of British foreign policy.

A final weakness of the populist-socialist position is its largely negative or conservative character. The almost conscious refusal to think through a socialist answer to the central problems facing Britain, the problems of inflation and a fair incomes policy, has encouraged a tendency to reject all attempts to work out relevant political policies as being middle-class, social democratic, elitist pastimes. A substitute has been found in the slogan that this is the worst Tory government in modern times—a slogan which is not only of dubious truth but one which avoids the real problem that almost all the government's policies have some sensible aspects which any future Labour government would have to retain. To admit this would involve the opposition in producing fair workable alternatives. The activists and far-left groups in some constituency parties and some unions encourage a negative approach, because they call for a blanket rejection of the entire Industrial Relations Act, the entire policy of joining the EEC, the entire Housing Finance

Bill and so on, a policy which would leave the next Labour government committed only to a return to the 1968–70 status quo.

The paradox is that the left, who prided themselves on being the most persistent critics of the last Wilson government, are now in practice working hard to ensure that the next Labour government is as like its predecessor as possible.

It is symptomatic of the curious reversal of roles not only between the parties but inside the Labour party that it is Roy Jenkins and his social democratic supporters who have been rethinking socialist policy in terms of how the next Labour government should tackle poverty, relative deprivation in the cities, the need for increased aid to the underdeveloped countries, and so on. They accept that the Labour party must be a party of change. They also accept that, in a highly complex society, government intervention to diminish class barriers in education or to end homelessness has to be carefully thought out if the desired results are to be obtained. They are prepared to face the reality of Britain's declining position as a nation state and our greater dependence on other countries, facts which mean that to achieve the maximum control of our own affairs, it is necessary to share sovereignty with and thus influence those powers whose policies most closely affect this country. It is also symptomatic that the left have not met these arguments with counter-arguments; they have not developed a policy or a position but have proposed changes in the Labour party's constitution whose practical effect would be to strengthen the power of those external activist groups in the party which in turn would vote for and bolster the position of the left inside the parliamentary Labour party.

The Tribune proposals

The only important pamphlet produced recently by the Tribune Group, or rather by Frank Allaun, Ian Mikardo and Jim Sillars on behalf of the Group (called *Labour: Party or Puppet? Making the Labour Party Fit for Democrats*) does not deal with policy questions but proposes four changes in the party's constitution or procedures. The first is that constituency selection conferences for parliamentary candidates should be narrower groups than at present, delegates only being allowed to attend if they have been present at a certain proportion of management committee meetings over the previous two years. Secondly, there should be no women's section on the National Executive Committee, the five women's places being allocated to the constituency parties (making twelve in all), but the constituency parties would then elect six MPs and six rank-and-file delegates to the NEC. Thirdly, MPs would be expected to 'sign an undertaking to carry out the programme and policy of the party as decided by Conference'. Finally, the leader of the party would be elected not by the parliamentary party but by the annual conference.

Two aspects of these proposals are interesting and reveal the attitudes underlying them. The first is the assumption that there is some kind of gap between the parliamentary Labour party, the bulk of the MPs and 'the real Labour party' in the constituency management committees and among shop stewards and trade union officials. In fact, MPs are usually selected by the biggest and most representative gatherings that ever take place in the constituency parties. Yet this is just what the Tribune pamphlet objects to; it wants to cut out the delegates who represent the large number of party members with broader interests than simply sitting on management committees: these are the people who turn out at elections to do the work, but who have other calls on their time as well as the Labour party between elections. This broader, more representative group of committed party members do such unforgivable things as vote for candidates who are articulate, who have some training in problems of public policy and who can put across a good case from a platform (all qualities, according to the Tribune pamphlets, which are apparently barely desirable in MPs). And this proposal to narrow the group who in fact choose the bulk of MPs is made in the name of democracy! There is the further point that because MPs then have to deal with the community at large, to meet, help and represent non-party members and to put up a case which carries conviction outside the confines of party executive meetings, it is alleged that these MPs somehow become less representative and increasingly out of touch with the mass of Labour voters.

In fact, the situation is the opposite. It is the small group of constant party activists who spend their entire lives inside the party with few other interests or conversation, who become less representative even of the bulk of Labour voters. On the other hand, MPs who have to have widespread contacts and who have to be re-elected, do keep in touch with these wider groups. It is fantastic to suggest that such MPs are less in contact with Labour voters than are trade union leaders who are often elected for life on grounds which have no relation to their knowledge of or capacity to represent the public at large. The second important and revealing aspect of these proposals is the idea that the Labour party and its parliamentary wing should not represent the mass of Labour voters but should be tied tightly to the interests of certain producer groups, namely, the larger unions. In practice, the Tribune Group's proposals would mean that the leader of the party would be chosen not on his capacity as revealed in parliament, but on his ability to meet the demands of a small number of trade union leaders.

The problem of union dominance

As the pamphlet admits, the unions have ten times the votes of the constituency parties at the annual conference and, if they selected the leader and if MPs had to sign promises to follow all conference decisions, this small group of union leaders, in no way responsible to or elected by the public, would determine the entire policy of any Labour government.

The objections to any such idea have to be stressed. First, there is no conceivable democratic defence for the block vote. The block votes of the unions bear no relation to the numbers of committed Labour voters in their ranks; the relationship is solely to the numbers for which the unions choose to pay affiliation fees. Union leaders at their own conferences deal largely with industrial matters and are often left a free hand or are only given broad guidance over political questions. This is why the change from a right-wing general secretary to a left-wing one (probably each elected on the quite different and, in the context, entirely proper grounds of their ability as wage bargainers) can mean that a million votes at the Labour party conference are switched from supporting right-wing resolutions to supporting left-wing ones. Aneurin Bevan, who belonged to the left wing in former days when its chief interest was in specific socialist policies and in campaigning to win over popular support for these political principles, strongly criticised the block vote as anti-democratic.

A second objection is that the conference, because it is union dominated, lays more stress on the interests of producer pressure groups than on the interests of consumers, citizens, taxpayers or the public at large. Yet the task of a parliamentary party is to represent these unorganised elements in the community. The best example is that it would be quite intolerable and contrary to the principles of parliamentary democracy for a Labour government to decide to try and limit inflation by restraining wage increases above a certain level, only to find that some of the unions could, by a majority on the National Executive and at conference, force a Labour Prime Minister to abandon this policy; a policy which had been adopted because it was in the interests of the nation as a whole and especially of the poorer rank-and-file workers. Although there was no such direct reversal of the Wilson government's policies, it is clear that trade union opposition was the main reason for the abandonment of the Prices and Incomes Policy in 1969–70. This led both to the inflation, which was a major cause of the Conservative victory at the polls, and to the redistribution of income away from those dependent on social security benefits and low wages, which undid the tendency to greater equality of incomes achieved by the Labour government between 1964 and 1968.

The real tasks

The task for those Labour party leaders who are labelled social democrats is now clear. They must preach the principles of socialism on which the Labour party was founded and explain the application of these principles to current social, economic and international conditions. This means a primary emphasis on putting the needs of the mass of the community before the interests of those with a monopoly-hold on economic power, be they financiers, multinational corporations or unions controlling key sectors of the labour force. The first task for the Party is to produce a social welfare, taxation and incomes policy which will reduce income gaps and the class system that derives from these gaps. This policy, aimed at eroding the class system, needs to be reinforced by government intervention to remove inequities in education and to end not only homelessness and slums but to prevent the growth of massive one-class estates in our cities. Urban development, with the serious problem of land and house prices, requires elaborate and careful government policies to create reasonable standards for all who live in built-up areas. Public transport and regional policies are needed to remove other forms of inequity. More resources should be devoted to the prevention of pollution and to aiding the underdeveloped world. A social democratic government that has come to terms with Britain's place in the world in the 1970s should pursue international policies designed to maximise our influence in those areas where Britain's interests and security are involved thus maximising our control over our own internal policies. These are objectives which will be achieved by a sharing of control over trade, investment and monetary policies in Europe rather than by the succession of attempts to act on our own followed by periods of being 'blown off course' that marked the last Labour government.

Social democratic policies of this kind must be backed by a renewed emphasis on parliamentary democracy and debate. The current drift to government by sit-in, confrontation and defiance of the law only aids those with special positions of power in the community and is utterly at variance with the social democratic belief that priority goes to those with a just case established by open debate and the process of representative government. As part of this, the Labour party should try to eliminate any position of special power accorded to pressure groups within its own constitution and should give each citizen who joins the Labour party an equal chance of influencing its policies.

If these objectives are not successfully pursued and if the Labour party drifts further towards the position where it has no ideology or idealism, it will become merely the puppet party of those powerful union leaders whose first interest is not socialism or social justice but simply the well-being of the particular groups of weekly wage-earners whom they represent. Then the Party will not only suffer further electoral defeats but it will deserve them.

The Character of a Moderate (Socialist)

BERNARD CRICK

Vol. 47, no. 1, January–March 1976

> *Gilnockie*: Aha, ha. But you *are* ane whoor?
> *Lady*: I'm no *your* whoor.
> From John Arden, *Armstrong's Last Night*.

'MODERATES stand up!', indeed—as Mr Roy Hattersley has just cried.[1] I am a moderate, indeed a rather truculent and aggressive moderate, someone who has always thought that the average citizen should have his sleeves rolled up and his fists lightly clenched, not sit wincing behind this or that newspaper. But I want to say something before I stand up: that I am a moderate *Socialist,* or rather a Socialist who is moderate. I hope I am still with Mr Hattersley, or probably a bit beyond him, keeping my distance but not too far ahead.[2] I am not moderate, however, in the sense that the editor of *The Times*, Mr David Wood, Mr Ronald Butt, Miss Nora Beloff, Mr Robert McKenzie, even, and all in the Liberal Party over the age of 40 are moderate. And Roy Hattersley should beware of the motives of these Greeks when they come bearing gifts, praising him as moderate. They have damaged the repute of Reg Prentice in the Labour Party by this. And when in September *The Times* called Mario Soares a moderate (catching correctly that he believes in parliaments and persuasion, but missing utterly that he wishes to achieve a planned egalitarian society) they drove the editor of *Tribune* into acute dialectical contortions: for Dick Clements seemed to accept that anyone whom *The Times* called moderate is not fit to be thought of as a Socialist.

This silliest usage of 'moderate', however, is simply to mean 'what I approve of'—or as the *Daily Telegraph* editorial writers use it to refer to any *others* whom they can on occasion mildly tolerate. The commonest use is to define an alleged centre of the political spectrum. (I always remember that Arthur Schlesinger Jr once wrote a book called *The Vital Centre*, which seemed to me to be simply dead centre.) This dead-centre-of-the-political-spectrum view soon gets muddied up with talk of coalition (immediately jerking several points to the right all those radicals who are flattered into that premature senility of being 'responsible fellows', that is unresponsive to popular pressures). What would they do with a coalition if they had one? Or 'moderate' can be given the more theoretical-seeming and less practical-politics import of 'consensus'—a belief that we must have 'fundamental values' in common in order to survive. This view is usually advocated by people without any belief in clear values themselves: so probably the moderate-as-consensus-politician needs to reformulate his case to say that other people, that is the People, should hold values in common (like a bit in the mouth of a horse), but that they are not necessary for us, pragmatists all.

Values should restrain (difficult) people, not animate them into positive citizenship.

Modes of moderation

The confusions arise because 'moderate' can be applied either to means or to ends, to goals or to values. And when it refers to substantive goals, it can refer to the centre of the national spectrum or to the centre of the Labour party—a rather different calculation. And when it refers to means or to procedural values (like parliamentarianism, toleration, respect for simple truth, liberty and democracy, not the contortions of ideology), it can treat them simply as means towards many different ends or it can treat them as ends in themselves—which is the most sophisticated argument, the argument that any pursuit of rational and clearly defined goals is ultimately going to prove coercive, so we should best carry on simply managing, administering, politicising, with decency and humanity, not hope for too much, and never treating men as if they could be better, either more altruistic or more rational, than they are.

Now there is much to be said for this view, if we believe in the myth of the Fall, are naturally pessimistic or rationally believe, through reading what Sir Keith Joseph calls 'the noble philosophy of Hayek', that there is little chance of us all bettering our lot in this world of scarce, indeed, diminishing resources, particularly in our British economy of today. I simply want to say that as a moderate and a socialist this is not my view for one. I believe that our society needs to be changed, should be changed and can be changed. But that it can only be changed in desirable directions through time and by what are essentially moderate means. When this has happened, there may be a point at which we can look back and say that there has been a revolution (as for world health or scientific technology, for example), that is both a change in the conditions that shape social and economic arrangements and in human consciousness. But revolution is rarely the most probable means to ensure a good end. Violent revolutions are a response either to the breakdown of government or to intolerable oppression: at best they create the opportunity, which then has to be taken deliberately and carefully, for comprehensive social change. More often revolution can only sensibly be understood as a process and not an event. In other words, moderate but naked and quite unashamed, I am an evolutionary (that is, revolution-through-time) Socialist. Please do not call me moderate at all, though call me tolerant and libertarian (if I deserve it) any day, if this then leads you to believe that I want to maintain the same kind of present society (cleaned up a little) as the centre of the political spectrum both desire and enjoy. Which of us would then have been deceiving the other? And please will the left stop deceiving themselves that socialist legislation without mass support can transform society (at least without an intolerably—and usually self-defeating—degree of coercion); and will they stop calling any who doubt this either backsliders or Fascist beasts?

Ordinary people still need convincing, and convincing freely, that socialist ideals are worth trying, perhaps not necessarily only in alternating electoral spasms, but always in such a way that while advance continues, the possibility of peaceful retreat is never closed. Yet if once ordinary people were convinced, then a democratic socialist regime would have far more power behind it to transform society genuinely than have the imposed socialist regimes of East Europe.

So let me try to restate in its broadest and most commonsensical terms the case for democratic Socialism (to use George Orwell's careful lower and upper case). But is this necessary—when we have had a Labour government for about a decade, with one short interruption?

Lack of thought

They (I mean the leaders of the Labour party) find it hard to think at all (apart from being too busy, except perhaps in August) because of (a) a constitutional debility; and (b) a mistake in logic. The constitutional debility is the castrating or muzzling (as the case may be) of leadership by the doctrine of collective responsibility. No minister may safely state any principles that the Prime Minister might dislike or might feel put himself in the shade, nor apparently produce any evidence which might ruffle the belief of the Sir John Hunts of that world that the least said the better. The Prime Minister himself may break the doctrine (a) by writing his memoirs (which contain no thought in the whole of the book, only a day-to-day celebration of his own cleverness); and (b) by the agreement to differ in the Common Market referendum campaign. But the others may not break it. And civil servants watch that they do not.

The others, it is said, collectively constitute (with a bit of ballast) the most intelligent, certainly the most highly educated, Cabinet in British political history; and yet they cannot talk freely and speculate publicly about the aims of political activity. They may only, by permission, defend set positions. Only the briefest and most enigmatic signals are allowed of what their basic beliefs and working theories may be. Whatever one thinks of Tony Crosland's general views or of those of Tony Benn (and I am a very tolerant moderate who can see the intense plausibility of both), there is no doubt that each of them would be more influential if out of government, perhaps even out of the House. The pen is mightier than the mace. We do not lack good administrators: we lack thinkers with an empathy towards real, ordinary people; and we lack sufficient politicians with integrity and almost any with a clear sense of purpose—or if they have it, we can only surmise it by occasional discordant phrases cutting across cautious department briefs, or by knowledge of what they said before they went silent and underground in high office.

The mistake in logic is, however, an even more important factor in explaining why a Labour government which has had the lion's share of power for the last decade yet lacks any publicly comprehensible sense of direction. 'Pragmatism' is believed to be a thing that wins elections (but only just, it seems). Pragmatism apparently means being practical, or vulgarly that 'truth is what works': the pseudo-philosophy of the careerist or of the manager of a going concern (and if it is not 'going', then not to question if one is in the right trade or working in the best way, but to borrow more and to pray for more oil). The fallacy of pragmatism is that it can only work within a known and accepted context of moral habits, beliefs and principles. It is not self-validating. To be 'purely practical', even, assumes that there are under-lying values which are known, shared and understood. If there is no such consensus, then pragmatism is fraudulent—both in the sense of being self-deceiving and of being imposed on others, itself masking an ideology while pretending only to mirror public opinion. The question may indeed be one, as the Archbishop has remarked, of basic values; but whose values and what values? It may not be a problem of the decay of 'good old values' (of competitiveness and individualism?), but of changing values—a search for more fraternity and sociability.

The pragmatist in a changing world is likely to make great mistakes by attempting, for all his hyperactivity, to conserve the unconservable. Pragmat-ists wasted our national resources by trying, like Alice, to run very fast to stay put in one moving place: the hanging on to 'East of Suez' for so long after there was anything to defend; the defence of the pound in the late 1960s; the belief in a free market for wages amid falling productivity; and the eco-nomically crippling belief that houses and jobs should be brought to people and all movements of population, as far as possible, frozen.

The pragmatic politician's contempt for doctrine is almost as misleading as the journalist's habitual attempt to reduce every idea to a personal interest. Journalists often say that the public will only grasp issues if they are personalised, but more often they themselves believe —as the daily quest for novelty amid long-term problems conditions them to believe—that personal factors predominate. So deep is this contempt for ideas and resulting ignorance about them that it is leading people to call almost any manifestation of real socialist thought 'Marxist'—as if the tradition of the Webbs, Cole, Tawney and Laski had never existed. Indeed, the genuine Marxists of the book had better watch out, for the very word is shifting its colloquial meaning to refer to anyone who believes in Liberty, Equality, Fraternity.

I am not a Marxist. I hold the amiable view that on some things that very great man was profound and right, on others wrong and that on still more issues he was so overgeneralised and abstract as to be virtually meaningless. If Marxism is a 'growing method', then it may just become another word for socialism. If Michael Foot is persistently called a Marxist by the right wing press (moderates?), he will end up by believing that, after all (all those long battles with his friends Bevan and Orwell against the Communist Marxists), he really is one. I do not much care. One can be a good man without being a follower of Christ, and a good democratic Socialist with or without the blessing of the censorious pedantic priests of Marxism. But I do care intensely for the theory and spirit of Enlightenment and of the French Revolution: that mankind will progress by applying reason to the ideals of liberty, equality and fraternity. Yet revolution is to be seen as a long and deliberate process of government and popular education and persuasion, not as a dramatic single event. And I am angry when non-Marxist social democrats refuse to argue with Marxists and take refuge behind a shallow technological scepticism about the importance of ideas at all—just as angry as when quests for doctrinal purity disallow any practical political action.

Socialism implies reason and example from both leaders and followers— not secrecy and perpetual personal exceptions. (That a *Labour* government could prosecute publishers of a book by a colleague and that a *Labour* government should flinch at limiting high incomes!) But a practical socialism means an intelligent appreciation of the different demands of the short-run and the long-run factors, the pursuit of neither without the other and also a tolerant recognition that a socialist party must act on different levels simultaneously. Great changes need more planning and time than do immediate responses to short-term problems. If it has been decided to rehouse the area completely in ten years' time, the ancillary services can be prepared; but in the meantime redecoration and repairs must continue, especially if the roof is blown off by one of those intercontinental storms really beyond the control of any government.

The right wing of the Labour party is in danger of making a cult of pragmatism and of realism not as means to ends, but as ends in them-selves—an hermaphrodite chasing its own tail. The left wing is in danger of forsaking political means to their ends, which is, in fact, recurrently destruc-tive of these ends—a phoenix far too frequent. Too many right wingers have become, indeed, simply careerist smoothies. Too many left wingers have simply retreated into sectarian fanaticism rather than face the lapsed, but perpetual and necessary, task of converting the public to socialist principles.

What is the common core of all types of genuine socialism? Basically it is both a theory and a doctrine. The theory is that the rise and fall of societies is best explained not by the experience of cleverness of elites (Conservatism), nor by the initiative and invention of individuals (Liberalism), but by the social relationships of the primary producers of wealth—in an industrial society, the skilled manual worker. The doctrine is that a greater equality will lead to more cooperation rather than competition, and that this will enhance fraternity and thus liberate from inhibition and restriction both individual personality and the productive potential of a society.

In the 1930s the Labour party had a bad spell when it wanted both to fight fascism and to disarm. We have recently been in a bad spell when we wanted both to maintain free collective bargaining and to obtain social justice for all. This may only have been a temporary aberration. Socialism began and rests on the belief that a free market in wages leads both to intolerable injustice and to a limitation both of productive and of human potential. But the message still has to be got across. A resolute socialist programme would still lose votes.

So if the politics of self-interest is not working and if people are plainly fed up with the ping-pong party electoral battle of 'Who's the better manager of the shop?', let us explore (if only for a New Year's Resolution) what a realistic and immediately relevant democratic socialist argument would be in terms likely to convince the unconvinced, not just the dwindling and thus somewhat touchy party faithful. Let us have a little less on programmes and manifestos and a little more on principles and long-term objectives.

Principles and directions

So I want to consider what a democratic Socialist (to use again Orwell's careful emphasis, the adjective distinguished from the noun, the means from the end) or a moderate Socialist (that is moderate about means, but not necessarily about ends) should be doing to develop his three basic values of liberty, equality and fraternity. I say 'develop', not work towards 'the goal', because values are not a kind of distant beacon that one day we may reach, thereupon rest, and in the meantime ignore: they are constant companions (if often quarrelsome among themselves and of varying influence upon oneself) on a journey which, while it progresses, yet never ceases. And this journey is governed not by some predetermined selection of an arbitrary point on a dubious map, but simply by agreement about a general sense of direction and how to behave towards each other on the way. Strictly speaking our goals are specifically socialist, but our values are not all specifically socialist—they include such values, good and common values, as truth, freedom, tolerance and fairness, none of which rules out our goals, but all of which may affect the means towards these goals.

Is any sense of direction realistic, however? Before a moderate socialist charges he wants (a) some idea of where he is going; and (b) some hope of being followed. Cromwell once remarked that an army never goeth so far as when it knows not where it is going. And there is an argument against any such politics of purpose at all. Is not the best any government can do simply to keep the ship afloat—as Oakeshott has taught (and Wilson is more the Oakeshott figure of a statesman than ever a Heath or a Thatcher)? The actual Labour party is, indeed, to be understood historically as a coalition of interests, primarily the wage-politics of trade unions, and any specifically socialist influence has been at the best marginal. Certainly it is untrue that once upon a time, in the days of the banners and the brass bands, it was socialist; and that it has fallen away by treachery, careerism and parliamentary nice-Nellyism. The myth of the Fall is poor history. There is no need to be a bad historian to be a good socialist. Look for socialism in the future of the Labour party, not in the past. For socialism is not a movement; it is a theory which sees the key to social progress in the character of the skilled working man's relations to the factors of production. The Labour party may not be socialist, but socialism may be more illuminating of its dilemmas and more useful in giving it self-respect and a sense of direction than the non-theory or the 'pragmatism' of the leaders of the moment.

The dilemmas of the Labour party, loss of membership, loss of support, loss of heart, increasing internal intolerance, may arise not from the lack of realism of its leaders but from their lack of theory and doctrine. Realism and pragmatism must be about something, they cannot feed of themselves; and plainly the customs and habits of the past are failing lamentably. Pragmatism, at the moment, is only concerned with how to keep the party in power. Reducing politics to that level, the electorate will simply judge in terms of immediate management of conventional values, self-interest and prosperity. And since no one can fully control the weather, not even Harold Wilson or Margaret Thatcher, each government will in turn, in these hard times for our country, be judged to have failed: so periods of alternating power will follow, rendering almost impossible any fundamental changes—which is just what opponents of adversary politics seem to want. Doctrine and publicly argued principles must be replenished and revivified if only to break from this truly liberal, capitalist, utilitarian vicious circle. Such doctrines must be realistic as well as heart-felt and clear—and the more heart-felt they are, the more one can compromise in the short run without destroying long-term hopes and integrity.

Socialist ideals are not to be restored; they are yet to be adopted. As one of the founding fathers wrote in 1911 in a once-famous Home University Library book, *The Socialist Movement*:

The Labour Party is not Socialist. It is a union of Socialist and trade union bodies for immediate political work. . . . But it is the only political form which evolutionary Socialism can take in a country with the political traditions and methods of Great Britain. Under British conditions, a Socialist Party is the last, not the first, form of the Socialist movement in politics.

Hardly strengthening my case to quote Ramsay MacDonald. But if he did not last the course himself, back then he happened to be right. Short-run realism and long-run idealism (plus middle-term planning) do not exclude or contradict each other: they complement each other. Even our short-run factors need not be a retreat from Socialism (as cuts in public expenditure are seen) but could be made a prelude to a more socialist system of rewards. A declining economy in crisis may yet produce strident calls for an equality-fraternity of sacrifice. Such a siege-socialism could prove social fascism, unless we look to our liberties too. But even given the opportunity, the worst of conditions and the best of motives, am I too not falling into the trap of advocating something that would hearten the faithful and lose the elections? What will it benefit a politician if he finds his own soul and loses the whole world? We are indeed fed up with the pharisaism and self-indulgent purity of so much left wing sectarian thought. But I am not arguing against their ideals, only against their believing that they can achieve them all at once or not at all. We have all been talking to each other in the Labour movement too long if we cannot see that long before the public will ever want nuances of socialist principle, they are right now very hungry for almost any kind of principles in politics. So great dangers as well as opportunities appear. Some sense of integrity, some sense of movement, some sense of common purposes and fraternity, some lessening of injustices in rewards—never mind quite precisely what—is what the public seems hungry for at this very time. The public seem to thirst for something positive, but all they get is people knocking on the doors with questionnaires asking them what policies they want their leaders to lead them with—some leaders! The present leader of the Labour Party seems like an ignorant nurse who believes that constant application of a thermometer will lower the patient's temperature.

Liberty

Leaders should just try what they believe in and find out if it is popular. But the manner in which socialist leaders try and in which they find out should be distinctively open, participative and subject to correction. The one easily recognisable mark of a democratic Socialist movement should be its almost fanatic commitment to more liberty and openness. The means are not the ends but they can make or break the ends. And even Rosa Luxemburg said of Lenin, a socialism that does not proceed through freedom becomes oppression. All talk of 'socialist liberty', as if it were different in kind from any other, is dangerous nonsense, often deliberate obfuscation. Far-away thoughts? I am no longer sure when one thinks of students howling down Sir Keith Joseph; or of campus bookshop assistants refusing to stock, order or handle books hostile to what they judge to be 'the student' cause.

More immediately, official talk of 'open government' is rhetorical nonsense when it goes with the maintenance of traditional, conservative controls over publicity: the belief of all autocracies and autocrats that government cannot work well if the reasons why decisions are made can be publicly known. In fact, there is a kind of British half-autocracy: Tony, Alan, Bernard, John, Robin, David, Peter and the statutory woman could have always read—and did—Crossman's Diaries without the Attorney-General or a High Court Judge's permission; but not the rest of you. And all schoolkids in the country can be taught that the ombudsman is a 'good thing'—they and their teachers seem captivated by him—but the government could reply to his criticisms last year of Mr Benn and Mr Shore not with honest and beguiling admissions, nor with reasoned rebuttals, but with the ignorant and ignoring contempt that seems to possess modern governments with even the slenderest of mere parliamentary majorities. And the government damps down the Poulson inquiries. And the Labour Party National Executive refused even a party inquiry into the affairs of the NE England Labour Party. Have we come all the way for this?

The right wing think that they can pick and choose what liberties to adopt, in their own interests—sound on Clay Cross, but hostile to workers' control:

very few are libertarians at heart. But those of the left wing who are libertarians at heart often get themselves trapped in bad Marxist logic: that only in the classless society after the revolution can there be true liberty—until then all we have is an instrumental 'bourgeois liberty' or an 'oppressive tolerance'. (Therefore no holds barred in your own strategies, but tactical howls of 'liberty in danger' every time the law comes near you.) But active liberty has a long history, and it was bourgeois in its origins. The fault is not in its paternity but in its prudishness. Liberty is all very well for the likes of us, but impossible *en masse*, for all of them. But we must be promiscuous in liberty if we have any faith in reason and human nature. 'The liberal bourgeois is genuinely liberal', said Orwell, 'up to the point where his own interests stop.'

What we must do is constantly to try to persuade people that their idea of self-interest is self-defeatingly narrow; and that ideals widen our horizon into the future, particularly our children's future. 'Do you want *them* to grow up into a world like *this*?' is the strongest practical socialist idealism. It is not so much that the impractical of today can be practical tomorrow, but that in the modern world the practical of today is always the impractical of tomorrow.

Socialist liberty is no different from liberal liberty, except that there is more of it for all: a humanistic faith that ordinary working people have to be drawn into participation and decision-making too, and not just in leisure time but in working life. Of course an incomes policy under Socialism, but ultimately a voluntary one—how else? How else, that is, without ever greater centralised controls and oppression in fewer and fewer hands. If from political democracy we cannot also create economic, industrial and occupational democracy, then we drift towards a 1984 kind of society—though more likely to be one, as Tocqueville imagined, in which the elite dole out welfare rather than privation; so long as they can make the decisions, the masses can have everything possible given to them, except freedom.

If socialist liberty does differ from liberal liberty in one respect, it is in that it goes back, like the men of the French Revolution, to a classical or Roman concept of liberty more than a *laissez-faire* one: not just being left free by the state, which is often to be left high and dry; but that each man and woman should exercise freedom aggressively. A state is neither as strong nor as just as it can be if its inhabitants do not act like citizens—nor is a union, a firm or a school. Citizenship and liberty is enhanced by example and by multiplying participative institutions in all spheres. We could stop short of 'extremist' Socialism and yet make some public stir about that. But what a long way from the practical policies of our great leader's fourth administration.

Equality

Equality is a value basic to any possible kind of socialism. Without a real desire to achieve an egalitarian society, any democratic Socialist movement loses its dynamic and lapses back into the alternating ping-pong politics of the

'I'm a better manager of the shop than Fred' kind (whatever trash the shop is selling, however badly built it is). But the concept has its difficulties. Literal equality, whether of opportunity, treatment or result (or of all three), is almost as undesirable as it is plainly impossible. But an egalitarian society is both possible and desirable. By an egalitarian society I mean a classless society, one in which every man would see every other man as a brother, a genuinely fraternal society with no conceit or constraint of class to limit fraternity. But it would not be a society in which everyone was exactly equal in power, status, wealth and ability, still less in humane end-products of happiness.

No difficulties about the concept are, however, so great as to warrant abandoning it or treating it as pure ritual of the Labour church—unless one wants to abandon it. One difficulty is that we want, rhetorically, to make something sound positive which is, intellectually, at heart a negative matter. There is no 'complete equality' which can 'finally be realised', unless genetic engineering was to come to the aid of economic planning (with about equal accuracy and predictability, one would hope). But there are so many unjustifiable inequalities—not just in theory but so flagrantly in practice. The boot should be worn on that foot. If we believe in the moral equality or the fraternity of all mankind, then all inequalities of power, status and wealth need explaining and justifying. They can be justified (here I follow Rawls and Runciman) only if these inequalities can be shown to be of positive advantage to the less advantaged. Some inequalities can be justified, more not — particularly if one adds the vital condition of liberty, actually to ask the disadvantaged. No precise agreement can ever be reached or, if so, for no more than a transitory time and a particular place. Nor can philosophy supply incontrovertible criteria for what is an unjustifiable inequality. But in an egalitarian society *all* inequalities will be called into question, constantly questioned and criticised: they will have to be justified precisely and for themselves; not as an acceptable, general side-product of status or power.

'Less Unjustifiable Inequalities!' may not be a slogan that warms the blood like wine, but that is as well. For there are other values to be preserved, which is always the difficulty. No one value, be it liberty, equality, fraternity, love, reason, even life itself, can at all times override all the others or be sure never to contradict them. Equality could certainly be maximised in a totalitarian society—but only at the expense of liberty so that genuine fraternity is destroyed. The Socialist, having a theory of society, looks at values together, in their social setting and in relation to each other. He no more postpones liberty *until* the classless society than he reserves egalitarian and fraternal behaviour and example *until* the classless society. If he does, he will not get there; and when he does, classlessness by itself will not have solved all problems and removed all possibilities of tyranny.

The moderate socialist as egalitarian should not get drawn into the parody argument of exact equality of income and wealth: that is somebody else's nightmare not his dream. Literal minded distributive socialism is very hard to find—since the time of the Gracchi at least. 'Soak the fat boys and spread it thin' may be good rhetoric, but most people know how thin it would be. Industrial relations are not as bad as they are because the men on the shop floor believe that the cow can make milk without grass or that 'vast profits' are there to be distributed to our direct advantage—about 6p a week more all round, once and for all, on Friday and bust by Monday—but they are bad because men think that it is *unfair* that they should be restrained while their bosses actually write to tell newspapers that in their cases incentives to do better do not begin until about £15,000 a year; and that they have no real incentive to work anyway if their children or the cats' homes cannot freely inherit all their wealth. Workers, oddly, use their eyes and see how much patriotic restraint is practised by those who at least look like ruling classes. They see clearly the gross extravagance of Ascot, of the West End and of the fashionable residential areas. (Photographs of such should be forbidden— they do far more harm 'our civilisation' than do those pictures of which Lord Longford complains and blames.) And working men do not miss the claim of top civil servants that their salaries should be competitive with industry (as if they, too, shared the Marxist–capitalist view of the exclusive importance of economic motivation), and should be inflation proof even, on top of a non-contributory pension. What servants of the state! What example! *Quis custodet custodes*, indeed. Nothing better illustrates the decline of the traditional restraints of the cult of the gentlemen and the growth of the moral standards of the speculators and developers.

Equality is, then, a demand for equal justice not for proportional distribution, But the parody is sometimes accepted, perhaps because some Labour leaders begin to have doubts, from the company they keep, as to the potential popularity of the ideal at all. Most people, they feel, want no more than equality of opportunity; and only then if they are among the disadvantaged in 'the great game', to transfer Kipling's phrase to the happy world of Keith Joseph. This destruction of socialist morals and morale earns newspaper praise as 'realism' or 'pragmatism'. Here the moderate socialist parts company with many right wing Labour MPs.

True, ordinary people will commonly get no further than 'equality of opportunity', if you put the question to them in such an abstract and general way. But suppose you ask them if they think it right that the top 20 per cent of incomes (before tax) had seven times greater a share in the total income than the bottom 20 per cent? Or (findings of the recent Royal Commission on the Distribution of Income and Wealth) that 67 per cent of the personal wealth in the country is possessed by the top 10 per cent? The answer may then differ. And answers will certainly differ in terms of perceptions of the justice or not of particular rewards and relativities. Here is an incredibly undeveloped area of liberty and openness. We are so full of taboos about disclosing incomes, even though civil servants and teachers are among obvious exceptions. Suppose all incomes were disclosed. Suppose it was a constant topic of debate in the mass media: 'Here's what this man or woman does, here's what they do, here's what they get. Is it fair?' If this happened, justifications for differences would have to be produced and discussed seriously—not as easy, however, as to knock the miners for their muscle tactics, or praise them for their temporary restraint, or to knock MPs for the crass folly of the timing of their own pay award last year.

Amid full openness, many differences and some injustices would remain. Surveys show that many unskilled and poorly paid people seem to believe that almost no salary is too high for the greedy medical consultants—so socialised have we all been about the long and worthy tribulations (investment) of medical education. (Do not let them leave the country, I say, unless they pay it back.) But it is likely that genuine knowledge, publicity and debate would help to raise the floor and bring down the ceiling. By itself it could not create an egalitarian society, but it would be a condition for it. There would emerge, whatever the justifications for particular inequalities and relativities, a public view of a minimum and a maximum income. An incomes policy would be acceptable if it was, thus, a genuinely socialist one; establishing what range of differentiation is tolerable to an informed majority.

Are there still some primitives who think that any income differentials are contrary to socialist principles? If there are, they are less in number, I suspect, than the hypocrites and careerists who can always find some reason for a Labour government not to enforce some fairly modest, middle middle-class income as a maximum income.

If socialism means anything, the theory is that with greater equality there can be greater fraternity, hence greater cooperation, hence greater productivity—since wealth basically comes from the worker. The record of British management of late hardly impresses one with the claim that only ever-continuing economic incentives lead to efficient management. Power and status count for a lot and so does having a clear and worthwhile job. Real managers like to produce, but the English upper middle class now prefer the City to industry. Their kind of mentality led even a Labour government to leave 'the white-hot heat of the technological revolution' for the paper battle of saving the pound. (The class of men who would do it better and do it for less are from the foremen, the junior managers, the technical teachers, that borderland between the old skilled workers and the old lower middle class, so many of whose sons and daughters are now, in beliefs and behaviour, so unexpectedly but clearly if precariously classless.)

So much scope for action remains in the direction of greater equality: not to be represented or misrepresented as levelling but rather as a constant, aggressive questioning of the reasons for and the justifications of both existing distribution of incomes and wealth and existing divisions of responsibility between 'workers' and 'management'. Such questioning could prove as popular as it is right. More important for socialism than abstract arguments about formal ownership is progress towards taking all wages and incomes out of the market and determining them by representative arbitration and open comparison of relativities. The media, even now, could give a lead in popularising knowledge of differences between jobs and of different incomes.

People are surely fascinated by this. And public policy should work towards complete openness of all incomes. Many differences can be justified. But they must be. We need to develop this as a whole new branch of applied social philosophy rather than of traditional economics. If we had shown one half of the energy in this direction that we have shown in educational policies, an egalitarian society would be appreciably nearer. Indeed, we must beware that, perhaps mainly out of frustration with national economic policies, we do not hope for too much from mere education nor drop out, as it were, from political economy into a fantasy of the comprehensive school as a model of the Socialist commonwealth. Especially in education we should not confuse literal equality of treatment with true egalitarianism. For true egalitarianism is no more—but no less—than the removal of unjustifiable inequalities; and it is a necessary condition, but not a sufficient condition, for fraternity.

Fraternity

To appeal for more fraternity and less fratricide within the Labour movement needs a thick skin as well as a clear head. The Labour movement used to be proud of exhibiting within itself the very fraternity it wished to create in society as a whole, but of late brother seems more eager to revile brother and sister sister than to argue with opponents and to seek to persuade the vast majority of the unconvinced.

Any advance towards a Socialist Britain needs, first, more democracy; a greater opening up to popular influence and knowledge of all the institutions that shape our lives—'liberty'. Secondly, it requires a constant public demand for justification (if any) of each particular inequality of reward, together with gradual but systematic and determined action to reduce those inequalities— not equality but 'egalitarianism'. But, thirdly, it requires an attitude of mind, a morality, a psychology, which gives equal respect and care to everyone, irrespective of class, kin, race, religion, office, talent or learning—'fraternity'. Our preachers should say: 'And now abideth liberty, equality, fraternity, these three; but the greatest of these is fraternity . . .'

Equality of respect does not, however, imply either—as Runciman puts it— 'equality of praise' or the confusion of sincerity with truth. Is it rational to treat all opinions as equal? And is it brotherly to treat all people as one would ideally have them rather than as they themselves are? Big brotherly, perhaps. But fraternity is treating all men as ends and not means, not just all societies. It does not mean treating everybody the same but according to their different personalities and needs; and it means reconciling conflicts by mutually acceptable, public political institutions.

An enforced equality is the destruction of brotherhood—the dark warning of Orwell's 1984. Fraternity can, indeed, exist amid great inequality, but only in times of emergency: the comradeship of the trenches, the Dunkirk spirit, and 'the years of struggle' of both left wing and right wing political movements. But a fraternity for everyday wear in all seasons is hardly imaginable amid great inequalities which limit common purposes. Doing things together for ourselves in common enhances fraternity—unlike having equal welfare given to us which, if personal involvement is lacking, too often creates jealousies rather than comradeship. Economic controls by themselves can never guarantee a more fraternal society. Simple arithmetical equality could create even fiercer competition. We must not oversociologise. Social conditions can help or hinder but they can neither guarantee the consumption of fraternity—nor even ensure its destruction. Fraternity is an ethic that can and should be chosen and pursued freely. It goes with simplicity, lack of ostentation, friendliness, helpfulness, kindliness and restraint between individuals, not just with the fierce memories of the great occasions, the times of struggle or the Sunday 'socialism' of Saturday afternoon demos.

Fraternity does not mean no leadership; it only means no permanent class of leaders tomorrow and no *noblesse oblige* today—no condescension, no giving favours, but rather receiving trust on account of peculiar skills of both empathy and action in helping common and commonly defined purposes. In Beethoven's *Fidelio* the king hails all men as his brothers. But the power and arrogance of a king or a modern leader who thinks that he had such a gift to bestow will of itself negate the brotherhood. Even Edmund Burke said that it is hard to argue on one's knees. Some still try. The boss in a small firm or office who drinks with the men and chats with the girls is only being matey, perhaps even condescending or politic, but not genuinely fraternal unless he seeks for their opinions and takes them seriously about how things should be run.

Nor does fraternity imply the necessity of pseudo-proletarian behaviour. Society is not altered as quickly as a change of costume on a bare stage. The oldest blue jeans will now attempt to hide the newest wealth. But that leaders of working-class parties are commonly bourgeois is neither surprising nor reprehensible. For bourgeois culture stresses individualistic skills of initiative, while working-class culture, in response to exploitation and oppression, stresses solidarity. The culture of the classless society is, indeed, more likely to be bourgeois in the best sense than proletarian. It will encourage and respect individual skills, talents, personality, character; not a new iron mould of conformity, however better than the one that went before. The virtue of class solidarity was an adaptation to class injustice and would become regressive if ever class differentiation vanishes to the point of irrelevance. So the cultural ideals of a democratic socialist movement must be more than the revival of a few folk songs and dialects: amid the new we should sift, refine, adapt, but offer the best of the old to all. And that best includes the moral seriousness of the puritan tradition of individualism as found in Lawrence and in Orwell, neither the purely acquisitive, competitive individualism of capitalism nor the indulgent, permissive, irresponsible individualism of anarchic socialism. Seriousness tempers personality into sociability.

BERNARD CRICK

Fraternity must begin at home but be extended to the workplace. It is not simply a luxury for schools or an indulgence for radical teachers. Indeed, beware of overstating the relevance of education to achieving an egalitarian and fraternal society. Far from being the spearhead of Socialist advance, as some hope and others fear, schools may be in danger of becoming the last refuge of noble and frustrated Socialist minds, baffled at the seeming uncontrollability of the national economy or of their national leadership. Beware of hoping for too much from schools and of overburdening them with the type of concern for 'character education' we all once attacked—not just because it was the wrong kind of character.

As I wrote the original articles on which this essay is based as serial parts in the *New Statesman* last August, correspondence almost entirely concentrated on the fact that I had admitted openly in a newspaper to sending my sons to a private school. My difficulty was (and still is) that I just do not see the issue as that important compared to gross inequalities of income and housing. State education is not yet a necessary shibboleth of Socialism. As a scholar, I have scholarly values. Some comprehensive schools do, some do not. Amid conflicting values, I make a local choice. I assume that scholarship is among the permitted range of human choices which will be found in a democratic Socialist society. But my generous critics seem to admit only one possible kind of motive in wanting such an education, that of social advance. Their sociology tells them that there is only one real reason for going to public schools; mine tells me that, in any case, the home is more important socially than the school. Fellow socialists seem more worried at individual cash choices involving education than about those involving housing. I am simply not as sure as my critics why, within the higher minimum income and the lower maximum income which I advocate as a socialist wages policy and as our first priority for action, some such choices are thought legitimate, some not; they would matter less if we had such a programme.

I am more worried at the educational fashion for 'mixed ability groups' right down the line in LEA schools. In some subjects the state sector is now almost doomed to inferiority. We may have got the worst of both worlds by leaving the private sector free but seeking to abolish the direct-grant grammar schools. I would hesitate long, however, in the name of liberty before abolishing the private sector in the name of equality until the public sector returns to the original ideal of the comprehensive school: that under one roof pupils would be treated differently according to their different abilities in different subjects or different skills, but never all in the same class for everything, never treated *en masse*. The doctrine of 'mixed ability' classes is either a bad confusion between literal equality and egalitarianism, or more likely a rationalisation of despair at having too few teachers and too many children to make the old ideal of 'to each according to his abilities' work. Knowledge can be used for social status, but limiting access to knowledge will not create equality of status. Do not destroy anything unless there is some-thing better to put in its place, and do not let us destroy education as we destroy privilege. My socialist ideal is a common educational system; but my moderation makes me see this as coming through time and through infinite gradations of different forms of both control and content in education, not through expropriation and proscription. These points are worth labouring because they touch on liberty as well as equality in a way difficult for many Socialists.

The state system has its problems too. Perhaps it is sometimes justifiable to bus children against their will away from their neighbourhood to satisfy intelligence-quotient planning. But at least recognise that 'community' suffers, which is also a great Socialist value (we may be making the same mistake as in the new towns policy and the high-rise flats); and recognise that no one knows if the policy of an initial equal distribution leads to a less discriminatory final result overall than would positive discrimination in the supply of teachers and resources for the less-favoured schools.

Of course, if all housing were state-owned and equitably distributed and if all environments were made equal. . . .

What we do know is that social stratification is still acute inside schools, not surprisingly, for the evidence is strong that schools have little effect on basic values and behaviour patterns compared to the influence of home, the media and society at large. Educational systems work badly, it is good to know, as vehicles for deliberate indoctrination, whether of the Rhodes Boyson and Ronald Butt variety or of the Revolutionary Socialist kind. Most guff is like unto water off a duck's back. Pupils react sceptically against any such abuse or extension of authority. But the schools work better at developing skills to understand the world: they are rather unlikely instruments to change it. If one wants an egalitarian educational system, first we must change society.

Let us get our priorities right. Fraternity is not something to be thrust on kids as a sacred episode before they are pitchforked into the real industrial word; it is something that has to be applied in the real industrial world. And fraternity is more concerned with individuality than is literal equality: but it is always endangered or frustrated by gross inequalities of power, wealth or status. Certainly education is among these inequalities. But as we are now and will be for some decades at least, once we leave the classroom or the ward meeting, the illusion is over. In the real world, however, there is vast scope for making far more of what is there already—the expertise and experience of the man who knows the job and who cares for the persons and views of his colleagues or workmates. Fraternity is simply taking common sense and common concern seriously.

The second chance

The long summer of national power, prosperity and self-conceit is nearly over and socialists in the Labour Party must face the fact that in times of relative ease we have failed; but that during a winter of crisis we may be given a second chance. (The first chance was squandered from 1945 to 1950.) We have failed not merely through failures of governments to use their power in socialist directions, but more basically through a failure in the days of affluence of the Labour movement itself to persuade an effective majority of the electorate that we should build a better Britain, not just on occasion manage the shop better. Our declining share of the vote (39.2 per cent in October 1974) is a pitiful basis for radical and freely willed social change. Individual membership of the party, even, continues to decline (probably now no more than a quarter of a million compared to a million in 1953)—despite the help of all those Reds whom Miss Beloff finds under other people's beds. The party now is too small either to reflect public opinion or to be able to influence it.

A genuinely socialist society needs the resolute use of centralised power, but that power is itself powerless, in any modern industrial society, unless it can carry with it popular support. And such support must be found both in the grass roots and in all those groups in which we work or spend our leisure, where our opinions do count (somewhat) and in which our opinions are influenced (somewhat) by our fellows. Only in war did we achieve a unity of purpose, great productive efficiency and (for a brief and memorable moment) a sense of fraternity. Yes, indeed, a fraternity that largely depended on external threat: none the less, it was on the home front between 1940 and 1945 that both the need and the practicality of a welfare state were proved. 'Equity of sacrifice' and 'Fair shares for all' became, instead of competitive individualism, both the official ideology of work and popular belief and behaviour.

We could be close to such a situation again. 'Equality of sacrifice' may be both a national need and a genuinely popular slogan. Perhaps it was always unlikely that the average person would be converted to socialism in relatively affluent times. Socialism does not aim at austerity, but it becomes plausible (particularly its value of fraternity), the idealistic suddenly appears practical, indeed necessary, in times of enforced austerity. Perhaps Socialism is, at heart, a prophecy of what could happen if the capitalist economy breaks down, rather than a safe prediction that it will. But while the free market in wages may not yet be quite beyond repair, its defects have proved so strong, both in terms of uncertainty and injustice, that many could now be persuaded that it is not worth repairing. A more planned and egalitarian society, albeit one hungry for and jealous of liberty, will avoid these savage oscillations of prosperity and depression which marked and marred classical capitalism and which now threaten even that minimal certainty of expectations on which the mental health of societies, as well as individuals, depends.

Ordinary working people cannot be expected to practise self-restraint and to suffer or to watch mass unemployment grow while businessmen and top civil servants enjoy huge salaries and the perquisites of office far beyond even middle-class standards; such luxury amid deprivation is not merely indecent and immoral, it grows politically untenable. If governing elites still wish to govern, they must set an example in the patriotism, public spirit and austerity that they preach to others, not themselves get in first in the endless claims for socially useless personal material advantage. The wiser of those new right-wing intellectuals of free-market liberalism see the difficulty and preach the need for restraint and example to the businessmen. But without sanctions they could save their breath to cool their porridge: they become either naive or hypocritical.

So an egalitarian incomes policy, setting a national maximum and minimum and establishing public machinery to arbitrate relativities between severe limits, should be Labour's policy for the crisis, and the greatest step forward ever towards democratic Socialism. Such arbitration would not be the bureaucratic imposition of 'objective' criteria, but rather publicity for and public discussion of what other people do and get. The object is to establish what people *think* to be fair and will accept as fair, to educate us all in making genuine comparisons, not to pretend that full objective criteria are possible, either of national need or of job specification. Such factors of job evaluation and of statistical evaluations of differentials are highly relevant, but not decisive; a greater sense of fairness is the greatest need. Complete openness about incomes and wealth and constant public debate would create the voluntary basis to emerge for an enforceable consensus on outer limits. And with lower and upper limits there could be a vast simplification of tax and welfare structures. Within such limits, market forces would work; prices can only reflect what people actually want to buy and sell.

A Socialist incomes policy calls for a left and centre alliance in the Labour party. As a moderate Socialist I find *Tribune* too wild and woolly and the Social Democratic alliance too class-conscious and complacent. The Left at last begins to emerge from the temporary delusion that a free market for wages and the industrial power of a few unions on behalf of their own members can lead towards social justice, or that prices can be controlled when we live by export and import. The left and the unions will accept incomes policy only if it strikes hard at high incomes and in this they are both just and sensible. The right of the party would regard this as impractical. Their version of incomes policy has only been aimed at the unions; and they have for long indeed abandoned any talk of Socialism—except for party workers at weekends—in favour of a kind of John F. Kennedy Democratic Party fantasy complex or complex fantasy.

Some of the right would actually prefer to do without the party at all and appeal directly to the electorate, rather as some of the left, for all their rhetoric of 'the people' (remember the Referendum) would prefer to do without the electorate (or elect another one). The centre of the Labour party is still warmly but rather vaguely socialist, but has, of late, either been too absorbed in practical work to think very much, living off some very run-down mental capital, or has actually lost hope of the practicality of Socialism in British conditions, but without quite losing their faith. This sleeping giant could be woken by the economic crisis.

Even the Fabian Society shows some glimpses of trying to think about general principles again, rather than the constant administrative war-game of arguing that this or that social service is scandalously underfinanced and if given more would be the key to a more healthy and salubrious future (the worst legacy—someone had to say it sometime—of the Titmuss school: worthiness, energy, dedication, indeed; but a complete lack of theory, hence of direction: *noblesse oblige* plus BSc (Econ)).

What the press call 'moderate' is usually the right of the Labour party; that is, the centre of the national spectrum. The true moderate in the Labour party, however, is anyone, whether of the left or the centre, who aims at transforming our society to a better one *by political means* and who sees the main priority as themselves persuading the unconvinced, not as enforcing dogmatic purity within the ranks or as threatening freedom of the press—as if a press wholly controlled by unions or syndics could convert a pliant public to Socialism, rather than that a more socialist public should be demanding, by how they spend their 10ps, a more socialist press. Political means are the acceptance of effective representative institutions, including Parliament, above all, but now needing to reach far more people in their own neighbourhoods and workplaces than ever Parliament did; and the need to persuade people openly and fairly; not to deceive or coerce them, even for their own good.

Democratic procedures cannot allow, for instance, MPs a property right in their seats; but equally parties must be no more immune than unions, indeed voluntary bodies of all kinds, from reform to ensure a greater and wider democracy (the only answer to infiltration is not less membership and less democracy, but more). But politics and democratic procedures are not ends in themselves. They are ways of pursuing ends. And fairness or social justice is not just the perpetual patchwork fairness of the best possible as we are: it could be something permanently better. All kinds of disputes may always remain; but they can be lifted to a higher level.

The opportunity now presents itself in crisis and in need. The affluent spree is over for ever. Guilt and remorse begin to replace sheer bewilderment; even some fear arises. For even if we can learn to live easily with ourselves again, Europe as a whole still has to come to terms with the Third World. But some hope, too, for there is a mood of seriousness and a thirst for principles. Clear and simple formulations of doctrine are needed as never before. Labour finds its basic principles in trying to create more fraternity and liberty for all, in denying all democratically unjustifiable inequalities, and in acting on the belief that ultimately it is the worker who creates wealth and that his cooperation and mutual aid create fraternity. If the party can show by behaviour and policy that it follows these, then it has a much more compelling and relevant rhetoric than the precarious 'our man is a better manager than yours' into which we have so despicably and foolishly descended.

The pure idealist is useless, but so is the pure pragmatist. We have to work on different levels, to look far ahead as we try to do the best we can right now;

to imagine people as they could be, while we deal with them as they are. Political compromises are not sell-outs nor debased pragmatism if the long term sense of purpose is clear and if we are taking clear steps forward. 'The man who striveth for the mastery', said St Paul (himself no mean proselytiser), 'is temperate in all things'—if he is really interested in mastery, not just in the negative power of keeping a label saying 'leader' on a private door or 'pure Socialist' on a banner of a purely propagandist weekly. Genuine Socialist leadership is collective. The 'long term' is being quickened by the crisis more than by our own exertions. But can the Labour Party be ready to seize the chance to demonstrate, for the first time since 1945, the relevance of Socialism to the majority not yet convinced? Advance by 'small steps' by all means, as Roy Hattersley argued, echoing Willi Brandt, but steps need to be placed deliberately on top of each other, not scattered surrealistically, one by one, over a landscape as opportunity arises. And we build at a moderate pace towards *Socialism*, not 'radicalism', please. Radicalism is only an attitude of mind, a style, an itch: Socialism is both a theory of society and a moral doctrine. It only needs to be taken seriously.

It needs to be argued. At a time of crisis and national self-doubt, the public are no longer impressed by the shopping-list electoral arguments of 'we did' and 'you didn't', whether based on left- or right-wing manifestos. It would be a grim irony if the Powells and the Keith Josephs carried greater weight, because of the greater clarity of their principles, than those of the traditional men of doctrine, the socialists of the Labour party, suddenly turned pragmatic, practical, that is with nothing to offer unless the winds blow fair—which they do not. And so much extreme ideology is the souring of good doctrine by the bland or contemptuous refusal of practical men of politics or administration to think long, to think systematically, to think morally, almost to think at all.

Notes

1 This is a much-revised and expanded version of five short articles which appeared in the *New Statesman* in August and September [1975].
2 Roy Hattersley, 'The Radical Alternative', in *New Statesman*, 31 October 1975.

Democracy in the Age of Science*

RT HON ANTHONY WEDGWOOD BENN, MP

Vol. 50, no. 1, January–March 1979

THE RELATIONSHIP between Science and Democracy is central to any discussion about the future. Unless they can be reconciled power may be abused, and the development of knowledge may be restricted. My thesis is that secrecy is the great enemy of democracy and science, and the key to the advance of both lies in the wider spread of knowledge. It is in the joint interest of the scientific community and the general body of citizens to formulate such clear demands for greater openness, and to press for them with such strength, that the present tradition of secrecy is broken down and replaced by an open system offering freedom of information. This is necessary if we are to reveal the issues, and the choices that are available, so that individual citizens may exercise their judgement upon them, and press their policies according to their interests and opinions within our democratic system.

Knowledge is the only natural resource which is increasing; while most natural resources are diminishing. Access to that knowledge, and control of the uses to which it is put, are therefore the key to the future. The choice between the private and the public ownership of knowledge is a major scientific and political issue. Science is rightly proud of its reputation as the liberator of mankind from the obscurantist superstitions of the past, and in its achievements it has increased mankind's control of the forces of nature by enlarging his knowledge of the laws of nature. Science and the scientific method, engineering and applied technology now permeate every part of a modern society. But they have also helped to create great power—and the organisations which control it. For good or ill. If the men and women who are now in charge of those big organisations—be they governmental, industrial or financial—are successful in shrouding their thinking, decisions and their policies in secrecy then it could be that the resources of science and engineering which they command could enslave humanity instead of liberating it. And if mankind is excluded from understanding the knowledge which is now available he will be deprived of his inheritance.

If we apply this test of the 'extent of knowledge' as an index of freedom for both citizen and scientist, we have to ask ourselves how society stands against that test in practice. Clearly, the record varies from country to country. But it is in general true that the most secretive societies are the most oppressive, and that even the least oppressive are still secretive.

*Full text of a lecture given to the Annual Meeting of the British Association for the Advancement of Science at Bath University on September 8, 1978. The Institute of Workers Control, Nottingham have reprinted it as a pamphlet.

The demand for knowledge

The demand for openness is a clear sign of democratic pressure. Throughout history this demand has had to be conceded albeit partially and bit by bit, by those with power in order to gain consent for the exercise of their power. Successive kings were forced by this means to concede knowledge first to the feudal barons, and then to the gentry, the merchants, and later still to the entrepreneurs in order to stave off the revolts against their power. 'Grievance before supply'—the right to be heard before money was voted by the Commons to support the King's Government—became an instrument for accountability to force the King to disclose his policy in order to win the support of his people. Later the struggle to secure the admission of the Press to the House of Commons and bring about the publication of Hansard reflected the demand of the voters to know what their MPs were doing in their name.

Similarly, the campaign for the franchise was accompanied by the demand for knowledge. As early as 1649 the Levellers were arguing that 'common people have been kept under blindness and ignorance, and have remained servants and slaves to the nobility and the gentry. But God hath now opened their eyes and discovered unto them their Christian liberty'. 'Open the books' has long been a demand of unions and employees. This demand for disclosure has been increasingly evident in the very areas that science has made the greatest impact. The whole range of government and industrial policies, especially in areas of high technology, where the impact of science on mankind is likely to be the greatest, has been the focus of the greatest campaigns for disclosure. The development of parliamentary democracy, universal education and the growth of the mass media have all increased the range of public understanding by the dissemination of knowledge about government, science and industry and have, in their turn both reinforced democracy and stimulated pressure for disclosure.

The growth of power

But it would be wrong to look at only one side of the balance sheet. For what also has to be considered, is the growth of industrial, financial and public power, which have all developed practices of secrecy which have effectively kept millions of people in ignorance of the biggest decisions of all which affect their lives.

First, the exponential growth of human knowledge in all spheres of learning has completely outpaced the capacity of any one human being to encompass its range. As the volume of knowledge increases the proportion of it that any one person can acquire in his life span has fallen and is now falling at an accelerating rate. However much a person may learn in a day, or a week, or a year, it is always a diminishing proportion of the increase in the sum of knowledge gained by humanity in that same day, week or year. It is a chastening, but an inescapable fact, that at the end of this British Association Meeting each of us will be relatively more ignorant than we were at the beginning however much we have learned, as individuals, during the course of the conference. This accelerating rate of relative ignorance may well mean that the expansion of knowledge by mankind as a whole—which is, in total, liberating in its effect—may in respect of any one individual have the effect of demoralising him as he comes to realise that knowledge is being used by others to control his life.

The arguments for secrecy

It is against that background that the arguments of secrecy that are made by those with power have to be examined. These arguments are of various kinds, each of them understandable but which, taken together, constitute an entrenchment of secrecy at a level which is becoming increasingly unacceptable.

1. *The security case*

Let me begin with the security case. This argument for secrecy is basic and runs like this: Every country is vulnerable to external attack and internal subversion and its defence requires it to prepare plans against these possibilities. Thus preparations must be kept behind the tightest veil of secrecy. The logic of this argument is, on the face of it, unanswerable and few will challenge it. To disclose defence secrets or internal security arrangements would be to invite those against whom we wish to be protected to find ways to evade the defences that otherwise they would have to meet. No Freedom of Information legislation proposed has ever been framed to include open access to security information. But having said that, limits of security have to be carefully defined to avoid a situation in which any, and every, action by government is justified by reference to security.

Every tyrant and dictator in history has always found that an appeal to security is the simplest way to win public acquiescence for his tyranny or dictatorship. And today the identification of 'enemies' at home, and abroad, is still the easiest justification for all sorts of actions that may limit civil liberties. The denial of human rights all over the world, including South Africa, Iran, Chile, China or the Soviet Union, is almost invariably justified in this way. But we all know that strong armed forces built up to resist foreign aggression may then be used to commit aggression abroad, or be diverted to suppress discontent arising from legitimate demands for human rights at home. Similarly, an internal security apparatus may be established in the guise of defending a free society and then become an instrument for eroding freedom in the society it is intended to defend. All these distortions of security can themselves be concealed behind the very veil of secrecy which the needs of security are supposed to justify.

External security. For example, total secrecy surrounded the preparations of the Anglo–French invasion plans for Egypt in 1956; the USA supported attack on Cuba at the Bay of Pigs in 1961; and the Soviet invasion of Czechoslovakia in 1968. But whatever the military case for preserving this secrecy in advance of an immediate military operation the real issues in every case were political, and related to the policies which led up to the situation in which Britain and France came to attack Egypt, America came to help attack Cuba or Russia came to invade Czechoslovakia. The proper public discussion of these critical policy issues was of course prevented by the same secrecy and was later justified by the need to protect the troops just about to go into action. Foreign policy choices cannot be excluded from proper public discussion on the grounds that they involve military security. For to do so would be to make foreign policy an instrument of the military, instead of military policy being the instrument of foreign policy, which must be maintained in a time democratic society. Thus any demand to extend military secrecy to cover foreign policy must be resisted.

Internal security. Exactly similar limits must be placed on the extent of legitimate secrecy in matters of internal security. Obviously the publication of plans to arrest a foreign spy or a domestic terrorist would frustrate the purpose of the operation and no one in his senses would advocate doing so.

But it is obviously important to draw a clear distinction between a spy and a critic; and between a terrorist and a dissident. If no such distinction is drawn the apparatus used to safeguard freedom can be used to suppress it. In countries which do not aspire to political liberty this presents no problem because the government is openly committed to the proposition that its own survival is in the interests of the people, and anyone who opposes the government is therefore an enemy of the people. But in societies which allow the people freely to decide who is to form the government no such argument can be sustained. Indeed, in such democratic societies the freedom of the people is the test by which freedom is judged—not the survival of the government. In such societies the decision by the people as to whether they wish the government to be replaced depends upon a free and an unfettered debate between supporters of the government and its critics and other dissidents.

There is always the risk that internal security measures, introduced to defend freedom, could be abused, and secrecy used to justify the harassment of dissidents; and if this were to happen it could destroy the very freedom these measures are intended to defend. The balance between freedom and security poses special difficulty in political democracies and requires wider public debate. First, it should be obvious that while the specific measures adopted for internal security may need to be protected, the policy, overall extent, cost, and methods of the security services are legitimate objects for public discussion. These are domestic policy issues comparable to the foreign

ANTHONY WEDGWOOD BENN

policy issues which should dictate the defence policy of the nation. And if we are to insist that the internal security services are to be under democratic control, then the policy they follow must be the subject of full public debate in the light of adequate information. In dictatorships of right or left such a proposition would not be entertained for a moment. But in democratic societies the issues are real and immediate. They require our attention because national security is still the major argument used for absolute secrecy covering foreign and defence policy and domestic police powers. Unless we can think through these difficult issues we could find that the term 'national security' could become a blanket excuse for secrecy on any matter which the government of the day wished to exclude from public scrutiny.

In Britain defence secrets are guarded by the Official Secrets Act. Foreign Policy is more widely discussed but is still subject to the protection of government position papers, diplomatic exchanges and negotiating briefs. As far as domestic security is concerned normal police activities are discussed, but the operations, policy and extent of the security services are completely blanketed out by tight secrecy. Only the Prime Minister is entitled to know the full extent of the operation of the security services. The only Prime Minister who has written about these matters in recent years was Harold Wilson, who devoted one chapter to them in his book *The Governance of Britain*. This whole chapter, which was only 446 words long, being the only authoritative report ever written by the only office holder able to know, merits full quotation.

The Prime Minister has the ultimate responsibility for the national security authorities at home and abroad, though the home and overseas organisations concerned come departmentally under the Home Office and the Foreign and Commonwealth Office responsibility. The Number 10 responsibility is exercised through the secretary of the Cabinet, who is the Prime Minister's link with the authorities concerned. The Cabinet Office account for the Secret Service vote which is published under the heading 'OTHER EXTERNAL RELATIONS: SECRET SERVICE being the estimate of the amount required in the year ending . . .',

In 1975/6 it amounted to £22 millions. No other details of estimates or expenditure are made available to Parliament either in the estimates or the accounts. By agreement with the Public Accounts Committee, the account is supported by the personal certificate of the Comptroller and Auditor-General in a unique form: 'I certify that the amount shown in this account to have been expended is supported by certificates from the responsible Ministers of the Crown.'

The Prime Minister is occasionally questioned on matters arising out of his responsibility. His answers may be regarded as uniformly uninformative. There is no further information that can usefully or properly be added before bringing this chapter to an end.

Against that background of officially supported public ignorance it is necessary to turn to the United States of America to find any serious public discussion about these matters. It is greatly to the credit of the Americans that faced with a clear abuse of power by the executive, they were determined to

S178

© 2011 The Author. The Political Quarterly © 2011 The Political Quarterly Publishing Co. Ltd

bring all these issues out into the open. Apart from the direct investigation into the Watergate Affair a proper inquiry was held into the conduct of the security services by Senator Church, and it brought to light information about matters which in Britain would never have been disclosed. I would like to read you a passage from a speech made on the subject by a member of the Church committee—a Senator Walter Mondale, who is of course now the Vice-President of the United States, and whose words acquire their importance by virtue both of his intimate knowledge of the investigative Committee of which he was a member, and the high position which he now occupies in the American Federal Government.

Our investigation showed [he said] that many of the abuses of the Nixon years could be traced back to the attitudes of the Cold War. Fastened on us was the fearful myth that America could not be defended without more deceit and illegality than democracy permits—and without more cynicism and hypocrisy than our beliefs would allow, For years, this assumption was used to justify actions abroad—from subversion of freely elected governments, to assassination attempts aimed at foreign leaders. And inevitably, in Macbeth's words, the invention returned home 'to plague the inventor'. The CIA came home to launch 'operation chaos'—a surveillance programme directed against American citizens—even though that agency is forbidden from exercising internal security functions. The law didn't matter.
   The army spied on the lawful democratic activities of groups ranging across the political spectrum—from Carl McIntyre's Conservative Christian Action Movement and the John Birch Society to the Urban Coalition, the Anti- Defamation League, and even the Chamber of Commerce. The law didn't matter. There was massive invasion of privacy. For years the FBI and the CIA illegally tapped phones and engaged in other forms of electronic surveillance. The law didn't matter.
   The FBI and CIA both opened the private mail of American citizens. Over 300,000 first-class letters were opened—the mail of people like John Steinbeck, Senators Church and Kennedy, and organisations like the Federation of American Scientists. The law didn't matter.
   The National Security Agency obtained from major international cable companies copies of all private telegrams sent overseas by American citizens in businesses. The law didn't matter.
   Legitimate law enforcement functions were twisted and perverted. In 1969 the Internal Revenue Service established a 'Special Services Staff' to examine the tax returns of individuals—not because they had violated the tax laws, but because some people in government did not like their politics. The law didn't matter.
   Eventually these agencies resorted to the Commission of Common Crimes to obtain what they considered necessary information. So the FBI and the CIA illegally broke into the homes and businesses of American Citizens—the so-called 'black bag jobs'. They even established official liaison with organised crime. The law didn't matter.
   Perhaps the most terrifying abuse of power during this period was what the FBI called Cointelpro. That ugly little acronym would have been at home in any police state in Eastern Europe or Latin America. It meant illegal investigations targeted against American law-abiding individuals or groups—and punishment administered not by a court but by a government agency —through harassment and tactics designed to break up marriages, destroy reputations, terminate employment, sabo-

tage political campaigns and even encourage violent retribution by falsely and anonymously labelling intended victims as government informers.

The United States has now made a serious effort to open up a discussion of the proper limits of security in a democratic society. There has of course been a long tradition in the United States Congress of Committees and Committee hearings at which members of the executive have been required to answer questions that in Britain we would never be allowed to ask. Now there is a Freedom of Information Act which has conferred a right to know on citizens. There are many people in Britain who would like to see the same openness here; and who cannot, in the absence of information, assess whether or not abuses of a comparable kind could occur here. Maybe the ultimate authority of the Prime Minister is effective in preventing it—but Harold Wilson said the public is not entitled to know more than he disclosed in his chapter.

I have dwelt on security at great length for obvious reasons. First, that political freedom must be secure. Secondly, that true security for that purpose must require secrecy. Thirdly, that the border line between legitimate secrecy, and the abuse of power in the name of security, is one that must be defined to prevent it justifying total secrecy. Fourthly, that since the technological instruments of persecution, manipulation and repression done in the name of security—which may amount to police state methods—inevitably bring science into bad repute, and could inhibit free scientific inquiry, it is a matter of concern to scientists as to how these issues are handled.

2. *The financial and commercial case for secrecy*

The second argument for secrecy that is commonly advanced is based upon the maintenance of financial and commercial interests. The main advocates of secrecy on these grounds are, of course, those whose own interests are involved. Banks are extremely secretive about their policy and practices; so are major business firms, and the decision-making of multinationals and international financial institutions is shrouded in such mystery that even governments do not find it easy to discover what is really going on. Pressure for full disclosure is likely to be met by a blank refusal accompanied by due warnings of the consequences if disclosure were to be enforced. There is no doubt that the publication, in advance, of details of specific negotiations by industrial or banking enterprises could frustrate the objectives the negotiations were intended to secure. Governments may be in a similar position. But having identified those narrow categories of information where the requirements of secrecy are strictly limited in terms of time, the rest could easily be released without damage to the organisation concerned. Indeed, without information it is impossible for the *policy* that lies behind the decisions to be properly discussed; and for the people who make these policy decisions to be held accountable for what they have done.

3. *The case for secrecy to protect the individual*

A third defence of secrecy that is advanced is that the records about individuals relating to their own personal affairs should be protected from publication. Since such records are of no interest in terms of public policy there is no pressure to include such categories of information within the scope of any Freedom of Information policy. Indeed, the argument works the other way. There is growing anxiety in many parts of the world that information may be accumulated about individuals for one purpose, and then grouped together in the centralised computer to form records that could be used for purposes other than the purpose for which the information was gathered. In plain English there is a fear that dossiers may be collected which if kept secret from the person to whom they relate could infringe his liberty by making it easier for him or her to be penalised, harassed or in some way disadvantaged. It is also possible for mistakes to be made and it is theoretically possible for untrue statements to be included in such records for malicious reasons. In this situation the only real safeguard is to confer a right upon all persons to know what is on their own files, so that they can correct errors, challenge unfair judgements and 'clear their names' literally. Such a remedy requires personal disclosure but not publication. We have not yet achieved that right.

Apart from these three arguments relating to military, financial and personal information which may need to be protected—and all of which require secrecy limited to the extent which is necessary, a whole host of other arguments are advanced for maintaining secrecy over a far wider range of subjects. These arguments need to be listed in order to reveal the extent of the opposition to openness that still persists in official quarters.

4. *The arguments for secrecy based upon administrative and ministerial and professional convenience*

These arguments are regularly used and appear in many forms. It may be said that the issues are too complicated for the lay public to understand; that the public are not really interested; that wide consultation will be costly and cause delay; or make administration more difficult; or that discussions will narrow the government's freedom of manoeuvre; or weaken its negotiating stance; or subject it to unhelpful external pressures; or undermine its negotiating strength; and sometimes that the publication of information collected by government would destroy the confidence of those who gave that information and inhibit people from speaking their mind. But if all these arguments fail to carry weight it may be asserted that the government has a duty to govern and that disclosure erodes the power necessary to do that duty. In the course of my life as a minister I have heard all these arguments used many times over, and in some shape or form, they constitute the real reason why open government is so strongly resisted. It is that disclosure weakens the prerogative of ministers and the role of officials who enjoy their greatest power when they alone know what is up for decision, what the choices are and what are the relevant facts. Then their advice is hard to challenge. Seen from an official or ministerial viewpoint these are obviously attractive arguments. But to accept them would be to accept that the convenience of the government is synonymous with the national interest; and that the national interest actually requires the exclusion of the public from enjoying any real role in formulating policy, or exercising any effective influence before decisions are made. These arguments are usually used to justify secrecy in areas of policy in which science and technology play a major role and if the public are precluded from participating in them the frontiers of democratic control would be sharply reduced. It is just because openness, by contrast, can actually extend the frontiers of democracy, that it is so important to press for it.

How secrecy is upheld

If these then are the arguments for secrecy that predominate in large organisations and especially within government how is it sustained? Various techniques are used and it is to them that I now want to turn.

1. *The Official Secrets Act*

This legislation covers everything from espionage designed to undermine the security of the state, to the protection of all official documents covering the whole range of government work. The workings of the Official Secrets Act have recently been the subject of a great deal of public discussion and inquiry, and the government has recently published a White Paper proposing changes in section 2 of the Act and indicating a readiness to consider some proposals for wider reform. However, at present it is an offence in law to disclose any documents or information acquired in the conduct of official duties. The proponents of reform fall into two categories. There are first those who want to confer the statutory right to know, subject to safeguards kept to a necessary minimum; and secondly there are those who want to make the minimum number of changes designed to stave off the pressure for real reform—leaving us with official secrets legislation that, unlike the present Act, would command sufficient public and judicial support to make prosecutions possible.

This latter school of thought, which is strongly held by the establishment, inside and outside the government, is also prepared to accept the need for greater disclosure of information than hitherto—so long as the decision as to whether, and what, to publish is strictly controlled by the executive as part of its prerogative. What this school of thought will not have is the statutory right to know entrenched in legislation that would pass the initiative to the citizen.

But it would be a mistake to regard the Official Secrets Act as being the sole, or even the prime, instrument by which secrecy is observed. There are in fact a number of equally important techniques and institutional arrangements which reinforce it.

2. *The 30-year rule*

The protection of public records under the 30-year rule merits separate consideration. Under this rule more than a generation has to elapse before the citizens are allowed to know the thinking that lay behind even the most major government decisions which affected their lives. The justification for this rule rests mainly on the argument that the knowledge of publication of minutes and papers and records of discussions, less than 30 years ago would inhibit the candid expression of opinion by ministers and officials and thus endanger the free exchange of views which good government requires.

These arguments are different from the arguments for protecting current discussions, the immediate secrecy necessary for diplomatic and other negotiations, or budgetary preparations. It is in fact an argument that is based on the *principle* that accountability by publication is incompatible with good government and hence that democracy which depends upon account-ability must be limited by a time gap of 30 years.

Since democracy can be properly described as the institutionalisation of a process, which a society can learn from its own experience—and especially by its own mistakes—a 30-year time gap before that experience, and those mistakes can be published in full, must necessarily make that learning process at best ineffective and at worst almost useless.

3. *Restrictions on ministerial memoirs*

It is in this context that attempts to restrict the right of ministers to publish their own experiences has to be seen as being especially relevant. This policy—in so far as it is effective—is intended to deny those citizens elected to serve in higher office from conveying their experience to those who elected them unless the Cabinet Office have approved the text.

4. *The Privy Councillors' oath*

All Cabinet Ministers are, upon appointment, sworn into the Privy Council by an oath administered in the presence of the Sovereign. This oath, which has now been published, imposes a special duty upon all ministers to preserve the secrecy of government and Cabinet business to which they become privy. It is a powerful reinforcement of the Official Secrets Act in relation to ministers.

5. Collective Cabinet responsibility

Similarly, the constitutional convention of collective Cabinet responsibility which is thought to be central to the working of the British Constitution has considerable implications for secrecy of government. Under this doctrine the myth of Cabinet unity on all matters discussed is fostered. Cabinets are, of course, rarely united in their views. Indeed, were it so there would be no Cabinet discussion at all. Why then is this myth fostered? In its origins it was a protection for the Sovereign's principal advisers against attempts, by the Sovereign, to pick out those ministers who were ring-leaders of advice unacceptable to the Crown. It must simultaneously have been clear that Parliament and the populace could best be kept quiescent if they were told that the Cabinet was solidly behind every policy announced by HMG; and thus dissatisfied groups could not nourish the hope of a change of policy based on the knowledge that their view was being advocated in the highest councils of the state.

Later, as the franchise extended the democratic influences, party unity became a major factor in securing electoral success. This, too, gave a practical reinforcement to the idea of collective Cabinet responsibility. It is certainly both right and necessary that Cabinet colleagues should meet to discuss the options before them, and should agree to stick together defending the choice made.

Common sense and ordinary personal loyalty must require defeated minorities to accept the majority decision and to explain and defend it. But there is no reason whatsoever why this necessary and sensible principle should be extended to the necessarily false pretence that no alternative policies were considered, no real debate took place, and that everyone present was convinced of the merits of the majority view—as distinct from accepting that it was the majority view and that as such it should be supported. The narrow interpretation of collective Cabinet responsibility denies citizens essential knowledge of the processes by which their government reaches its decisions.

6. The effect of patronage upon secrecy

In addition to these factors working for secrecy there is the effect of patronage in enforcing it. In this context the Prime Minister's powers to hire and fire ministers without any requirement to consult, or seek parliamentary approval of any kind, for either process, can naturally be used to enforce secrecy by the occupant of Number 10. The last Prime Minister, who formed four separate Administrations, over an eight-year period, appointed or reshuffled 100 Cabinet ministers and 403 ministers of state and junior ministers. And since all those who hold ministerial office depend upon the PM's continued approval for their positions, his view of what it is right to disclose, and right to withhold, is more likely to prevail than that of the minister's own assessment of what he—or the public as a whole—might think it was in the public interest to publish. A system of elected ministers would produce a very different result.

There are many other techniques open to any large organisation which can have the effect of protecting information from 'unwelcome' public interest. Vice-President Mondale referred to the more extreme abuses, but private pressure, deliberate mystification, the misrepresentation of criticism, and news management have all been practised to a greater or less degree by all those who have held power in all countries throughout the whole of human history.

These, then, are some of the means by which secrecy is maintained. But it would, of course, be entirely wrong to conclude from what I have said that the blanket on official information is in any sense effective—or is even intended to be effective. For the practices followed differ substantially from what the formal position suggests. A brief reference to these practices is therefore in order.

How information gets out

1. Official information officially released

Although much official information is withheld a great deal of it is officially released. The mass of White Papers, government publications, official statements of statistics and reports of commissions, working parties and committees, constitute a fair volume of output. There are ministerial speeches in Parliament and outside, press releases and press conferences and articles and broadcasts on radio and television. The volume of official publications has steadily increased. Ministers are, by long-established convention, permitted to read this information which they believe to be in the public interest to release.

2. Official briefings

In parallel with all this goes an equally well-established practice of ministers and officials giving unofficial background briefings to journalists—including the lobby. These non-attributable briefings at No. 10; or the House of Commons or in government departments are accepted by the correspondents concerned on the basis on which they are offered—namely that sources are not identified. The government can then fly kites, offer an analysis or explanation that advances their policy, or feed out selected pieces of information. But it should be noted that such practices all leave the discretion entirely with the government and are themselves secretly conducted.

3. Unauthorised disclosures

It is now well known that a great deal of information about government gets out as a result of unauthorised disclosures or 'leaks'. It is common knowledge that some ministers, officials or those who have come into the possession of information which they wish to become public knowledge have, as individuals, passed it on to journalists or others. The motives for these leaks could be to win public support for a particular policy by letting it be known that an important choice is just about to be made. A regular procedure exists for inquiring into leaks of this kind but they are rarely if ever successful in identifying the source or sources.

Much of the information that appears in the press derives from such sources and they can be as embarrassing for ministers as they are valuable for the shaping of a public understanding of government policy discussions.

It is rare for official documents to leak, but two examples, one for the United States and one for the United Kingdom, deserve a mention because of the motivation which lay behind them. The most famous and the most recent was the deliberate publication of the Pentagon papers by Daniel Ellsberg. He was so concerned by what he learned about the conduct of the Vietnam War by the United States administration that he resolved deliberately to make the facts known to help the anti-war campaign. For Ellsberg it was a matter of conscience and in defence as he saw it of the American National Interest.

The other case occurred in this country during the 1930s although the facts only came to light quite recently. *The Daily Telegraph* reported on November 30, 1976, under a headline that ran as follows; 'Whitehall Spies Fed Churchill Secrets in 1930s'. The story began:

Sir Winston Churchill received hundreds of secret documents surreptitiously removed from official files sent to him in breach of the Official Secrets Act when he was fighting appeasement as a back-bench MP.

Mr Martin Gilbert, Sir Winston's biographer, reported that these documents had been found at the Churchill Archives at Chartwell and said: 'there was total, consistent and persistent breach of the Official Secrets Act'.

Presumably those officials or serving officers who abstracted these documents and sent them to Mr Churchill were moved by the same motives as Daniel Ellsberg—namely a concern for the British National Interest and a fear that that interest was being betrayed by the then government.

Ministerial memoirs—in practice

After referring to the official attitude to ministerial memoirs I should draw attention to what happens in practice. Anthony Nutting, Dick Crossman and Selwyn Lloyd and others certainly committed technical breaches of the conventions in publishing what they did about events that occurred less than 30 years before the books they wrote were published.

Conclusion

This, then, is the balance sheet as best I can draw it up at this moment. The growing demand for open government is still being held back by the sort of arguments set out above whilst the present practices succeed in restricting disclosure to the prerogative of the executive, supplemented by briefings.

Meanwhile, evasions of the law and custom are growing, have been to some extent accepted, and few if any of them can be held to have inflicted serious damage on the national interest though governments may have been embarrassed for a time. But the question is not whether there are sufficient breaches of secrecy to satisfy the idle curiosity of the public or to furnish material for commentators to write their articles in the press. The real issue is whether the public interest is served by the present system as it is supposed to work. The answer must be 'no'. For when we discuss the subject it is not an arid constitutional technicality that we are considering but the central question of the method by which current decisions are made which affect the lives of all of us, and determine the deployment of massive financial resources and resources of highly skilled people. If we accept that the control of information about those decisions and how they are arrived at, are a prerogative of government then we are also accepting that democracy cannot become mature enough even to allow the people to share the thinking that precedes those decisions. The extent to which governments should become open cannot be left to the discretion of ministers alone. It should be entrenched in a statutory right to know which transfers the prerogative for initiating demands for disclosure to citizens and then Parliament. There must be absolutely adequate safeguards for information bearing on genuine questions of national security including protection for citizens about information relating to them. Any serious attempts to secure real democratic control in the age of science would require some major changes.

First
The development of a series of select committees covering the work of each and every department with an effective power to call ministers and officials to account and to see all relevant papers—save only for the narrow range of real security classified documents to which I have referred.

Second
The development of procedures which would allow the elective rather than the present appointive system to operate for ministers which would make them more sensitive to the demand of MPs for a greater role in decision-making.

Third
A comprehensive Freedom of Information Act conferring the statutory right to information upon Parliament and the electors.

I think I should mention two further changes that go wider than the issues which I have been discussing. For a fully mature democracy capable of true self-management must concern itself with the free flow of information in all its aspects. I therefore would add:

Fourth
Provision within the educational structure for the right of all citizens to real access to the main stream of knowledge in our schools and post-school institutions throughout the whole of their life.

Fifth
Provision within the mass media for greater and more systematic access to it by those representing the full range of interests, faiths and opinions in society in place of the present very narrow range of interests and opinions which now predominate. For all these reasons I appeal most strongly to the scientific community to join actively in pressing for greater openness by the passage of the full Freedom of Information Act and the strengthening of the rights of electors and of Parliament to hold government more fully to account for the decisions that it takes. These reforms are now urgently needed to safeguard democracy, and the scientific tradition of freedom which depends upon it.

Beyond Social Democracy

DAVID MARQUAND*

Vol. 58, no. 3, July–September 1987

IN BRITAIN, even more than in other western countries, the politics of the 1980s take place in the shadow of the 1970s. The 'Keynesian social-democratic' consensus,[1] which prevailed for most of the postwar period and to which the neoliberalism of the last eight years is a reaction, broke down under the Wilson–Callaghan Government of 1974–79, amid mounting inflation, swelling balance of payments deficits, unprecedented currency depreciation, rising unemployment, bitter industrial conflicts and what seemed to many to be ebbing governability. And just as the victorious freetraders' interpretation of the crises which preceded the repeal of the Corn Laws helped to shape the political agenda of the mid-nineteenth century, so today's political agenda is, to a large extent, the product of the victorious neoliberals' interpretation of the crises of ten years ago. The reason why Mrs Thatcher and her colleagues still have the political initiative after nearly a decade of office is that no one has yet mounted a successful challenge to that interpretation. The objects of this essay are to point the way towards a possible alternative, and to explore some of its implications.

The neoliberal interpretation

Despite the erudition and sophistication of some of its exponents, the neoliberal interpretation is, at bottom, simple. 'Keynesian social democracy' was, of course, a philosophy of the middle way. However strongly its adherents disagreed on other matters, they agreed in repudiating the dichotomies of market versus state; capital versus labour; private enterprise versus public ownership; individual freedom versus social justice. Central to it was the belief that it was possible to combine elements of traditional capitalism and traditional socialism in a synthesis more benign than either: to mitigate the hardships of unregulated capitalism without sacrificing consumer choice or entrepreneurial initiative. The neoliberal interpretation of its collapse rests on the assumption that no such synthesis is possible. For neoliberals, no less than for fundamentalist socialists, capitalism is capitalism and socialism, socialism. The notion of a mixed system, in which the state softens the rigours of the market, is a dangerous absurdity: without its rigours the market will not work. The policy failures of the 1970s merely confirmed that the middle way had always been a will-o'-the-wisp; and that even in the

* The author is Professor of Contemporary History and Politics at the University of Salford and has just been appointed joint editor of this journal. His *The Contradictions of Individualism* will be published by Jonathan Cape in January next year.

days when the search for it had appeared to be successful, success was sowing the seeds of eventual failure. Keynesian social democracy' collapsed, in short, because it was bound to collapse: because the attempt to transcend the dichotomies of market versus state and personal freedom versus social justice was vain, and because the policies it engendered were bound to generate a vicious spiral of 'overload', through which excessive expectations on the part of the electorate fostered and were, in turn, fostered by excessive commitments on the part of the state.

The most obvious weakness in all this is that it goes too wide. Britain was not, of course, the only western country which found it difficult to adjust to the economic upheavals of the 1970s. But in north-western Europe, at any rate, no other country found it anything like as difficult as she did. Yet in all the countries of north-western Europe, governments pursued policies similar to those pursued by Britain's 'Keynesian social democrats' in the same period. If the British policies were doomed to failure, so were their foreign equivalents. If the British state was weighed down by excessive commitments, and the British electorate inflamed by excessive expectations, so, presumably, were the states and electorates of Sweden, Austria and West Germany—all of them social-democratic mixed economies, with strong trade unions and generous welfare programmes, in which the share of GDP going to public expenditure was as high as or higher than in Britain.[2] But, by any conceivable reckoning, the Swedish, Austrian and West German economies withstood the upheavals of the 1970s more successfully than did the British.

It is true, of course, that the catastrophes which the British economy experienced in the 1970s had deep roots. Despite rapid growth by previous British standards, it had grown much more slowly than those of most developed countries throughout the postwar period. Like a chronic invalid exposed to a snowstorm, it was uniquely vulnerable to the foul weather of the 1970s because it had fallen further and further behind competing economies during the fair weather of the 1950s and 1960s. But this only pushes the problem one stage further back. If the origins of Britain's feebleness in the 1970s lie in her invalidism in the 1950s and 1960s, we need to know why she was an invalid then.

Here the neoliberal interpretation, having gone too wide to explain the 1970s, becomes too narrow. *Ex hypothesi*, it can address only the postwar period, when the political economy was run on 'Keynesian social-democratic' lines, or at most the period since World War One, when it began to take its postwar shape. Unfortunately, the long relative decline of the British economy is not a phenomenon of the postwar, or even of the post-1918 period, alone. It began in the last quarter of the nineteenth century, at a time when the British economy conformed more closely to the classical, market-liberal model than did almost any other major economy, and when the social-democratic Welfare State was barely a twinkle in Sidney Webb's eye. With occasional ups and downs, it has continued ever since—under *laisser-faire* market Liberals, protectionist Big Business Conservatives, top-down socialist planners and both Labour and Conservative 'Keynesian social democrats'. No account which purports to explain the latest chapters in the story while ignoring the opening ones can get us very far.

The triumph of individualism

Despite these flaws, however—indeed, in some ways because of them—the longevity and popularity of the neoliberal interpretation provide the best point of departure from which to start the search for an alternative. For it is based on two implicit assumptions, one concerning the sources of economic innovation and change, and the other the nature of politics and political man, both of which have been deeply embedded in Britain's political culture since the industrial revolution, and both of which help to account for the crises of the 1970s as well as for the way in which the political class reacted to them.

The first is that the motor of economic innovation is the 'undistorted' competitive market which the founding fathers of classical market liberalism thought they saw around them: that because the astonishing upsurge of innovation which created the first industrial society in history was driven by the market, technological and economic innovation must always be market-led. The second is that the conception of man and society which underpinned market liberalism applies to the polity as well as to the economy: that in politics, as in economics, the sovereign individual—voter or consumer—chooses his own purposes for himself that the choosing self is, in Brian Crowley's phrase, 'impermeable';[3] and that the choice of purpose is therefore a private act, with which politics and government have and should have nothing to do. Even in the heyday of 'Keynesian social democracy', these assumptions lurked in the subconscious of the political class like rocks hidden by a high tide. The turmoil of the 1970s only brought them back to the surface.

Of course, the doctrines from which they spring have always been in contest. Ever since it first began to capture minds and influence behaviour, market liberalism has provoked indignation and hostility; even when it seemed to be carrying all before it on the level of policy and decision, there was a strong undercurrent of dissent on the level of imagination and reflection. The inarticulate 'moral economy' of the eighteenth-century crowd, which held it to be '"unnatural" that any man should profit from the necessities of others', continued to inspire popular protests against the new political economy until well into the nineteenth.[4] Chartist publicists tried to develop a 'people's science' of economics, hingeing on the notion of a fair return for labour; High Tories campaigned for the aristocratic ideal of a harmonious, organic society; Carlyle, Cobbett, Dickens and the young Disraeli all tried to fill the 'moral vacuum' which they sensed in the prevailing economic doctrine.[5] Later in the century, Idealist philosophers tried to restate the values of community in an idiom partly derived from Hegel. In the twentieth century, the labour and socialist movements proclaimed the equally communitarian values of social justice and class solidarity. No doubt the same applies, even more strongly, to everyday life. *Homo economicus*, the rational calculator of the classical theorists, was a reified abstraction, not a creature of flesh and blood: not even Dickens's genius could make Mr Gradgrind more than a horrifying caricature.

But all this only qualifies the central point. The early nineteenth-century dissenters spoke to the heart, not to the head. They had feeling and imagination on their side; but they lacked a convincing theory to give the promptings of the heart an intellectual cutting edge. They could mourn the passing of the old world, and dream of a new one; but they could not make sense of the world which was actually taking shape around them—or not, at any rate, in a fashion which could tell the inhabitants of that world how, in practice, to prevent it from taking shape. Still less could they dislodge the individualistic ethos which made the doctrines they opposed resonate among practical men of all classes. Thus, Benthamite individualism and market liberalism both shaped and reflected the common sense of the age; and although the emergence of a regulatory state and the transition from liberal to corporate capitalism gradually undermined the latter, they hardly shook the intellectual and cultural hegemony of the former. Nor, for that matter, did the Idealists of the late-nineteenth century or the socialists and labour men of the twentieth. Despite the communitarian yearnings of the early Independent Labour Party and the Marxist legacy of the early Social Democratic Federation, mainstream twentieth-century British socialism has been essentially Benthamite in philosophy.[6] As for the British labour movement, it has never managed to transcend the defensive sectionalism of the craft unions—'joint stock companies for the sale of labour', as Robert Currie has called them[7]—from which it sprang.

Hence, one of the most revealing ironies of modem British history. As Karl Polanyi showed, the 'great transformation' from agrarian to industrial society followed a parabola rather than a straight line. In the first, market-liberal, phase, the laws and customs which impeded the growth of a market economy were repealed or done away with. But before that phase had run its course, a reaction had set in; and in the second, interventionist, phase, new laws and customs were introduced to protect society from the consequences of the previous one.[8] In Britain, however, the reaction against full-blooded market liberalism took place under the same philosophical aegis—and, more importantly, in the same cultural framework—as had the movement towards it. Contemporaries, anxious to come to grips with the changes through which they were living, naturally made much of the differences between the 'Collectivism' of the end of the nineteenth century and the 'Individualism' of the beginning. What stands out in retrospect is the continuity between the two. State intervention was tentative, hesitant and reactive; and although it was sometimes justified in other terms, the logic behind it was essentially utilitarian.

Models of innovation

Two consequences followed. The first and most obvious was that the political class failed either to grasp the true meaning of Britain's relative economic decline, or to devise strategies with which to halt it. As John Zysman has argued, the instinctive, two-centuries-old British assumption that economic innovation and adjustment are bound to be market-led is a gross over-simplification.[9] Even in the capitalist world, there are at least three 'models' of the process, not one. There is the market-led model of Industrial Revolution Britain or present-day Hong Kong. There is the state-led model, best exemplified by Gaullist France and by Meiji, and for that matter contemporary Japan. Finally, there is the negotiated model, found in Austria, Sweden and to some extent in West Germany. The differences between the last two of these models go deep, but for the moment they can be ignored. What matter are the differences between both of them and the first. The crucial difference is that they are both varieties of what Ronald Dore has called a 'developmental' state—of a political form designed, in his words, 'explicitly to promote the competitiveness of the nation seen as one actor in a cut-throat world economy'.[10] And, in the political culture which the neoliberal assumptions described above had helped to shape, the notion of a developmental state could not take root.

Hence, the great paradox of twentieth-century British economic history. Albeit in different ways and to different extents, the countries which first followed and then overtook Britain on the path to industrialism all shared at least some of the essential attributes of the developmental state. For all of them, the world economy was made up of nations seeking wealth as a means to power in the long term, and power as a means to wealth in the long term, not of individuals seeking only to maximise their satisfactions in the short term. They were not content with an economic pattern which condemned them to permanent inferiority in the most sophisticated activities of the time, and in all of them (not least, in the allegedly market-liberal United States) the state deliberately tried to change the pattern. Britain did not—perhaps could not—follow suit. The notion of a Welfare State was slowly accepted. The notion of a developmental state, using its power to compete more effectively with other states in the world market, met dogged and uncomprehending resistance. At most, the state's job was to distribute wealth. It was not supposed to create it. Thus, the public sector came to be seen as the domain of the non-economic—of the fair, the concerned and the tender-hearted in the eyes of its supporters, and of the sloppy, the profligate and the uncompetitive in the eyes of its opponents. The notion that it might be the ally of, or even a spur to, competitiveness remained alien to both. Even when governments began to intervene in the supply-side of the economy, first in the 1930s and more systematically in the 1960s and 1970s, essentially welfare considerations—the protection of existing jobs and existing industries—usually predominated over developmental ones.

The implications go wide. In a path-breaking essay, Alexander Gerschenk-ron once observed that the more 'backward' the society undergoing indus-trialisation, and the wider the gap between its level of technological sophistication and the level of the most advanced economies of the time, the more industrialisation depends on public authorities.[11] Thus, the German state intervened in the economy more than the British, and the Russian and Japanese more than the German, Herein lies the paradox—a paradox which echoes through the last century of British economic history like a tolling bell. The minimalist state of late-eighteenth- and early-nineteenth-century Britain was appropriate for an industrial pioneer, in which economic development could take place slowly and gradually, through a series of small, piecemeal steps within the capacity of a decentralised private sector. Once her old followers had begun to overtake her, however, roles were reversed. She was no longer a pioneer, and began to fall into relative backwardness herself. But the values and assumptions of her pioneering days survived, inhibiting her from overcoming her backwardness in the way that the backward countries of the previous generation had overcome theirs. Hence, the failure of Joe Chamberlain's campaign for Tariff Reform before 1914 and of Lloyd George's for home development in the 1920s, the defensive character of the National Government's internal economic management in the 1930s, the half-heart-edness of the Attlee Government's experiments in planning, the humiliating collapse of the National Plan in 1966 and the muddled, irresolute inter-ventionism of the 1970s. And hence also the long succession of economic crises which destroyed the 'Keynesian social-democratic' consensus, and the confusions and hesitations which ran through the response of the political class.

Public intervention and civic morality

The second consequence goes deeper. As well as being a philosophy of the middle way, 'Keynesian social democracy' was a philosophy of the mixed economy—of an economy in which resources are largely allocated through the market, but in which public power intervenes on a significant scale to supplement, constrain, manipulate or direct market forces for public ends. That sentence, however, raises as many questions as it answers. Public intervention implies a public purpose: otherwise, those who do the interven-ing cannot know what they are trying to achieve. But in a political culture shaped by the assumption that society is made up of separate, atomistic individuals, pursuing only their own private purposes, the notion of a public purpose which is more than the sum of private purposes is apt to seem dangerous, or meaningless, or both.

The result was an intellectual and moral vacuum at the heart of the 'Keynesian social-democratic' political economy. It had a substantial public sector and depended upon public intervention. But because the notion of a public purpose was alien to them, its managers had no philosophy of public intervention or of the public good. So long as things went well, no obvious damage followed. Hard choices were avoided, and predatory interests bought off. In default of active support, the system made do with passive acquiescence. But when the economic weather turned cold, passive acquiescence was no longer enough. Economic recovery entailed changes in behaviour; and in order to change behaviour, the state had to influence choices and purposes. In principle, there were two ways of doing this. It could have influenced them through a mixture of punishments and rewards—perhaps indirectly, by manipulating the punishments and rewards of the market, perhaps directly by regulation and prohibition. Or it could have influenced them through persuasion. But in order to persuade, it would have had to appeal to a civic morality of some kind, on the basis of which some choices and purposes ranked higher in the moral scale than others; and because they were imprisoned in the utilitarian intellectual framework inherited from their nineteenth-century ancestors, the 'Keynesian social democrats' could not develop such a morality.

Some of them sensed that an active state needed active citizens, willing to accept their share of the obligations it had assumed on their behalf, but they could not articulate that notion convincingly, or make it resonate in the society around them. Only rewards and punishments were left. Thus, 'Keynesian social democracy' became, for most of the time, a technocratic philosophy rather than a political one: a philosophy of social engineering, rather than of persuasion, negotiation and debate. In Peter Clarke's terminology, its view of government, and of the relationship between government and governed, was 'mechanical', not 'moral', emphasising outward changes of structure and law rather than inner changes of value and belief.[12] As the crisis deepened, however, social engineering became more and more difficult; and governments had to turn to argument and persuasion after all. Since the changes they sought were often painful, moreover, they had to argue on non-hedonistic grounds: on grounds of patriotism, or fraternal solidarity or the common good. But their philosophy gave them no basis for arguments of this sort and no language in which to couch them. It is not surprising that they became progressively more helpless as time went on. The neoliberal counter-revolutionaries of the 1980s have climbed to power on their helplessness.

Politics as mutual education

In this perspective, the long-drawn-out crisis of which the counter-revolution is the culmination is political rather than economic, and cultural rather than political. The failures of adaptation which lie behind it all reflect the stubborn survival, both on the 'micro' level of the individual enterprise or producer group and on the 'macro' level of the whole economy, of the ethos of market liberalism and of the reductionist individualism which underpins it. It is, in short, the crisis of a fragmented society—of a society in which, for the best part of two centuries, the dominant system of values has nibbled at any notion of community or common purpose like air pollution nibbling at an ancient building.

Hard questions follow. How can a fragmented society make itself whole? How can a culture permeated by reductionist individualism restore the bonds of community? One possible answer is that it cannot: that the social and political fragmentation which the current counter-revolution reflects will continue indefinitely. No one who has lived through the last fifteen years of British history could dismiss that answer out of hand. If this essay has any single thesis it is that the roots of Britain's predicament lie deep in her history and culture. Most past societies caught in a predicament of that sort have failed to escape, and there is no guarantee that Britain will be able to do so either. Yet this does not mean that escape is, by definition, impossible. The conventional British view that culture is in some sense given, impervious to argument and incapable of being changed, is as dangerous as any other sort of determinism. Inherited values and assumptions can be jettisoned; the institutions which embody and transmit them can be reformed or abolished. What it does mean is that changes of the sort that are needed are unlikely to come easily or quickly if they come at all. Above all, it means that they are unlikely to come through the methods of the recent past.

For the reductionist individualism which underlies those methods can encompass only two ways of living together in society, and therefore only two conceptions of politics and political man and only two modes of social change. One is the command mode, and the other the exchange mode. Change may be commanded from the top down, or it may result from free exchanges of one kind or another. People change either because they are told to, or because it is worth their while (or made worth their while). Society is either a kind of hierarchy, held together because those at the bottom obey those at the top, or it is a kind of market, held together by the calculating self-interest of its members. Thomas Hobbes painted a marvellously coherent, if chilling, picture of a society operating by the command mode. The seventeenth-century English Whigs, and their eighteenth-century American intellectual descendants, drove out their respective rulers in the name of the exchange mode. Both modes are, of course, omnipresent; it is hard to conceive of a society in which neither played a central part. Change can come by either of them, and frequently does. Almost by definition, however, neither can generate profound cultural changes—changes of value, belief and assumption—of the kind which will have to take place if Britain is to adjust more successfully in the future than she has in the past.

Once we abandon the reductionist straitjacket, however, we are no longer limited to these two modes. And in the real world there is also a third—more elusive, less often studied, but, potentially at any rate, much more hopeful. Charles Lindblom calls the relationships on which it depends 'preceptoral',[13] but they could equally well be called 'persuasive', 'educational' or even 'moral'. They are the relationships, not of masters to servants or buyers to sellers, but of pupils to teachers and teachers to pupils. Change in the

© 2011 The Author. The Political Quarterly © 2011 The Political Quarterly Publishing Co. Ltd

preceptoral mode comes neither from commands nor from exchanges, but from persuasion, discussion, indoctrination, conversion—in short, from learning. People change, not because they have been ordered to or given incentives to, but because they have learned to see the world and themselves in a different way: because, in some measure, they have become different people. If a society operating by the command mode would be rather like a regiment, and in the exchange mode like a bazaar, a society operating by the preceptoral mode would be more like a classroom, a debating chamber, a Quaker meeting or a Jewish Yeshiva. This does not mean that preceptoral relationships are, in themselves, morally superior to the others. They can be abused by tyrants and exploiters, just as the others can. If Gladstone's Midlothian campaign was one spectacular example of preceptoral politics, Mao Tse Tung's Cultural Revolution was another. But that is only to say that all human relationships have potentiality for evil as well as for good, and that all social ideals can be twisted and debased. The important point is that— although no society could operate by the preceptoral mode alone—it is as omnipresent in most real-world societies as the other two. Because reductionist individualism cannot make sense of it, it has eluded most of the theorists whose teachings the common sense of the last 200 years reflects. Yet it exists. Men and women do not only command and obey, and exchange one good for another. They also teach and learn, persuade and are persuaded.

Almost by definition, we cannot lay down in advance what shape a politics of community and mutual education might take. Yet one or two implications stand out. We cannot redefine our common purposes if we cannot have common purposes. We cannot educate each other if we have no spaces in which to speak to each other. We cannot learn from each other if we will not accept the responsibility for our mistakes. The notion of change through mutual education implies a notion of the political domain as a public realm, where the members of a political community listen to, argue with and persuade each other as equal citizens; of the citizen as a reflective and open-minded being, capable of rising above his particular interests in order to make a disinterested judgement of the general interest; and of man as a learning being, continually influencing and influenced by his fellows, and with immense potentialities for good and evil. Two classic insights help to point the way. One is John Stuart Mill's: 'We do not learn to read or write, to ride or swim, by merely being told how to do it, but by doing it.'[14] We learn the arts of government by practising them; we become responsible by taking responsibility. The other is Burke's: 'To be attached to the subdivision, to love the little platoon we belong to in society, is the first principle (the germ as it were) of public affections.'[15] Small groups are the building blocks for big ones: the feelings of mutual loyalty and trust which hold the wider society together have to be learned in the lesser collectivities of which it is made up.

It will not be easy to rebuild the Progressive Tradition whose achievements are now being dismantled. There are worse teachers from whom to learn how to begin.

Notes

1 I have borrowed the term 'Keynesian social democracy' from David Heald, *Public Expenditure: Its Defence and Reform*, Martin Robertson, Oxford, 1983.
2 For the details, see Rudolf Klein, 'Public Expenditure in an Inflationary World' in Leon N. Linberg and Charles S. Maier (eds), *The Politics of Inflation and Economic Stagnation*, Washington, DC, The Brookings Institution, 1985.
3 Brian Lee Crowley, 'The Limitations of Liberalism: The Self, the Individual and the Community in Modern British Political Thought with special reference to F. A. Hayek and Sidney and Beatrice Webb', London University Ph.D., 1985.
4 E. P. Thompson, 'The Moral Economy of the English Crowd in the Eighteenth Century', *Past and Present*, No. 50, 1971, pp. 76–136.
5 For the 'people's science' see Noel W. Thompson, *The People's Science: The Popular Political Economy of Exploitation and Crisis 1816–34*, Cambridge, Cambridge University Press, 1984; for the 'moral vacuum' see Gertrude Himmelfarb. *The Idea of Poverty: England in the Industrial Age*, London, Faber and Faber, 1984.
6 Except, among the leading figures, for Tawney.
7 Robert Currie, *Industrial Politics*, Oxford, Oxford University Press, 1979.
8 Karl Polanyi, *Origins of Our Time: The Great Transformation*, London, Gollancz, 1945.
9 John Zysman, *Governments, Markets and Growth, Financial Systems and the Politics of Industrial Change*, Ithaca, NY, Cornell University Press, 1983.
10 Ronald Dore, 'Industrial Policy and How the Japanese Do It', *Catalyst*, Spring, 1986, pp. 45–58.
11 Alexander Gerschenkron, 'Economic Backwardness in Historical Perspective' in A. Gerschenkron (ed), *Economic Backwardness in Historical Perspective*, Cambridge, MA, Harvard University Press, 1966, pp. 5–30.
12 Peter Clarke, *Liberals and Social Democrats*, Cambridge, Cambridge University Press, 1978, pp, 1–8.
13 Charles Lindblom, *Politics und Markets*, New York, Basic Books, New York, 1977.
14 John Stuart Mill, *Essays on Politics and Culture*, (ed. G. Himmelfarb), New York, 1963, p. 186, quoted in Carole Pateman, *Participation and Democratic Theory*, Cambridge, Cambridge University Press, 1970, p. 31.
15 Edmund Burke, *Reflections on the Revolution in France*, London, Penguin edition, 1982, p. 135.

Representative Democracy and Its Limits

PAUL HIRST*

Vol. 59, No. 2, April–June 1988

DEMOCRACY is the dominant idiom in political discourse in Britain, as in all other Western countries. Everyone is a democrat irrespective of their other political views; and anyone with the slightest concern for political success carefully avoids criticising democracy for fear of the political wilderness. Representative democracy is such a powerful tool of legitimation of the actions of government that no serious politician, even if they have just lost an election, will question it. Democracy is an unquestionable good and representative democracy is identified with democracy.

To challenge the dominant idiom appears to be political suicide, but such a challenge needs to be mounted in the name of democracy. The dominant idiom—representative democracy as democracy—in fact serves to legitimate modern big government and to restrain it hardly at all. Electoral victory serves as a means to stifle other claims to political competition, public pressure and governmental accountability. It permits governments to deny challenges to their authority which may in fact be necessary if government is to be made more effective and accountable. The following discussion is not an anti-democratic attack on representative democracy, but rather a criticism of its capacity to do the job it is supposed to do; supervise, restrain and control government. Part of the argument is that corporatist mechanisms of consultation and bargaining are a vital supplement to representative democracy in the era of big government and organised social interests. Corporatism, it is claimed, would strengthen rather than weaken democracy in the UK and assist in the solution of the problem of Britain's economic decline.

Despite democracy being the dominant idiom, most politicians and ordinary citizens are unclear as to its nature and purpose as a political mechanism. The term 'political mechanism' may appear odd, but it enables us to treat political institutions in terms of their functions and outputs.[1] If one asks people 'what is democracy and what is it for?' most of them are puzzled. They tend to treat democratic institutions as an unquestioned fact of obvious utility, as an ultimate value or as an end in itself. 'What do you mean, what is it for?' 'Democracy is obviously a good thing, how can you question it, just look at the places that do not have it?' And so on. But all political mechanisms are a means to do something, for example, to produce certain sorts of

*Paul Hirst is Professor of Social Theory at Birkbeck College, University of London. His most recent book is *Law, Socialism and Democracy*, London, Allen and Unwin, 1986.

decisions or to mobilise resources for certain objectives. After some more questioning one usually gets an answer like, 'to give expression to the will of the people'.

What can that mean? In a sense the answer has an obvious meaning: democracy is a decision procedure and the people use this political mechanism to choose those public actions they want done by government. But there is a mass of problems in this obvious meaning. For a start, democracy is presented as a single idiom: one is a democrat, one is in favour of democracy. But once one starts to ask what democracy is for, one uncovers the thorny problem of what democracy is. There is no 'democracy' in the singular, rather there are a variety of doctrines of democracy and a variety of political mechanisms and decision procedures which are claimed to be democratic.

Let us begin our quest with one of the simplest and most obvious definitions, that given by the Oxford English Dictionary as 'government by the people'. Democracy is a form of government or rule. In its simplest form it is the direct rule of the people themselves as a body without superior authority set over them. Such a direct democracy necessitates that 'the people' are very few (a few thousands of citizens at most), that the tasks of government are simple and do not require special training or continuous attention, and that the political body in question stands against all the world and recognises no higher authority. Such a democracy is inconceivable today. It became obsolete in Europe in the fourth century BC for the simple reason that tiny self-governing statelets could not compete militarily with larger, more complexly governed powers. If direct democracy is taken seriously today, it can only be in a different sense as a means of management of some relatively simple and stable activity within a larger political whole. It will always be a subordinate form of administration within a bigger system of government which is not itself directly democratic. Direct democracy should not be despised. Where appropriate as a level of administration, it tends to be cheap, efficient and it gives those members interested enough to be active in it great confidence which stems from a good training in basic administrative-political skills. But it can never be a doctrine appropriate to the main forms of modern politics.

The Oxford English Dictionary follows its bald initial definition thus: 'That form of government in which the sovereign power resides in the people as a whole and is exercised either directly by them (as in the small republics of antiquity) or by officers elected by them.' The OED thus treats direct and representative democracy as if they were varieties within a species. But they are different in kind, as Max Weber pointed out when he noted that the former is a type of rule, while the latter is actually a form of legitimation of rule.[2] The OED definition is interesting not because it embodies some special wisdom or authority about political concepts but, on the contrary, because it engages in the slippage absolutely characteristic of modern everyday democratic vocabulary, that is, to identify representative democracy with rule by the people. Lincoln's Gettysburg Address has the formula precisely: representative democracy is 'government of the people, by the people and for the people'. In the nineteenth century, the slippage was comprehensible, because autocratic monarchy and oligarchic rule based on wealth and privilege were still the predominant forms of Western politics—democracy in this context could mean rulers chosen from among formally equal citizens by some mechanism in which all these citizens could equally participate. But even so, by any stretch of the imagination, it could not mean rule by the people.

Let us consider the doctrines of popular sovereignty and representative government, not as espoused by any particular political theorist but at the OED level of public political discourse. Political authority is presented as a delegated power brought into existence by the expressed will of the people. I do not mean here some explicit doctrine of a social contract, but the implication of the claim that the sovereign power ultimately resides in the people and that the form of government gives expression to the will of the people. The ultimate sovereign power must be given expression in some representative body to which that power is delegated. The National Assembly or Parliament is 'sovereign' because it expresses the delegated power of the people and is legitimately so because it is 'representative' of the people's will.

The assembly or parliament is a sovereign legislature that makes laws that take the form of universally applicable general rules, which single out or disadvantage no individual citizen or group of citizens, The assembly then delegates a portion of its own power to an administrative apparatus in order to give execution to and to enforce these laws. The executive portion of the democratic government is answerable to the legislative assembly or to the judiciary as interpreters and guardians of the law. The sovereign will of the people expressed through the assembly and its laws will infringe the basic liberties of none of the citizens, because these laws are universally applicable to all and the people as a whole will not consent to infringe those inalienable rights which they each possess as individuals. The delegated power of execution and enforcement must put that legislation into effect *sine ira et studio*; therefore, it cannot damage the liberties of the law abiding. If the executive does act in an arbitrary or partial way, then it will be called to account by the assembly. Representation guarantees that the legislature expresses the will of the people, who cannot wish to harm themselves, and the doctrine of the answerability of the executive to the legislature ensures that the delegated power of government is not abused. Democracy and the rule of law are thus fully compatible.

Doubtless, when put in this form most people recognise such ideas as the bland evasions of elementary civics courses. The commonplaces of democratic political legitimation are the main themes of not-yet-defunct classical political theory. In fact they are still the substance of the popular doctrine of democracy prevailing in the West. Only by means of such classic archaisms can representative government appear today as democratic rule, as giving genuine effect to the will of the people. Stated thus badly the doctrine must appear incredible as a description of our political system to any person even casually acquainted with the workings of that system. But, incredible or not, it remains the dominant idiom of modern politics.

Contradictions in the doctrine

Several basic contradictions are built into the doctrine. They may appear 'obvious' to any competent political scientist, but 'stating the obvious' has its value. The commonplace level of political discourse, where the legitimation of existing institutions is politically effective, carries on in sublime disregard of academic political science and abstract political theory. The legitimation of existing institutions of representative government as 'democracy' *tout court* is an obstacle to the perception of the need for reforms to make modern government more accountable and, therefore, more effective. The contra- dictions between representative democratic doctrine and modern govern- mental practice need to be registered *politically*, for however 'obvious' they may be to the academy, they have not registered with most politicians or voters.

1. The first of these contradictions is the most important and that is, that it identifies a decision-procedure for selecting political personnel with one for selecting policies or laws. In choosing the one the people choose the other. But it is assemblies or parliaments which make laws and governments that make decisions and not the people. The electors choose some of the personnel involved in making the governmental decisions, but they cannot directly choose the decisions. The electors may reject personnel who submit them- selves for re-election as representatives for the choices they *have* made but always relative to some very limited set of alternative personnel and on the basis of no more than suppositions about the choices they in turn *may* make. Politicians can always plead changed circumstances, constraints on decision- making beyond their control or the unanticipated consequences of legislation or action when explaining why they failed to do what they promised or when what they promised turned out badly.

   A mass of investigations in political science show that voters do not pay much attention to the specific policy 'promises' or parties. Voters pick and identify with parties and party leaders, and they are usually ill-informed about the actual policy proposals of the parties. In practice voters understand the game far better than the prevailing doctrine of representative democracy would lead them to: they pick parties and people and do not attempt to 'pick' policies or decisions. At best the electorate rejects those politicians it deems to have failed, but its choice of alternatives is always limited. An election is not a pure expression of the peoples' will but a choice between a small number of political parties.

2. The second contradiction stems from the idea that laws are general rules, and that because they are universally applicable they cannot infringe indi-

vidual rights. The doctrine assumes that what the legislature does is pass general laws and that the executive is no more than an impartial agency of enforcement of those laws. As we have seen, the legitimating use of the notion of the rule of law supposes laws to have received genuine democratic assent, to apply to all citizens as norms for their conduct and to be fair. Actually most legislation consists in delegating powers of decision and action to executive agencies, that then have the derived power to make such rules as necessary and administer an activity as they see fit within some broad statement of objectives. Laws are less universal norms regulating conduct than legal sanction for specific administrative measures.

Likewise, in the doctrine government is supposed to possess a doubly delegated authority, from the people to the legislature and from the legislature to government. In practice, government is a continuing agency devising policies and pursuing objectives, and it is also a party government. Far from being a servitor of the legislature, government is the initiator of legislation: the legal requirements necessary for the policy programmes of civil servants and senior party members are brought to the legislature and carried through it by means of party discipline. The members of a party government must take a great deal of the continuing policy and decision-making initiated within the government's administrative machine as given; it can initiate, alter or superintend only a small fraction of it. Party rule means the governmental direction of the legislature; parties are an instrument of patronage and discipline controlled by the leading party figures in the government. The legislature typically carries through a governmentally sponsored legislative programme, extending the specific powers of action of the government and while shaped by various forces embodying some of the objectives of the party leaders. The actualities of continuing government and party government thus reverse the positions of legislature and executive. Legally sanctioned governmental rule-making and action is far from being universally applicable; it is often specifically targeted at definite groups to their benefit or detriment.

3. The third contradiction is that 'representation' is a circular process; there is no way of judging how representative of the people one particular scheme is without comparing it with another. There is no pure form of representation, only definite packages of political mechanisms: voting systems, means of determining constituencies, degrees of suffrage, types of assembly, laws governing parties, etc. These packages have very different political consequences. To challenge one package as 'unrepresentative' is always to measure it, even if implicitly, against some other.

Proportional representation is widely claimed to be better than our current first past the post system in the UK, because it enables the number of representatives in Parliament to correspond more closely to the votes cast for the parties. But the scheme proposed some time ago by the Liberals, for example, favours parties which obtain a substantial portion of the votes in a constituency. It means that a party may receive, say, 5% of the vote nationally and receive no seats. Again, why should representation for a national party depend on constituencies which often favour one party by reason of the way the boundaries are drawn and which can vary by as much as 20,000 electors in size? A national party list and the requirement that a party obtain no more votes than the current average number of votes in a constituency in order to obtain one MP would surely be more representative. Is it not unjust that on a national scale a large number of people, perhaps several hundred thousands, may wish to vote for the Ecology party or the National Front but see no point in doing so given the current system, with the consequence that they have no hope of electing an MP? Perhaps. But would national politics be more representative of the 'people's will' if, as a result of such a national list system with low qualifying quotas, coalition governments were to be end-lessly formed and re-formed from the leaders of perhaps a dozen parties and on the basis of bargaining to which the people cannot be privy? I happen to favour the principle of PR but I have no illusion that the various possible schemes will act evenly on electors or parties. Whatever happens, PR or no PR, the electors will never be able to choose decisions or policies, only personnel and parties.

It might be objected that, not only are these criticisms obvious, they are also pointless. Does the doctrine really matter if the system works? Who could seriously imagine that it would be possible actually to represent in govern-ment decisions the wills of electors, when these are diverse, changing and contradictory? But it is difficult to believe that many people can be happy with the fact that the supposed theory of the representative democratic system is so far at variance with its practice. Once one problematises the notion of 'representation' then modern democracy ceases to be a form of delegated rule by the people and instead becomes a form of rule by professional politicians and government officials over the people, in which some of those rulers are periodically changed by the mechanism of election. The standard commonsense response to such criticism is: 'better a system in which personnel are thus subjected to the threat of change and in which the electors have a choice between at least two parties than one in which neither of these things happens'. Yes, indeed, far better. But that is not the point. If we compare a system where there are at least minimal political competition and, therefore, some political choices with one in which they are absent the issue is not in doubt. Better a very defective system of representative government than the best autocratic government. But this comparison induces compla-cency, and appears again to make 'democracy' an unqualified political good, an end in itself—this is wholly by virtue of contrast with a form of rule not subject to political competition, public scrutiny or public influence.

The purposes of democracy

So what is democracy for? It can only be, once we have cleared away the myths of rule by the people, a set of political mechanisms for ensuring the benefits of competition, scrutiny and influence. These benefits are that governmental decisions be responsive to the needs of citizens, efficient because based on adequate information and subject to criticism, and not systematically oppressive of individuals. To talk in this way is to assume a government machinery which would otherwise start to behave very differently if it were not subject to such constraint. It is to recognise the existence of large-scale continuing government and to accept that it is not a mere device for executing the 'will of the people' but stands in authority over the citizens. In this sense 'democracy' becomes a set of political mechanisms, of which representation through elections is one, that exercise constraints on government. But it is not itself a form of popular government.

To talk in this way is radically to undercut the idea of democracy as government by a sovereign people, whether directly or through representatives. It is to pose modern government as a problem and not as a mere expression of the people's will. An important current of nineteenth-century liberalism did, indeed, perceive government as a problem: the less of it the better and the less it interfered with the rights of the individual the better. Constitutionalist liberalism sought to fetter the actions of government, but it also tended to oppose democracy. Conservative liberals opposed widening the electorate to include all classes of the adult population and also the legislation of such mass agencies of political pressure as the trade unions. They did so because they feared that the 'people' would demand forms of action by the government which would take the administrative machinery of state into areas where it threatened the rights of the individual, in particular the right to private property. Some conservatives feared that mass pressure for reforms would lead to such a growth of the governmental machine that it could no longer be controlled or superintended by a handful of parliamentary notables.

On both counts they were right, according to their own values, and yet their opposition was futile. The conservative liberal response was doomed because it set itself not merely against the masses but also against government agencies and official perceptions of the need for state action to assure the working of a complex industrial society. The calendar could not be kept at 1831 for ever. The liberal anti-governmental protest constantly re-emerges, as in Lord Hailsham's campaign for a Bill of Rights during the previous Labour government. Mrs. Thatcher's administration may use liberal anti-statist and free-market rhetoric, but its objective is to change the direction and the policies of big government, not to abolish it.

Big government is the creature of a large-scale and complex industrial society. In such a society, whether capitalistic or socialistic, the state must provide social and economic regulation and management; it must also directly deliver a host of necessary services. Big government exists and it will not go away. Fashionable Conservative remedies which drastically reduce the scope of state action in order to enhance the public's choice are in no sense an enhancement of democratic control.

There are two main reasons for this. First, reducing what is done in the name of the state matters not one whit if the tasks are taken on by large-scale private bureaucracies, organisations which dwarf many nineteenth- and twentieth-century states. In that case we merely substitute even less accountable big private government for big public government. Secondly the loss of public provision in health, education and welfare makes a significant proportion of the people less and not more able to influence public affairs. A healthy, well-informed and secure population is more likely to pay attention to the doings of government than an ill-educated one living in fear of the doctor's bill or the sack.

It is now radicals and left liberals, not Lord Hailsham, who hanker after a Bill of Rights. They see it as a means of checking governmental power. But proposing formally to endow citizens with 'rights' by law, to prevent the infringement of the 'private' sphere by the state is to try to remain in the early nineteenth century. It relies on an external 'check' upon government rather than on the transformation of governmental practices. It is a remedy after abuse of power, not a continuing control on the use of power. Moreover, it would be difficult today to claim that there can be any 'inalienable' rights for the individual in the strict sense, since the necessities of economic management, public health, social welfare and social control make the degree of regulation of individuals a matter of policy debate and public convenience.

If the dominant conception of the representative democracy as public control remains marooned in the nineteenth century and big government cannot be superintended on 'our' behalf by a handful of ministers and MPs, then we need to think again about our doctrine of democracy and its institutional framework. The constitutionalist liberal may propose obsolete remedies and may wholly misconceive the nature of modern government, but the objective of subjecting government to control and review—even if it is now that of the 'total' rather than the 'nightwatchman' state—is not absurd. One thing is certain, we cannot place an undue reliance on representative democracy in doing so.

Representative democracy has the limited virtue of enabling certain of the leading decision-making and policy-initiating personnel in the state to be changed periodically or be threatened with change. This should not be overestimated as a means of control. Firstly, our present system puts party leaders at the head of a hierarchical administrative machine; while limited in their capacities of control and supervision, they have the capacity to initiate policies over a period of years and push a number of them through. Representative democracy permits party government legitimated by a popular vote, even though that vote may 'represent' the choices of a minority of the active electorate. Most party leaders are complicit with big government and do not in practice favour the closer superintendence and control of its actions by 'outside' political forces, because this would restrict their own capacity for action. Party leaders are seeking to be the heads of an 'elective despotism' to use Macaulay's phrase. Secondly, parties can use their governmental position to extend and secure their rule: this can take mild forms such as choosing a favourable time for declaring an election or engineering one with, for example, a consumer spending boom; or less mild ones such as blatant gerrymandering, disqualification and harassment of voters, barring opposition parties, etc. Elected governments in multiparty systems may rule for decades at a time, in some cases because they are successful and popular such as the Swedish Social Democrats, but in other cases elections amount to no more than a farce from which the government claims legitimacy as expressing the 'people's will'.

Once we stop contrasting representative democratic political competition with the political processes of a closed bureaucratic autocracy we begin to see that the election of a limited number of personnel to government is like the periodic change in the top management of a large continuing enterprise; policies may change but the basic structure of authority remains. The real issue is to change the regime of business as usual in big government, without imagining we can simply turn it into small government.

Current areas of concern

But why is there a problem? Is not British government wholly unlike the corrupt, arrogant and authoritarian bureaucracies in some other states? Yes, but surely nobody is going to be satisfied because we do things better than a banana republic? There are some very real problems with our present system of control of government which makes it fall far short of an adequate 'democracy' in the sense of a political system in which the state is sufficiently responsive to public influence and debate about policy measures. There are four main areas of concern.

One, as outlined above, is the tendency of representative democracy to turn into the 'elective despotism' of party government. Politicians, far from being a primary defence against the governmental machine, exploit its potentialities of centralised and hierarchical administration to the full to drive through a limited number of their own objectives.

A second is that big government is, however, so big that a handful of party leaders and ministers cannot directly control or superintend more than a tiny percentage of decisions, and so the elective despotism of party government is accompanied by the largely unaccountable rule of the official.

A third issue is that the combination of party government and continuing official administration and policy initiation leads to a double pressure toward secrecy and the control of policy information. The party leaders want an administration which is loyal and responsive only upwards, and which reveals only those aspects of policy or the information pertaining to it which suit the government's political purposes. The officials in turn pursue long-term departmental policies. This leads to the rule of the unelected official, not only in matters of routine or detail but in major issues that either never come before elected representatives or only before a small number of senior ministers on a 'need to know' basis and with very strong pressure to pursue official policy. It is in 'national security' matters of such vital importance as to require widespread debate and which ought to be subject to the widest range of political pressures that this rule of secrecy and officialdom is most evident.

Finally, big government is now so big that it is difficult for a ministerial cabinet or governmental party pursuing a programme of policy change to coordinate effectively policy over a number of departments and policy areas; this is a function of administrative 'drag' but also of the existence of a number of quite different 'departmental views', some of which will contradict the overall policy. The upshot is that it is difficult to pursue large-scale programmes of social and political change, certainly within the lifetime of one parliament.

The result is a governmental system that grows by accretion, that is secretive and unresponsive, and difficult to direct toward large-scale object-ives in the face of rapidly changing circumstances. Britain's system of government is widely recognised to be bad in these respects compared to many of our European neighbours, but this seldom seems to register with politicians as a radical threat to democracy. What makes our situation particularly problematic is that it is less easy simply to pursue 'business as usual' in government because of the extent of our economic decline and the social strains it has brought in train. We do need large-scale social and economic changes to remedy this decline and such changes are very difficult to get out of the present system of dual government by parties and officials. Party government leads to the illusion of decisive action. Between 1963 and 1979 a succession of governments promised to modernise Britain effectively, according to their own perceptions of the causes of its economic decline and prescriptions for a remedy. These successive governments changed the policies of their predecessors in some important matters, but then came to grief at the polls and found their own policies being changed in turn. From 1979, we have had a prolonged period of Conservative government, but only the appearance of consistency in economic policy. Policy has shifted pragmat-ically with circumstances and with the needs of maintaining office. Mrs Thatcher quietly buried full-blooded monetarism, and discovered 'electoral Keynesianism' in time for 1983 and strongly revived it for 1987. What Conservative rule has not done is to reverse Britain's economic decline. What Mrs Thatcher has done is to reinforce the authoritarian tendencies of British party government. The Conservatives have also gradually made peace with officialdom, having partly reshaped it in their own image. A successor government of different political persuasion will certainly find itself con-fronted with the 'departmental view'. But if it continues the disastrous tradition of party government it will face more difficulties than the resistance of officials.

Any party seeking social change needs to make government both more accountable to and more responsive to society as a whole. This may seem a paradox; surely social change is best driven through from the top? But successive British governments, even those derided as seeking 'consensus' by Mrs Thatcher, have only mobilised the support of a fraction of society for a task that needs the support of the vast majority: the reversal of Britain's economic decline.

Making government more continuously accountable to and responsive to public debate and public pressure may actually help to make the process of policy formation and execution more consistent and effective. Parties, because they are periodically subject to electoral contests tend to 'buy off' selected groups; this is one of the dominant and most successful channels of public influence. But it is a discontinuous one and can have disastrous consequences on policy, as the process of accommodation of electorally influential national and local lobbies in the USA shows. Britain has its own equivalent in the middle-class subsidy state: mortgage interest relief, company cars, occupational pensions, etc. What party would dare to challenge this welfare state for the well-to-do? Such a process of concession and accommodation is perfectly consistent with a virtual absence of public scrutiny over or influence upon other major policy issues and areas. The sociologist Emile Durkheim defined democracy not in terms of a set of representative institutions but as a condition of effective mutual interaction based on adequate information between the state and civil society.[3] My argument so far has been that in practice representative democracy does not secure this to a sufficiently satisfactory degree and that the doctrine of representative democracy widespread among politicians and the public in Britain enables this failure to continue; the symptoms of failure are recognised but not the cause. Party politicians in particular have too great an interest in the present system either to wish to comprehend it or to change it.

Some remedies

At this point I am obliged to offer some remedies. Let me begin, however, by saying what I do not propose. Firstly, it would be foolish to imagine that we can abandon the mechanism of representative democracy or completely abandon the institution of party government. Most people would greatly fear losing the vote; at least it offers some constraint on the actions of government. Political parties are an inevitable consequence of mass electoral democracy; they are vote-getting bureaucracies, and parties also organise political opinion to the point where elections become relatively simple matters of choice between a small number of alternatives. Just as the electorate needs the relatively simple choices offered by party images, because it is neither well enough informed about or involved in politics, so we can see why more 'populist' proposals for making government responsive to the people are a non-starter. Referenda, for example. offer the spurious hope of a 'people's choice'. But in reality they are ideal tools for government or influential lobbies to acquire legitimacy for a policy or an institution. Most of the populist proposals for the reform of representative democracy are devices for the political mobilisation of opinion-fed masses by the elite. Populist politics generally wants to short-cut informed debate and opinion by a simple yes or no vote; Proposition 13 put to the electorate of the State of California is a very good example of the complex consequences of an issue being hidden in a simple and apparently attractive proposal to cut state taxes.

Populism is the enemy of the informed control of big government because it relies on the empty category of 'the people'. Western societies are democratic to the extent that they are, not simply because they have free elections and the choice of more than one political party, but because they permit effective political competition and debate. Not only parties but a plurality of trade unions and other corporate interest organisations, special issue campaigns, etc., compete to influence decisions. Representative democracy can actually be used to legitimate action against this pluralism; increasing the centralisation, hierarchy and closedness of state administration the better to give expression to party government. Reducing the capacity of independent action by non-state organisations like trade unions can be justified by the claim that only central government is fully democratic because only it fully expresses the people's will. Exactly the same justification as that used by the Jacobins in the French Revolution is being used by Mrs Thatcher's government today.

If we want a more democratic society we need more effective and widespread political competition and debate not an elective despotism claiming authority from a popular vote. How do we obtain this and how do we at the same time obtain greater continuity in policy and coordination between policy areas? There is no contradiction between seeking competition and continuity if that competition is public, continuous and arrives at a measure of consensus. Democracy's future at the national level rests less on the choices of individual voters than on the effective representation of organisations representing major social interests. Effective influence on government depends on organisation. But organised interests can act in different ways and some of the outcomes, while exhibiting strong political competition, do not ensure coordination or continuity in policy. Interests can be pursued singly and exclusively, with organisations lobbying for concessions and advantage over others. That this can lead to a virtual Balkanisation of national politics and the growth of a political culture obsessed with getting a good deal for one's own interest can be seen in the contemporary USA. An effective progress of democratic competition between organised interests is one in which they bargain corporatively, collectively and cooperatively in association with the state. In Sweden, for example, the leaders of industry, labour and the state have bargained in this way for much of the postwar period and generally with considerable success. There is no reason why such corporate bargaining should be restricted to tripartite determination of wage levels and macroeconomic policy, or why much broader social interests should not be included in a more formally corporative political system. For example, it would be possible to replace our present House of Lords with a corporatist second chamber. Such a continuously functioning chamber would permit continuity, consensus and coordination in policy—a programme which could pass such a chamber would have a much higher chance of lasting than any proposal of a party government.

Corporate organisations are in turn effective only if they say what their members will in fact be able to do and if the members are disciplined enough to do what their interest organisations say. Accepting a bargaining process and the need for continued compromise, taking an active interest in one's organisation and obeying it are the preconditions for corporate democracy. The norms and attitudes underlying such a democracy are less strong in the UK than in some European countries like Sweden, or Austria or West Germany. Perhaps if we all stopped imagining that 'our' party government will enable us to turn the corner out of economic decline after the next election we might start to think differently.

Corporatism has received a very bad press in Britain, from both academics and politicians. The reasons have less to do with the intrinsic limitations of corporatism than with the severely limited forms of corporatist bargaining practiced in Britain and public attitudes toward them. Corporate bargaining in Britain has been restricted in an agenda, largely to wage freezes, and has been confined to a restricted range of 'peak' organisations with poor control over their members. It has been widely perceived by both left and right as an undemocratic makeshift undermining the sovereignty of parliament, and, therefore, democracy. In some other countries the agenda has been wider; the bargaining continuous rather than a matter of emergencies; the organisations represented more inclusive and more disciplined; and public attitudes more positive, accepting policy based upon bargaining and corporatist representation as vital mechanisms of democratic influence.[4]

A system of political competition and bargaining in which corporate organisations play a major part has less need of a highly centralised and hierarchical state than one dependent on party government for its 'democratic' component. Party government wants the state to be responsive to it and therefore subordinate and coordinated in its action. A more pluralistic system of government, where distinct dimensions of authority representing different functions have more political autonomy, could be the outcome of a system in which government programmes enjoy wide consensus. Officials in a less hierarchical and more pluralistic system could be more open and 'political', more accessible to public debate because they are less concerned to hide things from or to please superior officials or politicians. One way to counter big government is to 'pluralise' it into its component functions. There is less risk of lack of coordination of and continuity in policy if these are then provided by the continuing process of corporate bargaining across a broad range of interests.

The UK is a much more centralised state than most of its European neighbours, and it is also a country with the weakest processes of open corporate bargaining. This is not to say our neighbours' political systems are without fault or that they do not subscribe to the notions of representative democracy I outlined and criticised at the beginning. Few of them, however, expect so much of party government or give that government so much of the work of democracy to do. That British parties have been a major source of the growth of centralised government should come as no surprise; that they should have been considered as its primary means of control ought to shock us. We should also be shocked that we have made so little progress in the political theory of democracy since the 18th century. Our democracy has been gravely weakened by this complacent archaism; it may be weakened still further if we do not do something soon and change the mental habits that lead to inaction.

Corporatism is now thoroughly out of favour across a good deal of the British political spectrum, Labour has no love of it and fears even to test the goodwill of the unions, favouring loose agreements rather than bargaining leading to binding norms. The Conservatives regard corporate bargaining as anathema, part of the wretched era of 'consensus' politics that nearly brought Britain to her knees. Bargaining between organised interests is seen as a weak alternative to vigorously pursued central government policy by both Labour and Tories. The problem is that bargaining is essential when the government requires widespread cooperation and consent to attain certain objectives. The Conservatives seek to avoid this by a *dirigiste* policy in the public sector, by privatisation, and by supporting the authority of private managements to manage. Labour has less of a clear governmental doctrine, but the Labour left has traditionally favoured directive planning for business and autonomy in collective bargaining for the unions. Each party favours great autonomy for its 'own' organisations and strict, legally enforced, orders for those on the 'other side'. This places an intolerable burden on democratic legitimation in order to sustain the government making such policies. It relies heavily on the legitimacy of its 'mandate' and thereby weakens representative democracy, by identifying it with policies significant social interests regard as inescapably partial.

The problem would not be so serious had Britain's economic decline been checked by the longish period of Conservative rule. However much the government had abused its (minority) democratic mandate it could claim justification in having delivered the goods. The enthusiasts for the Thatcher experiment boast of Britain's economic strength, yet industrial output is barely higher than in 1979 (and below 1973); the underlying trends in the balance of trade in manufactures are distinctly unfavourable; and levels of investment in manufacturing remain unsatisfactory.[5] The long-run implications of these facts are serious indeed. We are currently suffering balance of payments deficits even at the peak of UK oil production. Unemployment remains unacceptably high and poverty is widespread. To tackle these problems at root requires something different from clever economic policies driven through ruthlessly by a government claiming legitimacy from an electoral victory (on the basis of a minority of the electorate). It does not matter whether that government is Conservative or Labour. There are no specially 'smart' economic policies in our situation, certainly not ones that ignore or railroad major social interests. In fact the key to broadly based economic recovery and industrial renewal is political change, change that leads to a real and widespread commitment to get things done. To tackle mass unemployment, poverty, and industrial decline citizens will have to sacrifice short-term advantages and accept a considerable measure of redistribution of national income from consumption to investment. This is just what the UK political system has failed to orchestrate.[6] A long-run commitment of broad sections of the population through their organisations to substantive economic goals rather than to immediate benefits appears remote and to expect it naive. Which is another way of saying that Britain has had weakly developed processes of corporate bargaining and has failed to make corporatism a central part of democracy.

Notes

1 I have discussed the concept of 'political mechanism' and the wider issue of the democratic reform of British Government in 'Extending Democracy', Ch. 5 of *Law, Socialism and Democracy*, London, Allen & Unwin, 1986.

2 See Max Weber, *Economy and Society*, vol. III, p. 951, New York, Bedminster Press, 1969.

3 See his lectures on Civic Morals in *Professional Ethics and Civic Morals*, London, Routledge & Kegan Paul, 1957.

4 For a positive account of corporatism in the economic policies of certain European states like Austria and Sweden, see Peter J. Katzenstein, *Small States in World Markets*, Ithaca, Cornell University Press, 1985.

5 See Williams *et al.* 'Facing Up to Manufacturing Failure' in P. Hirst and J. Zeitlin (eds.) *Reversing Industrial Decline*, Leamington Spa, Berg, 1988.

6 See P. Hirst 'The Politics of Industrial Policy' in Hirst & Zeitlin.

The Future of Political Biography

BEN PIMLOTT*

Vol. 61, no. 2, April–June 1990

WHAT is wrong with British political biography? The obvious answer is very little. 'Read no history, nothing but biography', wrote Benjamin Disraeli, 'for that is life without theory.'[1] In a nation traditionally suspicious of theory, many people seem to agree, and the most popular kind of book—not only among politicians and journalists, but also among scholarly authors, heavy-weight reviewers, the general public and, hence, publishers—has long been biography. Political biographies, moreover, have in some respects been getting better. In the early 1970s, Roy Jenkins—himself a distinguished biographer—commented on the rise of a generation of young academic biographers, who investigated in greater depth than their predecessors. He added that their work had yet to bear fruit.[2] Since that time, there has been a remarkable outpouring of twentieth-century British biography—charac-terised by close attention to unpublished papers, the more or less systematic use of interview and a large number of references and notes.

Political biographers might, therefore, consider themselves entitled to a sense of achievement. Yet biography is, at once, the most flourishing and—in intellectual and cultural terms—the least confident form of political writing. Here is a curiosity, and also perhaps a responsibility. Many people with a deep interest in politics, including quite a few practitioners, look to biography for knowledge and insight. But what is on offer so frequently disappoints.

Part of the reason may be that, while readers take biography seriously, nobody else does. Biography is at once the most avidly consumed, and the least analysed, form of political writing. A glance at the subject index in any university library reveals the lowly status of the political biographer's art. Literary biography has an honourable, if meagre, place: political biography, apart from a handful of essays, almost none at all. Thriller writers, film-makers, wood-carvers receive a great deal more attention than the unfortu-nate political biographer whose aims, style, methods and ethics are almost never examined. Reviews of biography generally do little more than summar-ise the life in question, with a pat or a kick for the author. How seldom do critics pause to wonder why so many people, with such eager patience, wish to discover the often unimportant and usually forgettable details of subject after subject, as each one makes his or her repetitive progress from cradle, via career, to grave. And how seldom do biographers themselves—political or any other kind—think about their craft, or take risks with it. All but the very

*The author is Professor of Politics and Contemporary History at Birkbeck College, London. This article is based on his inaugural lecture. His books include *Hugh Dalton*, which won the 1985 Whitbread Biography Award.

best titles of the last decade give one a sense, less of creative adventure, than of conservatism and stagnation. What is notable about most recent biographers is their impeccable authority; but also the straitjacket of unspoken, unwritten convention within which they operate. Indeed—for all its popularity and rising standards—biography in our own generation has been the least adventurous of the arts. That is a pity and in need of remedy. I should like in this article to offer, if not a political biographer's manifesto, then at least a call to action.

One reason why biography is so frequently dismissed is that it is a hybrid. Though firmly based in the historical method, it frequently involves the use of psychology, sociology and much else. More than the specialist historian, the biographer needs to be a jack of all trades, and hence is liable to be considered the master of none. Unlike, say, a medievalist or a poststructuralist, the jobbing biographer is not an expert. Yet this should scarcely be grounds for an inferiority complex. For biography's most important relationship—and the one which is central to its claim to separateness—is with another literary form that is no less dilettante, yet escapes the charge: the novel. 'Biography is fiction', Aneurin Bevan is alleged to have said. It is possible strenuously to deny the accusation, and yet to celebrate the actual link of biography with what is, undoubtedly, its first cousin. In biography as, typically, in the novel, there is narrative, characterisation, birth, love, death and moral dilemma. In biography, as in the novel, the author often succeeds by providing a central figure with whom the reader can identify. Many novels—from *Jane Eyre* to *Ulysses* to *The Satanic Verses*—are fictionalised biographies or, very often, only lightly fictionalised autobiographies. If biography combines academic disciplines, its authors often straddle cultural ones. It is a sign of the intimacy of biography and fiction that biographies are as often written by novelists as by historians. Do biographers make good novelists, or novelists good biographers? Evelyn Waugh's life of Gabriel Rossetti, his first book, is better than several of his novels. Among contemporary writers, Peter Ackroyd has won awards for both biography and fiction, and last year's Whitbread biography prize-winner was the novelist, A. N. Wilson, for his life of Tolstoy.

Of course, there are also important biographers—though less frequently readable ones—who consider themselves scientists, pursuing knowledge about an individual with the kind of rigour that a microbiologist devotes to the study of a cell. Such biographers are not to be disregarded, and in their insistent demand for evidence they set standards for the rest of us. My own view, however, is that even the most ascetic of these truth-seekers deceive themselves. For all their belief that biography is about telling the truth and nothing but the truth, their actual dependence on the novel is greater than they appreciate. Bernard Crick, whose biography of George Orwell does *not* fall into this trap, nevertheless castigates Wyndham Lewis for declaring that good biographies are like novels. 'Lewis did not intend', remarks Crick, 'to let the cat out of the bag.' It could be that we should not now be afraid to let the cat right out of the bag, and permit it to roam around the biographer's study.

Crick's point was to criticise an older type of mellifluously written biography in which evidence was a minor extra. But that battle is now won. Whatever else, serious biography does not suffer from inadequate research. Biographers need now to show their independence, by holding firm to the historical method, yet seeking to emulate the novelist's imagination.

There is a chasm that separates the biography from the novel: it is the gap between fact and invention. It is deep, it is logical, and no biographer can ever cross it. When one speaks of biography as having an affinity to the novel, that does not mean, of course, that biography should be taken away from a vigilant adherence to sources. It is certainly possible to agree with Crick when he writes that 'a biographer has a duty to show how he reaches his conclusions, not to pretend to omniscience; and he should share things that are moot, problematic and uncertain with the reader.'[3] Scholarly biographers clearly have no interest in the type of book known as 'faction', in which the author uses a true story as the basis for his own imaginative theme, deliberately rearranging or inventing minor facts. Such a book is always a novel, albeit a curious and sometimes confusing one, and has nothing to do with historical biography. It is *truth* that gives biography its poignancy—what Virginia Woolf called 'the creative fact; the fertile fact; the fact that suggests and engenders'. In the novel, the author builds castles in the air; in biography, the author can use only the building blocks of reality. 'The novelist is free', as Virginia Woolf puts it, 'the biographer is tied.'

Yet, and this is a dangerous but important point, that is the only difference. Everything else is mere convention, and convention exists to be broken. It is convention that seems to compel so many biographers to regard a life as a race-track, to be followed in a straight line from birth to death. It is convention to regard a biography as an encyclopaedia or school report. It is convention which labels some matters as 'public' and others as 'private' and frequently builds chapter walls between them. It has recently become a convention to see the biographer as a kind of super-sleuth, with a duty, by fair means or foul, to ferret out the 'whole truth' about a character. It is a convention that requires the biographer, somewhere along the line, to make moral judgements. It is convention that seems to make so many biographers take on the role of literary nannies, alternately clucking at their charges for minor transgressions, and stoutly defending them against nasty critics in the outside world for major ones.

The biographer is tied by the truth, and has a duty to seek it out and not suppress it. But that does not make him primarily an investigative reporter. Newspapers, publishers, and possibly the public, have an appetite for the new: but biographers should not confuse this demand with their own artistic responsibility. With many public figures, indeed, shortage of material is not the problem: there is often quite enough already in the public domain. The main job of the biographer is to tell a story that will make the reader happier, sadder, even a bit wiser. In this, his purpose is no different from that of the novelist, and this is the only convention that matters.

Story-telling is the one consistent convention of biography. Probably, it is as old as language itself. Certainly, we cannot consider the future of biography without a glance at a history that preceded the parvenu novel by millennia. If modern biography now plays second fiddle to the novel, historically the influence was the other way round. Originally, all biography was propaganda. The first Western biographies are to be found on Hittite and Egyptian tombs. Biography provides the core of Homer, as of the Nordic legends. The Christian religion itself is based on four, sometimes complementary, sometimes competing, biographies. In the middle ages, the lives of saints and kings provided the bread and butter of historical scholarship, and the tradition of uplifting, or exhortatory, biography long survived the reformation. If Foxe's *Book of Martyrs* in the seventeenth century constitutes the vulgarisation of hagiography, the biographical writings of Isaak Walton provide its apotheosis.

Samuel Johnson was the first in the British tradition to suggest, not that the purpose of biography was to look through keyholes, but that it should explore, and not necessarily praise. Johnson's definition of the profession serves, indeed, as a model for our own time. 'The business of the biographer', he wrote, 'is often to pass slightly over those performances and incidents which produce vulgar greatness, to lead the thoughts to domestick privacies, to display the minute details of private life.'[4] Yet, despite Johnson and despite Boswell, in the following century biography seemed to return to an older, reverential mode. The Victorian era was a time when the popularity of the massive, multivolume biography threatened to suffocate the art with complacency. 'How delicate, how decent is English biography', wrote Carlyle, 'bless its mealy mouth.'[5] How much does modern biography derive from the eighteenth century, and how much from the nineteenth? We are taught that Johnson is the father of modern biography, but contemporary biography may owe more to the decent and delicate Victorians than we commonly allow.

The twentieth-century anarchist was Lytton Strachey, whose *Eminent Victorians*[6] and life of Queen Victoria[7] exploded a large bomb beneath the decorous architecture of the elegant apologists of great statesmen, the Morleys, Moneypennys and Buckles. Yet Strachey's lesson has only been half-learned. The point about Strachey is not, or not just, that he took the lid off the old hypocrisies, exposing the ambitions of a Cardinal Newman and the pederasty of a General Gordon; still less that he was a crusader for the 'whole truth', which—emphatically—he was not. The point of Strachey's work is that it belongs to the author, not to the subject. Strachey's portraits are aesthetically confident, in a way that other biographies seldom are. They are 'true' because they are wickedly pleasing. Strachey's camped-up Victoria with her middle-class habits and Highland passions is obviously not the whole truth. A sombre historian, armed with the same facts, could produce an alternative Queen Victoria, and several have. Strachey's *Victoria* succeeds and survives because it uses the facts as he knew them, to present a personality at once engaging and intolerable, who is both believable and symbolic of attitudes that needed to be challenged. Like the markings on the pyramids, it is propaganda, but propaganda of the best kind: it persuades us. The result, as Virginia Woolf puts it, 'is a life which, very possibly, will do for the old Queen what Boswell did for the old dictionary maker. In time to come, Lytton Strachey's *Queen Victoria* will *be* Queen Victoria, just as Boswell's Johnson is now Dr Johnson. The other versions will fade and disappear.'[8] In my opinion, *that*, and not a proliferation of footnotes, is the mark of biographical achievement.

Strachey was a political and social iconoclast—whether he was a successful revolutionary is more doubtful. Certainly, there has been no equivalent innovator, and modern biographies—in weight and implicit flattery—seem to belong to the age he denounced. An important name in postwar biography is Michael Holroyd, whose own biography of Lytton Strachey[9] broke down some of the final barriers of reticence which Strachey had undermined, making not merely the facts of. 'domestick privacies' but also the 'minute details of private life' virtually a requirement. Where Strachey had hinted, Holroyd laid bare. Holroyd's achievement was to introduce private details, including hitherto well-hidden sexual ones, in order to explain, without diminishing, his subject. It was a major breakthrough but not, perhaps, one which has changed the direction of biography.

Strachey, no doubt, would have relished the prospect of being, as it were, hoist by his own petard. Yet I wonder whether this really ever happened. Holroyd's *Lytton Strachey* is likely to be, and remain, Strachey, just as Strachey's *Queen Victoria* is Victoria. But it does not make one feel critical of the Bloomsbury Circle, in the way that Strachey makes us critical of the Victorians. If anything, it leads us to romanticise them. If the effect of Strachey's *Eminent Victorians* was to knock a whole mausoleum of Establishment idols off their pedestals, the effect of Holroyd's *Strachey* has been to inspire a succession of biographies of ever more minor actors in the Bloomsbury soap opera, not to mention a colour supplement industry in Bloomsburyana. What we have today is a new species: the warts-and-all hagiography, in which the warts are redefined as engaging quirks or even as beauty spots. Most modern biographies, indeed, for all their revelations of promiscuity and personal disorder, have barely departed from the Victorian, and medieval, tradition of praising famous men. Though Strachey may have exploded a bomb, much of the old masonry remains intact and nowhere more so than in the comparative backwater of political biography.

Many political biographies, of course, are still stuck in the pre-Holroydian age—partly because they encounter obstacles which, on the whole, impede literary biographies less. In death, as in life, public figures are jealous of every aspect of their reputations, and so are their executors. Virginia Woolf makes something of this point. 'The widow and the friend are hard taskmasters', she wrote. 'Suppose, for example, that the man of genius was immoral, ill-tempered and threw the boots at the maid's head. The widow would say, "Still I loved him—he was the father of my children; and the public must on no account be disillusioned. Cover up; omit''.'[10] Robert Skidelsky, who is definitely post-Holroydian, makes entertaining use of Virginia Woolf's comment in the introduction to his own splendid life of Maynard Keynes. Keynes, he points out, had many widows—including, in effect, a whole school of disciples, who had a collective interest in preserving his reputation and presenting him to the world in unsullied, heroic clothing.[11] These guardians determined the choice of the official biographer, Roy Harrod, who conceived his role as that of an evangelist of the faith and of its messiah. In Harrod's book any reference to Keynes's homosexuality is avoided, and the hero is deftly rescued from his various financial and political scrapes.[12]

Harrod was himself not only a Keynesian, but also a sub-Bloomsburyan, and his biography is marked by elegant style and a lack of footnotes—a literary work indeed, though not in the sense which is here recommended. A more recent example, which takes the principles of the academic school of biography to its limit and possibly beyond it, is that of Philip Williams's enormous, invaluable, and in some ways magnificent biography of Hugh Gaitskell.[13] Williams found himself in a dilemma of a kind which, I think, well illustrates the impossible difficulty facing the biographer who believes himself to be an objective truth-seeker. Williams was a passionate Gaitskellite, who had spent many years actively fighting the Bevanite heresy; he was also a dedicated and meticulous scholar, who deplored what he saw as the casual use of evidence in Michael Foot's life of Aneurin Bevan.[14] Williams, therefore, produced a book of great detail and erudition, in which every sentence is accounted for with a reference, and which contains a novel scholarly device— the two-tiered end-note. It is impossible to fault Williams's scholarship, and researchers will be using his book as a work of reference for as long as history is written. Yet it is, in the outcome, quite as prejudiced as Foot on Bevan, and it casts a discreet veil over Gaitskell's private life. Curtly, in the preface, Williams explains that he is writing a 'political' biography—thereby absolving himself, Pontius Pilate fashion, from any need to ask about his private world. 'I think' he writes, 'I have omitted no important influences on his intellectual and political development.'[15] Well, that is a matter of opinion. But, as Crick said, such problems and uncertainties need to be shared with the reader. We cannot automatically regard Gaitskell's relationship with a leading aristocratic lady, who mixed in high Tory circles, as irrelevant to Gaitskell's thinking; especially as the Labour leader was, at the time, involved in bitter controversies within his working-class party.[16] Williams's motives and principles were always of the highest, and it is likely that family pressure was involved. The case is worth mentioning, however, partly because it is arguable that the public–private division is impossible to make; if close companions and dancing partners are irrelevant, what of wives? Should the biographer of Macbeth miss out the Queen? And partly because it illustrates once again how pointless is the search, in biography, for the whole truth. Williams's *Gaitskell* runs to over a thousand pages, of which two hundred are devoted to reference notes: yet a dimension of the subject's life which may have been immensely important to his happiness, feelings about the world, and—yes—his intellectual and political development, is treated with euphemism and coyness when it is touched on at all. This may not diminish it as a chronicle, but it certainly limits it as art.

But to press, with Holroyd, for lack of censorship, is not the same as equating revelations with good biography. Nor, to return to an earlier point, should we think that the unreserved biographer automatically escapes the clammy grip of the Victorians. If Williams may be guilty of *suppressio veri*, there is also another, post-Holroydian school which considers—no less culpably—that its duty of criticism is discharged as soon as exposure is complete. Once the 'domestick privacies' have been unearthed, the biographer feels free—perhaps even more free—to return to the serious business of doling out praise and explaining away faults. Thus Richard Ellman's recent life of Oscar Wilde certainly does not spare his reader's blushes.[17] Yet the book, paradoxically, is nonetheless a work of devotion—the author persistently batting on his subject's side. Like Williams, Ellman seems to take it for granted that his role is to defend his subject against attackers. In this he is out of time. Gaitskell and Wilde, in death if not in life, can stand up on their own, without help from their friends. We live in an anti-heroic age: characters are more interesting, and hence actually more admired, if the author shows less anxiety to convince us. Williams and Ellman are cited, not because they are worse than other biographers, but because they are better—master craftsmen whose work stands way above the generality. They are sensible, sensitive, meticulous and fair. What they illustrate, however, is the limitation of the tradition from which they stem: a tradition in which, partly out of admiration, partly because of familial pressure or authorial gratitude, but mainly out of an ingrained, centuries-old habit of mind, biographers take it for granted that their task is to portray their subject as more worthy than he or she might otherwise be thought to be. Whether a modern biographer hides relevant facts, like Williams, or exposes them, like Ellman, he almost always sees it as his role to do as well for his subject as the facts allow. It may be protested, isn't that the gentlemanly way? Why else write a biography? To denigrate? There is seldom much point in that. If the object of biography is not to reveal the whole truth, and not to glorify, what is it?

One answer is that the best biography—like the best play, novel or poem—must be the egotistical creation of its author. It is indeed significant that 'portrait' should be the common metaphor. We have compared biography to fiction: let us now consider painting. The aim of the biographer is not to build an exact photographic likeness—that is logically absurd. It is to build an impression, using evidence as the paint. The impression should be recognisable and revealing, and the portrait is of particular interest if the sitter is well known. Yet, as in painting, sitters, however grand, are in the end merely models, more or less idiosyncratic representations of the human species. Focusing on the subject, the author attempts to build, not a distillation of important facts, still less a logical argument, but a verbal image, using a *pointillisme* of detail and comment. The aim is to create a picture, not to display the paint: the choice of colours and their arrangement will be highly selective. In the process of creating the image, public and private details will be mingled according to need and the artist's fancy. You do not leave out one colour altogether, because it might cause offence; nor do you feel a crusading urge to splash the canvas with scarlet, just because that colour is available.

In biography, as in portraiture, and as in the novel, the aim is not the abstraction truth, except in the artistic sense, but *understanding*. The aim is, or should be, to understand an individual life, the forces that shape it and the motives that drive it, in the context in which it is placed. If the quest is for truth, the biographer is liable to become diverted into an obsessive pursuit of sources—and biographies will get longer and longer, *ad infinitum*. But if the search is for understanding, then the biographer's and novelist's eye have much in common. Here what matter are not just the events in the life under scrutiny; also important are facts about friends, enemies and society in general, and the wider stock of ideas and debate. As in the novel, so in the biography, the hero's life should be the focus of intensive study: yet also the vehicle for a wider observation of human nature and the human condition.

Certainly, if the quest is for understanding, it is apparent that public and private facts cannot be put in separate boxes. Real life accepts no such partition. It is apparent that every publicly expressed passion—of patriotism, class sentiment, concern for the poor or whatever, has a private dimension; and that 'political character' is always a package in which public and private traits are intertwined. If it is relevant to a biographer of Churchill that he was a failure at Harrow, it is relevant to a biographer of Attlee that he had a difficult wife and to a biographer of Lloyd George that he kept a mistress. If the quest is for 'truth' the biographer may decide to examine one category of truth, and separate it from another, and may feel a compulsion either to conceal or to reveal; if the aim is understanding, everything goes into the pot.

If biography is about 'understanding', it is both part of the discipline of history, yet distinct from it. If biography is about scientific truth, what matters is the historical school to which the biographer may be attached. If, in the words of Carlyle, 'history is the essence of innumerable Biographies',[18] and individuals are to be counted as significant for the influence they exert, then the interest of a biography may be ranked according to the status of the subject. If, on the other hand, the Marxist view of history as the product of vast impersonal forces is accepted, then the truth-seeking chronicler of the individual has little to offer. But if biography is about understanding, then it matters little whether the subject is a prime minister or a labourer—provided the material for a story is there—any more than it matters in a novel. Here it is interesting to note a revival of biography across the Continent of Europe associated more with the lives of the ordinary than of the great, or at any rate of adjutants rather than of generals. The movement, in the West—in France, Germany, Italy—is linked to a growing historical curiosity about the Second World War. Biography has become the fertile means of reappraising former enemies and collaborators—in short, of understanding. In the East, a fashion for modern biography is part of a conscious rejection of the old determinism. A new school of Russian biography—carefully researched, anecdotal and consciously departing from Marxist tradition—is seeking to reinterpret the era of Stalin and Brezhnev.

It would be nice to imagine that, in place of the traditional work-place to War Cabinet biography, future biographers might be permitted to tackle mundane lives, and make them interesting. Alas, there are restrictions. The first is a lack of sources: a biographer needs his paint. A great man leaves a trail behind him—press reports, letters, official records, and a wide circle of acquaintances who also have letters and the rest, in which he is mentioned. One golden rule, if you want to be remembered, is to keep a diary: increasing numbers of politicians obey it, scribbling in shorthand during Cabinet meetings, or talking into tape-recorders late at night. In the age of the video-recorder it may not be long before compulsive diarists speak their thoughts direct to camera: an intriguing, or nightmarish, possibility for the biographer. Among the ungreat, however, record-keeping of any kind is rare.

The second restriction is the market place. Here the public differentiates sharply between novels, which can as easily be about dustmen or stock-brokers as about princes, and biographies which have to be about the famous. Among book-buyers, celebrity is the draw, quality is secondary. It is, perhaps, this market pressure that is most responsible for making the generality of political biographers valets to the famous. A finite number of suitable subjects gives widows the advantage. Whether or not they provide full access to papers, or set conditions on their use, they will naturally seek out an admirer. But the limitation of subjects does not inevitably limit the imagination; and widows—to their credit—are becoming less restrictive.

This article is called the *future* of political biography, because it argues that it is time for a change. In general, compared to novelists, the life of the biographer is a cushioned one, in which the pressure for innovation is slight. Publishers, reflecting public taste, want orthodox lives spiced with colourful details, of orthodoxly famous people: the best contracts go to those who provide them. In universities, where the majority of political biographers earn their living as teachers, academic pressure encourages humility, the thesis approach, an acceptance of the status of a disciplinary poor relation. Neither in the ivory tower, nor in the garret, is there much sign of a will to experiment. Neither in the universities, nor outside them, does anybody bother much about composition, structure, shape, dramatic effect, sub-plot—kindergarten stuff for any fiction-writer. Hugh Trevor-Roper on Sir Edmund Backhouse,[19] Tony Gould on Colin MacInnes[20] are two examples of biographers who, whether deliberately or not, gave their well-researched books the shape and feel of fiction. Such instances are exceptional, however, and in the field of high politics, extremely rare. Pick up any political biography, and you will find it built like a Wimpey house, with almost identical segments and proportions—as if, somehow, the Great Biographer in the Sky had ordained them.

Biographers, I believe, are in danger of becoming complacent about their audience, public and academic, as our Victorian forebears were before us. We are in danger of regarding our activity as a minor, respectable branch of the public service. And our work, unless we do something urgently about it, is in danger of ending high on the shelves of second-hand bookshops—magisterial, dusty and forgotten. Yet biography can and will change, and may do so drastically. A single book could make the difference: what is needed now is a radical with the arrogance of a Picasso or a Joyce to smash our encrusted expectations. Such an innovator, and such a deliverance, may yet be produced by the present restless market-place, in which the urgency of demand is met commercially, but not aesthetically, by the hectic expansion of supply. When the moment does come, the revolution will be rapid. It is possible that biography may then once again become the most advanced, instead of the most conservative, of the literary arts—and even the most admired.

Notes

1 Benjamin Disraeli, *Contarini Fleming. A Psychological Autobiography*, London, John Murray, London.
2 Roy Jenkins, 'Modern political biography, 1945–1970', reprinted in *Gallery of Twentieth-Century Portraits*, London, David and Charles, 1988, p. 197.
3 Bernard Crick, *George Orwell: A Life*, London, Secker and Warburg, 1980, p. x.
4 *The Works of Samuel Johnson*, London, 1787, vol. 5, p. 385.
5 Cited in *Chambers Encyclopedia*, London, George Newnes, 1970, vol. II, p. 323.
6 Lytton Strachey, *Eminent Victorians*, London, Chatto and Windus,1920.
7 Lytton Strachey, *Queen Victoria*, London, Chatto and Windus, 1921.
8 Virginia Woolf, *Essays*. London, Hogarth Press, 1966–7.
9 Michael Holroyd, *Lytton Strachey: A Critical Biography*, London, Heinemann, 1967–8.
10 Virginia Woolf, *op. cit.*
11 Robert Skidelsky, *John Maynard Keynes: Hopes Betrayed, 1883–1920*, London, Macmillan, 1983, p. xx.
12 Roy Harrod, *John Maynard Keynes*, London, Macmillan, 1981.
13 Philip Williams, *Hugh Gaitskell: A Political Biography*, London, Cape, 1979.
14 Michael Foot, *Aneurin Bevan*, vol. 1, London, Four-Square, 1966; vol. 2, London, Denis Poynton, 1973.
15 Williams, *Gaitskell*, p. xiii.
16 See Mark Amory (ed.), *The Letters of Ann Fleming*, London, Collins, 1985, for evidence of Williams's missing ingredient.
17 Richard Ellman, *Oscar Wilde*, London, Hamilton, 1987.
18 Thomas Carlyle, 'Essay on history', in (ed. 'G.H.P.'), *Prose Masterpieces from Modern Essayists*, London, Becker & Sons, 1884.
19 Hugh Trevor-Roper, *Hermit of Peking. The Hidden Life of Sir Edmund Backhouse*, London, Macmillan, 1979.
20 Tony Gould, *Insider Outsider. The Life and Times of Colin MacInnes*, London, Chatto and Windus, 1983.

Modern Conservatism

DAVID WILLETTS, MP*

Vol. 63, no. 4, October–December 1992

THERE are two strands to modern Conservatism. On the one hand there is the commitment to the free market—with its appeals to the individual, to initiative, to enterprise and to freedom. On the other hand there is the trust in community, with its appeals to deference, to convention and to authority.

Some commentators believe that these represent two fundamentally incompatible views of the world, and that free-market *arrivistes* have taken over the party of deference and authority. In reality, both approaches can be traced right back to the origins of Conservatism. Edmund Burke, eloquent in his defence of tradition, was also the free-market follower of Adam Smith. Disraeli, who invented the idea of Empire, never allowed it to interfere with the principles of free trade. The One Nation Group of the postwar period not only accepted the principles of the welfare state, it also argued against government intervention in the economy. Mrs Thatcher never accepted the crude simplicities of *laissez-faire*; in her more reflective speeches such as her address to the General Assembly of the Church of Scotland she showed that she understood we had moral obligations to others. The Conservative agenda for the 1990s must show how these two strands of thought can be reconciled.

The political cutting edge of Conservatism is its commitment to the free market. That has provided the hard intellectual core of modern Conservatism. It has given the Conservative party its drive and purpose. And it has played a large part in the Conservatives' recent political success: the slogans of freedom, choice, opportunity, ownership meet the mood of the times and the mood of the electorate.

A crucial task for the Conservative party is therefore to ensure that the free-market agenda remains as substantial and vigorous in the 1990s as it was during the 1980s. There is no disguising the difficulties in doing this. In the heroic early Thatcherite period there were enormous virgin lands, areas of government policy untouched by free-market thinking. Over the years those have been brought under the harrow. Now there is hardly an area of government policy which has not already been reviewed, White Papered, enacted since 1979. A successor of mine at the Policy Unit might well think that the waters had been well and truly muddied.

Another difficulty is that, after the extraordinary rollercoaster ride of the Thatcher years, many people now simply want a quiet life. They think that after the turbulence and change of those years we can now put our feet up.

*David Willetts is Conservative MP for Havant. This article is based on his book *Modern Conservatism*, published by Penguin in March 1992.

But a politician's work is never done; there are always new problems to address. Moreover, a party which ceases to believe that there is anything useful for it to do in office will rapidly find itself with nothing useful to do in opposition.

The prime task for the Conservative government is therefore to set out its free-market agenda for the 1990s. This has already been addressed in some powerful speeches from John Major, together of course with the election manifesto itself.

A free-market agenda for the 1990s

One can identify four strands which, woven together, make up the fabric of a Conservative free-market agenda for the '90s.

The first of these is, of course, the development of internal markets within the public sector, bringing the good features of choice and competition into publicly financed services. That is what lies at the heart of the Citizens' Charter. It constitutes a substantial policy agenda. It takes various specific initiatives from the 1980s such as competitive tendering, the internal market in the Health Service, open enrolment in schools, and applies them vigorously across the whole public sector. The purchaser/provider distinction is gradually being recognised throughout the public sector. (Indeed, there is the story of a man run over by a bus, lying on the pavement. Someone jumps off the bus and rushes towards him saying, 'Don't worry; I work in the NHS, I can help you', whereupon the injured pedestrian gasps, 'But are you a purchaser or a provider?') There are still, however, some crucial general questions about the role both of purchasers and providers, which need to be addressed.

Purchasers of services—be they Health Authorities, Local Authorities or Whitehall departments—still need to learn the art of good buying. As more contractual relationships appear in the public sector, more skill is needed in deciding what is to be put into the contract and how good buying is to be set about. Too many contracts can be very long on exactly how the job is to be done, whilst at the same time imprecise on what the final output is to be. They specify how the job is to be done in such detail that there is no real scope for the provider to contribute any independent managerial skill.

Many of the new free-standing providers within the public sector—self-governing hospitals, grant-maintained schools, Next Steps Agencies, TECs—are relishing their new-found freedom. Yet there is scope for considerable tension here as entrepreneurial public sector agencies are not clear how much power the centre will retain over them. We will need a new constitutional settlement in effect setting out the reserve powers of the NHS Management Executive or the Secretary of State for Education in dealing with schools and hospitals that enjoy greater independence within the framework of a public service. There are powerful traditionalist forces pushing ministers to keep these institutions on a very tight rein. How else are they to be properly accountable to Parliament? If the Public Accounts Committee is properly to inquire into their use of public money, then elaborate centralised record-keeping is going to be needed. How will ministers handle the politics of diversity if provision in one part of a unitary state becomes very different from patterns of provision in another part of the kingdom? Yet, if these forces are allowed to triumph, the freedoms of the Next Steps Agencies, the self-governing hospitals, etc. are likely to be more apparent than real.

There is a more radical approach and that is for ministers to regard their duties to taxpayers and to users of public services as being discharged through the purchasing function. They do not need to establish direct lines of managerial control over institutions provided there is a clear contractual relationship with them establishing what services they are meant to provide at what cost. That is the more ambitious interpretation of the purchaser/provider split and of the agenda in the Citizens' Charter. It will be very interesting over the next few years to see which model emerges in practice.

Deregulation

The second element in the Conservative free-market agenda for the 1990s is deregulation. Despite the stress laid on deregulation in the Thatcherite rhetoric of the 1980s, the problem of excessive regulation, in which the benefits far outweigh the costs, is if anything getting worse. Part of the explanation may be that governments rightly trying to hold down public expenditure try instead to achieve their public policy objectives 'off balance sheet', by regulation. Instead of the economic costs being obvious and measured as higher taxes and a higher expenditure bill they are instead disguised as they are transferred to the private sector. The classic example of this is rent control. This was an attempt to ensure that poorer people could afford their rents, but instead of all taxpayers paying for this through social security benefits it was achieved in effect by partially expropriating private landlords.

Sadly, we have seen several examples of excessive regulation during the 1980s. The Financial Services Act continues to have a serious impact on the retailing of financial services in this country. The regulation of food safety after the salmonella and listeria food scares put outrageous burdens on food retailers and food preparers. The implicit cost placed on a bout of diarrhoea in these regulations is enormous. Throughout the country there are schools, hospitals and restaurants spending tens of thousands of pounds completely replacing their old kitchens so that they can meet the latest regulations. A third example of excessive regulation is the Children Act of 1989. In the interests of raising the standards of regulated child care even higher, the government has restricted its availability. More children will be left without proper child care at all. These new regulations are often believed to be the result of heavy-handed interference from Brussels, whereas the problem is much closer to home.

All the examples above point to the need for rigorous review of the economic impact of regulation to establish whether or not the benefits justify the costs. The impact of government on the economy is not just measured by taxes and expenditure.

Technology and individualism

The third strand in a free-market agenda for the 1990s is the impetus which comes from technological advance. In a way the Marxists were right when they saw the importance of technology in shaping political and social structures. But the mistake which the left then made was to associate itself with a particular stage of technology—the period of mass manufacturing when thousands of workers would stand side-by-side on one enormous production line. That sort of mass production did indeed help to drive collectivism and egalitarianism in politics. Now technology is helping to drive a very different sort of political agenda—one which is much more individualistic and market-orientated.

Technology is making free-market individualism ever easier. The government's reviews of broadcasting have been driven by a recognition that a regulatory regime suitable for a period when there were relatively few channels simply would not apply to a world of many more TV and radio channels together with satellite and cable broadcasting.

Changes in medical technology will gradually undermine the traditional district hospital. Instead of sending samples to enormous pathology labs, individual GPs will be able to put sensors to our skins and get a reading straight away. There will be much more non-invasive surgery which will be carried out at day case units or even the GP's clinic. All this will encourage the GPs and other small scale providers.

Alan Walters began his career as a transport economist and as early as the 1960s he was advocating road pricing. At the time this was seen as an eccentric idea; but with the development of sophisticated technology it is now feasible that crowded conurbations will see road pricing within the next twenty years. The technological scope for free-market solutions is becoming ever greater.

Spreading ownership

The final strand in the free-market fabric is the spread of capital and ownership. As societies become richer so they have a larger and larger capital stock. Ultimately all capital belongs to people and so on average people have more wealth, a greater stake in society. The trouble is that often people do not have a strong personal sense of owning the assets which belong to them—most notoriously of course in the case of occupational pension funds.

The 1980s failed to reverse the trend for more and more shares to be held through institutions—share-holding may have become wider during the

1980s, but it also became even shallower. Indeed, the Financial Services Act and the changes in the City after the Big Bang probably made the life of the small personal share holder even trickier. So we still need a Conservative agenda to encourage more direct personal ownership of assets. One way to achieve this is to require that pension funds, at least notionally, unitise their assets, so that individual members of a scheme get an annual statement of the value of their part of the pension fund. Actuaries like to claim that such a calculation is impossible; but if they are now able to calculate transfer values for members of pension funds they should also be able to calculate the value of one stake in an accumulated fund, with suitably cautious allowances for contingency reserves etc. At the same time we need to encourage more direct personal holding and trading of shares. The eventual arrival of TAURUS should make this more possible as we will be able to hold our shares in the form of computerised entries, with a statement of our holdings being produced like a bank statement. This should lower the transaction costs of buying and selling shares. It may provide the basis for a long-awaited resurgence of personal share ownership and trading.

There is a meaty free-market agenda here for John Major's government—developing the purchaser/provider split in the public sector, deregulating, pursuing the individualistic impulse of technological change, and encouraging personal ownership. It is striking that in the only countries in the English-speaking world where Labour parties came to power during the 1980s—Australia and New Zealand—they achieved this by leap-frogging over the right-wing parties and being more free market, more reformist. The Conservative party is making sure there is no chance of the Labour party doing this in Great Britain.

The need for community

This free-market agenda needs to be set within a Conservative framework. Conservatives are not simply economic liberals and certainly not libertarians. A Conservative understands that, in Quintin Hogg's neat expression, economic liberalism is 'very nearly true', It offers a host of valid insights into the operation of the economy, but it just will not do as a complete political philosophy. The market (like patriotism) is not enough. Free markets need conservatism. Economic liberals have fought an admirable and successful battle for our interests as consumers to be given priority over our interests as producers. But that then leaves the question of who these consumers are; what there is to them apart from their immediate appetites; what they are loyal to; what duties they believe they have. An understanding of our position in historic communities is essential to answer these deeper questions.

The Conservative understands the importance of the institutions and affiliations which sustain capitalism. There may be a universal instinct to 'truck, barter and exchange', but it only generates a modern advanced economy if it is expressed through a particular set of institutions such as private property, a law of contract, an independent judiciary and legislation to ensure consumers have accurate information. These institutions need to be sustained by ties of loyalty and sentiment. We do not accept markets and price mechanisms everywhere. You cannot sell your children. You cannot sell your vote. The state does not raise revenue by auctioning places on a jury. Royal weddings are not commercially sponsored (yet). The market system is constrained and limited by other values.

Perhaps the most sophisticated postwar attempt at capturing this idea of the mutual dependence of markets and the community is the German concept of the social market. Its intellectual origins show that it is not just some woolly expression of a commitment to the mixed economy. It was originally formulated by the German economic liberals of the Freiburg school, who saw the government's role as ensuring open competition. A social market was one addressing the needs of consumers, rather than being subject to political control. It was competition which made markets fulfil their social purpose.

A Conservative may be wary of some versions of the idea of the social market. For instance, it is often assumed that the social element of the market must mean state action and public spending. But the state does not embody society. Indeed big government is perhaps the biggest single threat to any sense of community. High spending, high taxing governments lead us into a Hobbesian competition of all against all as we try to get favours, tax breaks and subsidies from an ever-expanding state.

Moreover, Britain's different historical experience means that we must inevitably have rather different views of the ties which hold us together. For the Germans, faced with the destruction of so much after the war, the social market was above all a *Gesamt Konzept*—an over-arching idea, behind which the parties could unite in reconstructing Germany. It was important in creating a new basis for German political culture. But Britain has never experienced such a deep break in its political traditions. We have a much longer continuous history as a nation state. For us, therefore, the ties of community need to be much less explicit—they are ties of affinity and of a shared culture.

These ties are so elusive and intangible that many would think that there was no distinctive political agenda which any government could implement aimed at sustaining them. It was Wittgenstein who observed that: 'trying to repair a broken tradition is like a man trying to mend a damaged spider's web with his bare hands'. But in practice there are specific things which governments can try to do which constitute a distinctively Conservative political agenda for sustaining our sense of community.

The first example is the National Curriculum in education. It establishes that there are some areas of knowledge and some skills which we should all share by virtue of being citizens of this country and so it reverses some of the fracturing of our traditions brought about by education experiments in the postwar period. It is not just an attempt at maintaining standards but also at defining the shared knowledge which will bring us all together.

The second example is David Mellor's new Ministry of National Heritage, bringing together everything from Manchester's Olympic bid to the Royal Opera House and the BBC. It recognises the power of culture, in its broadest sense, in sustaining national identity. This is not just high culture—it includes not only looking at Impressionist paintings but engaging in all the activities which the Impressionists themselves painted.

The third example is perhaps the most ambitious—Family Law. Although we do of course have an elaborate structure of family law in this country, developed further in the 1989 Children Act, we are much more reluctant to set out explicit obligations in the way that continental countries in the Christian Democratic tradition have been prepared to do. Germany has the most rigorous family law, formulated by the Allies after the war to ensure the strength of the family as an institution. There are provisions which oblige middle-aged children, for example, to contribute to the maintenance of their elderly parents if they are in nursing homes. In France, parents may lose some of their entitlement to family allowance if their child is regularly absent from school. We may find in this country that we slowly become more willing to accept that obligations, which previously were unquestioned and implicit, should now be made explicit and buttressed by the force of law. We have already seen some examples of this with the much more rigorous system of ensuring that absent parents make a contribution to the maintenance of their children and the extension of the legal responsibility of parents for the criminal actions of their younger children. More such measures setting out obligations across generations within the family could well be introduced during the 1990s.

Market and community

Conservative thought at its best conveys the mutual dependence between the community and the free market. Each is enriched by the other. It is the point at which modern conservatism comes close to the most sophisticated liberalism. Hayek is a good example. Although he famously denied that he was a Conservative, his essay 'Individualism: True and False' shows such an awareness of the weakness of most progressive liberal ideas of the individual that it must be regarded as a classic Conservative text.

There is no disguising the sheer political difficulty of getting across both the message of free-market radicalism and also the message of Conservative belief in the community. Chris Patten admired the German social market idea so much partly because it had achieved this political trick of combining the two messages in one slogan. He observed that all the marketing men told him that you could sell shampoo by showing that it cured dandruff, or you could sell shampoo by showing that it left your hair particularly lustrous, but you could not convince people it did both. It is perhaps the distinctive strength of the Conservative party now that we understand that we do have to get across both halves of the message—that is indeed the core of modern Conservatism.

This preoccupation with linking communities and markets is part of a continuing Conservative concern with national integration. Disraeli's two nations, Salisbury's fears of national disintegration, the One Nation Group, John Major's opportunity society—all address the question of how to ensure that all British citizens feel that they participate in national life.

It is a fine point of political judgement, indeed of political principle, how much to expect us to share with our fellow citizens. Socialists are too ambitious: their egalitarianism is wrong in principle as well as destructive in practice. Nor can one expect any longer, if one ever could, uniformity of belief to weld us into one moral community—the nation as a monastic order writ large. Those extreme communitarians, like socialists, demand too much. We have to rub along together on these islands and that requires tolerance of diversity.

It is also wrong to demand too little—the libertarian error. Without shared loyalties to institutions we lose any basis of legitimacy for the state. Our shared historic culture is the most powerful force for national integration. Education can give everyone and anyone access to our literary and historical tradition. It is a sad irony that those progressive thinkers so keen to criticise Thatcherite individualism and the privatisation of industry—where it makes obvious sense—have themselves encouraged the privatisation of our culture. Look at the changes in a typical school curriculum over the past thirty years and one can see the fracturing of our literary tradition as the trivial and the meretricious jostle alongside the great. Similarly, a sense of the shape of our history has been lost, to be replaced by a miscellany of theses and special subjects. No longer can we be confident that someone emerging from our schools will have come across the novels of Charles Dickens or know who Winston Churchill was. As Prince Charles rightly observed, that is indeed cultural disinheritance. It is real deprivation. The battle for educational standards is perhaps the most important single battle for a Conservative to fight.

A market economy with low inflation, a welfare state in which we all share, and prudent constitutional reform are all part of the successful working of a modern free society. Any sensible Conservative attends to such arrangements. The threat to our precious national life comes from those on the left who try to do too much—giving government a role in detailed management of the economy, using the welfare state as an instrument of egalitarianism, or transforming our constitution. More recently we have seen a new threat from those who want to create a federal Europe, developing EC institutions beyond the underlying economic and cultural integration necessary to sustain them.

Limiting the power of government is essential in holding us together as a nation. We need to be permanently on our guard against the temptation of arguing that if something is bad, it should be illegal; and if something is good, it should be subsidised. We do not want to live in a country in which everything which is not forbidden is compulsory. If we all are perpetually fighting to take resources from others, or to coerce others, using the state as our weapon, then we will indeed experience national disintegration. Perhaps Edmund Burke might have the last word:

It is one of the finest problems in legislation, and what has often engaged my thoughts whilst I followed that profession. 'What the state ought to take upon itself to direct by the public wisdom, and what it ought to leave, with as little interference as possible, to individual discretion.' Nothing, certainly, can be laid down on the subject that will not admit of exceptions, many permanent, some occasional. But the clearest line of distinction, which I could draw, whilst I had my chalk to draw any line, was this: that the state ought to confine itself to what regards the state, or the creatures of the state, namely, the exterior establishment of its religion; its magistracy; its revenue; its military force by sea and land; the corporations that owe their existence to its fiat; in a word, to everything that is *truly and properly* public, to the public peace, to the public safety, to the public order, to the public prosperity. In its preventive police it ought to be sparing of its efforts, and to employ means, rather few, infrequent, and strong, than many, and frequent, arid, of course, as they multiply their puny politic race, and dwindle, small and feeble . . .

. . . the leading vice of the French monarch . . . was . . . a restless desire of governing too much. The hand of authority was seen in everything, and in every place. All, therefore, that happened amiss in the course even of domestic affairs, was attributed to the government; and as it always happens in this kind of officious universal interference, what began in odious power, ended always, I may say without an exception, in contemptible imbecility.[1]

Note

1. Edmund Burke, *Thoughts and Details on Scarcity*, quoted in Ian Hampsher-Monk, *Philosophy of Edmund Burke*, Longman, 1987, pp. 278–9.

Britain in the European Union: A Way Forward

SHIRLEY WILLIAMS*

Vol. 66, no. 1, January–March 1995

WHEN Norman Lamont, the former Chancellor of the Exchequer, declared at the Conservative Party Conference in October 1994 that 'there is not a shred of evidence that anyone accepts our view of Europe', he was stating, with the possible exception of Denmark, no more than the truth. But his additional assertions, in a remarkably frank and coherent speech which deserved more detailed analysis than it was accorded, are harder to sustain. 'All the other member states want a European state', he claimed; 'Britain does not need European integration to underpin our democracy'; and, most significantly, 'opposition to further integration is the only basis of unity'.[1] This was, of course, the culmination of his argument. The fragile unity of the Conservative party depends upon the Prime Minister opposing any substantial further progress towards European integration at the intergovernmental conference (IGC) to be held in 1996, a date that coincides with the probable run-up to the next British general election.

Parties and policies

The position of the main opposition parties adds piquancy to this coincidence. Both national opposition parties, Labour and the Liberal Democrats, support some measure of further integration, in particular the strengthening of the European Parliament, without necessarily supporting a fully federal Europe. Both parties, for instance, accept the European Union's social policy, and would probably reverse the opt-out John Major negotiated at the Edinburgh Summit in December 1992.

A succession of opinion polls over many months has shown a persistent lead for Labour over the Conservatives. According to the Gallup 9000 poll, since October 1993 Labour has been supported on average by 50 per cent of the British electorate, the Liberal Democrats by 20 per cent and the Conservatives by 24 per cent. The Conservative party is therefore governing with the support of only a quarter of the electorate. Yet this is the government that will negotiate for Britain at the IGC, still wielding on many matters the power of the veto.

*Baroness Shirley Williams is a Liberal Democrat peer and Professor of Elective Politics at the John F. Kennedy School of Government, Harvard University.

Published by Blackwell Publishing Ltd, 9600 Garsington Road, Oxford OX4 2DQ, UK and 350 Main Street, Malden, MA 02148, USA

If the government takes any account of the views of the other parties, as it should on a matter so profoundly affecting the future of the nation, no final disposition concerning Britain's future relationship with the European Union should be confirmed by the government or ratified before a general election. If the other member states agree to make substantial changes to the EU's present institutional structures or to transfer further functions of national governments to the EU, then a consultative referendum should be held prior to ratification. But that commitment should apply equally to any further opt-outs or special arrangements made by the British government. The future relationship of Britain to the European Union must not be determined by a discredited and unpopular government in the dying months of its mandate.

There are in principle three policy options for Britain in relation to the European Union. The first of these is to pull out of the Union, while seeking to remain within the European Economic Area.

The second is to muddle through, as Britain has been doing for many years now, opposing further moves towards integration for as long as possible, opting out where feasible, but also weighing up the long-term costs of exclusion from the decision-making process of the Union against the short-term benefits of being seen to defend British national independence.

The third option, which is advocated in this article, is for a new kind of constitutional engagement between Britain and its fellow member states, one that would be acceptable to the main British political parties and one that might enable Britain to play a more constructive role than it has done hitherto.

British exceptionalism

The attractions of the first option lie deep in Britain's geography and history. They have enabled Britain to isolate itself from the continent of Europe, and to see itself as an exception to the cultural and historical movements that shaped that continent. Britain has involved itself only to correct what it perceived as a serious imbalance of power arising from the pursuit of hegemony on the part of some European power—France or Spain, Russia or Germany.

The history of these islands has also fed belief in British exceptionalism—in Shakespeare's 'island built by nature for herself, against infection and the hand of war'—occupied by no foreign power for nearly a thousand years, undefeated in war in this bloodstained century, maintaining the appearance of international influence with permanent membership of the UN Security Council and membership of the Commonwealth.

So it is not surprising that Britain has been, from the beginning of the history of European integration, ambivalent about its relationship to the continent of Europe. In his Spaak Memorial Lecture at Harvard University on 16 October 1994, Roy Jenkins (Lord Jenkins of Hillhead) compared the behaviour of British governments in this respect to that of a man watching a train pulling out of a station. At the last minute, the man runs after it and leaps aboard the very last coach, only to complain bitterly that all the seats in the restaurant car have been taken.

The pattern has repeated itself, from the European Coal and Steel Community, the European Defence Community and the Messina conference to the Treaty of Rome. Even after Britain became a reluctant member of the EEC in 1972, there came the Labour government's insistence on 'renegotiation'—a rather ineffective attempt to prove that it held national interests dearer than did Edward Heath—and then Mrs Thatcher's insistence on unanimous voting for all but the laws that underpin the single market.

The first option: quitting the Union

The first policy option, leaving the European Union, would require a huge economic adjustment, even if Britain were able to become a member of a reconstructed European Economic Area. Over half of Britain's trade is now conducted within the Union.[2] The common external tariff, reduced as it has been by a series of GATT rounds, might not be much of an obstacle; but on the whole range of non-tariff barriers to trade, Britain would lose whatever leverage it now has. Foreign investors—and 40 per cent of direct foreign investment in the European Union has been in Britain—would be unlikely to increase their stake in Britain; indeed, some would almost certainly move elsewhere.

There would be other consequences, too. The City would be permanently outside the European monetary union; the border between Northern Ireland and the Republic would become the border between the EU and Britain; and membership of a European Economic Area would still mean exclusion from the institutions that shape Europe—an exclusion that Austria and the Scandinavian countries concluded was not in their interests.

The special relationship

The heaviest costs, however, would be political. What enabled Britain to maintain its isolation from the European movement towards closer union was the 'special relationship' with the United States. Through that relationship, Britain continued to exercise disproportionate influence on world events, even after its own relative military and economic power resumed their long decline after the Second World War. But the special relationship served another, less benign, purpose: it enabled Britain to pretend to itself that it could remain aloof from the affairs of the European continent.

President Charles de Gaulle perceived that relationship as a deadly danger to the French-led *Europe des patries* that he wanted to construct. He would have vetoed Harold Macmillan's application for membership of the European Economic Community in 1961 in any case, but the Nassau agreement on Polaris in 1962 gave him the justification he wanted. Yet the Nassau agreement was itself evidence of the attenuation of the special relationship. The Kennedy administration had cancelled Skybolt without accommodating British sensibilities, although Skybolt was the chosen means to modernise Britain's nuclear deterrent. Polaris was more expensive than Skybolt, yet was seen as a second-best by the military. The Nassau agreement showed how dependent Britain had become on a United States that no longer saw it as vital to its own interests.

Today, only Britain believes in the special relationship as anything more than the easy discourse of countries that share a language and parts of a culture. That, of course, is very important; but it does not constitute significant political influence. Furthermore, the impact of the discourse will diminish as the United States becomes more diverse, with its Hispanic and Asian minorities growing in size and increasing in political influence.

Britain's influence in the United States is waning, after a brief period during which American media attention focused on Margaret Thatcher as the first woman Prime Minister of Britain, a Prime Minister moreover with a powerful personal influence on the US Presidents with whom her period of office coincided, Ronald Reagan and George Bush. Yet President Bush, despite this close personal association, had emphasised that the European Community was the western partner the United States needed in the post-cold war world, to help construct a 'new world order'. In particular, President Bush underlined the importance of Germany in his talks with Chancellor Kohl on the subject of German reunification in Washington on 17 May 1990.

President Clinton's relations with the Major government were soured from the beginning by the Conservative party's foolish offer of campaign help to his opponent, George Bush, in the 1992 presidential election. He therefore had no compunction in openly recognising the importance of the German–American partnership. 'Germany is now the powerhouse of Europe,' he declared in Bonn on 11 July 1994. To a crowd at the Brandenburg Gate in Berlin a day later, he vowed: 'America is at your side, now and for ever.' He has addressed no such heroic affirmations to Britain.

The President's judgement about the respective significance of Germany and Britain for the United States is shared far beyond the confines of government. The media's interest in Britain, apart from the arts, is confined to stories about the Royal Family and occasional reports on domestic politics, mainly focused on such embarrassments as ministerial resignations for various kinds of impropriety. What makes this lack of interest more surprising is that Britain continues to be the largest single foreign investor in the United States—but even that fact is little known outside financial circles. It may, however, help to explain the persistence of the British belief in a special relationship, whatever the evidence to the contrary.

Without the special relationship, a Britain that opted out of the European Union would become at best a larger and less well-endowed Norway, outside the mainstream of global relationships and without influence in international organisations. Once Britain lost its seat on the UN Security Council, as it would, there would be no compensation in the form of a European Union seat. Furthermore, as the EU develops its defence dimension within the Western European Union, the WEU, not Britain, will become the linchpin of European defence, the second pillar of NATO. The central theme of British postwar policy, to prove its indispensability as the premier ally of the United States, will be seen as the anachronism it is.

The second option: muddling through

But, it will be argued, John Major in his William and Mary Lecture at Leiden University on 6 September 1994 did not propose any such drastic action as opting out of the European Union. He knows that such a proposal would split the country, divide his own party, offend his American and European allies alike, and damage international confidence. His position is the second option: muddling through, the option Britain has pursued for the last twenty years ever since joining the European Community. At Leiden, the Prime Minister outlined his own vision of Europe, one in which each member state would, beyond the common commitment to the single market, be free to opt into or out of further moves towards integration.

The Prime Minister distinguished Britain's position sharply from two other explorations of what a future Europe might look like, one set out by Edouard Balladur, the French Prime Minister, in an interview on 30 August,[3] the other outlined in a paper published by the CDU/CSU parliamentary group in Germany on 1 September.[4] Each attempted to influence the deliberation that is now and will continue until the intergovernmental conference in 1996, on the next stage of European integration.

M Balladur described a Europe of concentric circles, with a central homogeneous core composed of France and Germany. The CDU/CSU paper, prepared for the parliamentary group by Wolfgang Schauble and Karl Lamers, went further, calling for a Europe built around a core of countries committed to European integration which it boldly named: France, Germany and Benelux. That core, the document stated, 'must not be closed to other member states; rather, it must be open to every member state willing and able to meet its requirements'.

John Major's vision of Europe stands in sharp contrast to that of Helmut Kohl, the German Chancellor, whose governing party was re-elected, albeit with a smaller majority, on 16 October. Chancellor Kohl is not one for muddling through. He has two objectives for what is likely to be his last period in that office: the attainment of European political union and the enlargement of the EU to include as full members the Visegrad countries of eastern and central Europe: the Czech Republic, Hungary, Poland and Slovakia. Indeed, he has told close colleagues that he believes this to be his personal mission, as the last of the political generation shaped by the experiences of the Second World War. Joachim Bitterlich, Chancellor Kohl's adviser on foreign policy, summed it up: over the next four years, Herr Kohl will be 'preparing Germany for the twenty-first century and making European integration irreversible'.[5]

The Schauble/Lamers paper is blunter. 'If European integration were not to progress, Germany might be called upon, or be tempted by its own security constraints, to try to affect the stabilisation of Eastern Europe on its own and in the traditional way [i.e. by pursuing Germany hegemony] . . . Hence Germany has a fundamental interest both in widening the Union to the East and in strengthening it through further deepening.'[6]

One of the arguments John Major made most forcefully in his Leiden lecture was this: 'To choose not to participate is one thing; to be prevented from doing so is quite another.' Yet, paradoxically, in saying so he echoed the CDU/CSU paper: 'It is essential [it says] that no country should be allowed to use its right of veto to block the efforts of other countries more able and willing to intensify their cooperation and deepen integration.' If the British government were to attempt to veto further moves by others towards integration at the IGC, it would mock the Prime Minister's own words.

There is no support for the use of such a veto in the other member states. That is not to say that none sympathises with Britain in slowing down the momentum towards further integration. Rather, they find the complaints, threats and abusive speeches made by British ministers increasingly hard to take. Other countries drag their feet or fail to implement directives they dislike; or they discreetly let it be known, at an early stage of the Commission's deliberations, that they cannot support such and such a proposal. Some ministers in the British government, however, often for domestic party reasons, ventilate their criticisms and concerns crudely, publicly and without finesse.

Yet our fellow European member states do not take Britain's dogged opposition to further integration altogether seriously. One is reminded of the story of the boy who called 'Wolf!' when no wolf threatened the flock of sheep he was guarding, until on the occasion when a real wolf attacked the sheep no one responded to his call, believing the boy to be bluffing.

In 1985 Britain threatened to veto further moves towards integration. In December 1990, at the intergovernmental Council in Rome on the Treaty of European Union, rather than attempting another veto, Britain chose instead to opt out of the social policy.

In 1985 the British government, in the discussions on the single market initiative, indicated its opposition to qualified majority voting. Instead, voluntary abstention from the use of the veto, a 'gentlemen's agreement', was proposed. President Mitterrand spoke darkly of a 'two-tier Europe'. At the June 1985 meeting of the European Council in Milan the British stuck to their position; but British opposition was bypassed when the Italian president of the Council, Signor Craxi, called an unscheduled vote on the holding of an IGC on the single market, a decision that required only a simple majority. Outmanoeuvred, Britain participated in the IGC.[7]

So other member states have reason to believe that a firm intention to proceed will drag Britain along, late and reluctant, in its wake. For Britain, it is the worst of both worlds: having to conform to rules in the making of which it exercises little influence.

The imperative of party unity

John Major, is, to use an American expression, caught between a rock and a hard place. His European colleagues want to press ahead with strengthening the EU's institutions as a precondition of further enlargement to the east. The right wing of his party opposes any such strategy. Trying to placate both, the British government agrees to the enlargement, but resists the institutional changes that are inescapable in a Union of nineteen member states, indicating that, at most, it would support the minimum changes necessitated by enlargement.

The Prime Minister proposes a Europe of 'variable geometry', not because that is an attractive option for the country to adopt, but because the party and public opinion that he and many of his colleagues have done their best to shape is suspicious of the EU—and of the Commission in particular—and antagonistic to any further transfers of powers to Brussels. As it approaches a close and difficult general election, the government will do nothing to counter anti-EU propaganda, for a xenophobic campaign based on the *état-nation*, already foreshadowed in the utterances of the Tory right, may be all it can fallback upon, It will not, however, opt out of the Union entirely, for the reasons given above.

Such a campaign, grudgingly conceding an *à la carte* Europe as the most that could be offered, would win little support abroad. The United States, anxious to see a European defence pillar capable of bearing much more of the burden of western security, would see it as a retreat by Britain. European colleagues would see it as sabotage of the European ideal. Even the Conservative party's closest allies in the European Parliament would have no sympathy for such a stance. For instance, Gerhard Rinscher, leader of the CDU party group in the European Parliament, said of Major's Leiden speech, 'One wonders how he differs from Mrs Thatcher. He remains faithful to the idea of an *à la carte* Europe, in which each chooses the sectors in which it will participate. This is a deadly danger for European integration.'[8]

A European hard core?

However, it is also the case that the proposal for a hard-core Europe of five countries, as made in the CDU/CSU paper, has won few adherents. All the existing member states excluded from that hard core have protested, Italy with particular vehemence as one of the founding six. Spain's Prime Minister, Felipe Gonzales, wrung from President Mitterrand of France at the Franco-

Spanish summit on 20 October a joint statement that the proposal floated in the CDU/CSU paper for a two-tier Union was unacceptable. That opened up a certain difference in tone between the French President and the French Prime Minister.

It is indeed difficult to see how European institutions could operate on the basis of some member states voting on some issues and others on others. It is just about possible to ring-fence one particular area like monetary union or social policy, though even in these cases the boundaries drawn between one area and another are often artificial. Opting out may work as a temporary expedient, but permanent opt-outs will eventually give rise to different and incompatible fragments of Europe, reversing much of what the single market has achieved.

A single-track, multi-speed Europe, with each member moving towards agreed common objectives at its own pace, is a more attractive proposition. It is also not new. Transitional periods before entering into the full rigours of the single market have been operated successfully for several of the twelve, and are prerequisites for the early membership of the Visegrad group, let alone other east European countries.

So a compromise will have to be hammered out at the IGC. What is already clear is that no one European country can expect to be able to stop other member states who want to move ahead more quickly, be it towards monetary union or the integration of their defence forces.

Shared suspicions

If John Major were to abandon his proposal for Europe à la carte and instead seek at the IGC acceptance for a new constitutional engagement based upon a variable-speed Europe, Britain would not be without allies. Public suspicion of the European Union, and in particular of the European Commission, is based on more than inflammatory speeches and tabloid newspaper attacks on straight bananas and curving cucumbers. Nor is it confined to Britain, as the French and Danish referenda on the Maastricht Treaty so clearly demonstrated.

The Union's institutions are in M Balladur's phrase, 'opaque in the eyes of its citizens'.[9] Regulations and directives emerge from an intricate network of committees, intra- and intergovernmental and institutional negotiations, and negotiations within the two—a multi-level game from which Europe's citizens are largely excluded. The European Council, which acts as a legislature for much of the time when it discusses whether to accept amendments proposed by the European Parliament, and whether to accept or reject amended laws, still conducts its business in secret—the only legislature in the democratic world so to do. In the later stages of the games, this is the one player privileged not to show its hand.

The third option: a new constitutional engagement

A new constitutional engagement would have three elements: first, more precise delineation of the respective powers of the Union and of the member states, drawing upon the principle of subsidiarity to determine the balance between them; second, a strengthening of the role of national parliaments; and third, greater democratic accountability within the Union's own institutions, with in particular an enhanced role for the European Parliament.

No law can by itself set final bounds to the Union, for integration has its own dynamic. But the proposals set out here, backed by member-states and parliaments asserting their own jurisdictions, would restrain the forces of centralism.

Defining the limits of the acquis communautaire

Suspicions of 'Europe' encompass more than the intricacies of Union decision-making. The Commission, abetted by the Council and the Parliament, has promulgated a large number of regulations and directives under articles of the treaties that prescribe majority voting, that is to say articles relating to the establishment of the single market. The European Court has usually upheld the choice of legal bases made by the Commission, even when their scope is extended to the outer limits of what the articles meaning might bear. These regulations and directives then become part of the *acquis communautaire*. To take just two illustrations of the point, directives on working hours have been formulated by the Commission under articles covering the health and safety of workers; and proposals to ban most tobacco advertising have been proposed under articles on the free movement of goods.[10]

On this central issue of the limits of the Union's competence, a British government would not be without other member states to share its concerns. Among these would be Germany itself. The German Constitutional Court, in its verdict on *Brunner* v. *European Union* (12 October 1993), based the legitimacy of all European laws squarely on the decision of the parliament of the German Federal Republic to accede to the European treaties. Thus 'the validity and application of European law in Germany depend on the instruction to apply that law expressed in the act of German accession'. The court went on to specify more exactly the limits of Union competence: 'Thus, if the EU institutions and agencies were to treat or develop the Union Treaty in a way that was no longer covered by the Treaty in the form that is the basis for the Act of Accession, *the resultant legislative instruments would not be legally binding within the sphere of German sovereignty.*'[11]

Indeed, just because the legitimation of the European Union is rooted in the democratic legitimacy of the national parliaments that voted to transfer their powers to it, those national parliaments must retain their own integrity. 'What is decisive', says the Constitutional Court, 'is that the democratic bases of the European Union are built up in step with integration, and that as integration proceeds, a thriving democracy is also maintained in the member states . . . From all that it follows that functions and powers of substantial importance must remain for the German Bundestag.'[12]

Germany's constitutional relationship to the EU is grounded in its Basic Law, the Gundgesetz, under Article 23 of which the Federation, with the consent of the Bundesrat as well as the Bundestag, may transfer sovereign powers to the EU. The judges in the Brunner case were concerned about the fuzziness of the boundary between the respective competences of the EU and Germany. They called for 'precision and certainty' as to the powers being transferred. Indeed, the limited nature of these transferred powers, and their 'legally ascertainable' scope, were seen as essential to their democratic legitimation.

The Constitutional Court's concern extended to the past and to the future. As to the past, the Court committed itself to review the legal instruments of EU institutions and agencies to see if any transgressed the limits of Community competence; for the future, the Court stated clearly that the EU remains essentially an economic union, 'the common authority of which is derived from the member states'. Any change in this status, such as creation of a federal Europe, would require a new treaty. In the case of Germany, such a treaty would have to be compatible with the requirement that 'functions and powers of substantial importance' remain with the Bundestag.

In France, too, following the referendum on the ratification of the Maastricht Treaty, only narrowly carried, the Senate brought pressure to bear on the government to clarify the respective powers of the Union and the member states. The constitution of the Fifth Republic was amended by the addition of a new article (Article 88.1) which asserts that the European Union rests upon the exercise of competences conferred by the member states and exercised in common.

Without analysing the positions of all the other member states, it is clear that there is concern in Germany and France, as well as in Britain, for a clear definition and delineation of the respective competences of the Union and the member states. That concern has greatly increased since majority voting became the norm for determining a wide range of EU legislation. But it is obviously unsatisfactory for each country to define these limits for itself, since the national courts may not reach compatible conclusions.

The European Court of Justice pursued an activist role as a Community-builder in the 1960s and 1970s, laying the foundations of the *acquis communautaire* in its landmark judgements in *van Gent en Loos*, *Costa v. ENEL*, *Cassis de Dijon* and other cases. While the Court has adopted a lower profile in recent years, some of the more sceptical member states would not trust it to weigh their interests sufficiently in determining where EU competence begins and ends.[13]

Sir Leon Brittan, the EU Trade Commissioner, ingeniously proposed in his recent book *Europe: The Europe We Need* a new mechanism.[14] A committee of representatives of national parliaments should be charged with the duty of enforcing the principle of subsidiarity; should be given the right to challenge the legal bases on which laws are drafted; and should scrutinise any laws taking the EU into new territory. The attraction of the proposal is considerable for those concerned about the democratic deficit, in that national parliaments would become much more fully engaged in the decision-making procedures of the Union. The difficulties are also considerable, however. How would differences of opinion between members of different national parliaments be resolved? Would the European Court of Justice be acceptable as the final adjudicator where reconciliation of views proved impossible?

An alternative possibility, suggested by Professor Joseph Weiler, would be a special court, dealing only with these issues of competence and subsidiarity, composed of judges drawn from each member state's highest national court. In either case, however, consideration by a committee of representatives of national parliaments would provide a new and valuable input into the deliberations on competence and subsidiarity, if only because national representatives tend to be closer to public opinion than MEPs, and subsidiarity is essentially a political concept.

The European Parliament, meanwhile, has changed its rules of procedure to enable it to request the Commission to modify a proposal if the Parliament concludes that the principle of subsidiarity has not been respected. But the Parliament, like the Commission and even the Court of Justice, is seen in some quarters as *parti pris*, judge in its own cause. Certainly the European Parliament has supported the Commission in basing Community law on articles which require majority and not unanimous voting.

A federal constitution would deal with these issues by defining the respective powers of the federal state and of the member states, and any concurrent powers they might share. But it is plain that much of Europe is not ready for a federal constitution. The new EFTA members will have had little time to accommodate themselves to the post-Maastricht Union by 1996; the Visegrad group is only at the stage of close association, though at Copenhagen a pledge was made of full membership at an unspecified date. The European Union, if it holds together, is therefore likely to continue to develop incrementally. Hence the need for a new mechanism to determine the respective competences of the Union and the member states.

Subsidiarity

Subsidiarity has emerged as a general accepted guiding principle in a Union that has no constitution. It is a powerful idea, and one that may help the Union through its differences. It is not, of course, a new idea in the evolution of the EU. As long ago as 1984, the draft Treaty of European Union proposed by the European Parliament, the so-called Spinelli draft, attempted to formulate a definition of subsidiarity: 'The Union shall only act to carry out those tasks which might be undertaken more effectively in common than by the member states acting separately, in particular those whose execution requires action by the Union, because their dimension or effects extend beyond national frontiers.'[15]

But subsidiarity is more generally defined as acting at the lowest level compatible with effectiveness. Combating pollution of the seas is clearly not an appropriate area for action by local governments, for example, but combating pollution of springs and wells may indeed be. It is a principle that sits well with the emphases on empowering citizens, building public and private partnerships, and working with non-governmental and community-based organisations that characterise so much contemporary political discourse. Its implications are radical, not just for the EU, but for highly centralised national governments like those of Britain or Greece, and for regional and local government also.

Subsidiarity is a principle already well established in Germany, The Netherlands, Belgium and Italy, and rapidly gaining ground in Spain and France also. The German *Länder* are all represented in Brussels; more significantly, they have won the right not only to be consulted through the Bundesrat, but to be involved in the decision-making process wherever they would be similarly involved in an internal matter (Article 23(4) of the German Basic Law, amended in 1 993). Education is one obvious function in which the *Länder* will be involved.

Regional policy

The European Commission itself is fully engaged in operating on the principle of subsidiarity in its administration of the structural funds. The former Commissioner for the Regions in the Delors Commission, Bruce Millan, established direct lines of communication with regional and local authorities, bypassing national governments. In most instances, this relationship is regarded benevolently; most member states have supported the consultative Committee of the Regions established in a protocol to the Treaty of European Union.

The British government, however, fought bitterly against the principle of additionality—that EU regional funds were to be additional to the funds the national government would provide. It refused to cooperate in regional initiatives such as RECHAR, the Community's programme for the rehabilitation of districts dependent on coal-mining, until pressures from local MPs and councils made it relent.[16] The British government's attitude on regional policy has been in all but name a second opt-out.

Strengthening the role of national parliaments

If the principle of subsidiarity is to be invoked in a new constitutional engagement as the basis on which the delineation of Union and member-state competences is to be determined, member-state governments have to accept its relevance to their own constitutional structures. Britain is today the most centralised state in the European Union, along with Greece; one in which the powers of local government have been deliberately and drastically curtailed. There are implications therefore for this country in the negotiations to take place at the IGC.

In Britain, much disquiet has been articulated about the threat to parliamentary sovereignty, though one might have more sympathy for those who express such concern if they had ever shown any interest in strengthening parliamentary control over the national government. It was Lord Hailsham who described the British political system as 'an elected dictatorship', and he wasn't far off the mark.

Leon Brittan's proposal would be one way to engage national parliaments in the process of EU decision-making. Since the Maastricht Treaty was debated, the scope and authority of parliamentary scrutiny committees on European legislation have been enhanced in several states, including Germany, Britain and France. Making the proceedings of the Council of Ministers public when it acts in the role of a legislature would make the work of these parliamentary scrutiny committees even more effective. Increasingly these committees are cooperating with MEPs; members of the appropriate committees of the European Parliament can work with national scrutiny committees when proposals relevant to them are being considered.

A basis for bargaining?

A strict delineation of the respective competences of the Union and the member states, together with the active application of the principle of subsidiarity and a more prominent role for national parliaments, could go a long way to meet public unease about the erosion of national sovereignty. Once intergovernmental and interinstitutional bargains could be reached on these matters, the 'deepening' of the existing European institutions would become less difficult to negotiate, for member states would be assured that their own competences would be respected.

The enlargement of the Union from twelve member states to fifteen and then nineteen will in any case demand changes; it also provides the opportunity for strengthening the accountability of the Council and the Commission to the European Parliament. But that will only happen if the Parliament asserts itself more strongly than it has done so far. The Santer episode, when the Socialist group tried to prevent the nomination of Jacques Santer as Commission President, showed a European Parliament willing to wound but afraid to strike. Under the Maastricht Treaty, the Parliament already has considerable powers in European decision-making; but its views are often taken insufficiently seriously by the Council.

The reasons for this weakness lie to some extent with the Parliament itself. Absolute majorities are required to amend or reject legislation under the cooperation procedure, or to reject a Council text in the event of a breakdown in the conciliation procedure under co-decision-making. Such majorities are hard to obtain in a Parliament from whose sessions many members are often absent—some because of their commitments as national political figures. National political leaders are often placed high on their parties' lists for the European elections, to enhance the party profile with electors and to assure them of a salary and a position should they not be elected at the national level. The dual mandate may mean that the European Parliament takes second place to national commitments. In addition, the domination of the Parliament by the two big groups, the Socialists and the Christian Democrats, may discourage members of other parties from playing a full part in parliamentary activities.

Deepening the European Union

There are nevertheless strong grounds for enhancing the Parliament's powers. The co-decision procedure adopted at Maastricht is extremely cumbersome. Under this procedure, the European Parliament can reject the common position adopted by the Council of Ministers if it produces an absolute majority against that position; but if it proposes amendments with which the Commission does not agree, the Council can only override the Commission by a unanimous vote. If such unanimity is not forthcoming, the amended law has to be considered by a Conciliation Committee convened by the Presidents of the Council and the European Parliament. If the Conciliation Committee agrees on a joint text, it must be approved by both within six weeks; if a joint text cannot be agreed, the proposed law falls unless the Council reaffirms its original common position, and that is itself approved by an absolute majority of the European Parliament.

The procedure is a good example of the opacity that characterises so many of the Union's decision-making procedures. Whenever decisions are made under the treaties by qualified majority vote, as in the case of directives concerning the single market, the European Parliament should be able to veto by absolute majority, after a period for conciliation. It should not be open to the Council to submit a further text. The Parliament is in these instances the sole organ of accountability, since governments responsible to national parliaments may have been overridden in the Council's vote.

Democratising the European Union's institutions

The central obstacle to the effective scrutiny of ministers in their European-level decision-making remains the secrecy of the Council's proceedings. National parliaments are promised consultation, which usually means listening to their views on the agenda prior to Council meetings, and then announcing the outcome afterwards. The European Parliament can amend or reject proposals for regulations and directives, but it cannot hold the Council accountable. Open debate once the common position is established in the Council, on amendments and on the final decision, would enable national parliaments to scrutinise the actions of ministers speaking in their names. It would, of course, be inconvenient for executives, but executives have substantially increased their power *vis à vis* legislatures in European decision-making.[17] The Maastricht debacle shows the dangers that arise when ministers distance themselves from the public and its representatives.

The European Parliament should be empowered to confirm the appointment of Commissioners individually after their nomination by a member state. Some national governments have been insisting on significant portfolios—or even specific portfolios—for their Commissioners, to the point where the Commission President's right to allocate them to being undermined.

The only way to counter such pressures on the President is to give the European Parliament a more prominent role in the appointment of Commissioners. Once nominated and allocated a specific portfolio by the President, Commissioners would come before the appropriate committee of the Parliament for confirmation. Not only would this requirement influence member states in their choice of Commissioners; it would also discourage governments from trying to strong-arm the President into allocating portfolios on the basis of such pressure rather than the candidate's qualifications for the job.

There has already been extensive discussion about the size of the Commission, and the difficulty of accommodating additional Commissioners from the new member states. Several proposals have been put forward for restructuring the Commission. Britain, for example, has proposed reducing the number of Commissioners to one from each member state; but even a Commission of fifteen or nineteen will not have enough significant portfolios to go round.

One proposal is that there should be senior and junior Commissioners. This is much more attractive than the alternative suggestion that smaller states should group together to appoint a Commissioner; The Netherlands and Greece do not have a great many interests in common. The advantage of the former proposal is that it would still leave each country with a Commissioner, and outstanding junior Commissioners—in effect, ministers of state—would have an opportunity to be promoted to a senior portfolio in their second term. There might be ten such portfolios, of which seven would be held by countries with populations exceeding 30 million, and three by the small countries. The other five Commissioners in a Union of fifteen, or ten in a Union of nineteen, would be junior Commissioners.

A further argument for this proposal is that ministerial cabinets would be drawn from a more diverse national background than at present. Another is that the EU, if it wished to be bold, could agree to the potential new members from central and Eastern Europe appointing acting junior Commissioners prior to full membership. (The analogy is with the invitation agreed by the European Council to be extended to the Visegrad countries to take part in seven ministerial meetings and one European Council meeting each year.)

There is one other part of the Union where accountability to national parliaments needs to be asserted much more strongly than at present, if only because the European Parliament has no *locus standi* in the matter beyond being informed and consulted. I refer to the intergovernmental pillars of the Treaty of European Union, and in particular to Title VI on 'Cooperation in the Field of Justice and Home Affairs'. Some of the areas covered under Title VI have direct and important consequences for our citizens, especially those belonging to ethnic minorities—immigration policy, visa policy and policy regarding nationals of third countries; others are of great importance for our civil liberties, including how drug addiction is combated and police cooperation on such matters as the processing of personal data.

Because the intergovernmental pillars do not fall within the scope of the Community, the European Parliament has the right only to be informed and consulted. Documents coming before the Council of Interior and Justice ministers would not be in the public domain, as formal Commission proposals are. Beyond texts or proposals that might require primary legislation, the provision of documents is made at the discretion of ministers, though in some countries proposals are subjected to parliamentary scrutiny—notably Denmark, where proposals made by the Danish or other governments are submitted to the European Scrutiny Committee of the Folketing. But there is a troubling lacuna here, the more so since Article K3 of Title VI lays down that the Council may 'adopt joint action in so far as the objectives of the Union can be attained better by joint action than by the member states acting individually, on account of the scale or effects of the action envisaged; it may decide that measures implementing joint action are to be adopted by a qualified majority'.

This sounds like as good a defining case as one might hope to find of the principle of subsidarity weighing in favour of Union action. In practice, that common action is properly accountable neither to the European Parliament nor to the national parliaments.[18] At the very least, documents tabled by governments with significant effects on their populations should be debated by their parliaments before any joint action is taken.

Conclusion

It is beyond the scope of this article to attempt an exhaustive list of the institutional reforms that may be discussed at the 1996 IGC. Those proposed here are directed only at some of the changes made necessary, or possible, by the enlargement of the Union to fifteen, and then probably nineteen, member states. The arguments is that there is at least a basis for a mutually acceptable bargain between member states, one in which the deepening of the European institutions is balanced by a clear definition of their competences based on the principle of subsidiarity; and in which the power of veto for the European Parliament over all legislation approved by a majority vote in the Council of Ministers is coupled with a stronger role for national parliaments in scrutinising and overseeing the actions of their own governments as they engage in European decision-making.

Finally, the British government should consult the opposition parties and invite public discussion on its own proposals for the IGC before committing itself to any final positions with regard to the future structures of the European Union's institutions. A repetition of the Maastricht debacle would not only damage the European Union; it would damage the credibility of Britain's own democratic institutions.

Notes

1 The Rt Hon Norman Lamont MP 11 October 1994, at Selsdon Group meeting, Bournemouth.
2 European Commission Document 12, *Intra-EU trade*, 1992.
3 Interview in *Le Figaro*, 30 August 1994.
4 Wolfgang Schauble and Karl Lamers, CDU/CSU discussion document, *Reflections on European Policy*, 1 September 1994.
5 Quoted in Agence Europe, September 1994.
6 Schauble and Lamers, *Reflections on European Policy*.
7 Andrew Moravscik, 'Negotiating the Single European Act' in Robert O. Keohane and Stanley Hoffman (eds), *The New European Community: Decisionmaking and International Change*, Boulder, CO, Westview, 1991.
8 Rinscher. chairman of CDU European parliamentary group.
9 *Le Figaro*, 30 August 1994.
10 Council directive no. 89/662, 1989, reported in EC *Official Journal* L 359; quoted in Joseph Weiler, 'The Transformation of Europe', *Yale Law Journal*, vol. 100, 2403.
11 *Brunner* v. *European Union Treaty*, 1 C.L.M.R. 57 1994.
12 Ibid.
13 Joseph Weiler, 'Journey to an Unknown Destination: A Retrospective and Prospective of the European Court of Justice in the Arena of Political Integration', *Journal of Common Market Studies*, vol. 431, no. 4, December 1993.
14 Leon Brittan, *Europe: The Europe We Need*, London, Hamish Hamilton, 1994.
15 Quoted in Emil Kirchner, *Decision-Making in the European Community*, Manchester, Manchester University Press, 1992.

16 See Gary Marks, 'Structural Policy and Multilevel Government', in Alan L. Calruny and Glenda G. Rosenthal (eds), *The State of the European Community*, vol. 2: *The Maastricht Debate and Beyond*, Lynne Rienner Publishers and the Longman Group, 1993.
17 Andrew Moravscik, 'Why the European Community Strengthens the State: Domestic Politics and International Co-operation', paper presented at the Conference of Europeanists, Chicago, April 1994.
18 Select Committee on the European Communities, *House of Lords Scrutiny of the Intergovernmental Pillars of European Union*, 2 November 1993.

Defining British National Identity

BHIKHU PAREKH

Vol. 71, no. 1, January–March 2000

THE SO-CALLED 'problem of British national identity' has been a subject of agonised debate in Britain since the early 1960s, triggered off initially by the loss of empire, then by the rise of the welfare state, postwar black and Asian migration and entry into the European Community, and more recently by the devolution of power to Scotland and Wales. Although the debate has been fascinating, it has often tended to avoid large questions, such as what we mean by national identity, why we need a coherent view of it, whether it might not become a vehicle of authoritarian cultural engineering and illiberal politics, where the national identity is to be located, and how we can resolve the inevitable differences about shared values, common political goals, visions of British society and views of British history that lie at the heart of national identity. In this article I shall step back from the actual debate, address these and other questions that it has taken for granted, and suggest how the debate might more profitably proceed.

Personal and national identity

The term 'identity' is of relatively recent origin. Its cognate 'national identity' is even more recent and seems to go back no further than the 1950s, when it replaced such earlier terms as 'national character', 'national soul' and 'national genius'. The term 'identity' primarily refers to individuals and is analogically extended to human collectivities including nation-states. It would therefore be useful to begin with a brief discussion of individual or personal identity.

To ask what is our identity as individuals is to ask what defines us or makes us the kind of persons we are and distinguishes us from others. As individuals we possess countless attributes and qualities and stand in a host of relationships with others. Some of these attributes and relationships are contingent and transient, whereas others are central and tenacious and shape us profoundly. The fact that we are golfers or members of a particular club is a contingent fact of our lives; we would not become altogether different persons if we ceased being either. By contrast our humanity, gender, culture, religion, values, moral commitments, dominant passions, psychological and moral dispositions, and so forth are constitutive of us in the sense that we either cannot abandon them at all or cannot do so without becoming different kinds of persons. Since they constitute us, they are an integral part of us, making it almost impossible to define ourselves independently of them. This is not to say that some or many of these characteristics and relationships do not change over time, for as reflective and self-determining agents we can and do redefine and change ourselves, but rather that when they do, we ourselves change, however imperceptibly, and recognise ourselves as different from what we were before.

Identity refers to those features and relationships that are constitutive of us and define and distinguish us as certain kinds of persons. We are necessarily the products of countless influences. Some go back to our childhood and are largely unknown to us, and many others operate so surreptitiously and unconsciously that we can become aware of them only after a most rigorous self-analysis. A part of our identity thus always remains a mystery to us, and we are constantly surprised by what we say and do. It also contains large areas of ambiguity, contradiction and fluidity, and we can never fashion ourselves into entirely coherent and transparent wholes. Our identity is neither fixed and unalterable nor wholly fluid and amenable to unlimited reconstruction. We can alter it, but only within the constraints imposed by our inherited constitution and necessarily inadequate self-knowledge. Since our identity evolves over time and is often marked by several identifiable turning points, it has an inescapable historical dimension and is best told in the form of a story or a narrative of how we came to be who and what we are.

Although identity is closely related to difference, the two are not the same, and much confusion is created by conflating them. Obviously, to know who I am is also to know who I am not and how I differ from others. And since the need to define my identity arises partly because I wish to distinguish myself from others, every statement of identity is also a statement of difference. However, it is wrong to suggest that my identity consists in my difference from others. I differ from them because I am already constituted in a certain way, not the other way round. My differences from them are derivative from and not constitutive of my identity. If others became like me, my differences from them would diminish, but it would be absurd to say that my identity has changed, for it is they who have changed and not I. In order to preserve my identity, all that is necessary is that I should remain true to what I take to be central to it. I do not need to struggle to remain different from others at all cost, both because this has no bearing on my identity and because others then determine my identity and undermine my autonomy.

Identity is not always a matter of pride. As we discover who we are, we might not like some or even most aspects of it. We might find that we harbour deep sexist, racist and other prejudices, or that we are mean, jealous, greedy and unable to respond to others' achievements in a spirit of generosity. We then feel ashamed of ourselves, and even of our culture which encouraged these prejudices and moral traits in us, and explore ways of reconstituting and reforming ourselves. It is rare for an individual to be wholly proud or totally ashamed of his identity; the former breeds narcissism, the latter self-hatred, and both alike are recipes for psychological and moral disintegration. For the most part we are both content with and critical of our identity in different degrees. To say 'this is my identity' is not to say that this is how I wish to or should remain for ever, for I need to ask if I am happy with it and approve of what it entails. Just as I can evaluate my identity, so can others. While my identity deserves their respect, the respect cannot be uncritical, for they might legitimately question and even refuse to respect some aspects of it.

In the light of our discussion it would be helpful to draw a threefold distinction between identity or inherited constitution, self-understanding or self-knowledge, and self-conception or self-evaluation. Identity refers to the way we are constituted, including the totality of passions, fears, hopes, aspirations and the residues of countless past influences that form part of us and make us a certain kind of person. Self-understanding refers to the way we understand ourselves and is a product of our attempts to make some sense of ourselves. Self-conception is parasitic upon self-understanding, and refers to our critical assessment of who we think we are and what we wish to make of ourselves. Identity refers to who we really are, self-understanding to who we think we are, and self-conception to what we would like to be. The three are dialectically related, and both shape and are shaped by each other.

In the light of what I have said about personal identity, it is relatively easy to see what national identity is. National identity is the identity of a political community and refers to the kind of community it is, its central values and commitments, its characteristic ways of talking about and conducting its collective affairs, its organising principles, and so forth. National identity is too complex and elusive to be reduced to a set of easily identifiable features or summed up in a few neat propositions. Every definition of it highlights some features, ignores or marginalises others, and is inherently partial and partisan.

National identity is neither unalterable nor a matter of unfettered choice. It is alterable within limits and in a manner that harmonises with its overall character and organising principles. It is not wholly transparent either, and parts of it remain opaque and inaccessible to even a most searching self-examination. No one had expected the allegedly reserved British to express their grief in a relatively uninhibited manner on the occasion of Princess Diana's death. And the surprise was further compounded when it was discovered that nearly 40 per cent of them had not bothered to watch her funeral on television. National identity, again, is not always a matter of pride. In the aftermath of the Nazi era, many Germans intensely disliked what they discovered about themselves. Deeply afraid to trust themselves, they decided to restructure and regulate their identity by tying themselves closely to a federal Europe. In Britain, too, not all the country's citizens feel comfortable with its imperial history. While some are very proud of it and others moderately so, yet others feel deeply ashamed of the aggression and the hypocrisy with which their country conquered and justified its rule over weaker societies.

National identity, then, is both given and constantly reconstituted. We might not like parts of it, and might think that even those we do like need to be changed to suit new circumstances. Such changes as we make in it must be consistent with the rest of its constituent elements, as otherwise they cannot graft and take root. All such redefinitions and changes require a deep historical knowledge of the country and a feel for its past, as well as a rigorous and realistic assessment of its present circumstances and future aspirations. While remaining firmly located in the present, we need to make a critical appraisal of our history and use its resources to develop a new sense of national identity that is faithful to the past and yet resonates with present experiences and aspirations. National identity can neither be preserved like an antique piece of furniture nor discarded like an old piece of clothing. It needs to be constantly reassessed, adopted to changing circumstances and brought into harmony with our deeper self-understanding and ideals. To freeze it, to refuse to evaluate and change it, out of inertia, uncritical pride or a mood of nostalgia, is the surest way to subvert it.

The paradox of national identity

Every political community needs to—and, as a rule, tends to—develop a view of its identity, of the kind of community it is and wishes to be. Its view of its identity serves several purposes. It satisfies the intellectual curiosity of its members as to what makes it the kind of community it is, why it is this and not some other community, and how it differs from others. The shared view of national identity unites its members around a common self-understanding and gives focus to their sense of common belonging. It also inspires them to live up to a certain self-image and cultivate the relevant virtues, helps them make wise choices in matters affecting their collective life, facilitates the community's self-reproduction and intergenerational continuity, and so forth.

Every conception of national identity, however, also has its dark underside and can easily become a source of conflict and division. Every long-established political community includes several different strands of thought and visions of the good life. Since any definition of its identity is necessarily selective, it stresses some of these and excludes others, so that individuals and groups sharing the latter are delegitimised and reduced to a second-class status. The history, traditions and values of the community can also be read and interpreted in several different ways, and again every definition of national identity shows partiality towards some of these and denigrates others. The dominant definition of national identity can also become a vehicle for moulding the entire society in its image, for there is nothing more important to a society than to maintain its identity, and that leads to an intolerant and authoritarian politics. Again, every definition of national identity has a tendency to distinguish the community concerned fairly sharply from others, and in so doing to offer a highly distorted and unflattering view of the latter and to discourage intercultural borrowing. A view of national identity also tends to prevent or corrupt political debate by introducing a pseudo-ontological mode of reasoning. Some public policies, rather than being discussed in terms of their likely consequences, are dismissed on the ground that they are too incongruent with the national

character or identity to be taken seriously. Advocates of the policies concerned are then either reduced to silence or forced to engage in an inherently
inconclusive discussion about the community's true identity. As I will show
below, these and related dangers are not at all imaginary and have in fact
shadowed much discussion of British national identity.

We are then confronted with what I shall call the paradox of national
identity. Every political community needs some shared view of its collective
identity; but every such view has an exclusivist, authoritarian, repressive and
ideological thrust and a tendency to demean those outsiders who constitute
its acknowledged or unacknowledged point of reference. A view of national
identity is a force for both unity and division, a condition of the community's
survival and reproduction which can paradoxically also become a cause of its
fragmentation and even disintegration.

I suggest that the only way to resolve the paradox is to ensure that a
political community's conception of its identity satisfies the following criteria.
First, it should be inclusive and respect the prevailing ethnic, religious,
cultural and other diversities and visions of the good life. If it were to be
heavily biased towards one of these groups or visions, it would alienate the
rest and fail to serve its main purpose of providing a basis of political unity.
Obviously no definition of national identity can be purely formal and
culturally neutral, but its content should be as widely acceptable as possible.

Second, we must fully acknowledge that since no statement of national
identity can ever capture the immense richness and complexity of the
community's history and way of life, it is inevitably partial and even partisan.
We must accordingly regard the current conception of national identity as
inherently tentative, and welcome (and give to others) opportunities to
criticise, contest and revise it.

Third, since national identity is a historical product and can only be revised
within limits, any statement of it should be fully sensitive to and, whenever
possible, continuous with the community's history. Since national identity is
also intended to equip the community to face challenges to come, it has a
futuristic dimension and must not remain trapped in the past. In other words,
it should provide a bridge between the past and the future in order that
members of the community can confidently and judiciously both carry and
break with its past.

Fourth, the definition of national identity is intended not only to unite but
also to inspire members of the community to live up to an idealised vision of
how they should live, to evoke and mobilise their sense of collective loyalty,
and to make it a matter of pride and joy to belong to the community. Not all
the qualities of character the community displays are worthy, and hence a
statement of its identity involves critically reflecting on these qualities and
determining which of these are noble and worth cherishing.

Fifth, the definition of national identity should be self-contained or
autonomous, constructed in terms of what the community is and not how it
differs from some other. As noted above, much of the popular and philo-

sophical discussion of identity mistakenly conflates it with difference. A community differs from others because it has a certain identity, not the other way round. And the fact that it differs from them in certain respects does not mean that it may not share other features in common with them. The definition of its identity should not therefore be contrastive and exclusive and make the mistake of seeing others as wholly different, let alone inferior. In order to say that fair play or individualism is part of British national identity, one does not need to say, as Margaret Thatcher did, that these qualities are missing among the French or the Germans, her frequent points of reference.

Sixth, the rationale behind wanting a clear sense of national identity is domestic—to unite and inspire members of the community, to articulate and focus their collective self-understanding. A shared national identity is their vital collective asset and structures and nurtures their relations. It is not meant to impress foreigners, help domestic corporate interests promote their products abroad, or attract tourists. These are at best incidental advantages and do not form the *raison d'être* of, let alone heteronomously determine, the content of national identity.

Seventh, the statement of national identity cannot be given from above by the government or political leaders or the intellectual elite. It must grow out of a vigorous democratic debate so that it represents the widest possible range of views, articulates the deepest aspirations of citizens, and can be enthusiastic-ally endorsed and owned by them all. However seductively it might be presented, an officially fabricated view of national identity has no emotional roots, lacks democratic legitimacy, is unlikely to convince all, and needs enormous moral and cultural engineering to overcome resistance.

Finally, national identity is the identity of a political community and has a political basis. It is located not in what its members personally like or dislike, but what constitutes and defines them as a political collectivity. The fact that the British like animals, tend to prefer tea to coffee, spend Sunday at home, are not given to expressing their emotions, frown on self-promotion, etc. are their contingent cultural characteristics. Not all of them share these, and even if they do the qualities concerned are politically irrelevant. Their national identity is embedded in the beliefs, practices and institutional structures that constitute and regulate the conduct of their political life. In other words, national identity should be defined in politico-institutional rather than ethno-cultural terms.

Two visions of national identity

The debate on British national identity has been going on since at least the early 1960s, and has given rise to a wide variety of views, of which two have enjoyed considerable popularity. For convenience I shall call them the New Right and the New Labour views of British national identity.

The New Right view was first articulated by Enoch Powell. For him the British national identity had four essential and interrelated components. First, it involved parliamentary sovereignty. The House of Commons was 'the personification of the people of Britain; its independence is synonymous with their independence'. Second, Britain was a fundamentally individualist society and had always cherished the rights and liberties of the individual. This was more true of it than of any other society, and the roots of its individualism went as far back as the beginning of its history and were deeply embedded in the character of the British people. Third, the British national identity was grounded in and constantly nurtured by the ethnic and pre-political unity of the British people. The British were a cohesive people, intensely aware of their ethnic identity, and bound by deep ties of kinship and loyalty to those of their kind at home and abroad. They had a strong sense of 'the homogenous we' and instinctively knew who was 'one of them' and who was an 'outsider'. Fourth, thanks to the country's geography and history, the British national identity was distinctively singular and unattached. Britain was an island, not a part of the continent of Europe; a self-contained and detached entity with its centre of gravity located within itself. Its history reflected its geography and was uniquely global. For long periods of history that were crucial to its development, Britain 'had stood with her face to the oceans, her back to Europe'. And even when it crossed the oceans to rule the world, like the imperial Rome it never left home and struck roots elsewhere. Since it had always remained itself and belonged to no larger entity, it was able both to be true to itself and to remain open to the world.

Powell used his conception of British national identity to arrive at important conclusions concerning the political issues of the day. He condemned the devolution of power to Scotland and Wales on the ground that it detracted from the sovereignty of Parliament, gave power to 'anti-parliaments', and destroyed both the unity and the identity of the country. He condemned large parts of the welfare state because they were incompatible with British individualism and the moral virtues associated with it. He was convinced that British people would never accept and assimilate black and Asian immigrants, as their sense of who they were 'instinctively revolted' against the alien cultural presence. Powell therefore suggested that either the ethnic minorities should be repatriated or their rights should be retrospectively reduced. He would not allow their wives and young dependants to join them and regretted his earlier advice to the contrary.

Since British national identity was singular, Powell concluded that it would be suicidal for Britain to join Europe. It was not a European nation, and its geographical proximity to Europe was a contingent matter of little political and cultural significance. Its history had always been enacted within its own borders and on the high seas, never in Europe, and its cultural, political, economic and other institutions as well as its pattern of historical evolution were also distinct. Powell conceded that other European states did not feel threatened by the European community, but insisted that that was so because their identities were different from the British. Since their democratic institutions were of more recent origin and did not have deep historical roots, they did not feel deeply attached to them. The continental states were also quite similar to one another, both because they had sprung from the Napoleonic wars and subsequent historical events and because they had a common social basis in peasant agriculture. They also had similar legal and administrative institutions and shared a common outlook on politics and society. The federal idea therefore came naturally to them and did not damage their national identity. Since Britain was quite different from them in these and other matters, its destiny lay elsewhere. Unlike many of his successors, Powell did not think that Britain shared much in common with the United States either, and placed little value on a close Anglo-American alliance.

Margaret Thatcher shared Powell's view of British national identity—with one important difference. She too stressed parliamentary sovereignty, individualism and the ethnic unity of the British people. Although not entirely happy with blacks and Asians and the concomitant cultural pluralism, she took the view that they can and should be assimilated into the British 'stock' and way of life. Although as convinced as Powell that the British national character was 'quite different from the characters of people on the continent' and that the country 'has little resemblance to the rest of Europe', she valued British membership of the European Community, partly to civilise the latter and partly to prevent it from becoming a federal state and posing a threat to vital British interests. Unlike Powell, she insisted that British 'character' and 'culture' were very similar to those of the United States and that Britain was bound to it by the closest ties of history, language and 'race'. As she put it recently in an extraordinary remark, all British problems in her lifetime had originated in Europe and their solutions had come from English-speaking nations. Like Powell, she was a British nationalist, but while his nationalism had an ethnic core, hers had a racial dimension; and hence the deep differences in their attitudes to the United States.

Thatcher's view of British national identity became the operative philosophy of her administration, giving her a sense of direction and self-confidence as well as a body of non-negotiable convictions. She obviously could not *deduce* specific policies from it, for that depended on contingent circumstances, but it did help her decide what issues or aspects of a situation were significant, why and to what degree. For Thatcher Britain had a distinct genius, identity, soul or essence, and nothing that went against it could ever succeed. She enjoyed a privileged access to and was the high priestess of national Being. For decades successive political leaders, pathetically ignorant of the national character and identity and victims of false self-consciousness, had misled the nation and passively presided over its decline. She was determined to be different. All this gave her politics a quasi-religious character and generated an almost messianic mode of public discourse.

The New Right view of British national identity runs through the speeches and writings of John Major. He moderated its tone but not its content, and added the Orwell-derived references to warm beer, long shadows across the country grass, green suburbs, old maids bicycling to Holy Communion through the morning mist, etc. while studiously avoiding any reference to the industrial towns of the north, queues outside the Labour Exchanges, etc. which were for Orwell just as integral to British identity. The New Right view was also reaffirmed by Charles Moore in his 1995 lecture at the Centre for Policy Studies. He added little new, except to demand full integration of Northern Ireland into the United Kingdom and to blame, like Powell, the perfidious administrative elite who had 'persuaded' Thatcher to sign the Single European Act. Michael Portillo, who evidently considers the Church of England central to British national identity, John Redwood, David Willetts, Simon Heffer and others have all expressed similar views of British identity.

In a major speech bearing the title 'Identity and the British Way', William Hague asks 'what it means to be British' and gives an answer that unmistakably belongs to the New Right tradition. He stresses parliamentary sovereignty, 'the core of our national identity', and the spirit of enterprise and individualism powerfully encapsulated in 'Thatcherism' which 'preceded Margaret Thatcher by eight hundred years'. Like Thatcher, he sees Britain as a part of Europe but not a European country because of the differences in their experiences during the last war and their manner of articulating their identity. Unlike other European countries Britain has not suffered from 'invasion and tyranny', and has wisely invested its national character in and been well served by its political institutions. This was why, according to Hague, visitors to Paris headed for the Eiffel Tower or the Louvre rather than the Assemblée Nationale, whereas those to London preferred Big Ben, the Houses of Parliament and Buckingham Palace.

Departing from Powell and Thatcher, Hague adds two new elements to his definition of British national identity. Britain is an 'open and mobile society' which welcomes talents from all backgrounds, as seen in the rise of Ted Heath, Margaret Thatcher, and Hague himself from modest origins to high positions. The other 'defining characteristic' of British identity is that it is a 'country of neighbourhoods not of regions, of local not regional loyalties, as seen in the traditional British involvement in charities, church groups, voluntary clubs and local institutions. Unlike Powell, Thatcher, Moore and several others, Hague values Britain's multi-ethnic character but does not think it an integral part of its national identity.

Like Powell and Thatcher, Hague uses his view of British national identity to rule out several policies and to attack the Prime Minister. Devolution of power, especially to Scotland, militates against parliamentary sovereignty, and hence is unacceptable. The same is true of a closer European Union. Proportional representation takes power away from the people, and hence is 'threatening to British identity'. Regionalism is inherently inconsistent with local loyalties and has no place in a 'country of neighbourhoods'. On each of these issues, there is very little argument, only assertion: what Hague dislikes is against national identity and the character of the British people. And Tony Blair, accused of nothing less than undermining all the four constituents of

British national identity, is turned into the principal enemy of the British people.

The New Right view eloquently illustrates the dangers of discussing politics in the elusive language of national identity. Its political reasoning is abstract and *a priori*, relying on an ideologically convenient statement of national identity to legitimise politically acceptable policies and avoid the arduous process of making out a reasoned case for them. The New Right definition of British identity meets none of the eight criteria mentioned earlier and is deeply flawed. Parliamentary sovereignty is not unique to Britain, cannot be equated with democracy because of the unelected House of Lords, means little when the ruling party has a large majority, and is being increasingly eroded by the process of globalisation. What is no less important, we need to ask if it is *desirable* in the current economic and political context, and whether pooling it with that of other European countries may not represent the best way to regulate global forces, promote Britain's vital interests, and preserve its relative independence and identity. Again, individualism is an important part of British identity; but so is the spirit of mutual concern and social solidarity. The New Right spokesmen talk of Britain as a cohesive nation without realising that the nation is a community of sentiments and fate and cannot be based on individualistic foundations. As Michael Oakeshott, the most eloquent twentieth-century spokesman of English conservatism, put it, British history, like that of all other European countries, has long been marked by both individualist and communitarian impulses, each regulating the other, neither able to defeat its rival, their constant interplay and uneasy balance providing the key to its institutions and policies.

As for Europe, Britain is a European country whose history has long been closely tied up with that of the rest of Europe and whose language, culture, etc. have profoundly influenced and been in turn influenced by it. If Britain did once turn its back on Europe, we need to ask if that stance does not now need reassessment. As for Hague's social mobility, it is far less extensive than he pretends and goes back no further than the past three decades. If Britain can discard its centuries-old class structure and redefine its identity, there is no reason why it cannot do the same with its other dimensions as well. In short, the New Right definition is narrow, exclusive, dogmatic, intolerant, backward-looking and uninspiring. It also lacks democratic legitimacy, encourages the kind of collectivist social engineering we saw under Thatcher, and takes an unjustly demeaning view of major European countries.

During the past few years we have witnessed the emergence of a new view of British national identity advanced by the spokesmen of New Labour. In an influential and well-argued monograph Mark Leonard, an eloquent New Labour representative, stresses Britain's global connections and European roots, and rightly sees these as complementary. Like the New Right he highlights Britain's individualism, but balances it with an equal emphasis on its sense of justice, fair play and ethic of sharing. Unlike Powell and

Thatcher and to a much greater degree than Hague, he accepts Britain's multi-ethnic and multicultural character as an essential component of its identity and rejoices in it. Like all three he stresses Britain's commercial dynamism and technological spirit—but also its cultural vitality and creativity.

In several speeches as Prime Minister, Tony Blair has expressed similar views and also emphasised several additional aspects of British identity. As against the New Right view, he argues that Britain's plural political structure is based on the equal partnership of England, Scotland, Wales and perhaps Northern Ireland, and underplays the role of parliamentary sovereignty. As he rightly implies, it is not parliamentary sovereignty but parliamentary democracy that is central to British identity, and the latter is fully consistent with and indeed requires devolution of powers. Blair also stresses Britain's long tradition of tolerance, cultural plurality, hospitality to different ways of life, social compassion and youthful spirit. His view of British history is largely free of the Thatcherite gloating over how the country 'civilised' the inferior races in Asia and Africa and 'saved' the rest of Europe from its internal barbarians. As against Hague, Blair also appreciates that Britain has long been and still remains a class-ridden society and needs to be far more open and inclusive.

Although the New Labour view of British national identity as outlined by Mark Leonard and others is more inclusive and tolerant, more in tune with the history and aspirations of the British people, and more sensitive to the contemporary economic and political context than its Conservative rival, it leaves much to be desired. It is eclectic, largely rhetorical and lacks philo-sophical depth. It tends to reduce national identity to a corporate brand, as if Britain were a political corporation needing a new image to sell itself abroad. It is essentially London-based, celebrating the city's 'coolness', competitive-ness, design and financial services, etc., taking only passing note of the rest of the country—and then only if it measures up to London's standards. The New Labour view also contains seeds of exclusion and intolerance, tending as it does to imply that those citizens who do not display enterprise, creativity and other desired qualities are not fully British, even perhaps a drag on the country's progress and a moral embarrassment. It takes little account of the place of England within a radically reconstituted Britain and the need to provide a new overarching redefinition of British identity with which the English can feel comfortable and which can arrest the growth of narrow English nationalism.

Leonard and others draw an untenable contrast between tradition and modernity, between old and new Britain, and their view of British identity has a deeply anti-traditional thrust. While the New Right spokesmen are too obsessed with the British past to face its future with fresh eyes, the New Labour view seems to dispense with the past altogether and lacks historical depth and resonance. It is also largely celebratory, stressing aspects such as Britain's inventive genius, and taking only a cursory look at its weaknesses. Since it lacks a critical and reflective dimension, its definition of British identity remains somewhat superficial. Leonard's proposal that Britain should mobilise all its institutions to project his view of its identity at home and abroad is troubling. It homogenises British identity, ignores the great British virtues of modesty, scepticism, self-mocking irony and self-effacement, and is likely to prove morally suffocating.

Although Tony Blair is more sensitive to these dangers, he too tends to see British national identity in terms of how Britain should be projected abroad. Calling Britain young when a quarter of its population is over sixty does not offer a sufficiently inclusive vision of it. Nor is it advisable to aim to become a beacon to the world or its moral leader. If others find something worth learning from the way we solve our problems, we should be pleased. But to imagine that we have some special talents in this area and that the rest of the world eagerly looks to us for moral guidance is to invite disappointment and the charge of hubris. To say that every nation has a 'purpose' is to make the Thatcherite mistake of taking too simplified a view of its history and identity and suppressing its inescapable diversities and disagreements.

Although the new view of British national identity that we need to develop will draw on the insights of New Labour, it must also go beyond it. It must be grounded in a critical interpretation of British history, identifying parts of it that we have reasons to be proud or ashamed of, and forming a coherent and balanced collective self-understanding. We also need to engage in a vigorous democratic debate on the kind of Britain we wish to and can realistically hope to create in its current historical circumstances. Although we can reasonably be expected to agree on some aspects of that vision, we would disagree on others. Such disagreement is not only inescapable but also desirable, for it reflects the vitality of British political culture and prevents the hegemonic domination of any one view. The search for national identity is an unending process, both because a rich and complex society cannot be reduced to a crisp definition and because new circumstances constantly call for new definitions.

The process of British self-definition, then, is a conversation between different and conflicting views, and at best yields an inherently temporary and tentative consensus that for a while forms the basis of its political life. The more it satisfies the criteria listed earlier, that is, the more inclusive, tolerant, culturally plural, open-minded, historically grounded, inspirational and democratically based it is, the greater is its power to mobilise all Britons around a set of common purposes. New Labour cannot hope to win the enthusiastic loyalty not just of 'middle England' but of the entire and increasingly pluralised country unless it undertakes the intellectually demanding task of articulating such a broad and generous view of the British national identity. It has the required cultural and moral resources, but lacks the patience and a reflective and critical impulse. As for the New Right, little can be expected of it, at least at present. Hague and his associates are too heavily trapped within the Thatcherite past and too nervous to rethink the fast-changing British and European political reality to do anything more than retail the old nationalist and libertarian banalities.

State and Market: Towards a Public Interest Test*

GORDON BROWN

Vol. 74, no. 3, July–September 2003

SINCE 1997 the New Labour government's central objective, the heart of our vision for a prosperous Britain, has been to promote opportunity and security for all. Our first priority was to address the country's chronic long-term failures in macroeconomic policy. In government we had the strength to take difficult decisions, including to freeze public spending for two years as we constructed a new monetary and fiscal regime.

A sound macroeconomic framework, nevertheless, is a necessary but not a sufficient condition to achieve, in an increasingly competitive global economy, a Britain where there is opportunity and security not just for some but for all. So successive budgets have sought to promote, on the one hand, competition, innovation and the enterprise economy, and, on the other hand, the New Deal, tax credits and public service reform as the routes to an efficient and fair Britain in which individuals can realise their potential.

Achieving these objectives demands the courage to push forward with all the radical long-term reforms necessary to enhance productivity and to improve public services; and, as we do so, we must have the strength to face up to fundamental questions that cannot be sidestepped about the role and limits of government and markets—questions, in fact, about the respective responsibilities of individuals, markets, communities and the state.

Indeed, in almost every area of current controversy—the future of the Private Finance Initiative, of healthcare, of universities, of industrial policy, of the European economic reform agenda, of public services generally—the question is, at root, what are the best relationships between individuals, markets and government to advance the public interest, and whether it is possible to set aside, and indeed move beyond, the sterile and debilitating conflicts of the past.

Take the health service. The essential question in a world of advancing technology, expensive drugs and treatments, and rising expectations is whether efficiency, equity and responsiveness to the patient are best delivered through a public healthcare system or whether, as with commodities generally, market arrangements, such as the hospital selling and the patient buying, are the best route to advancing the public interest.

* This is an edited text of a speech delivered by the Chancellor of the Exchequer, Gordon Brown to the Social Market Foundation at the Cass Business School on Monday 3 February 2003.

GORDON BROWN

Take higher education. Our universities operate in an increasingly global marketplace and at the same time their excellence depends upon drawing upon the widest pool of talent—both factors making change inevitable and necessary. One of the central questions in higher education systems round the world concerns the extent to which the university should become, in effect, the seller, setting its own price for its service, and the prospective graduate the buyer of higher education at the going rate, whether through an up-front or deferred system of payment, and what the consequences of such arrangements would be for equity and efficiency, as well as choice.

Take the Private Finance Initiative. The argument is whether, at a time of unprecedented need for investment in our public infrastructure, for example in hospitals and schools, the private sector can provide the benefits of efficiency and value for money to promote what most agree is the public interest: schooling and healthcare free for all at the point of need.

Take industrial policy. The essential question is whether, when global competition is challenging every industry, the state should replace market forces where they fail (the old Labour policy); whether the state should refuse to intervene at all even in the face of market failure (the old Tory *laissez-faire*); whether we should second-guess the market through a corporatist policy of supporting national champions (a policy I also reject); or whether, as I would propose, the best industrial policy for success in a global economy is to help markets work better.

Or take European economic reform. The question is how far, in a world where business must respond quickly and people must adapt to change, Europe is willing to go beyond old assumptions that flexibility is the enemy of social justice and recognise that the right kind of flexibility in European labour, capital and product markets can advance not only economic efficiency but also social cohesion.

In each area the questions are, at root, whether the public interest—that is, opportunity and security for all—and the equity, efficiency and diversity necessary to achieve it, are best advanced by more or less reliance on markets or through substituting a degree of public control or ownership for the market; and whether, even when there is public sector provision, there can be contestability.

Every modern generation since Adam Smith counterposed the invisible hand of the market to the helping hand of government has had to resolve this question for its time: what are the respective spheres for individuals, markets and communities, including the state, in achieving opportunity and security for their citizens?

The New Deal in the United States in the 1930s and—in a different way—nationalisation and the welfare state in Britain in the 1940s established new paradigms. Whole areas traditionally left to markets became regulated or owned by the state in the avowed interests of efficiency and equity. In the 1960s and 1970s Labour's story could be summed up in the story of the breakdown of that relationship as—in the way Anthony Crosland predicted—

old forms of collectivism were seen to fail. And, when Labour refused to update its conception of the respective roles of markets and state, and take on vested interests, the government also failed.

In the 1980s there was an attempt—in some areas largely successful, as in utilities, and in some areas unsuccessful, as in health—to withdraw the state from areas where previously the public interest was seen to be equated with public ownership. But by 1997 major questions about the relationships between individuals, markets and communities, including the role of the state, remained unanswered. On the other hand, it is also true that in every single postwar decade—on both sides of the political spectrum—the centralised state was wrongly seen to be the main, and sometimes the sole, expression of community, often usurping the case for localities and neighbourhoods taking more responsibility for the decisions that affect their lives.

The question I want to focus on specifically here is how, for a new decade in which globalisation and technology are challenging traditional assumptions anyway, we renegotiate the relationship between markets and government.

Assessing the market's performance

Agreeing on where markets should have an enhanced role and where market failure has to be addressed is, in my view, absolutely central to the next stage of the New Labour project. To hold to old and discredited dogmas about what should remain in the public sector and how the public sector operates, or to confuse the public interest with producer interests, makes no sense for a reforming party and, as technologies and aspirations change, would lead to sclerosis and make it impossible to obtain our enduring goals. We must not adhere to failed means lest we fail to achieve enduring ends.

Equally, to fail to put the case for a reformed public sector where the case is strong not only leads directly to the allegation from our opponents that New Labour merely imitates old conservatism but also makes it impossible to achieve the efficient and equitable outcomes we seek.

As long as it can be alleged that there is no clarity on where the market requires an enhanced role, where we should enable markets to work better by tackling market failure, and where markets have no role at all, an uncertain trumpet sounds; we risk giving the impression that the only kind of reform that is valuable is a form of privatisation, and we fail to advance—as we should—the case for a renewed and reformed public realm for the coming decades.

On the other hand, by stating our vision clearly, we can bring to an end the sterile and self-defeating argument over PFI, where producer interests have often been wrongly presented as the public interest; move forward from what has been a debate insufficiently explicit on the role of public and private providers in some of our public services; and, most of all, open up a broad and challenging agenda for prosperity and social reform.

In the last parliament we overturned old Labour shibboleths, rejected an old-style Keynesian assumption that there was a trade-off between inflation and growth, and, in making the Bank of England independent and applying fresh rules, procedures and systems of accountability in a new monetary and fiscal regime, sought to make Labour the party of stability and economic competence.

Now we need to affirm a yet more radical break with Labour's past, and in this parliament go further. By drawing the proper distinctions between those areas where markets require an enhanced role; those where, by tackling market failure, we can enable markets to work better; and those where markets cannot deliver opportunity and security for all, we can, with confidence, make New Labour the party not just of social justice but of markets, competition and enterprise, and show that advancing enterprise and fairness together best equips our country to succeed in the global economy.

I have said that the respective role of markets and the public sector has been the underlying, even if sometimes the unspoken, divide at the heart of British political arguments for nearly a century. But let us be clear at the outset where there is at least consensus.

Left and right have always agreed that there is a sphere of relationships—which encompasses family, faith and civic society—that should never be reduced to transactions, either buying or selling, or to diktat, state command and control. The new Archbishop of Canterbury, Dr Rowan Williams (in his recent Dimbleby lecture on the market state) and the Chief Rabbi, Dr Jonathan Sacks (in his recent book *The Dignity of Difference*)—profound and influential thinkers who have led the debate—tell us that while there are areas where the market is legitimate, there are areas where to impose market transactions in human relationships is to go beyond the bounds of what is acceptable; indeed, where to do so corrodes the very virtues upon which markets rely for success.

Markets, they would suggest, may be the best way of constructing exchanges, and thus providing many goods and services, but are not good ways of structuring human relationships. They also argue that while, generally, markets are good at creating wealth, they are less good at guaranteeing fairness and opportunity for all—and certainly not normally good at dealing with their social consequences. And they conclude that many of the choices we make cannot be made through markets alone, and to have faith in markets cannot justify our sidestepping fundamental moral questions. Quite simply, it is an unacceptable market fundamentalism that leaves markets to take care of all their consequences.

The political philosopher Michael Walzer talks of blocked exchange: some things that are not and should not be for sale and are off limits. In the same way, the economist Arthur Okun has said that the market needs a place and the market needs to be kept in place. Everyone but an economist, he says, knows without asking why money shouldn't buy some things. But this agreement between left and right extends beyond a proper distinction between the sphere of relationships and that of transactions, and a recognition of what Michael Sandel calls 'the moral limits of markets'. Both left and right generally agree also that markets are best seen as a means and not as ends. Of course, some on the right have argued that because market exchanges are freely entered into markets define freedom; and the left has often slipped into arguing that because markets cannot cope with their social consequences, they are a threat to equality, liberty and the realisation of human potential; but both left and right say that for them markets or the public sector are means not ends.

There should indeed be a legitimate debate between left and right about values and the stress we place on opportunity and equity, while safeguarding the importance of liberty. But the debate between left and right need not be any longer a debate about whether there should be a market-based economy or not.

Beyond this consensus, it is the respective role of markets and the public sector that has been the greatest dividing line between left and right. For the left, historically it has been a matter of dogma that to define the public interest—opportunity and security for all—as diminishing the sphere of markets; and for the right it has been, historically, a matter of ideology to expand the role of markets.

Why? Because, for the left, markets are seen as too often leading to inequality, insecurity and injustice. In this view, enterprise is the enemy of fairness, and the interests of social justice are fundamentally opposed to the interests of a competitive economy. The left's remedy has therefore been seen to lie in diminishing the impact and scope of the market—through greater public ownership, regulation and state intervention. Indeed, for nearly a century the left in Britain wrongly equated the public interest with public ownership, and at times came near to redefining one means—public owner-ship—as a sole end in itself.

For the right, on the other hand, it is the absence rather than the prevalence of markets that is to blame for the ills of society and economy. This benign, neoliberal view of markets sees them as sufficient to produce a combination of liberty, equality, efficiency and prosperity. And so, as a civil servant said in a conversation during the 1980s recorded by Professor Michael Barber, 'It doesn't really matter what the issue is; we know that the question we have to ask is, "How do we create a market?"' It was, he said, 'the prescription on every occasion: deregulation, marketisation and the withdrawal of the state.'

So, for the left, the goal of opportunity and security for all is prejudiced by reliance on markets; for the right, opportunity and security for those who deserve it can be achieved only by greater reliance on markets. These views—too much market on the one hand, too little market on the other—have defined the terrain of political debate in Britain and elsewhere in the postwar period.

Yet, for all their differences, both views reflect the same doctrinaire approach to the question of the role of markets. Whether markets are seen as the cause of or the solution to inequality of opportunity and insecurity, they have been seen by left and right alike as universally so: the vices and virtues of markets apply everywhere or nowhere. The result is that neither left nor right has been able to contribute to a considered view, and therefore a viable policy agenda, as to where markets can serve the public interest and where they cannot.

So we start from a failure on the part of the left: that the left has too often failed to admit not just that, in order to promote productivity, we need markets, but also that we should normally tackle market failure not by abolishing markets but by strengthening markets and enabling them to work better. But we also start from a failure of the right: the right's failure to understand that there are some areas where markets are not appropriate and where market failure can be dealt with only through public action.

So the argument that is often put as public versus private, or markets versus state, does not reflect the complexity of the challenges we face: that markets are part of advancing the public interest and the left are wrong to say they are not; but also that markets are not always in the public interest and the right is wrong automatically to equate the imposition of markets with the public interest.

The challenge for New Labour is, while remaining true to our values and goals, to have the courage to affirm that markets are a means of advancing the public interest; to strengthen markets where they work and to tackle market failures to enable markets to work better; and instead of reverting to the left's old, often knee-jerk, anti-market sentiment, to assert with confidence that promoting the market economy helps us achieve our goals of a stronger economy and a fairer society.

So, in this article I want to achieve three purposes.

- First, to show how a progressive government seeking a strong economy and fair society should not only support but positively enhance markets in the public interest.
- Second, applying that same public interest test, to recognise that there are limits to markets—not only where, as a matter of morality, we have always accepted they have no place, but also, as a matter of practicality, in those areas where they do not and cannot be made to work, and hence where we should support public provision as the more equitable, efficient and responsive solution.
- Third, to set out how we can avoid the trap of simply replacing market failure with state failure and, applying the same public interest test, achieve equity, efficiency and diversity by reforming and modernising the public realm for the decades ahead, in particular through devolution, transparency and accountability.

Enhancing markets in the public interest

In 1994, just two days after Tony Blair led the abolition of Clause Four of the party's constitution, I announced our decision to revamp Labour's competition policy. We did so because we recognised that competition—not the absence of it—was essential not just to an efficient economy but also to a fair society. Indeed, in a break from a hundred years of Labour history, I said that the public interest required a pro-competition policy that would deliver efficiency, choice and lower consumer prices. Some asked us why we were extending markets when all around us we saw the failures of the market economy. I argued that where there was insufficient competition our aim should be to enable markets to work better.

I also said then that we needed not just a new pro-competition policy but also a new industrial policy, which aimed not to second-guess, relegate or replace markets but to enable markets to work better. People asked me why I proposed this when it was clear that in Britain short-termism and low investment were glaring examples of chronic market failure. My opponents within Labour argued that the last thing we should do was to extend markets. The best industrial policy, they said, was the old one: as markets fail, to replace them with state action—national investment banks, national enterprise boards; import controls to protect big companies; even nationalisation of financial institutions.

But I said that markets here failed because special interests were undermining their dynamism. The new industrial policy, in setting out to enable markets to work better, should aim to extend them successfully, to harness the initiative, creativity and innovation and benefit from the coordination that can arise from the decentralisation and dynamism of properly functioning markets. For this to happen, there must be:

- first—if not perfect information—fair and accurate information possessed by the consumer;
- second—if not perfect competition—fair competition among many suppliers with low barriers to entry, and producers that are not monopolists with the power to dictate prices;
- third, mobility: capital and labour that are free, like consumers, to go elsewhere.

Today it is even more important that markets are strengthened. While twenty years ago, even ten years ago, it was just about possible—if costly and wrong—to protect and insulate companies, sectors or whole economies from global competition, there is now no longer any safe haven from the inefficiency and uncompetitiveness of the past. With hardly a good or service not subject to intense global competition, it is not only unwise but impossible to shelter our goods and services markets by subsidies or by other forms of protectionism without incurring long-term damage. Indeed, competitiveness abroad is best served by competition at home; so, in the modern global economy, stronger markets become more and more necessary.

Our new approach leads to fundamental changes in direction from the old policy approach.

Instead of being suspicious of competition, we should embrace it, recognising that without it vested interests accumulate; and, instead of tolerating monopoly or cartels which were never in the public interest, or appeasing special interests, we should systematically extend competition—forcing producers to be efficient, extending the choices available to consumers and opening up opportunity for the ambitious and the risk-takers.

Instead of being lukewarm about free trade, we should embrace it: free trade, not protectionism, is essential to opportunity and security for all, and instead of the old protectionism we advocate open markets. Instead of being suspicious of enterprise and entrepreneurs, we should celebrate an entrepreneurial culture, encouraging and rewarding the dynamic, and enthusing more people from all backgrounds and all areas to start up businesses—here again enabling markets to work better and strengthening the private economy.

Instead of thinking the state must take over responsibility where markets deliver insufficient investment and a damaging short-termism in respect of innovation, skills and environmental protection, we must enable markets to work better and for the long term. Here again, the case for state intervention is not to extend the role of the state but wherever possible to tackle market failure and help make markets work better.

Instead of the old centralisation that characterised industrial policy—promoting 'national champions' or 'picking winners' or offering subsidies to loss-makers—our industrial policy should reject special privileges for anyone, lay out a level playing field for all, and aim to deliver higher growth and jobs in every region with a new decentralising regional policy that addresses market failures in skills and innovation at the local level.

Instead of extending regulation unnecessarily to restrict the scope of markets, we should systematically pinpoint services where regulation does not serve the public interest and can be reduced.

Instead of thinking of employment policy as maintaining people in old jobs even when technological and other change is inevitable, we should pursue the best route to full employment, which is to combine flexibility—helping people move from one job to another—with active intervention to provide skills, information and income support.

And instead of viewing flexibility as the enemy of social cohesion, we should recognise that the right kind of flexibility in European labour, capital and product markets is becoming ever more essential for competitiveness, and that while government does have a role to play in easing the transition for those affected by change, it should not involve itself in resisting change.

So what are the next steps on the economic reform agenda that will help us towards higher productivity and thus towards a Britain of opportunity and security for all?

First, in testing times for every national economy it is ever more important to pursue policies for monetary and fiscal stability. The recent volatility in global stock markets, which saw US markets (S&P 500) down 44 per cent since their peak, UK markets (FTSE 100) down 49 per cent, French (CAC 40) down 58 per cent and German (DAX) down 66 per cent—has demonstrated once again that no country can insulate itself from the ups and downs of the world economy.

I understand the concerns that uncertainty causes for investors and consumers alike. Indeed, it is because we have always understood that monetary and fiscal regimes must work well in challenging times as well as good times that—with tough decisions in 1997 on deficit and debt reduction, including a two-year freeze on spending in the late 1990s—we sought to ensure that Britain was better placed than it had been in the past to deal with economic challenges and ongoing risks. And we still have—and will continue to have—the strength to take the tough decisions. Instead of being, as in previous downturns, first into recession and last out, the country that normally suffers most, Britain has gone on growing in every quarter over the past six years while other major economies have been in recession.

The true test of economic policy is whether it can cope with difficult as well as good times, and I am confident that, tested in adversity, our system will demonstrate its credibility and resilience. With our fundamentals sound and debt low, we have met, are meeting and will continue to meet our fiscal rules. With interest rates, inflation and unemployment at record lows, this is indeed the right time, building on that underlying stability, to push ahead with competition, enterprise and productivity reforms in our economy, so that in an increasingly competitive and uncertain world we can secure higher levels of long-term growth.

Second, then, in every product and almost every service we must do more to open up competition. Having already in the past six years gone a long way, conferring independence on the competition authorities;

- as Dr Irwin Stelzer proposed, introducing trust-busting incentives and criminal penalties for those engaging in cartels;
- giving the Office of Fair Trading a proactive role in investigating markets;
- dealing with a range of professions where regulation has been an excuse for vested interests and exclusions from entry; and
- in the EU, demanding improvements to the functioning of the single market

—we have a long way still to go.

The Independent Office of Fair Trading is currently investigating the markets in liability insurance, private dentistry, estate agents, taxis and doorstep selling. It has reported on many industries, including most recently the market for prescription drugs, recommending reforms that expose them to the bracing winds of competition. We look forward to tough pro-competition decisions and to continued scrutiny of areas where we expect them to do more.

But the competition test should apply to the public sector as well as the private sector. And I hope that the OFT will use to the full its new powers to investigate all those areas where the public sector, through regulation or its actions, unjustifiably restricts competition.

We recently published our progress report on European economic reform, with detailed proposals, based on the pro-market principles I have set down, for further labour, product and capital market deregulation; for a new approach to state aids; for support for private finance initiatives in Europe; for action to prevent British firms from being excluded from European markets, from energy and telecommunications to agriculture; and for extending the principles of a strong, proactive and independent competition regime to the EU. Similarly, we will progressively seek to tackle barriers to a fully open trading and commercial relationship between Europe and America, strengthening joint arrangements to tackle competition issues.

Third, we must take far more seriously the need for urgent progress in the world trade discussions after Doha. In the case of Europe, sooner or later Europe's leaders must come together to tackle, at root, agricultural protectionism, which imposes enormous costs on taxpayers, consumers and the world's poorest people.

Fourth, the government will continue to be on the side of small business, recognising that around one-third of our country's productivity gains come from new entrants challenging and then replacing existing companies. We will continue our work of removing barriers to business success,

- helping to cut the cost of starting, investing, hiring and training;
- continuing our reforms of the business tax regime for enterprise and entrepreneurs and capital gains;
- opening up public procurement to small firms; and
- moving forward with measures to encourage the entrepreneurial culture.

Fifth, where markets by themselves cannot deliver the long-term returns from investing in skills and new technologies, and cannot safeguard the environment for the long term, it is right for the government to act. So where firms, large or small, cannot themselves make the large investments needed in basic research, it is right for government to attempt to safeguard their intellectual property rights more fully and to share the costs. It is also right to build on the new employer skills pilots and to forge a new partnership of government, employee and employer with a view to making labour markets work more flexibly. Where there are barriers to the unemployed getting back to work, it is right to extend both the opportunities and the compulsion of the New Deal, ensuring labour markets are more flexible as we tackle the social and economic causes of unemployment.

Where capital markets are short-termist and fail in the long term we should press ahead with the Cruickshank, Myners and Sandler reforms and be prepared to build on our capital gains tax reforms (moving from short-term rates at 40p to long-term rates at 10p) to encourage the long-term view. And our approach to the environment must not be restricted to efforts to prevent environmental damage but must extend to offer incentives to invest in environment-friendly technologies.

Sixth, this emphasis on market solutions to market failures—and rejection of old-style centrally imposed industrial policies—demands a new regionally based policy focusing on local enterprise, skills and innovation. Our new regional policy consultation document urging greater devolution of powers from the European Commission will be published shortly. We are removing the last of the permanent, ongoing subsidies for operating costs in coal, shipbuilding and steel, and, as the DTI Secretary of State, Patricia Hewitt, is showing, the old days of the 'sponsorship' department are over, freeing up resources to enhance the DTI's role in promoting competition and enabling markets to work better.

The pursuit of equity

The measures for competition, trade, enterprise, science and skills, and regions take us along the road towards a Britain of opportunity and security for all. They mean a more efficient economy that delivers more opportunity. But the extent to which we go further and ensure opportunity and security for all depends upon a further set of political choices. Let me give a few examples.

A party that does not care about opportunity for all need be at best neutral towards those excluded from it. But for a party for whom equity matters, a central element of a pro-competition policy is the removal of all the old barriers that prevent new entrants; and integral to a skills and education policy is drawing on the talents of not just some but the widest range of people and their potential. In both cases the most equitable solution is also likely to be the most efficient.

A party unconcerned about equity would be neutral about the need for regional policy or be against it. I have suggested that an effective regional policy is economically efficient, but those who are most concerned about divisions between regions and the inequalities that result will wish to demonstrate that balanced economic growth is not only in the interests of the least prosperous regions but in the interests of regions where prosperity can bring congestion, overcrowding and overheating.

Too often in Britain—unlike America—opportunities to start a business have seemed accessible mainly to a closed circle of the privileged; so those of us who believe in opportunity for all will wish to go furthest in promoting enterprise for all. In the poorest areas in Britain, where only one business is created for every six in the wealthier areas, and where not only family savings but also bank capital at the right price are often unavailable even where men and women show initiative and dynamism, our whole approach must radically change. Enabling markets to work better for the enterprising demands that we remove the old barriers to enterprise that discriminate against lower-income groups and hard-hit unemployment blackspots, where the enterprise culture is already weakest, and open up wider access to capital, management expertise, telecommunications and financial advice: that is, that we intervene actively to widen individuals' economic opportunities irrespective of their background.

In tackling these market failures—especially failures in the availability of information and the mobility of capital—a new agenda opens up that helps markets work better and delivers opportunity for all. Here is our answer to those who allege that we can pursue equity only at the cost of efficiency; a demonstration that equity and efficiency need not be enemies but can be allies in the attainment of opportunity and security for all. Here social justice— equality of opportunity and fairness of outcomes—is not bought at the cost of a successful economy but is achieved as part of such a success (a point I made when I gave the Smith Lecture six years ago). This agenda must continue to be at the centre of our thinking and policy-making.

I have sought to show that markets can sometimes fail. We also know that public services can fail too. The experience of telephones, gas, electricity and water was of public sector monopolies created to guarantee supply of service but over time coming to embody not the empowerment of the consumer but a restriction of their choices. In opposition, Labour had to come to terms with and accept the privatisation of telecommunications. We saw that with the right framework—regulation only where necessary and with a light touch wherever possible—we could create the conditions in which markets could work in the public interest and deliver choice, efficiency and a fair deal for consumers.

Too often the Tory approach was pro-privatisation but not pro-competition: privatising without liberalising, or regulating in conditions where private vested interests replaced public vested interests and denied the consumer choice, thus undermining the public interest. Our insight was to see that the Tory solution was a private sector solution at the expense of markets and, in the end, of the public interest.

In this and other areas we knew that if we could ensure competition, proper flows of information, and mobility of labour and capital—and thus help markets work better—then the consumer would gain from the resulting efficiencies and extension of choice, and that, over time, the regulation necessary to ensure security of supply for all could be diminished.

But, interestingly, the Tory solution was to equate support for private sector and private business with support for markets. They adopted a pro-private sector policy which replaced public sector monopolies with private sector monopolies, and failed to develop a pro-market policy where there was genuine competition, the possibility of new entrants, and a proper flow of information to, and choice for, consumers. Indeed, when they privatised they often failed to put in place the conditions for effective markets. Instead, they privatised rather than liberalised, and the old monopolies returned—but this time in the private sector.

It has been for New Labour to insist in opposition and in government that utility reform must promote a market economy (and not just a privatised economy), and that we liberalise where possible and regulate where necessary so that the needs of the consumer are best advanced.

So, while some on the left still say we should be anti-market and renationalise, in these areas our values can best be advanced through markets working in the public interest. This, then, is our approach to utilities:

- we are opening up to greater competition utilities like water and postal services;
- as markets fully develop, we will withdraw unnecessary regulation, while never putting at risk opportunity and security for all;
- we will ensure that the new consumer watchdogs now in place—for example Postwatch, Energywatch and Water Voice—represent and empower consumers effectively, and that regulators make regulatory impact assessments including assessment of effects on competition—standard practice for all significant new proposals; and
- we will press in Europe for the same liberalisation for energy and utility services.

At all times our approach is shaped by our view that the public interest can best be guaranteed with market means of delivery through the price mechanism. Nor can we hold to old ideas about what should be in the public sector when there is no justification for it. This demands that we look at services to consumers where traditionally the public sector has been used and where markets are seen to have failed—but where, in future, markets, with their dynamism, capacity for innovation and enhancement of choice, can better respond to new technology and rising aspirations than a public sector context.

Already we have proposed a Shareholder Executive bringing together all government shareholdings, and have insisted on all government assets being publicly accounted for. Where there is no justification for their being in the public sector—indeed, where the answer to market failure has wrongly been seen to be public ownership—we must be honest with ourselves about the changes necessary (as we have been already with a range of industries and services, from the government's shares in privatised companies and in organisations from Qinetiq to the Tote) when the public interest is best advanced not by government ownership but by markets.

Enhancing markets will mean reducing government. But, as I suggested in a series of articles and speeches last autumn, and as the Chief Economic Adviser to the Treasury also argued in his *New Localism* pamphlet last year, we must also have the courage to recognise where markets do not work. Our clear and robust defence of markets must be combined with a clear and robust recognition of their limits.

The limits of markets

For most consumer goods, markets adjust to preferences and thus to demand and supply on a continuous basis. But what about situations where this not only does not happen but the market failures cannot be corrected through market-based government intervention to make the price mechanism work? What of situations where there are clear externalities and clear social costs that cannot, even with the use of economic instruments, be fully captured by the price mechanism? What of situations also where there are multiple distortions in the price and supply disciplines and where even the removal of one distortion to create a purer market may turn a second-best outcome into a third-best outcome? Take healthcare—the successful delivery of which has proved to be a mammoth challenge in every modern industrial country.

The economics of healthcare are complicated and difficult. No sensible person pretends to have all of the answers to all of the complex, interrelated and excruciatingly difficult policy problems that rapidly rising demand, expectations and costs create. The only thing that is certain is that, as technologies change and needs change too, changes will follow in healthcare delivery, now and for the foreseeable future. But those of us in positions of responsibility cannot afford the luxury of inaction: we have to come up with the best system we can devise and be prepared to adapt it in the light of changing technology and the rapidly changing needs of citizens.

The modern model for the British NHS—as set down by the government and the Secretary of State for Health, Alan Milburn—embodies not just clear national clinical and access standards but clear accountability, local delivery of services, independent inspection, patient choice, and contestability to drive efficiency and reward innovation.

The free market position which would—on the proposals of Conservative health spokesman Liam Fox—lead us to privatised hospitals and some system of vouchers and extra payments for treatments, starts by viewing healthcare as akin to a commodity to be bought and sold like any other through the price mechanism.

But in healthcare we know that the consumer is not sovereign: use of healthcare is unpredictable and can never by planned by the consumer in the way that, for example, weekly food consumption can. So we know:

- that the ordinary market simply cannot function, and because nobody can be sure whether they will need medicinal treatment and, if so, when and for what, individuals, families and entire societies will seek to insure themselves against the eventuality of being ill;
- that in every society, this uncertainty leads to the pooling of risks;
- and that the question is—on efficiency grounds—what is the best insurance system for sharing these risks?

Early in 2002, when the government examined the funding of healthcare, we concluded that, with uncertainty about risk, insurers often have poor information on which to base their risk assessment of the customer; and that, as a result of these uncertainties—and with many citizens considered too high a risk, too expensive and therefore excluded—there are serious inefficiencies in private pricing and purchasing.

Indeed, in the United States, some insurance policies are now thought to have a 40 per cent loading simply to cover the administrative costs involved in risk profiling and billing, and today premiums average around $100 a week, are rising by 13 per cent a year, and even then often exclude high-cost treatments. Forty-one million Americans are uninsured.

In my Social Market Foundation lecture a year ago I argued that on efficiency and equity grounds, private insurance policies that by definition rely for their viability on ifs, buts and small print and can cover only some of the people some of the time should not be preferred over policies that can cover all of the people all of the time.

But I also argued, on efficiency as well as equity grounds, that the case for such a comprehensive national insurance policy was greater now than in 1948, when the scientific and technological limitations of medicine were such that high-cost interventions were rare or very rare—there was no chemo-therapy for cancer, cardiac surgery was in its infancy, intensive care barely existed, hip and knee replacement was almost unknown—and thus health-care, compared with now, was relatively inexpensive.

I argued that today the standard of technology and treatment is such that some illnesses or injuries could cost £20,000, £50,000 or even £100,000 to treat and cure, and I suggested that because the costs of treatment and of drugs are now much higher than ever, and the risks to family finances much greater than ever—not just for poorer families but for comfortably off families well up the income scale—therefore the need for comprehensive insurance cover of healthcare is much stronger than ever.

The very same reasoning which leads us to the case for the public funding of healthcare on efficiency as well as equity grounds also leads us to the case for public provision of healthcare. The market for healthcare is dominated by the combination of, on the one hand, chronically imperfect and asymmetric information, and the potentially catastrophic and irreversible outcome of healthcare decisions based on that information, and, on the other, the necessity of local clusters of medical and surgical specialisms.

This means that, while in a conventional well-functioning market the price set by the producer is the most efficient, in health not only is the consumer not sovereign but a free market in healthcare will not produce the most efficient price for its services or a fair deal for its consumer.

Take the asymmetry of information between the consumer as patient—who may, for example, be unknowingly ill, poorly informed of available treat-ments, reliant on others to understand the diagnosis and/or uncertain about the effectiveness of different medical interventions, and thus is not sover-eign—and the producer. With the consumer unable (in contrast to a conven-tional market) to seek out the best product at the lowest price, and information gaps that cannot (even over the long term) be satisfactorily bridged, the results of a market failure for the patient can be long-term, catastrophic and irreversible. So even if there are risks of state failure, there is a clear market failure.

Further, market failures exist not only because of asymmetry of information and the irreversibility of decisions but also because local emergency hospitals are, in large part, clusters of essential medical and surgical specialities and have characteristics that make them akin to natural local monopolies:

- 50 per cent of admissions and 75 per cent of hospital beds are accounted for by emergency, urgent or maternity cases, i.e. non-elective cases where patients are generally unable to shop around;
- the need for guaranteed security of supply means that, generally, a local hospital cannot be allowed to go out of business;
- there is a need also for clusters of mutually reinforcing specialities (trauma, pathology and emergency medicine, for example);
- a high volume of work is required to guarantee quality of service;
- the economies of scale and scope make it difficult to tackle these market failures by market solutions; and
- as the US system has demonstrated, it is also difficult for private sector contracts to anticipate and specify the range of essential characteristics we demand of a healthcare system.

So the many market failures in healthcare, if taken individually, challenge the adequacy of markets to provide efficient market solutions. But what could happen when these market failures—the asymmetry of information between consumer and producer, clusters of local specialisms, and the difficulty of contracting—are combined with a policy that puts profit maximisation by hospitals at the centre of healthcare?

It is then that the consumer, the patient, would be at greatest risk of being overcharged, given inappropriate treatments for financial rather than medical reasons, and offered care not on the basis of clinical need but on the basis of ability to pay, with some paying for care they did not need and others being unable to afford care they did need, as a two-tier healthcare system developed.

One response would be to regulate a private healthcare market, as we do in the case of utilities which are privately owned but independently regulated. But let us list what, in Britain, a private sector healthcare regulator would have to do to safeguard the public interest fully. It would fall to a regulator:

- to control entry to the market by setting, specifying and policing basic standards for quality, workforce, facilities, governance and customer service,
- to maintain an inspection regime to protect patients by ensuring these standards were met,
- to step in when inadequate service was provided,

- to ensure security of supply and training provision,
- to police the market to guard against abuse, monopoly pricing and unfair competition,
- to adjudicate in disputes, and
- to ensure that information supplied to patients and consumers was honest and accurate;

and it would fall to a commissioner to attempt to specify every aspect of the service purchased in a contract.

It is hardly surprising that in every advanced private healthcare system in the world, clinical negligence litigation is a great and growing problem; complaints of bureaucracy are legion; attempts by insurers to standardise entitlements and restrict choice are controversial; huge government subsidy is reluctantly seen as essential; and allegations of two-tier care are divisive.

Conventionally, regulation copes best in situations where we insist on minimum standards. But when there is an explicit undertaking that medical treatment must be given at the highest level to every patient on the basis of health need and not ability to pay, then one is led to the conclusion that, even if that task of market regulation could be practically accomplished, public provision is likely to achieve more at less cost to efficiency and without putting at risk the gains from the ethic of public service which, at its best, sees dedicated public servants putting duty, obligation and service before profit or personal reward.

So equality of access can best be guaranteed not just by public funding of healthcare but by public provision.

The case for non-market solutions for education and other public services can also be made, and there is a debate that will continue about what equality of access means for the coming generation; but my point here is that we can make the case on efficiency as well as equity grounds that market failures in healthcare, as in some other services, are not easily subject to market solutions.

So, in health:

- price signals don't always work;
- the consumer is not sovereign;
- there is potential abuse of monopoly power;
- it is hard to write and enforce contracts;
- it is difficult to let a hospital go bust; and
- we risk supplier-induced demand.

Having made the case for the limits of markets in healthcare for both finance and provision, I do not accept that the future lies in a wholly centralised service; that we should rule out contestability or a role for the private sector in the future; or that we need devalue or ignore the important issue of greater consumer choice.

Even in a world where healthcare is not organised on market principles with consumers paying for their care, it is in the public interest to have devolution from the centre and to champion decentralised means of delivery. This includes contestability by providers on the basis of cost and efficiency. Accordingly, the Secretary of State for Health is matching the record increases in investment with further far-reaching reforms:

- devolution with multi-year budgets for primary care and hospital trusts;
- more payment by results;
- NHS foundation hospitals with greater management flexibility;
- increased choice for patients through booked appointments and using NHS Direct and walk-in centres; and
- to ensure that the money invested yields the best results, independent audit, independent inspection and independent scrutiny of local and national provision.

These reforms are essential not only to promote contestability but to decentralise control to where it can be exercised most effectively in the interests of citizens and patients. Where the private sector can add to, not undermine, NHS capacity, and challenge current practices by introducing innovative working methods, it has a proper role to play in the NHS—as it always has. But it must not be able, when there are, for example, overall capacity constraints, to exploit private power to the detriment of efficiency and equity—which is why the areas in which Alan Milburn is introducing a greater role for the private sector are not those areas where complex medical conditions and uncertain needs make it virtually impossible to capture them in the small print of contracts, but those where the private sector can contract with the NHS for routine procedures, where we can write clear, accountable contracts to deliver NHS clinical standards, where private capacity does not simply replace NHS capacity and where we ensure that patients are given treatment solely on the basis of clinical need.

Indeed, the case I have made and experience elsewhere lead us to conclude that if we were to go down the road of introducing markets wholesale into British healthcare we would pay a very heavy price in efficiency and equity and would be unable to deliver a Britain of opportunity and security for all.

Because we are clear about the limits as well as the uses of markets in healthcare, we can now put the debate about PFI in its proper context.

In my view the Private Finance Initiative is in the public interest. It must be right that government seeks to secure, over the long term, the most cost-effective infrastructure for our public services. PFI enables us do this by binding the private sector into open and accountable long-term relationships with the public sector, aimed at securing a proper sharing of risk and access to private sector managerial expertise and innovative ideas, in order to secure better public services.

The public sector has always drawn on the expertise and experience of the private sector. But, whereas in the public procurement of the past, private companies built and then walked away, PFI seeks to ensure that the companies involved are held transparently accountable for design faults, construction flaws overruns and long-term maintenance, so that value for money is achieved.

Those who say that PFI is privatisation have got it wrong because, while the private sector is rightly helping in public service delivery, the public interest is paramount. PFI is thus quite distinct from privatisation. For example, in privatised healthcare or education it would be the market and the price mechanism, not the public (sector), that defined the service and provided it directly to those customers that could afford it, and thus the public sector could end up sacrificing both fairness and efficiency in the delivery of these core services.

But under PFI the public sector can harness the efficiency that can come from contestability and the private sector in pursuit of better-quality public services and, throughout, retain control of the services it runs, enabling these services to be comprehensive, efficient, universal and, where it is our public policy decision, provided free of charge.

So there should be no principled objection against PFI expanding into new areas where the public sector can procure a defined product adequately and at no risk to its integrity, and where the private sector has a core skill from which the public sector can benefit and learn—as in the provision of employment and training services, the renovation of schools and colleges, major projects of urban regeneration and social housing, and the management of prisons. And in each of these areas we can show that the use of private contractors does not occur at the expense of the public interest, nor necessarily at the expense of terms and conditions of employees but, if we can secure greater efficiency in the provision of the service, is one means by which the public interest is advanced.

Towards decentralisation

And this leads to my third theme. Even when a market is inappropriate, old centralised, command and control systems of management are not the way forward; instead, we are seeking and should seek—in the NHS and other public services—a decentralised means of delivery compatible with equity and efficiency.

It is the assumption that the only alternative to command and control is a market means of public service delivery that has obscured the real challenge in healthcare and other public services—namely, the challenge to develop decentralised non-market means of delivery that do not have to rely on the price mechanism to balance supply and demand.

Indeed, it is only by developing decentralised non-market models for public provision that respond to people's needs, extend choice, and are equitable and efficient that we will show those who assert that, whatever the market failure, the state failure will always be greater that a publicly funded and provided service can deliver efficiency and equity and be responsive to the consumer.

This opens up a challenging agenda for modernisation and reform: more radical devolution of responsibilities from Whitehall as we give the role of Whitehall a sharper focus; greater attention to the conditions favouring a new localism in delivery, with greater transparency, proper audit and new incentives. It demands an honest appraisal of the ethic of public service which, at its best, is public servants seeking to make a difference and, at its worst, just the defence of vested interests. In this new world we need to ask about the next steps in matching responsibility and reward in the Civil Service as we encourage professionals who welcome accountability and whose ethic is about maximising the difference they make; and we will need a better appreciation of the important role local, voluntary and charitable community organisations can play in future delivery.

Our approach to public services has been to move away from the old system of controls:

- from a narrow centralism that had dominated public expenditure control ever since the days of the Plowden Report to devolution to regions, localities and communities;
- from a focus on inputs and process to a focus on outputs and results;
- from annual and incremental spending decisions that ignored investment needs to long-term, usually three-year, allocations based on proper policy analysis of consumption and investment requirements;
- from a crude departmentalism that put the consumer's needs second to a focus on how, by breaking down departmental boundaries, consumer needs can best be met; and
- from ad hoc policy initiatives and postcode lotteries that failed to meet public expectations for lower waiting times, better exam results and better service generally to national targets set in public service agreements within which local authorities, hospitals, departments and others have the incentive to innovate and the discretion to do so.

The four principles of public service delivery set down by Tony Blair correctly require a balance to be struck between national standards and local autonomy. Our long-term objective has always been to match the attainment of ambitious national standards with the promotion of local autonomy so that we can achieve efficiency, equity and choice.

Far from targets being a tool for centralisation, the modern company has lean headquarters that set clear targets, set the incentives and rewards, provide the freedom for local managers to deliver, and then collect the information so that results can be monitored and assessed.

So too in the public sector: where objectives are clear, well-defined targets can provide direction; where expectations are properly shaped, they provide the necessary ambition; where people can see and assess the impact of policy, and where national standards are achieved and can be seen to be achieved, targets can foster the consistency, accountability, equity and flexibility to meet local needs that the traditional delivery of public services has often seemed to lack.

Without targets providing that necessary focus and discipline for achieving change, recent public service improvements—from literacy and numeracy performance in primary schools to reduced waiting times and improvements in care for cancer and heart disease in the NHS—could simply not have been achieved. There is thus a critical role for targets, now and in the future, in shaping expectations of what can be delivered on what timescale and in avoiding the trap of low ambition on the one hand and—when faced with decades of chronic under-investment—overpromising on the other.

We know that national targets work best when they are matched by a framework of devolution, accountability and participation—empowering public servants with the freedom and flexibility to make a difference: first, to tailor services to reflect local needs and preferences; second, to develop innovative approaches to service delivery and raise standards; and third, to enable, as we should, a bonfire of the old input, interventionist, departmentalist controls over front-line public service managers—which is too often what they still find frustrating. And so it is right to consider greater local autonomy, and its corollary, greater local democratic oversight.

Where next?

What, then, are the next steps as we prepare for our next spending review and as targets are achieved and national standards established? One way forward is that local communities should have the freedom to agree, for each service, their own local performance standards—choosing their own performance indicators and monitoring both the national and local performance indicators—with national powers to step back in held as a backstop, to be used only in the last resort. Accountability would be enhanced, with local and national performance indicators published and tracked, and—as pioneered in New York—the local community expecting their local managers to continuously monitor and learn from their performance.

Further reforms flow from such improvements: greater flexibility for local pay and conditions of service; the reduction of ring-fenced budgeting; the reform of both inspectorates and monitoring regimes to recognise the benefits of local discretion; and work with service providers and user groups on performance indicators, to help community groups and local residents, especially in poor areas, build their capacity to hold local services to account. Thus the accountability of local service providers to patients, parents and local communities would be improved through greater transparency and a deeper democracy, tailoring services to needs and choices expressed both individually and collectively.

But we have also to get the balance right between responsiveness to choice and efficiency on the one hand, and equity on the other. Local autonomy without national standards may lead to increased inequality between people and regions, and the return of the postcode lotteries. The view we take on the appropriate balance between efficiency/diversity and equity will be shaped by the values we hold. The modern challenge is to move beyond old assumptions under which equity was seen to go hand in hand with uniformity, diversity to lead inevitably to inequality. Instead, we should seek the maximum amount of diversity consistent with equity.

Indeed, we are, in my view, already developing non-market and non-command-and-control mechanisms for service delivery and championing diversity by devolving further and faster to local government, the regions and the voluntary sector, and I want to suggest the next steps here too. In local government, with clear and concise information about each council's performance across its local services, with inspection regimes now more proportionate and with interventions concentrated on the small number of failing councils, John Prescott has moved us far from the destructive centralism—the universal capping, inflexible borrowing, the poll tax—of the 1980s and early 1990s. As we move forward we propose more freedoms and flexibilities—a 75 per cent cut in the number of plans; reduced ring-fencing; local PSA agreements that give localities more discretion; more targeted and thus more limited inspection; more freedom, with a fairer prudential regime, for borrowing; greater freedom to trade; more scope to use self-generated income, including new rates income from the growth of new businesses—freedoms and flexibilities that reflect a government that enables and empowers rather than directs and controls.

And in return for reform and results, and as an incentive to all the rest, the best-performing localities will soon have even more freedoms and flexibilities:

- the removal of both revenue and capital ring-fencing;
- the withdrawal of reserve powers over capping;
- the reduction of sixty required plans to just two—the Best Value Performance Plan and a Community Plan; and
- a three-year holiday from inspection.

Freedom and flexibility matter just as much as we innovate with a new regional policy, with its emphasis on indigenous sources of economic strength and thus genuine devolution of power from the centre.

There has been more devolution to English regions in the last few years than in the preceding one hundred years. This localism involves the freedom to determine local needs in Regional Development Agency budgets worth £2 billion a year, including in economic development, regeneration, tourism, planning, and—since April 2003 in selected pilots—the management of skills, training and business support.

Soon 90 per cent of the £7 billion a year learning and skills budget, 50 per cent of the small business services budget and the vast majority of housing capital investment will be devolved to the freedom and flexibility of local decision-making as we pioneer non-centralist means of delivering these services.

The financial freedoms and flexibilities are matched by greater account-ability through the role of regional chambers and, for those who in time choose to have them, elected regional assemblies. Having, in the NHS, already devolved 75 per cent of health budgets to primary care trusts, we have also established strategic health authorities. There is already discussion of democratic arrangements in these areas.

There is greater freedom and flexibility, too, for charities and for voluntary and community organisations as they take a bigger role in the delivery of services. At the heart of each of the new services we have played a part in developing—Sure Start for the under-fours, the Children's Fund, IT Learning Centres, Healthy Living Centres, the New Deal for jobs, the New Deal for Communities, the Safer Communities Initiative, Communities Against Drugs, the Futurebuilders programme and gift aid—is a genuine break with the recent past: services, once centrally funded and organised, can and should now be led, organised and delivered by voluntary, charitable and community organisations.

This new direction—this agenda for prosperity and social reform—moves us forward from the era of an old Britain weakened by the dictum that 'the man in Whitehall knows best' towards a new Britain strengthened by local centres awash with initiative, energy and dynamism. And the next steps should include not just further reform of local government but reform in the Civil Service as we map out the full implications of extending choice, equity and efficiency in individual public services.

Of course, in each decade the relationship between individuals, markets and communities will evolve as technology and rising expectations challenge each generation's vision of what is possible and best. But I am suggesting here that, today and in the future, in the large areas of the economy I have highlighted, our mission must be the relentless pursuit of stronger markets to maximise efficiency; and, in those areas where market failures are chronic, redoubled efforts to pioneer more decentralised systems of public service delivery.

An agenda founded on British values

This agenda I propose—one where we advance enterprise and fairness together—not only meets the contemporary challenges of competitiveness and equity but is, in my view, wholly in tune with British traditions and enduring British values. Indeed, this agenda for prosperity and reform is the modern means of applying enduring British values. For centuries Britishness has been rightly defined to the world as a profound belief in liberty and in the spirit of enterprise, combined with a deep civic pride that has emphasised the importance of what Orwell called decency: fair play and equity.

It is this long-standing commitment to both enterprise and fairness that, having shaped our past, now should define not only our economic policy but Britain's modern mission as a nation. Some continents are defined to the world as beacons of enterprise but at the cost of fairness; others as beacons of fairness or social cohesion at the cost of efficiency. In our time, Britain can be a beacon for a world where enterprise and fairness march forward together. It is this very British idea and patriotic purpose, and its enormous potential for shaping our country's future prosperity that should give us the strength to make all the tough and demanding reforms now necessary to create a Britain of opportunity and security for all.

A Sovietological View of Modern Britain

RON AMANN

Vol. 74, no. 4, October–December 2003

From 1994 to September 2002, Professor Amann spent eight and a half years in public service, first as Chief Executive of the Economic and Social Research Council (1994–9) and then as the founding Director General (Permanent Secretary) of the Centre for Management and Policy Studies in the Cabinet Office. Prior to that he held the Chair of Comparative Politics at the University of Birmingham, specialising in Soviet science policy and the politics of economic reform in centrally planned economies.

This is the second of two public lectures which Professor Amann delivered at the University of Edinburgh in December 1995 in his role as Montagu Burton Visiting Professor of International Relations. Despite the time lag of nearly eight years, the editors recently invited Professor Amann to publish the lecture in The Political Quarterly *because of the light it still sheds on the continuing struggle to find the right balance between trust and accountability in public management. The text of the lecture, which represented Professor Amann's personal view, is reproduced here in full without amendment or updating.*

WHEN the Soviet Union finally collapsed in 1991 a thoughtful academic colleague drew my attention to a cartoon which had appeared in the press. It depicted two ragged tramps hanging about on a street corner swapping hard luck stories. One was saying to the other: 'I used to be a leading Kremlinologist.' It proved to be a prescient reminder of my predicament. Clearly, most of my professional skills were now redundant, or would soon become so. There was no longer any need to read between the lines of *Pravda* for nuggets of truth or to scrutinise the order of precedence at (increasingly frequent) state funerals. Marxism–Leninism as a vision and a framework of analysis was defunct. The party was well and truly over in every sense. Politics was now to be found in the raw conflicts between emerging elites, in new subcultures and on the streets—not in institutions and formal rules.

However, although it was not apparent at the time, this cloud had an unexpected silver lining. Having become a pro-vice-chancellor at my university and, after that, Chief Executive of the ESRC, it gradually dawned upon me that the careful study of Soviet central planning which had absorbed my attention for over twenty years, far from being a waste of time, had instead provided me with unique qualifications—not so much in technical expertise but certainly in understanding. The growing managerial pressures in the public sector in Britain, which caused dismay and incomprehension to many colleagues, were instantaneously recognisable to an old Soviet hand. More-

Published by Blackwell Publishing Ltd, 9600 Garsington Road, Oxford OX4 2DQ, UK and 350 Main Street, Malden, MA 02148, USA

over, in their historical aspect my former studies had taught me that broken eggs do not necessarily an omelette make; that during a period of revolutionary change the means can come to dominate and distort the ends. These were sobering thoughts. In short, I had seen the future—but, unlike H. G. Wells after his pilgrimage to Moscow, I had some pretty serious doubts about whether it would work.

The observation that employees in Britain today have to meet more specific targets and cope with more paperwork is, of course, commonplace. But this is only a superficial aspect of central planning. What is much less widely understood is the fact that central planning, in its most highly developed form, comprises a distinctive culture with deeply established and norm-governed patterns of behaviour, socialisation processes and even its own special language. Furthermore, since the official justifications which accompany a system of central planning exhibit a high degree of 'false consciousness' and self-deception, we can also detect in it the ingredients of a powerful and invasive ideology. In many ways it is this socio-psychological aspect of central planning which represented the very essence of state socialism. Marxism–Leninism has gone. So, too, has the Communist Party of the Soviet Union, together with its alleged 'leading role'. But the culture of central planning remains—the 'vampire ideas', as Milovan Djilas would have called them,[1] which live on after death to suck the blood of later generations. It is against precisely *this* past that Russia is now struggling.

Now, however, I want to turn to Britain. It goes without saying that the origins and scale of planning in contemporary Britain are very different from those that lay behind Stalin's industrialisation drive of the 1930s. There are, however, some striking resemblances. My main argument is that—paradoxically and inadvertently—Britain may have set out on a road whose final destination is very different from that which was originally contemplated. With that thought in mind, I should like to highlight some of the early milestones along that route which are now coming into view.

We need to begin the story, however, with a fuller understanding of the sociological character of central planning. At this point I shall be talking specifically about the former Soviet Union. There are, though, implicit points of comparison here which will be brought out more fully later.

The sociology of Soviet central planning

Soviet central planning was based on a system of physical resource allocations which in theory, though never in practice, led to an overall materials balance. One might imagine the Soviet economy as a gigantic input/output matrix. There were no official markets to speak of and money was merely a unit of accounting. It was, as Joseph Berliner succinctly put it, a 'documonetary economy'. Each level and unit of production received a plan which laid down extremely detailed output targets and cost constraints, and equally detailed entitlements to raw materials and other resources for production and investment, which were obtained subsequently from a chain of specialist supply organisations (under Gossnab) in return for official certificates. The overall national plan, which had the force of law, was the end product of a complex process of negotiation between different administrative levels, during which the preliminary targets of the plan were first disaggregated and then reaggregated. For ease of understanding I have mapped the administrative levels of the UK higher education system on to those of the Soviet machine-tool industry, since the principles of plan formation are not fundamentally dissimilar (Figure 1). This is all that need be said for our purposes about the strictly formal aspects of central planning.

Now we come to the real story. Within such a planning system the volume of transactions was so huge and the interdependent relationships were so complex that real control was quite impossible. However, for a variety of political and psychological reasons, it was necessary to pretend that it was possible. Indeed, Pareto would have been gratified to observe that the traumatised inability of the political elite to continue to believe in its own mythology was a critical factor in the system's final collapse.

The key point was that no level of the administration *really* knew what the level below it was actually doing or was capable of doing. The periphery knew that the centre didn't know and the centre knew that they knew. Around this fundamental core of dishonesty grew a series of ever more elaborate controls and stratagems which brought an entire social system to its knees.

Since the centre (Gosplan or the ministry) did not know the true capacity of individual enterprises they guessed at it, typically adding on a standard percentage to the previous year's performance. This was the infamous 'ratchet effect'. In anticipation of that future tactic enterprises would, of course, conceal capacity and confine present output to bare plan fulfilment while at the same time pressing for more investment resources in their negotiations with the central authorities. Success here would give them the basis of an 'easy plan'. The aggregate result of this interplay was that the economy systemically underproduced and overconsumed. It also tended to produce goods that nobody actually wanted because in place of real customers enterprises faced crude plan targets, often expressed in terms of the volume or weight of materials used. The result was a stream of bulky and unattractive goods: for example, baggy trousers, and machine tools so heavy that they occasionally fell through the factory floor. In sharp contrast, improvement in product design, choice or innovation, which deflected effort from achievement of gross performance indicators, was avoided, in Brezhnev's memorable phrase, 'as the devil flies from incense'. The crazy distortions of such an economic system are virtually endless, but because they formed such a logical part of the whole they were a source of intellectual delight to western Sovietologists.

However, when we come to the intriguing question of why such an extraordinary system persisted for so long we touch upon matters closer to

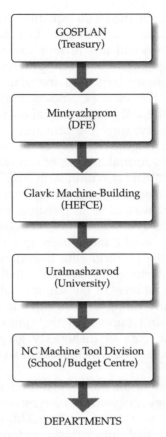

Figure 1: The Soviet machine-tool industry and British higher education: a structural comparison

home and our laughter may turn out to be premature. The most immediate factor was that all actors in the system at each level succeeded in 'fulfilling' their plans. It was a huge triumph of micro-rationality over macro-rationality. Through the peculiar prism of central planning's internal logic (and further obscured by large quantities of ideological clap-trap), the system did not *seem* to be failing. Also, powerful sources of self-interest and self-deception were at work. Over the decades since the 1930s an entirely new social stratum had formed, whose members were able and willing to modify established professional values and cope with this exotic 'management challenge'.

Recognising that performance indicators were so numerous that many were in conflict and could not be achieved, they became masters of prioritisation and learned to absorb huge amounts of administrative pressure. They discovered semi-legal ways around formal rules; they accumulated key contacts in strategic positions; they were adept at tactical deference, bluffing, deception, bullying and bribing. All these were essential survival skills and, in the aggregate, constituted a powerful and very system-specific form of human capital. It was an investment which the owners wanted to protect.

By the 1960s much of the original driving force of central planning had largely evaporated, to be replaced by a succession of lame and improvised ideological justifications that few actually believed. It had become a huge game, beyond the power of any one individual to change. As such it had accumulated an overwhelming number of rules and regulations—both formal and informal—which the players had learned to navigate with varying degrees of skill. It is in the language which the Soviet insiders use to describe this game that we perhaps begin to feel the first sharp chill of recognition (see Figure 2). Is this so very different from what *really* goes on these days in universities, hospital trusts, schools or—even—research councils?

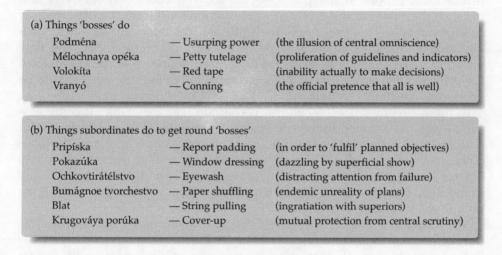

(a) Things 'bosses' do		
Podména	— Usurping power	(the illusion of central omniscience)
Mélochnaya opéka	— Petty tutelage	(proliferation of guidelines and indicators)
Volokíta	— Red tape	(inability actually to make decisions)
Vranyó	— Conning	(the official pretence that all is well)

(b) Things subordinates do to get round 'bosses'		
Pripíska	— Report padding	(in order to 'fulfil' planned objectives)
Pokazúka	— Window dressing	(dazzling by superficial show)
Ochkovtirátélstvo	— Eyewash	(distracting attention from failure)
Bumágnoe tvorchestvo	— Paper shuffling	(endemic unreality of plans)
Blat	— String pulling	(ingratiation with superiors)
Krugováya porúka	— Cover-up	(mutual protection from central scrutiny)

Figure 2: Soviet bureaucracy: some useful terms

How could it happen here?

The origins of a planning culture in modern Britain lie at the very opposite end of the political spectrum from those which inspired the creation of Soviet central planning. The philosophical basis of Soviet planning is to be found in Lenin's critique of 'economism': the view that a politically mature organisation of professionals (the Bolsheviks) was essential in order to secure the *real* interests of the working class rather than reflect their spontaneous interests, which were ephemeral and potentially divisive. In more down-to-earth economic terms, the Communist Party under Lenin's successors saw itself as imposing a general 'social interest' through its supervision of the planning process; as Jerry Hough has shown,[2] the Party's own direct role in setting overall priorities and reconciling conflicting demands for resources at the regional level was a fundamental source of its power.

In Britain, by contrast, the growth of a planning (or audit) culture stems paradoxically from the desire to strengthen the market. When Mrs Thatcher came to office in 1979 a principal objective of the new Conservative administration was to reduce the high prevailing levels of public spending, to create more incentives for private initiative and thereby to inject a new element of dynamism into what was perceived to be a failing economy—a failure to which, most damagingly, many ordinary people and leading figures in the major institutions had become reconciled. The high levels of public spending were conceived to be the result of a widespread 'dependency culture' which was becoming progressively unrestrained as a new generation of benefit claimants came along who had no collective memory of the prewar period. More central to our argument, however, was the assumption that many professional people in the public sector enjoyed cushioned lifestyles and pursued their own agendas which were disconnected from the real needs of ordinary people. This professional self-interest was quite slippery and typically clothed itself in eloquent expressions of high-mindedness. The new Thatcher government, however, refused to be charmed or deflected from the principle that producers of any good must not determine what should be produced; customers should.

In these circumstances, a cultural revolution was inevitable. It came as a rude shock. As a young university teacher in the late 1960s and early 1970s I had a total lecturing load of four hours per week (sufficiently large, in those days, to excuse me from classes and tutorials) and an earmarked travel budget so large that it was literally impossible to spend. I shall be eternally grateful for the privilege of having experienced that 'golden age', with all the time in the world for humane reflection—but it *was* a privilege.

Mrs Thatcher's answer to professional and institutional self-interest was not, of course, the countervailing force of Bolshevik intervention but the radical introduction of quasi-markets into the public sector, with a clear division between purchasers and providers. The critical point here is that these were not *real* markets with *real* customers buying services with *real* money. The purchasers were an organisational proxy for the final customer, using their allegedly superior inside knowledge (yes, there are vestiges of Bolshevik ideology here!) to secure value on society's behalf. From such little acorns do the great oak trees of planning grow.

As public institutions—such as universities, for example—began to construct 'bids' for resources to their central funding bodies (in Bristol, in this instance, rather than Moscow), it was of course appreciated in a vague sort of way that some kind of quality control would be required, otherwise the more unscrupulous institutions would 'play games'. Doubtless it was hoped initially that this would be a lightly managed process. However, the official fiction of the economical response, which is still maintained by many purchasing organisations, stands in dramatic contrast to the actual volume of the documentation which they demand and receive, and the time taken to produce it. The fact that space in aircraft hangars was required to house the aggregate university response to the last HEFCE Research Assessment Exercise makes that point in graphic terms. Inevitably, in manoeuvring for advantage in circumstances of information overload but imperfect knowledge, these complex proxy relationships between organisations have led to 'games'—on both sides of the purchaser/provider divide.

With the foundations of classic central planning relationships in place—even though the origins and institutional context in Britain were very different from those in the former Soviet Union—it was equally predictable that through the interplay of inherent mutual mistrust between centre and periphery the 'games' would become deeper and more intricate. The plot was bound to thicken. It is within this context that one can understand the emergence of an even more extensive and invasive 'audit culture' with its paraphernalia of quangoes, regulations, regulators, 'outposts', charters and codes of practice. Like the horizon, the objective of assured institutional accountability receded as one paddled clumsily towards it. Indeed, in a remarkable dialectical inversion, the audit process itself has been transformed by institutional providers from a means of attack into a means of defence. Since audit in many contexts measures systems and processes rather than conducting a detailed inspection of performance, audit reports can turn out to be little more than highly formalised 'comfort certificates',[3] legitimating what the organisation does but having little to do with the real quality of its core business.

These changes came as a profound cultural shock to a wide variety of professional groups; it now seemed that, after all, 'the gentlemen from Whitehall' no longer 'knew best'. Scientists sensed a distinct loss of autonomy as funding procedures and priorities cut across the Mertonian norms which governed their academic communities; teachers lost control of the curriculum; and even that most exalted and self-confident of all professional groups, medical consultants (uniquely enjoying both high income and public esteem), found their clinical judgements impertinently circumscribed by financial contingency. As a result of the Citizen's Charter and other such codes, a newly 'empowered' public began to challenge 'professional authority' and complain more vociferously. It is little wonder that many established professions began to feel somehow proletarianised.

As Michael Power has perceptively argued,[4] the 'audit explosion' is a form of cultural colonisation and is *intended* as a political challenge to professional autonomy. But, despite a great deal of demoralisation and grumbling, that point of principle is not widely recognised. These new administrative relationships have not, for the most part, been theorised or contested in systemic terms. Why not?

The answer to that question is both interesting and complex. It is, of course, tempting when viewing the British professions under siege today to see parallels with the unfortunate Soviet 'bourgeois specialists' of the 1920s: a group of engineers and managers who in their own eyes were far too sensible, pragmatic and conscious of their worth to take up a fundamental political challenge—until it was too late and they were wheeled out of their factories in barrows! But that would be a harsh judgement. In any event, groups which are subject to a concerted political and ideological attack of this kind frequently make a psychological adjustment which they are usually too proud to own up to. It is the classic dilemma of the persecuted minority, torn between the decision to fight (or, in this case, to challenge the new orthodoxy) and that to acquiesce gracefully, grab what advantage they can, and keep their powder dry. Many are the vice-chancellors and public sector chief executives, facing the new bodies which encroach upon their traditional autonomy, who might echo Cyril Washbrook's definitive view of fast bowlers: 'Nobody likes 'em but it's not everybody as'll let on.'

Yet even this line of explanation is insufficient since it does not account for the enthusiasm for the new values and procedures in some professional quarters. The constant drumbeat of ideological repetition, described so vividly by Arthur Koestler in his classic article in *The God that Failed*,[5] can produce conversion and consensus. After sixteen years of Mrs Thatcher's revolution, this is almost certainly a factor. But there is a sense in which business schools and consultancy organisations, which are crucial inter- mediaries in the socialisation process, have improved upon the old Commu- nist Party techniques. Staff development modules on time management, leadership, customer care and business process, for example, do more than improve technique; they impart the deep institutional values which are part of the new rule-governed and indicator-driven order. The most sophisticated and effective planning today is 'communicative planning',[6] which seeks to embed values organically rather than devolve specialist information hier- archically. When, as professional employees, we 'own the process', we signal our conversion. Just as in Stalin's Russia, a new stratum of able individuals has come forward who can best manage both the pressures and the technic- alities of hospital trusts and university budgets under the new arrangements. Those who keep faith with the traditional values are often treated with pity and contempt—as relics of the old world who have not quite 'got their act together'. Hannah Arendt, the great theorist of totalitarianism,[7] would certainly recognise, in the arrogance of the new world towards the old, the former's deep insecurity and irritation at having its conscience pricked.

The 'filling in' of the state

Rod Rhodes has described persuasively how, as a result of globalisation on the one hand and privatisation on the other, the British state is becoming 'hollowed out'.[8] While this insight is in many respects true, it should not be taken to imply, in my opinion, that a vacuum has been created which necessarily gives more scope for individual freedom. What may appear as a 'hollowing out' of initiatives at the macro-level looks very different at the micro-level, where the proliferation of new control systems has a distinctly 'filled-in' feel to it. This tightening of control is confirmed by the everyday experience of those working in large organisations, in both the public and the private sector. Britain has come a long way since the early 1980s, when Lord Dahrendorf could observe that Britons worked long hours but went to work primarily to spend an agreeable day.[9] A recent Demos pamphlet, *The Time Squeeze*, leaves us in no doubt that work in Britain is no longer the social occasion it once was.[10]

It may be appropriate at this point to describe the rather elaborate 'games' and pressures with which large numbers of people in Britain, particularly those working in the public sector, have to contend. The parallels with Soviet central planning are painfully obvious.

Contract negotiations across the purchaser/provider divide have become a complex and nail-biting battle of wits against an adversary who (unlike a real customer) controls both price and quantity. The 'ratchet effect' of incessant pressure for efficiency gains, irrespective of objective possibilities (which cannot be known) is endemic in the National Health Service and higher education. Concealing capacity in order to achieve an 'easy plan' is, inevitably, the calculated response. To get a better grip, purchasing and regulatory bodies stipulate more and more performance indicators, amounting in the case of the NHS trusts to an intrusive form of micro-management, accompanied by official rhetoric about vibrant managerial autonomy. (You always know that something is up when official protestations of this sort occur—this is pure *vran'yo*, almost on a par with agitprop statements about Soviet 'democracy of a new type' which allegedly stimulated turnouts of around 99 per cent on the part of an enthusiastic and grateful electorate.) Whenever the provider institution looks as if it may be gaining the upper hand, the goalposts can be moved with alarming speed. Universities which 'went down the access route' to expand student numbers and invested heavily in new student accommodation were caught the following year when targets were cut and penalties for over-expansion were introduced. Hospital trusts which have committed themselves to the development of expensive specialised facilities can be left high and dry when the purchaser places the 'business' elsewhere or unilaterally lowers the contract price for the activity. The resulting inability to take a long-term decision with any degree of assurance is a deep and widespread source of frustration.

A central feature of contemporary work culture is that the audit process in all its various guises must relate to an activity that is auditable. As a result, what is of high value (in commonsense terms) but not auditable tends to be neglected, while on the other hand what is auditable, but of little real value, can come to dominate the collective consciousness of institutions. In this way the audit process does not simply function as a narrow technical exercise in measurement but *defines* the core activity of an organisation and shapes the priorities of those who work within it.

In the school classroom, the preparation of elaborate written assessments and objectives (which nobody, inspectors apart, reads or refers to) eats into time needed for the preparation and conduct of high-quality teaching; in

RON AMANN

universities, auditable assessments replace substantive personal interaction between staff and students—indeed, the wholly bogus and inappropriate criterion of 'fitness for purpose' which formed the basis of the initial round of assessment of teaching quality in universities was an absolutely classic example of audit insularity. No wonder it has begun to unravel, not least because prospective employers have demanded reassurance about the *real* quality of what universities provide in terms of content and intellectual level—not what processes they have in place or whether they satisfy their own bureaucratised objectives and purposes.

The recent [1995] controversy regarding the Prison Service provides another striking example of the disparity between real objectives and auditable processes. In his critical report on the escape of prisoners from Parkhurst (prevention of which should surely be the core business of the Prison Service), General Sir John Learmont observed that 'Any organisation which boasts one Statement of Purpose, one Vision, five Values, six Goals, seven Strategic Priorities and eight Key Performance Indicators without any clear correlation between them is producing a recipe for total confusion and exasperation'. One might go further and hazard a guess that closer correlation between the various parts of this management model would not necessarily have alleviated that confusion.

As one might expect, 'games' to do with institutional performance indicators are endemic across the British public sector, as provider institutions seek to maximise the funds they receive from purchasing authorities, or at the very least to store up brownie points for future negotiations. Universities, to quote only a few examples, typically seek to reclassify students between different subject areas in order to attract a larger unit of resource for them; they convert what was previously extra-mural education into rather unconvincing (and certainly very long-term!) award-bearing courses in order to accommodate themselves to a new funding regime; postgraduate teaching assistantships have been created whose cost can be partly offset by an increased income stream which flows out of the Research Assessment Exercise. In that latter connection we have seen in the last year or so the growth for the first time of a feverish national transfer market in academic researchers. This is a perfect example of micro-rationality subverting macro-rationality, since in the aggregate none of the players has changed—all that has changed is their salary bill, which has increased at the taxpayer's expense.

In the face of all this indicator-driven behaviour, it is the extensive range of activity which *cannot* be measured or which is *not* eligible for material rewards that loses out; yet this is often the glue which holds institutions together. Collegiality is overtaken by stilted and instrumental behaviour which represents almost a form of moral coarsening. Fortunately, the point has not yet been reached when inner-city hospitals turn away emergencies because they have fulfilled the purchaser's contracted numerical requirement and will thus receive no extra payment—though such a response is a theoretical possibility.

Indicator-driven behaviour at the institutional level reproduces itself at the individual level, since, under the new managerial structures, institutional objectives cascade downwards into the job plans of individual managers. Thus, individuals come to see themselves, in a sense, as a kind of budget centre, allocating their time in a calculated fashion in order to maximise personal advantage in terms of salary and promotion. With the introduction of elaborate job evaluation schemes such as the Civil Service 'JEGS' (Job Evaluation and Grading Scheme) exercises, this game has become considerably more sophisticated. In negotiating their job plans and specifications with line managers, individuals will seek to incorporate 'JEGS-salient' activities (such as span of control, size of budgets for which one is formally responsible and grade seniority of those with whom one comes into direct regular contact) while jettisoning 'non-JEGS-able' activities. The pursuit of personal visibility, and narrow focusing of time and resource in order to notch up brownie points, are inimical to that barely visible collegiality and cooperation on which the collective well-being of complex organisations so crucially depends. Paradoxically such schemes, which are being introduced into many large organisations in both the public and the private sectors in order to remove traditional grade inflexibilities, can have quite the opposite effect. Individuals can come to assess their relative positions in terms of 'JEGS-ability' and resist moves which would weaken their standing from this perspective. Senior managers in whose gift lie the allocation of responsibilities now have in their hands a very modern form of patronage.

All this represents—and is probably intended to represent—a fundamental departure from the collegiality, solidarity and service values which once characterised large parts of the British workplace. Employees at all levels of seniority are now attuned to the administrative 'games' that are being played, are more calculating and are more wary of all manner of hidden agendas. The 'nanny state' has come to an end; but so, too, has 'nanny society'. In a wider sense, society may no longer be a resource upon which the state can easily call in its hour of need. There must be a sense, consistent with the spirit of the age, in which calls for loyalty and sacrifice are seen as expressions of the state's (or an organisation's) dependency culture.

The bureaucratisation of opportunity

A separate but closely related feature of the contemporary scene is the degree to which the rights and opportunities of minorities (a concept which has more to do with political salience than numerical size) are increasingly promoted by an elaborate administrative framework and ideological superstructure. Though still in their infancy in Britain, these arrangements have the potential to go well beyond the crude proletarian quotas which were introduced in the Soviet Union in the late 1920s and early 1930s. They probably have their origin in the desire to create an 'opportunity society' without incurring a significant increase in public spending, since administrative 'empowerment' is a relatively resource-free strategy. Whatever the underlying cause—and this must remain an open question—these new arrangements appear to be acquiring an irresistible momentum.

Consider the following true story, which Barbara Amiel described in a recent article in *The Sunday Times*. A young Canadian professional man, obviously white and middle-class, applies for a job in the Government Service. Though highly qualified, he is told by his interviewer that he is ineligible because the positions are reserved for applicants from ethnic minorities. The young man insists on his rights, announcing to the astonishment of the panel that he is a woman and a Cree Indian—and is given the job because, according to the procedures, his identity must be what *he asserts* it to be. To contest such an assertion would be to erode self-esteem.

Consider another example which I came across in my former unenviable role of pro-vice-chancellor responsible for student discipline at a large university. Alas, it was one of several such cases. To protect anonymity, this brief account is a composite of several actual incidents, but this does not detract from the main point. The incident in question took place at a late-night party held on campus in a student residence. As is often the case at such parties, everybody was extremely drunk. In the main lounge, where most of the students were scattered around, Miss X was lying on a settee on top of a fellow student. Her short skirt had worked its way up over her hips (I shall omit further details at this point). Stumbling past on his way to the toilet, Mr Y, a very young and junior member of staff with whom Miss X had had a romantic attachment, was seen to place his hand on her exposed thigh— though Miss X was unaware of this at the time and the evidence was inconsistent.

So much for the facts. It is the subsequent sequence of events that mainly concerns us. When she was told what had had happened the next day, Miss X accused Mr Y of sexual harassment. She insisted that the university take action on the strength of her assertion that harassment had taken place (according to her interpretation of the formal guidelines) but did not want to be personally involved in any formal disciplinary proceedings since this would make her feel 'threatened'. Mr Y, in the meantime, had constructed an elaborate, modern form of defence, positing ulterior motives on the part of Miss X and arguing that accusations of sexual harassment are themselves a form of sexual harassment.

At this point the university resolved to cut through all these slippery accusations, uncontested assertions and perceptions in order to establish good old-fashioned truth. This step, however, incurred some costs. Miss X (and her parents) now accused the university of a form of 'rape' because it had not met her wishes and had not accepted her assertion at face value. Witnesses who had supported her accusation also, apparently, felt 'abused' and 'threatened'. When the disciplinary hearing was finally arranged, it was dominated by references to the university's codes and procedures, which had been requested and minutely scrutinised by all sides in advance. Since both Miss

X and Mr Y had defined themselves as victims, both were accompanied at the hearing by their specialist sexual harassment counsellors, tutors and, in Mr Y's case, trade union representatives. Many of the 'abused' witnesses had also sought counselling and were similarly supported. There was much talk about rights but none about responsibilities. The incident itself became secondary.

The events described above, and in particular the forms of discourse which pervade them, suggest that the admirable aim of protecting rights and expanding opportunities is somehow being weakened and distorted. As the uninitiated would put it, 'You just can't understand where people today are coming from.' Further reflection, however, provides an answer. What can be observed, in essence, is the confluence of a victim paradigm and an audit culture.[11] Rules, procedures, codes and restraints on language replace judgement and common sense because the latter are dismissed as culturally contested categories. Inevitably, the new regulatory framework, as well as establishing important safeguards in genuine cases, provides a wonderful environment for covert battles of spite and for personal advancement not based on true merit. The application of complex social indicators can produce 'games' and distortions quite as well as economic indicators can.

Ironically, the reason why these elaborate codes of practice relating to 'equal opportunities' or 'harassment' are gaining such a foothold in the public sector is that purchasers request them as proof of good practice, and they thus become part of the wider economic game. First come the codes themselves, then compulsory staff training (which is a precondition for promotion), then a quasi-autonomous monitoring committee to enforce the codes and, finally, 'imaginative suggestions' about how the codes might be developed (i.e. getting round legal stipulations against positive discrimination, for example, by setting targets rather than quotas). There is no reason why such an arrangement should not work quite effectively—but that would depend on moderation and common sense, which are in relatively short supply. I can think of a professional association within the general domain of the social sciences, for example, whose elaborate code of practice is much more concerned with which minority groups gain entry on to postgraduate training courses than with the upholding of professional standards of competence embodied in the *content* of the training itself. I could name (but I won't) a university whose equal opportunities policy, widely regarded as a model of its kind, even makes provision for gender and ethnic prioritisation in the issuing of campus parking permits. The real danger, as exemplified by some 'progressive' local authorities, is of an ideologically driven monitoring committee—an inquisition searching for non-existent heretics. Tragically, when inquisitions are created they *do*, in order to justify their existence, tend to uncover 'heretics', just as the NKVD exposed 'enemies of the people'.

The final question must be whether such a contrived rule-governed approach, even if it did not produce a public backlash, could *actually* enhance rights and opportunities on a broad front. There seems no clear answer to that question yet; but the machinations of some large organisations in the private sector with elaborate customer care arrangements and Citizen's Charter standards suggest that counter-ploys are possible. Institutions can use their codes and procedures to deflect complaint and criticism. It's a two-edged sword. It may be true, for example, that banks forced many small businesses into liquidation during the recession, that insurance companies have organised special seminars to train their staff to negotiate claims downwards, and that many existing borrowers from building societies are locked into high interest rates in order to cross-subsidise irresistible introductory offers to first-time buyers. However, the customers of these institutions need not be distressed! When the next glossy brochure plops through their letterboxes, they can be sure that the keynote article illustrated by the smiling face of the chief executive will celebrate, in a number of cogent bullet points, the added value they have received.

Chto Delat'?

Raising critical questions about audit, public accountability and the new apparatus of equal opportunities is rather like expressing doubt in earlier times about the existence of God or the ultimate triumph of the working class. This is sacred territory. One should tread warily and be of sober countenance. However, given my own academic background, the temptation to raise these questions was too great to resist—and I have not always been as sober as I ought. The core of the argument, to remind you of it, is summarised in Figure 3.

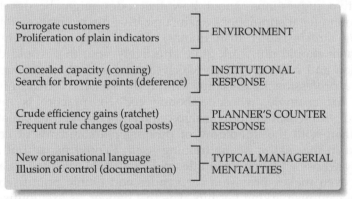

Figure 3: Central planning: life after death?

If I may paraphrase Chernyshevskii and Lenin, 'What is to be done?' I don't have a convincing answer to this question. What I *am* clear about, however, is that we are situated at present precisely where we don't want to be. Undoubtedly, the social revolution in Britain over the past sixteen years has brought significant gains in the performance of public and private sector institutions, but it is an *incomplete revolution*: and out of that very incompleteness have arisen all the indicator-driven distortions and humanity-sapping working environments that I have tried to describe.

Although I don't have any firm answers, as the head of a research council I have, you will not be surprised to learn, a couple of research proposals in mind. Each is aimed at a different kind of solution to the problems that confront us. Project A calls for a detailed cost-benefit analysis of the contemporary culture of audit and accountability, having in mind the restoration of a higher degree of professional trust and judgement and asking how, in practical terms, that might be achieved. Project B seeks to explore the possibility of transforming quasi-markets into real markets where proxy institutional customers are abolished in favour of real customers. These are very different kinds of projects, both intellectually and politically, and we shall have to await the final evaluation reports.

In the meantime, as chief executive of a non-departmental public body operating in the very environment which I have described, I keep my spirits up with one final thought, drawn from a long exposure to Marxist regimes: that freedom is, after all, the recognition of necessity.

Notes

1 Milovan Djilas, *The Unperfect Society: Beyond the New Class*, London, Unwin, 1972, p. 12.
2 Jerry F. Hough, *The Soviet Prefects: The Local Party Organ in Industrial Decision-Making*, Cambridge, Mass., Harvard University Press, 1969.
3 Michael Power makes this point in a forthcoming article entitled 'Audit and the Decline of Inspection'. It builds upon his original and perceptive analysis in *The Audit Explosion*, London, Demos, 1994.
4 Michael Power, 'The Perils of the Audit Society, paper presented to London School of Economics/Cabinet Office joint seminar, June 1995.
5 Arthur Koestler's chapter in Richard Crossman, ed., *The God that Failed*, London, Hamish Hamilton, 1950, pp. 25–82.
6 Judith E. Innes, 'The Role of Information in Communicative Planning', paper prepared for annual conference of the Association of European Schools of Planning, Glasgow, 16–19 August 1995.
7 Hannah Arendt, *The Origins of Totalitarianism*, New York, Harcourt Brace, 1951.
8 Rod Rhodes, *The New Governance: Governing without Government*, ESRC, 'State of Britain' seminar series, Jan. 1995.
9 Ralf Dahrendorf, *On Britain*, London, BBC Publications, 1982, p. 45.
10 Geoff Mulgan and Helen Wilkinson, 'Well-being and Time', The Time Squeeze, *Demos Quarterly*, no. 5, 1995.
11 On the 'victim paradigm', see Robert Hughes, *Culture of Complaint: The Fraying of America*, Oxford, Oxford University Press, 1993.

What Will Follow the Demise of Privatised Keynesianism?

COLIN CROUCH

Vol. 79, no. 4, October–December 2008

SINCE the end of the Second World War two regimes have successively dominated the political economies of advanced capitalist economies; both lasted around 30 years before ending in some disarray.[1] We now stand at the brink of a third, largely unknown one; what will its shape be? The first was the Keynesian strategy of demand management (assisted in several countries by neo-corporatist industrial relations systems). This more or less collapsed under the weight of the inflationary pressures from commodity price rises in the 1970s. It gave way to something generally called neo-liberalism, but which following the crisis of autumn 2008 we can now see to have been a regime of privatised Keynesianism.

Under original Keynesianism it was governments that took on debt to stimulate the economy. Under the privatised form individuals, particularly poor ones, took on that role by incurring debt on the market. The main motors were the near-constant rise in the value of owner-occupied houses and apartments alongside an extraordinary growth in markets in risk. This regime collapsed, partly during a repetition of energy and other commodity inflation, but largely because of certain internal contradictions.

Both regimes have had to manage an important contradiction, or at least tension: that between the insecurity and uncertainty created by the requirements of the market to adapt to shocks, and the need for democratic politics to respond to citizens' demands for security and predictability in their lives. That there are tensions in the relationship between capitalism and democracy may surprise those who, particularly in the USA, use those terms as virtual synonyms, but over the issue of security in working life it is fundamental. There is a further, related, tension within advanced capitalism itself, which needs on the one hand consumers on whose confidence firms can depend when planning their production, and on the other a capacity to respond to periods of declining demand by reducing the quantity and wages of labour, which in turn undermines consumer confidence. The tension can never be 'resolved' as it is endemic to the only successful form of political economy that we know; it has to be managed, by a series of regimes that will always in the end wear out and need to be replaced by something else.

The basic conundrum was the ambiguous gift that democracy gradually presented to capitalism during the twentieth century. Before that time the great mass of populations had been sustained on low incomes that rose only very slowly. Ideas of consumer confidence, if understood at all, applied to small, wealthier parts of the public. Demands by the mass of the population for a better life seemed impossible to accommodate, and although early social policy in Germany, France, Britain and elsewhere tried to put a basic floor under the insecurity of working-class life, its ambitions were limited. Fears about the revolutionary implications of democracy still led many elites to rely on repression, initially of a reactionary, later of a fascist and Nazi kind.

As is well known, the first answer to the problem came in the early twentieth century from the mass production system of manufacture associated initially with the Ford Motor Company in the USA. Technology and work organisation could enhance the productivity of low-skilled workers, enabling goods to be produced more cheaply and workers' wages to rise, so that they could afford more of the goods. The mass consumer became a reality. It is significant that the breakthrough occurred in the large country that came closest to a basic idea of democracy (albeit on a racial basis) during that period. Democracy as well as technology contributed to construction of the model. However, as the Wall Street crash of 1929, coming just a few years after the launch of the Fordist model, showed, the problem of reconciling the instability of the market with consumer-voters' need for stability remained unresolved. This is where what became known as the Keynesian model came in, as will be briefly described below. How its successor squared the circle is more complex; analysing it will take us to the heart of the current crisis. Finally, we shall try to peer into the future.

The ingredients, achievements and vulnerability of the Keynesian model

How the Keynesian demand management model was supposed to operate is widely understood. In times of recession, when confidence was low, governments would go into debt in order to stimulate the economy with their own spending. In times of inflation, when demand was excessive, they would reduce their spending, pay off their debts, and reduce aggregate demand. The model implied large state budgets, to ensure that changes within them would have an adequate macroeconomic effect. For the British and some other economies this possibility occurred only with the vast rise in military expenditure required by the Second World War. Previous wars had seen large rises in state spending, always followed by a major reduction afterwards. World War II was different, in that military spending was replaced by that on the new, growing welfare state.

The Keynesian model protected ordinary people from the rapid fluctuations of the market that had brought instability to their lives, smoothing the trade cycle and enabling them gradually to become confident mass consumers of the products of a therefore equally confident mass production industry. Unemployment was reduced to very low levels. The welfare state not only provided instruments of demand management for governments, but also brought real services in areas of major importance to people outside the framework of the market: more stability.

Arm's-length demand management plus the welfare state protected the rest of the capitalist economy from both major shocks to confidence and attacks from hostile forces, while the lives of working people were protected from the vagaries of the market. It was a true social compromise. As conservative critics pointed out from the start, there was always likely to be a ratchet effect in the mechanism: it was easy for governments to increase spending in a recession, bringing lower unemployment, more public services, and more money in people's pockets. It would be far more difficult at times of boom in a democracy to reverse these trends. This was the seed of destruction at the heart of the model. We shall come to it shortly. First we must take a look at the political circumstances that ushered the model into practical reality, for the ideas that were incorporated in it had been around for 15 to 20 years.

Karl Marx famously wrote that at particular moments of historical crisis particular social classes were in a position where their particular interests coincided with the general interest of society. Such classes triumphed in the revolutions in which the crises ended. Marx's error was to believe that when the class concerned became the international proletariat there would be an end to the process, because the proletariat was the generality of society and not just a particular interest within it. This was an error if only because it is impossible to imagine anything as vast as the global proletariat producing organisational forms that could express a shared interest. Be that as it may, the Keynesian model did represent a temporary coincidence between the interests of the industrial working class in the global north-west and a general interest of the politico-economic system. This was the class likely to threaten political and social order. It was also potentially the class whose mass consumption, if facilitated and made secure, could fuel economic growth of a kind unprecedented in human history. It was also a class that had produced political parties, trade unions and other organisations, as well as associated intellectuals, to shape and press its demands. The Keynesian model, combined with Fordist production, was a response to these demands that reconciled them with a capitalist system of production.

Behind these generalisations rests a more diverse picture. The basic approach was embodied in public policy a decade before the end of World War II in two places—Scandinavia and the USA—in both cases as the result of coalitions between forces representing industrial workers and small farmers. The US New Deal in this complete form was only a temporary arrangement. The Scandinavian labour movements, far more powerful than the US one, were able to take the model forward to its welfare-state form, joined for a time in that effort after the war by the then also powerful British labour movement.

The labour movements of continental Europe, crushed by war, fascism and Nazism, and divided among themselves by religion, were far weaker. The Keynesian model as such developed more slowly, and governments took different means to stabilise economies. In some countries, particularly France and Italy, there were real possibilities of communist domination of the labour movement. Governments had to ensure that working-class life escaped the insecurity of the 1920s and 1930s. State ownership of important parts of the economy, combined with agricultural subsidies to ensure that still large peasant populations would not join the radicalism of industrial workers, were used to provide the stability in the early years. They were not as subtle as Keynesian policies, and permitted considerably more state intervention in the economy, while consumer demand was slow to rise. However, the outcome was similar in terms of protecting workers' incomes from market fluctuations. In time, demand management and strong welfare states also appeared in these economies. Meanwhile, the vast injections of Marshall Aid from the USA meant that public spending—in this case another country's public spending—further stimulated the economies and maintained the security of working people's lives.

Germany was even more of an outlier. It benefited fully from Marshall Aid, but did not formally adopt Keynesianism until the late 1960s, when the model was nearing the end of its period of dominance. The initial German economic recovery did not depend on domestic consumer demand but on capital goods production (to re-establish production facilities) and exports. The country's own formal economic policy stance depended on balanced budgets, an autonomous central bank, and a high priority on avoiding inflation: major ingredients of the neo-liberal model that was to succeed the Keynesian one. It can however be argued that the German economy was during this period dependent for its stability, not on pure markets, but on a general Keynesian environment, or on other countries' Keynesianism: US public spending through Marshall Aid and rising consumer demand in the USA, UK and elsewhere.

Germany was not however an outlier in a further ingredient of the demand management model: neo-corporatist industrial relations. This had not been anticipated in Keynes's own writings, and it featured hardly at all in US and only fitfully in British approaches; but it was fundamental to the Nordic, Dutch and Austrian cases. Under neo-corporatist industrial relations trade unions and employers associations have regard to the impact of their agreements on labour costs on the general level of prices, and particularly on export prices. This can work only if these organisations have sufficient authority over all firms to ensure that the terms of the deal are not significantly broken. The countries listed, where this kind of collective bargaining has been particularly important, are all small economies, heavily dependent on foreign trade. Broadly similar arrangements developed in Germany, the only large country involved, as part of the priority on export- as opposed to domestic-led growth of that economy.

The importance of neo-corporatism for present purposes is that it addressed the Achilles' heel of Keynesianism: the inflationary tendencies of its politically determined ratchet. Countries that had Keynesian policies but no

COLIN CROUCH

or weak or neo-corporatism—before all others the UK and (though with less reliance on Keynesianism) the USA, but by the 1970s France and Italy too— were highly vulnerable to the inflationary shocks unleashed by the general rise in commodity prices during the 1970s, particularly the oil price rises of 1973 and 1978. The wave of inflation that then affected the advanced countries of the West, though nothing like what had been experienced in Germany in the 1920s, or in various parts of Latin America more recently, more or less destroyed the model.

On to privatised Keynesianism

An intellectual challenge to Keynesianism had long been ready. The advocates of a return to 'real' markets had never ceased to be active, and a range of policies was in readiness. The key objective was to have governments withdraw from accepting overall responsibility for the economy. While for the purposes of this article we are concentrating on demand management, Keynesianism had become emblematic of a far wider range of policies of regulation, welfare provision and subsidy. The opposing set of ideas required an historical moment to justify their installation in the approaches of governments and international organisations. The 1970s inflationary crisis provided this. Within a decade or so such ideas as the absolute priority of near-zero inflation at whatever cost in terms of unemployment, the withdrawal of state assistance to firms and industries in difficulties, the priority of competition, the predominance of a shareholder maximisation as opposed to a multiple stakeholder model of the corporation, the deregulation of markets and the liberalisation of global capital flows had become orthodoxy. Where governments in countries with weak economies were unwilling to accept them, they were imposed as conditions for assistance from or membership of such international bodies as the International Monetary Fund, the World Bank, the OECD or the European Union. When the Soviet Union collapsed in 1989, the more westerly of its former allies were brought within the scope of the new model.

A further change that had taken place was the declining autonomy of the nation state. The postwar political economy had been founded on the basis of governments that could exercise considerable discretion in how they managed their economies. By the 1980s the process generally known as globalisation, both a producer and a product of the deregulation of financial markets, had eroded much of that autonomy. The only actors capable of rapid action at global level were transnational corporations, who preferred their own private regulation over that by governments. This both advanced and even rendered necessary the new model.

Just as a class—that of industrial workers—can be seen as the bearers of the Keynesian model, so we can identify a class whose particular interests seemed to embody the general interest in the new model: the class of finance capitalists, geographically grounded in the USA and the UK but extending

S306

——

across the globe. If the world was to gain from the liberation of productive forces and enterprise that the spread of free markets would bring, the class of those who dealt in the unregulated finance that massaged and helped those markets to grow would benefit particularly. Whereas the tight labour markets and regulated capitalism of the Keynesian period had seen a gradual reduction in inequalities of wealth in all advanced countries, the following period was to see a sharp reversal of these trends, with the highest rewards (at least in the western world) going to those working in and owning financial institutions.

Two questions are immediately raised by this. First, what had been the fate of the industrial working class, whose interests had seemed so politically urgent in the 1940s and 1950s? And what become of the need to reconcile the instability of markets with people's demand for security in their lives, which had been both politically and economically so important?

The initial crisis of Keynesianism in the 1970s had been accompanied by an extraordinary wave of industrial militancy, such that one might have thought that the challenge of that class was becoming more rather than less important. But this was an illusion. Rising productivity and the globalisation of production were in fact undermining its demographic base. Starting in the USA, the UK and Scandinavia, the share of employment in mining and manufacturing began to decline throughout the West. The militancy of the 1970s served only to encourage governments that were so inclined to lend their hand to hastening that decline, as occurred in the UK with reference to the coal and some other industries during the 1980s. Industrial workers had never constituted a majority of the working population anywhere, but they had been the growing class; now they were declining. By the 1980s they had been replaced as leaders in industrial militancy by public employees, with whom governments could deal directly without disturbing the market economy much. The main growth sectors of the new economy, private services, were usually not organised and had developed no autonomous political agenda, no organisations to articulate their specific grievances.

In the regime of largely unregulated international finance that was instituted during the 1980s, governments were far more worried about capital movements than labour movements: positively, in that they wanted to attract investment from free-floating capital with short time horizons; negatively in that they feared that such capital would move away if they did not provide conditions in which it was happy.

However, as we have noted, the Keynesian model had met an economic demand from capitalists themselves for stable mass consumption as well as workers' demands for stable lives. In the newly industrialising countries of South Asia and the Far East this was not a problem. Until very recently these largely undemocratic countries have depended on export markets rather than spending by the mass of their populations. But this was far from possible in the existing advanced economies. Indeed, dependence there on increased domestic consumption rather than exports had intensified rather than weakened. As the industries making many of the products bought in mass markets moved to new producing countries, or, if they remained became dependent on less and less labour, employment growth came to depend on markets in personally delivered services, which are not so subject to globalisation. It is easy to buy a Chinese T-shirt in a western shop and benefit from low Chinese wages; it is hardly feasible to travel to China to get a cheap haircut. Immigration is the only way that globalisation affects such services, but its impact is limited by controls of population movements (which have not benefited from market liberalisation but have in general been intensified), and by the fact that immigrants' wages, though usually low, are not as low as in their home countries. So the puzzle remains: if the instability of free markets had to be overcome to usher in the mass consumption economy, how did the latter survive the return of the former?

During the 1980s (or 1990s, depending on when the neo-liberal wave hit a particular economy) the answer first appeared to be a negative one, as rising unemployment and continuing recession became the dominant experience. Then things changed. By the end of the twentieth century the UK and the USA in particular were demonstrating declining unemployment and strong growth. One explanation might be that, in a really pure market economy, the rapid alternations of boom and bust associated with the earlier history of capitalism do not occur. In the perfect market there is perfect knowledge, rational actors can therefore perfectly anticipate what is going to happen, and can adapt their behaviour to produce a seamless web of adaptation. Did the USA and the UK really enter this nirvana at the turn of the century?

No. Knowledge is far from perfect; exogenous shocks, whether hurricanes, wars or the actions of irrational people who do not behave as theory says they should, continue to impact on economies and to disturb calculations. As we now know, two things came together to rescue the neo-liberal model from the instability that would otherwise have been its fate: the growth of credit markets for poor and middle-income people, and of derivatives and futures markets among the very wealthy. This combination produced a model of privatised Keynesianism that occurred initially by chance, a real case of market entrepreneurship, but which gradually became a matter for public policy so important as to threaten the entire neo-liberal project.

Instead of governments taking on debt to stimulate the economy, individuals did so. In addition to the housing market there was an extraordinary growth in opportunities for bank loans and, particularly important, in credit cards. It was common for people to hold cards from more than one credit card company as well as several store-specific ones.

This explains the great puzzle of the period: how did moderately paid American workers, who have little legal security against instant dismissal from their jobs, and salaries that might remain static for several years, maintain consumer confidence, when European workers with more or less secure jobs and annually rising incomes were bringing their economies to a halt by their unwillingness to spend? US house prices were rising every year;

the proportion of the value of the house on which a loan could be raised was also rising until it reached more than 100 per cent; credit card possibilities were growing. With some exceptions European property values remained stable. Credit card growth was slower.

Europeans were told by orthodox experts that the answer to their economic problems lay in producing more and more labour insecurity and cutting back on their welfare states. They eventually more or less obeyed, but found few positive results. No one told them that these insecure workers would need to be enabled to take on unsecured debt in order to boost consumer spending.

In Anglo-America the anti-inflation bias of public policy further encouraged the model. Anti-inflationary policy bears down on the prices of goods and services that lose their value as they are consumed. Producers of food, material goods and services like restaurants or health centres confront an environment hostile to rises in their prices. This is not the case with assets, things that do not lose their value in this way: real property, financial holdings, some art objects. A rise in their price is simultaneously a rise in their value, and does not contribute to inflation. It was seen as an act of political manipulation when the UK government removed mortgage repayments, but not rent, from its calculations of inflation, but it was technically quite correct. Therefore assets, and earnings based on assets, have not been the objects of neo-liberal counter-inflation policy. Anything that could be switched from prices and wages derived from the sale of normal goods and services to an asset base therefore did very well. This applied to proportions of salaries paid as share options and to spending funded by extended mortgages rather than by salaries and wages.

Eventually governments, especially British ones, began to incorporate privatised Keynesianism into their public policy thinking, though the phrase did not occur to them. While a reduction in the price of oil would be seen as good news (because it reduced inflationary pressure), a reduction in the price of houses would be seen as a disaster (as it would undermine confidence in debt), and government would be expected to act through fiscal or other measures to get prices rising again. There had been an initial implicit public policy boost to the model back in the 1980s when the privatisation of council housing enabled large numbers of people on moderate incomes to take on mortgages and, later, to explore the scope for extended mortgages. But the move to more explicit policies to have house prices constantly rising crept up during the first years of the twenty-first century until the massive interventions into housing finance and the banking sector in general during 2007 and 2008.

Most of this housing and consumer debt was necessarily unsecured; that was the only way in which privatised Keynesianism could have the same counter-cyclical stimulant effect as the original variety. Prudential borrowing against specified collateral certainly would not have helped the moderate-income groups who had to keep spending despite the insecurity of their labour market positions. The possibility of prolonged, widespread unsecured debt was in turn made possible through innovations that had taken place in financial markets, innovations which for a long time had seemed to be an excellent example of how, left to themselves, market actors hit on creative solutions. Through markets in derivatives and futures the great Anglo-American finance houses learned how to trade in risk. They found they could buy and sell risky holdings provided only that purchasers were confident that they could find further purchasers in turn; and that depended on the same confidence. Provided markets were free from regulation and capable of extensive reach, these trades enabled a very widespread sharing of risk, which made it possible for people to invest in many ventures that would otherwise have seemed unwise.

An inability to share risks widely had been at the heart of the economic collapses of 1929 and the 1870s. In the 1940s it had seemed that only state action could solve this problem for the market. But now, absolutely in tune with neo-liberal ideology and expectations, there was a market solution. And, through the links of these new risk markets to ordinary consumers via extended mortgages and credit card debt, the dependence of the capitalist system on rising wages, a welfare state and government demand management that had seemed essential for mass consumer confidence, had been abolished.

After privatised Keynesianism: the responsible corporation?

In the event it was only abolished for a few years. All theories of market economics depend on the assumption that market actors are perfectly informed, but privatised Keynesianism depended on what were presumed to be the very smartest actors concerned, the financial institutions of Wall Street and the City of London, having highly defective knowledge. This is the Achilles' heel of this model, corresponding to the inflationary ratchet of original Keynesianism. Banks and other financial operators believed that each other had studied and calculated the risks in which they were trading. But during autumn 2008 it became clear that had they done so they would not have entered into many of the transactions they undertook. The only calculations made were that there was a good chance that someone else would buy a share in the risk. The only mystery is why, if they all behaved like that, they somehow believed that all the others were not doing the same. Bad debts were funding bad debts, and so on in an exponentially growing mountain.

Some people became extremely wealthy in the process, but this does not mean that they were parasites. They continued to be the class whose particular interests represented the general interest, because we all benefited from the growing purchasing power that this system generated. At least, this is true in the UK, USA and one or two other places. French, German and most other continental European citizens may feel differently, as their financial elites joined in the act, while they experienced little of the growth in credit.

Once privatised Keynesianism had become a model of general economic importance, it became a kind of collective good, however nested in private actions it was. And given that necessary to it, powering it, was irresponsible behaviour by banks in failing to examine their asset bundles, *that very irresponsibility became a collective good*. This in itself explains why governments had to bail out the firms involved, more or less nationalising privatised Keynesianism.

And so a second regime to reconcile stable mass consumption with the market economy ended. Both Keynesianism and its privatised mutant lasted 30 years. As regimes in a rapidly changing world go, that is probably as good as it can get. But the question arises: how are capitalism and democracy to be reconciled now? Also, how will the enormous moral hazard established by governments' recognition of financial irresponsibility as a collective good now be managed? The public policy response has not been 'now stop all this', but 'please carry on borrowing and lending, but a little bit more carefully'. It has to be so; otherwise there will be a danger of real systemic collapse.

Two things characterised the transition from prewar economics to Keynesianism and that from original to privatised Keynesianism: the availability of alternative ideas and the existence of a class, serving whose interests would serve a general interest. It is fashionable to claim that at the present juncture we lack the former, while not noticing the latter. This is wrong on both points.

Many of the ideas that constituted neo-liberalism had been lying around for more than 200 years when they were refashioned for public policy use during the 1970s. Today many of the components of the much younger mix of demand management and neo-corporatism are still around in the economic strategies of small states, usually today combined with portions of neo-liberalism too. Most widely noted, though not unique, is the Danish way of combining a strong welfare state and powerful trade unions with very flexible labour markets. That seems to square the circle of market flexibility and consumer confidence, as well as powering a dynamic and innovative economy. There is no shortage of policy mixes; only of coalitions of political forces capable of supporting them in the larger economies; and this returns us to the question of significant social classes.

Just possibly the current arrogance of the financial sector, demanding the right to privatise gain and socialise loss, is an equivalent of the industrial militancy of the 1970s, the pride that went before an historical decline. But this is doubtful. Economic prosperity continues to depend on supplies of capital through efficient markets far more than it then depended on the industrial workers of the western world. A difference of geographical reach is part of the explanation. The decline of the western industrial working class does not mean a decline in that class globally. More people are engaged in manufacturing activities today than ever before; but they are divided into national, or at best world regional, lumps with very different histories and trajectories.

Finance capital does not come in solid lumps but more like a liquid or gas, capable of changing shape and flowing across jurisdictions and regions. We remain dependent on both labour and capital, but the former is subject to *divide et imperia*, the latter is not—unless we see a major return to economic nationalism and limitations on capital movements that will lead to the breakup of the major corporations that dominate the global economy and probable major economic decline.

The most likely new model is one that in fact depends increasingly on those corporations; the logic of globalisation that imparted an important role to TNCs has not disappeared with the financial system. There has always been a tension at the centre of neo-liberalism: is it about markets or about giant firms? They are far from being the same: the more that a sector is dominated by giant firms, the less it resembles the pure market that in principle lies behind nearly all of today's public policy. There may well be intense competition among giant firms, but it is not the competition of the pure market. This is supposed to be characterised by very large numbers of actors, such that each remains incapable of having an effect on prices by its own actions, and certainly incapable of wielding political influence. In the pure market everyone is a price taker; no one a price maker. The kind of strategic action—such as selling short—that has characterised contemporary financial markets simply cannot happen.

Even while the neo-liberal epoch was just beginning, economists at the University of Chicago, usually considered to be the main centre for the generation of neo-liberal ideology, were preparing a new doctrine of competition and monopoly that was soon to influence the US courts, undermining the old principles of anti-trust legislation that were at the heart of US and, more recently, European competition law. It was not necessary, the doctrine argued, for there to be actual competition for customer welfare to be maximised. Sometimes a monopoly, by its very domination of the market, can offer customers a better deal than a number of competing firms.

This is not the place to examine the merits of this argument in detail. It is being used here only to show the fundamental ambiguity within neo-liberal thinking itself over what are usually seen as its fundamental characteristics: competition and freedom of choice. The recent banking crisis has seen, on both sides of the Atlantic, governments supporting, and gaining the support of competition authorities for, mergers and acquisitions that considerably reduce competition and choice.

The financial markets failed when the fundamental criterion of complete knowledge and transparency ceased to characterise banks' relations with each other. If we now add to that a sector with considerably reduced competition, as well as extended guarantees of support from the state in the event of irresponsible behaviour, we have a potentially serious problem of system legitimacy. At the same time, unless a country's political structure is likely to support something like a 'Danish' solution, we remain dependent on the financial system to resume privatised Keynesianism if capitalism's other problem with democracy is to be resolved.

The initial answer is a return to more regulation to compensate for declining competition and to avoid moral hazard, and in the immediate term this is happening. But we have been here before very recently. After what was in retrospect the first sign that the financial markets were not as effective at automatic self-regulation as was claimed on their behalf, the Enron and World.com scandals at the beginning of the century, the US Congress tightened regulations on company auditing in the Sarbanes-Oxley Act. It quickly produced complaints from the sector that enterprise was being stifled, and threats that finance houses would leave New York for the more permissive regime in London.

The same has been happening after the bout of regulatory measures being visited on the financial sector as part of the deal with governments to save it. How can the derivatives markets get to work in supporting high levels of borrowing if they are to be subject to rules that make much of that borrowing more difficult? Meanwhile, low- and medium-wage insecure workers will not be able to carry on spending unless they can get their hands on unsecured credit, even if at less manic levels than had been occurring. Furthermore, this will be a financial sector with a reduced number of major players, with very easy access to government and often shaped by government itself during the course of the 2008 rescue packages. One assumes that most governments that have been acquiring banks in the bout of unforeseen nationalisation that followed the October 2008 collapse do not intend to hold on to them according to the old model of controlling the 'commanding heights' of the economy. The fact that big banks operate internationally will itself be a disincentive to that. It is however also unlikely that these banks will be privatised through general public share issues. They will most likely be levered into the hands of a small number of leading existing firms deemed responsible enough to run them in good order. There will overall be a gradual slip towards a more negotiated, voluntary regulatory system. Justified by arguments about flexibility and of reducing burdens on the taxpayer, actual regulation will be exchanged for lightly monitored guarantees of good behaviour by the large financial firms.

To predict this is hardly crystal-ball gazing: it is a general trend in government–firm relations right across the economy. Sharing neo-liberal prejudices against government as such, frightened at the impact of regulation on growth, and believing in the superiority of corporate directors over themselves at nearly everything, politicians increasingly rely on corporate social responsibility for the achievement of several policy goals. The UK government even has a minister with responsibility for the subject.

Hardly a regime shift; just an adjectival shift from unregulated privatised Keynesianism to self-regulated privatised Keynesianism. But some implications of the change have more radical implications. First, the system will less and less be legitimated in terms of the market, freedom of choice and an absence of government involvement. Rather, there will be partnership between government and firms, or autonomous actions by firms commended by governments, with largely informal attempts to reconstruct trust. It will be 'big firms are good for you', rather than 'markets are good for you'. In some respects this resembles neo-corporatism, but with two major differences. First, organised labour will not be present, except as a token actor, as it has little power or competence at the level of global finance. Second, firms participated in corporatist deals as members of associations, which provided something of a level playing field among different firms. Today's giant, global firms have little time for associations, and seek anything but a level playing field when they build relations with governments. The new 'responsible corporation' model will however resemble corporatism in being limited to nation-state (just possibly EU) level, to which level governments' competence is limited, while the firms remain global and retain a capacity to regime-shop.

Second, and less important economically but more significant politically, this model will see a considerable enhancement of current trends towards a displacement of political activity from parties to civil society organisations and social movements. The model brings firms to prominence, not just as lobbies of governments, but as makers of public policy, either alongside or instead of governments. It will be firms that decide the terms of their codes of behaviour and responsible practices. Firms therefore become political subjects and objects in their own right, ending the sharp separation between governments and private firms that is the hallmark of both neo-liberal and social democratic politics. At the same time, as governments of all parties have to make similar deals with firms, and equally fear for their country's ability to attract liquid capital if they are too demanding of them, differences among parties on core economic policies will shrink even further than they have already. Party politics will still have much with which to concern itself: the relative share of public spending; questions of multi-culturalism; security. But it will vacate the former heartland of basic economic strategy. In reality it vacated this some years ago in most countries, but shreds of it remain in some parties' rhetoric.

It is already the case that for nearly every major corporation there is a website revealing details of its conduct, assessing its fulfilment of its social responsibility claims. As this remains a no-go area for party conflict, it will grow in importance in civil society politics. It will have the major advantage that it will not be so trapped at the nation state level as party politics; many of these groups are transnational. But it will be an unsatisfactory politics, as it lacks the formal citizenship egalitarianism of electoral democracy, while retaining many of the bad habits of parties. Activist groups are capable of grabbing attention with exaggerated claims or (in contrast) cuddling up to corporations in exchange for various resources just as much as are parties. It will also be a highly unequal struggle between them and the corporations. It is not a regime that either neo-liberals or social democrats want; but it is what we are all likely to get; and it may well reconcile again the capitalism economy and the democratic polity.

This is the kind of social forecasting that depends on an extrapolation of current trends. Can one not do better than that and peer further forward? Before very long the global economy will start to need the purchasing power, and not just the labour power, of the billions living in Asia and Africa. That will require serious thinking about the transfer of spending power, not to mention an increase in the price of T-shirts, and a completely different kind of global regime. What would trigger such an emergence of something finally resembling Marx's global proletariat? Probably not his own ideas; more likely radical Islam. But this is likely to become really serious politics after the next 30 years.

Note

1 I am grateful to Noel Whiteside for comments on an earlier draft of this article.

Index

Note: page numbers in italics refer to tables and diagrams; alphabetical arrangement is word-by-word.

The Political Quarterly © 2011 The Political Quarterly Publishing Co. Ltd